A CATALOGUE OF THE FIFTEENTH-CENTURY PRINTED BOOKS IN THE HARVARD UNIVERSITY LIBRARY

VOLUME III

Medieval & Renaissance Texts & Studies

Volume 119

A CATALOGUE

OF THE

FIFTEENTH-CENTURY PRINTED BOOKS

IN THE

HARVARD UNIVERSITY LIBRARY

VOLUME III

Books Printed in Italy
with the exception of Rome and Venice

By James E. Walsh
Keeper of Printed Books
The Houghton Library

ΩEÐIEVAL & RENAISSANCE TEXTS & STUÐIES
Tempe, Arizona
1997

A generous grant from the National Endowment for the Humanities,
an independent federal agency,
has helped meet publication costs for this volume.

Library of Congress Cataloging-in-Publication Data
(Revised for vol. 3)

Harvard University. Library.
  A catalogue of the fifteenth-century printed books in the Harvard University
  Library.
     p. cm. — (Medieval & Renaissance texts & studies ; v. 84,   )
  Includes indexes.
  Contents: v. 1. Books printed in Germany, German-speaking Switzerland, and
    Austria-Hungary — v. 2. Books printed in Rome and Venice — v. 3. Books
    printed in Italy with the exception of Rome and Venice.
    1. Incunabula—Bibliography—Catalogs.   2. Incunabula—Massachusetts—
Cambridge—Bibliography—Catalogs. 3. Harvard University. Library—Catalogs. I.
Walsh, James Edward, 1918- . II. Fifteenth-century printed books.
Z240.H37 1991   011'.42'097444   90–6658
ISBN 0–86698–096–2 (v. 1: alk. paper)
ISBN 0–86698–111–X (v. 2: alk. paper)
ISBN 0–86698–174–8 (v. 3: alk. paper)   CIP

∞

This book is made to last.
It is set in Baskerville, smythe-sewn,
and printed on acid-free paper
to library specifications.

Printed in the United States of America

Contents

Preface

With the great printing centers of Rome and Venice disposed of in volume II of this catalogue, we now come to the smaller cities and towns of Italy, some of them (Florence, Milan) not so small, with a fairly extensive output, others (Foligno, Genoa), with but one or two printers who produced very few books. These smaller presses are not too well represented in the various Harvard libraries, and indeed some of them (such as those at Mondovì and Como) are not represented at all. But it is in the nature of small enterprises to print editions in limited numbers and for the sale and circulation to remain for the most part local. Rarity can therefore be taken for granted, and not only in our own time. Richard Ashhurst Bowie, whose library is one of the great treasures of Harvard, noted in 1881 that it had taken five years for a German bookseller to find him a copy of Curtius Rufus's *Historia Alexandri Magni* (see no. 3061); and on another occasion he complains, "I sent an order for [Censorinus, *De die natali*] to Germany in 1875, but nearly five years elapsed before a copy was offered for sale" (see no. 3234). One hesitates to think how long Mr. Bowie would have to wait for his order to be filled were he to be trying to acquire such books today.

These small presses did not always restrict themselves to pamphlets or books of local or occasional interest, however. An example is the Foligno Dante of 1472, of which Harvard, despite Charles Eliot Norton's collecting efforts in the 19th century, does not have a copy; nor was Oppian's *Halieutica* (Colle de Valdelsa, 1478) included in Daniel B. Fearing's extensive collection of books relating to fishing, gathered by him over a long period of years, largely in the late 19th century. And were such rarities to come on the market today, they would probably be priced far beyond our means, for gone are the days when a Harvard librarian could record the acquisition of

an incunable in 1837 with the laconic notation "Cost 50 cents." Neverthe-
less, despite lacunae of this kind, the Harvard collection of non-Roman,
non-Venetian Italian printing can be considered distinguished, with a number of books of which no other copies are recorded in the United States and
even one or two that appear to be unique (see, for example, no. 3124A).
Many of the greatest rarities are to be found in the magnificent collection of
incunabula formed by James Frothingham Hunnewell and deposited in the
Harvard College Library by his son, James Melville Hunnewell.

A glance at the list of references prefixed to this volume will reveal how
deeply I am indebted to Dr. Dennis E. Rhodes of the British Library for his
many books and articles dealing with printing in the smaller cities and towns
of Italy. Over nearly forty years Dr. Rhodes has been using his sharp eye and
inquiring mind to shed light on and solve many a problem of dating,
type-identification, and assignment of books misdated and misassigned by
authorities less acute than he. All incunabulists are in his debt; it is a
pleasure to acknowledge my own.

I continue to be grateful to my colleagues in other Harvard libraries for
their cheerful cooperation in making the incunabula in their care available
to me, and to the administration of the *Gesamtkatalog der Wiegendrucke* in
Berlin for their willingness to answer my numerous queries. Once again, I
thank Dr. Paul Needham for giving me the benefit of his expert knowledge
in matters of provenance.

James E. Walsh
Cambridge, Massachusetts
15 March 1993

References

(Additional to those in vols. I–II)

I. Abbreviated References

Amelung (Trionfi) Amelung, Peter. "Die Florentiner 'Trionfi'-Ausgaben des 15. Jahrhunderts." *Ars impressoria: Entstehung und Entwicklung des Buchdrucks. Eine internationale Festgabe für Severin Corsten zum 65. Geburtstag.* Hrsg. von Hans Limburg, Hartwig Lohse, Wolfgang Schmitz (München, 1986): 251–65.

Balsamo Balsamo, Luigi. *Giovann'Angelo Scinzenzeler, tipografo in Milano (1500–1526).* Firenze, 1959. (Biblioteca bibliografica italica, 20)

BSB-Ink Bayerische Staatsbibliothek. *Inkunabelkatalog. Band 2: Brey-Gran.* Wiesbaden, 1991.

Fava Fava, Domenico. *Modena-Reggio Emilia, Scandiano.* Modena, 1943. (La Cultura e la stampa italiana nel quattrocento, 1)

Fava-Bresciano Fava, Mariano and Giovanni Bresciano. *La stampa a Napoli nel XV secolo,* vols. 1–2. Leipzig, 1911–12. (Sammlung bibliothekswissenschaftlicher Arbeiten, 32.-33. Heft)

Ganda Ganda, Arnaldo. *I primordi della tipografia milanese: Antonio Zarotto da Parma (1471–1507).* Firenze, 1984.

Gasparrini Leporace Gasparrini Leporace, Tullia. "Notizie e documenti inediti sul tipografo Antonio Carcano (1475-1525)." *Miscellanea di scritti di bibliografia ed erudizione in memoria di Luigi Ferrari* (Firenze, 1952): [327]–56.

Hirsch	Hirsch, Paul. *Katalog der Musikbibliothek Paul Hirsch. Bd. 1: Theoretische Drucke bis 1800*. Berlin, 1928. (Veröffentlichungen der Musikbibliothek Paul Hirsch, 2. Reihe, Bd. 1)
Kristeller	Kristeller, Paul. *Early Florentine Woodcuts. With an Annotated List of Florentine Illustrated Books*. London, 1897.
Manzoni	Manzoni, Giacomo. "Annali tipografici torinesi del secolo XV." *Miscellanea di storia italiana* 4 (1863): [237]–357 + 8 plates.
Rhodes (F)	Rhodes, Dennis Everard. *Gli Annali tipografici fiorentini del XV secolo*. Firenze, 1988. (Biblioteca di bibliografia italiana, 113)
Rhodes (M)	—— "A Bibliography of Mantua." *La Bibliofilia* 57 (1955): [173]–87.
Rhodes (S)	—— "The Incunabula of Siena." In his *Studies in Early Italian Printing* (London, 1982): [217]–28.
Rhodes (T)	—— *La stampa a Treviso nel secolo XV*. Treviso, 1983. (Quaderni di "Studi Trevisani," 1)
Rogledi Manni	Rogledi Manni, Teresa. *La tipografia a Milano nel XV secolo*. Firenze, 1980. (Biblioteca di bibliografia italiana, 90)
Veneziani	Veneziani, Paolo. *La tipografia a Brescia nel XV secolo*. Firenze, 1986. (Biblioteca di bibliografia italiana, 107)

II. Other References

Amelung, Peter. "Drei Inkunabeln, die es nicht gibt." *Beiträge zur Inkunabelkunde*, 3. Folge, 3 (1967): [178]–83.

Bühler, Curt Ferdinand. "The First Edition of Ficino's *De Christiana religione*: a Problem in Bibliographical Description." In his *Early Books and Manuscripts* (New York, 1973): [307]–12.

—— "The Two Issues of the First Edition of the *Manipulus florum*." In his *Early Books and Manuscripts* (New York, 1973): [198]–204.

De Marinis, Tammaro. *Appunti e ricerche bibliografiche*. Milano, 1940.

Fattori, Daniela. "Per la storia della tipografia da Verona." *La Bibliofilia* 92 (1990): [269]–81.

Goff, Frederick Richmond. "The Four Florentine Editions of Savonarola's *Predica dellarte del ben morire*." *The New Colophon* 3 (1950): 286–301.

Hind, Arthur Mayger. *Catalogue of Early Italian Engravings Preserved in the . . . British Museum. Edited by Sidney Colvin.* London, 1910.

Lohr, Charles H. "Medieval Latin Aristotle Commentaries." *Traditio* 23 (1967): 345–48.

Olschki, Leo S. "Un volume con postille autografe ed inedite dell'umanista Sebastiano Serico." *La Bibliofilia* 1 (1899): 12–17.

Pescasio, Luigi. *Pietro Adamo de'Micheli, protoeditore mantovano.* Mantova, 1972.

Rhodes, Dennis Everard. "Ancora per lo Stampatore del Mesue." *Studi offerti a Roberto Ridolfi* (Firenze, 1973): [407]–12.

——. "Filippo Nuvolone of Mantua." In his *Studies in Early Italian Printing* (London, 1982): [144]–48.

——. "Lilies and a Library." *The Book Collector* 24 (1975): 417–20.

——. "Notes on Early Florentine Printing." *La Bibliofilia* 84 (1982): [143]–62.

——. "Towards an Identification of Proctor 7393." *Gutenberg-Jahrbuch* (1963): 47–48.

Ricciarelli, Giocondo. "I prototipografi in Perugia." *Bollettino della Deputazione di storia patria per l'Umbria* 67,2 (1970): [77]–161.

Ridolfi, Roberto. "Incunabuli contrastampati." *La Bibliofilia* 51 (1949): [131]–44.

——. "Il processi del Savonarola." *La Bibliofilia* 46 (1944): [3]–41.

——. "Ancora i processi del Savonarola." *La Bibliofilia* 47 (1945): [41]–47.

——. *La stampa in Firenze nel secolo XV.* Firenze, 1958.

——. "Lo 'Stampatore del Mesue' e l'introduzione della stampa in Firenze." *La Bibliofilia* 56 (1954): [1]–20.

——. "Sulla data di un'edizione di Bartolomeo de'Libri." *La Bibliofilia* 52 (1950): [38]–40.

Saulnier, Verdun L. "Boccace et la nouvelle française de la renaissance." *Revue de littérature comparée* 21 (1947): 404–13.

Scapecchi, Piero. "Note sulla tipografia trevisana del secolo XV." *Studi trevisani* 2,4 (1985): 23.

Varnhagen, Hermann. *Ueber eine Sammlung alter italienischer Drucke der Erlanger Universitätsbibliothek.* Erlangen, 1892.

Veneziani, Paolo. "Pietro da Colonia e il *Tipografo del Robertus Anglicus.*" *La Bibliofilia* 75 (1973): [45]–65.

Watson, Andrew G. "A Varese Library-Stamp Identified?" *The Library*, 5th ser., 28 (1973): [147]–48.

A CATALOGUE OF THE
FIFTEENTH-CENTURY PRINTED BOOKS
IN THE HARVARD UNIVERSITY
LIBRARY

VOLUME III

Foligno

JOHANN NEUMEISTER

2762   **Procopius Caesariensis**: De bello Italico adversus Gothos gesto [Latin]. 1470.

f° and 4°. [74] leaves (1 and 74 blank); 288 x 208 mm.

A condensed translation by Leonardus Brunus Aretinus, who here claims to be the author. There are variants in the colophon; see BMC and GW.

In this copy sheets [a]2 and [d]1 are quarto, the rest folio; the colophon agrees with the BMC transcription. Large initials with white vine stem and floral bud extensions illuminated in gold and colors at beginning of books; illuminated coat of arms within a wreath in lower margin of [a]2r; initial on [a]3r added in blue, capital strokes in red; MS quiring, partly trimmed away. 19th-century red morocco, edges gilt. MS ownership notation, partly eradicated, in upper margin of [a]2r, "Di Galiotto Baglione"; leather booklabel of Edward Vernon Utterson (no. 249 in the Sotheby sale catalogue of his library, 19 April 1852); bookplates of Charles Lemuel Nichols and of William King Richardson. Blank leaves not present.

HC 1558; Pr 5721; BMC 6:599 (IB.25403); Pell 1112; GW 5600; IGI 2188; Goff B–1234; BSB-Ink B–937.

1951—Bequest of William King Richardson. WKR 1.4.9

Ferrara

ANDREAS BELFORTIS

2763 **Guarinus, Baptista**: De ordine docendi ac studendi. ca. 1475.

a1r: Batista Guarinus ad Maffeum Gambarã ‖ Brixianũ Adolescẽtẽ generosũ discipulũ ‖ suum de ordine docendi ac studendi. ‖ c4v, line 21: ... Vero‖nae .xv. kal'. Martii. 1459. ‖ c5v, line 21: ... Quod si feceris: uaticinor te alterũ ‖ Italiae florem futurum. obtempera mihi ‖ obtempera Fili carissime ‖

4°. a–b⁸, c⁶ (c6 blank); [22] leaves (22 blank); 200 x 140 mm. a2r: 25 lines, 144 x 80 mm. Type: 2:116R. Initial space on a1r.

The signatures are hand-stamped far down in the right-hand lower corner of the page, and some have been trimmed away. Initial on a1r added in red and blue, with marginal extension; leaves numbered in MS 111–32. MS marginalia. 19th-century calf. Bookplate of Alexander Peckover, baron of Wisbech.

H 8128*; Pr 5730; IGI 4519; Goff G–528.

24 December 1945—Bought with the Bennett Hubbard Nash fund. Inc 5730

2764 **Plutarchus**: Problemata. ca. 1477?

4°. [66] leaves; 196 x 138 mm.

Latin translation by Johannes Petri Lucensis; edited by Johannes Calphurnius.

Initial space on a2r, with guide-letter, not filled in; without rubrication. 19th-century red morocco. Initials of H. G. Curtis on front flyleaf, with his date of acquisition "17/4/[18]90."

BMC 6:603 (IA.25628); IGI 7919; Goff P–829; CIBN P–487.

1 June 1917—Gift of Horatio G. Curtis. Inc 5732.5

2765 **Seneca, Lucius Annaeus**: Tragoediae. 1484.

f°. [174] leaves; 265 x 198 mm.

BMC records signatures through sheet n2 hand-stamped far down in the right-hand corner of the page; in this copy they have been trimmed away. Initial spaces, with guide-letters, not filled in; without rubrication. Modern blind-stamped brown morocco, edges gilt, by Rivière. MS note by Louis H. Silver on front flyleaf, "From the C. W. Clark Collection" (p. 68 in vol. 3 of the 1914–22 catalogue).

HCR 14662; Pr 5731; BMC 6:603 (IB.25621); IGI 8905; Goff S–433; CIBN S–200.

15 June 1954—Gift of Louis H. Silver. Inc 5731

2766 **Guarinus, Baptista:** De ordine docendi ac studendi. ca. 1484?

4°. [18] leaves; 196 x 138 mm.

Initial space, with guide-letter, on a1r not filled in; without rubrication. Modern sprinkled calf. MS ownership (?) notation on front flyleaf, "Montemariorú."

HCR 8129=H 8130; Pr 5732; BMC 6:603 (IA.25626); IGI 4520; Goff G–529.

27 June 1918—Bought with the Constantius fund. Inc 5732

2767 **Savonarola, Michael:** De balneis et thermis naturalibus omnibus Italiae. 10 November 1485.

f°. [40] leaves (1 blank); 305 x 206 mm.

BMC records the register on f4v as headed "Registrū quinternoƶ huius libri"; this copy omits "quinternoƶ." Initial spaces, most with guide-letters, not filled in; without rubrication. Old vellum. Blank leaf not present.

HC 14493*; Pr 5748; BMC 6:603 (IB.25701); IGI 8805; Goff S–290; CIBN S–152.

Countway Library

2768 **Bernardus de Gordonio:** De urinis et de pulsibus. 4 March 1487.

f°. [24] leaves; 253 x 185 mm.

Initial spaces, with guide-letters, not filled in; without rubrication. Bound in part of a vellum leaf of 15th-century Latin liturgical MS containing musical notation.

HR 7804=7803(1); BMC 6:604 (IB.25705); Pell 5280; Polain 1667; GW 4087; IGI 1573; Goff B–454; Sack 582.

Countway Library (William Norton Bullard Collection)

2769   **Honestis, Christophorus Georgius de:** Expositio super Antidotario Mesue. 20 March 1488.

f°. [48] leaves (48 blank); 280 x 203 mm.

Includes his *Tractatulus de aqua ordei.*

Initial spaces, with guide-letters, not filled in; paragraph marks added in red in the first three quires. Half modern vellum and tan boards.

H 8799*; BMC 6:604 (IB.25706); IGI 4806; Goff H–320; Sack 1863.

Countway Library (William Norton Bullard Collection)

2770   **Alfraganus:** Compilatio astronomica. 3 September 1493.

4°. [30] leaves; ill.; 212 x 156 mm.

Latin translation from the Arabic by Johannes Hispalensis.

Initial spaces, with guide-letters, not filled in; without rubrication; woodcut on a1v colored. Half brown cloth and modern paste-paper boards.

HC 822*; Pr 5753; BMC 6:605 (IA.25717); Pell 513; GW 1268; IGI 351; Goff A–460; BSB-Ink A–310; Sander 279.

1948–Gift of Harrison D. Horblit. Inc 5753 (A)

2771   ——Another copy. 196 x 146 mm.

Initial spaces not filled in; without rubrication; woodcut uncolored. Modern blind-stamped brown morocco. Booklabel of Adriana R. Salem.

1965–Gift of Ward M. Canaday. Inc 5753 (B)

2772   ——Another copy. 200 x 145 mm.

Initial spaces not filled in; without rubrication; woodcut uncolored. Old vellum.

Countway Library (William Norton Bullard Collection)

2773   **Guarinus, Baptista:** Oratio funebris in reginam Eleonoram Aragoniam. After 12 October 1493.

4°. [6] leaves; 190 x 142 mm.

Half 19th-century vellum and decorated boards. "Bibliotheca Heberia-na" stamp on front flyleaf (no. 3153 in pt. 1 of the Sotheby sale catalogue, April 1834); bookplate of Gilbert R. Redgrave (no. 125 in the Sotheby sale catalogue of his library, May 1926), with a slip of his MS notes inserted at front.

HC(+Add) 8132; Pr 5754; BMC 6:605 (IA.25719); IGI 4522; Goff G–527.

6 May 1950—Bought with the Duplicate fund. Inc 5754

2774 **Collenucius, Pandulphus:** Pliniana defensio adversus Nicolai Leoni-ceni accusationem. 1493.

4°. [52] leaves; ill.; 189 x 144 mm.

Includes a poem by Lucas Ripa.

Initial spaces, with guide-letters, not filled in; without rubrication. Old limp vellum. MS ownership notation "Stephanus Baluzius Tutelensis" on title page; bookplate of James Frothingham Hunnewell, with his MS notation "Sunderland Library. Rec^d Dec 2/[18]82" (no. 9944 in pt. 4 of the Puttick & Simpson sale catalogue, November 1882).

HC 5483*; Pr 5755; BMC 6:605 (IA.25723–24); Pell 3854; Polain 4295; GW 7164; IGI 3055; Goff C–754; BSB-Ink C–470; Sander 2034.

January 1919—Deposited by James M. Hunnewell. Inc 5755

2775 ——Another copy. 207 x 147 mm.

Initial spaces not filled in; without rubrication. Half old vellum and paste-paper boards. Bookplate of William Norton Bullard. Imperfect: four leaves at front wanting.

Countway Library (William Norton Bullard Collection)

AUGUSTINUS CARNERIUS

2776 **Boccaccio, Giovanni:** Teseide. 1475.

f°. [166] leaves (5 and 165–66 blank); 340 x 235 mm.

In some copies the fifth leaf contains Boccaccio's dedication to Fiam-metta; and the date in the colophon appears as either ".M°.CCCC°.LXXIIIII°." or as ".M°.CCCC°.LXXV." Includes a com-mentary by Pietro Andrea di Bassi.

In this copy the fifth leaf is blank, and the date in the colophon appears as ".M°.CCCC°.LXXV." Initial spaces not filled in; without rubrication; MS quiring. 19th-century brown morocco, elaborately gilt, by Thouvenin; green morocco doublures and lining leaves, blind- and gilt-stamped. Booklabel of Adriana R. Salem.

HCR 3308; Pr 5735; BMC 6:606 (IB.25638); Pell 2461; GW 4499; IGI 1810; Goff B–761.

August 1959—Gift of Ward M. Canaday. Inc 5735

S E V E R I N U S   F E R R A R I E N S I S

2777   **Trottus, Albertus:** De vero et perfecto clerico. 23 December 1475.

4°. [117] leaves; 214 x 154 mm.

Some copies have a dedication to Cardinal Bartolommeo Roverella, others to Jacobus Zeno, bishop of Padua.

In this copy the dedication to Zeno is headed "Ad Reuerendissimum .D. Iacobum Zenum Pontificem Pa‖tauinum Excellentiss. prefacio in libellum de uero & perfec‖to clerico: que & quot concurrere opporteat in eo: per Alber‖tum trottum Iuris utriusq₃ interpretem." 18th-century vellum. MS ownership notations on front flyleaf, "1731 Di Giaco: Soranzo" and "M. Wodhull Feb. 21ˢᵗ 1791. Robson's sale" (no. 2610 in the Sotheby sale catalogue of Wodhull's library, January 1886); bookplate of James Frothingham Hunnewell. Tipped in at front is a typescript of the Roverella dedication. In this copy the "23." in the month date at the end of the table has dropped out. Imperfect: the inserted half sheet following leaf 3 (see BMC) is wanting.

HCR 588; Pr 5740; BMC 6:609 (IA.25673–74); Pell 397; Polain 3855; IGI 9727; Goff T–478; CIBN T–336.

January 1919—Deposited by James M. Hunnewell. Inc 5740

L A U R E N T I U S   D E   R U B E I S

2778   **Averroes:** Colliget. 5 October 1482.

f°. [116] leaves; 285 x 205 mm.

Latin translation by Bonacosa. There are variant colophons, one specifying "Venice" as the place of printing, though the book was undoubtedly printed in Ferrara; see BMC 6:xi and GW.

This copy has "Venecijs" in the colophon. Initial on a2r illuminated; those elsewhere, paragraph marks, and capital strokes added in red. Half modern vellum and cream boards. MS ownership notations in upper margin of a2r, "Ladislaus Steiff [?]" and "Su[m] ex lib. Brnd. Pergerj Med. Doct." MS marginalia.

HC 2189*; Pr p.316 (under Venice; no copy seen; reference to Hain only); BMC 6:xi; Pell 1655; GW 3107; IGI 1107; Goff A–1411; BSB-Ink A–952.

Countway Library (William Norton Bullard Collection)

2779 Andreae, Antonius: Quaestiones de tribus principiis rerum naturalium. 11 May 1490.

4°. [126] leaves; 200 x 148 mm.

Preface by Laurentius Ruscius. Edited by Petrus Malfeta. Includes: Franciscus de Mayronis, *Expositio super octo libros Physicorum. Formalitates eiusdem. Tractatus eiusdem de principio complexo. Tractatus eiusdem de terminis theologicis.*—Thomas Aquinas, *Tractatus de ente et essentia.*

Initial spaces, most with guide-letters, not filled in; without rubrication. Shabby paste-paper boards. MS ownership notations on blank a1r, "Barth° Doria Roberti" and "Isnard medicinae doctor."

HCR 989; Pr 5759; BMC 6:612 (IA.25737); GW 1668; IGI 477; Goff A–589.

Countway Library

2780 Hugo Senensis: Expositio super Aphorismos Hippocratis et Galeni commentum. 15 November 1493.

f°. [190] leaves; 298 x 212 mm.

Printed by De Rubeis with Andreas de Grassis.

Initial spaces, with guide-letters, not filled in; without rubrication. Old vellum. Bookplate of William Norton Bullard. MS index on two inserted leaves at end; vellum leaf of 15th-century Latin legal MS inserted at end.

H 9011*; BMC 6:612 (IB.25743); IGI 4944; Goff H–540; Sack 1917.

Countway Library (William Norton Bullard Collection)

2781   **Jacobus Philippus de Bergamo:** De claris mulieribus. 29 April 1497.

f°. [6], III–CLXX (i.e., CLXXII) leaves (CXXII and CLIX repeated; LXIII, LXVIII–IX, and CXXVIII misnumbered LXII, LXIX–LXX, and CXXX); ill.; 305 x 210 mm.

Edited by Albertus de Placentia and Augustinus de Casali Maiori. In some copies the word "Prologus" is repeated at the end of the third line of the caption on A2r, in others it is printed as a fourth line.

This copy has "Prologus" at the end of the third line. Without rubrication; woodcuts uncolored. Modern brown morocco, gilt, by Capé; edges gilt. Booklabel of Henry Huth (no. 597 in pt. 1 of the Sotheby sale catalogue, November 1911); bookplate of William King Richardson.

HC(+Add) 2813*; Pr 5762; BMC 6:613 (IB.25752); Pell 2069; Polain 1497; IGI 5071; Goff J–204; Sack 2006; CIBN J–140; Sander 915; Schäfer 186.

1951–Bequest of William King Richardson. WKR 1.2.6

2782   ——Another copy. 310 x 205 mm.

This copy has "Prologus" at the end of the third line. Without rubrication; woodcuts uncolored. 19th-century vellum. Booklabel of Adriana R. Salem. Imperfect: sheet f1 wanting, sheet s1 duplicated in its place; A1 inserted from another copy.

December 1962–Gift of Ward M. Canaday. Typ Inc 5762

2783   ——Another copy. 315 x 212 mm.

This copy has "Prologus" printed as a fourth line of the caption on A2r. Without rubrication; woodcuts uncolored. Contemporary blind-stamped leather over wooden boards, rebacked and repaired; brass latches on back cover, clasps and thongs gone. MS ownership notation on title page, "M. F. Sauolio ... 1618"; booklabel of Philip Hofer. Imperfect: leaf A1 badly mutilated; leaf a1 wanting.

28 February 1942–Gift of Philip Hofer. Typ Inc 5762.2

2784   ——Another copy. 298 x 200 mm.

This copy has "Prologus" printed as a fourth line of the caption on A2r. Without rubrication; woodcuts uncolored. 18th-century vellum.

Imperfect: leaf z6 (colophon, register, and printer's mark) wanting; in its place has been substituted a forged leaf containing a colophon "Ferrariae Laurentius de Rubeis M.cccclxxxxiii" and a mark not recorded as used by this printer, though it contains the initials "L D R"; the book was sold to the Harvard Library by Quaritch in 1883 as a "unique copy of an unknown first edition, issued four years prior to the regular well-known issue of 1497"; sophisticated, the leaves having been assembled from several different copies; a woodcut border from another book has been pasted around the title on A1r.

24 October 1883–Bought. Fogg Art Museum (Print Room)

2785   **Hieronymus, Saint:** Epistolae [Italian]. 12 October 1497.

f°. [6], III–CCLXIX, [1] leaves (XIII, XVI, XXXV, LVIIII, XCII, XCIX, CLXX, CXCI–II, CXCVI, CCII, CCIX–X, and CCXXXXVIIII misnumbered XVI, XIII, XXXIIII, LXI, XCI, XCXI, CLXIX, CXCVI–VII, CXCVIII, CCIIII, CCII–III, and CCXXXXVIII); ill.; 340 x 230 mm.

Includes Lupo de Olmeto, *Regula monachorum ex epistolis Hieronymi excerpta* in Italian translation by Matteo da Ferrara. There are variants on a1v; see BMC.

In this copy leaf a1v has a dedication not recorded by BMC, within BMC border 3a: "ELEONORAE. ES‖TENSIS. DVCIS. ‖ FERR. AC LISABEL‖LA'E. EIVS. FILIA'E ‖ MANTVA'E. REGI‖NA'E. MVNIFICEN. ‖ AC. LIBERALITA‖TE. DIVI. HIE‖RONŸMI. DIVI‖NVM. HOC. OPVS ‖ IN. LVCEM. PRODIIT ‖ ANN. M.CCCC.LXXXXV." Of the five leaves containing woodcut borders three have been colored, and four have a coat of arms added in the lower compartment, beneath the first of which is written "Semper uiuat semper: ANTONIVS: VLASTVS CRETENSIS Patauini Studij discipulus." 18th-century diced russia, with the arms of Michael Wodhull stamped in gilt on front cover and with his autograph and date of acquisition on front flyleaf, "Pinelli Auction. M: Wodhull Feb. 4th 1790" (not located in the Pinelli sale catalogue, 1789–90; no. 1284 in the Sotheby sale catalogue of books from Wodhull's library, January 1886). Several leaves at front and back remargined, without loss of text.

HC(Add) 8566; Pr 5765; BMC 6:614 (IB.25759); IGI 4746; Goff H–178; CIBN H–109; Schäfer 155; Sander 3404.

4 May 1921–Bought with the Duplicate fund. Inc 5765 (A)

2786   ——Another copy. 340 x 227 mm.

In this copy leaf a1v has the full-page woodcut of S. Jerome writing as described by BMC; the border is 3b. Woodcuts uncolored. Contemporary (?) wooden boards, crudely rebacked in black leather; back cover split; marks of clasps, no longer present. Ownership stamp in red in lower margin of a2r, "C O G" with coronet. Imperfect: four unsigned leaves at front and quire c wanting.

4 May 1905—From the library of Charles Eliot Norton. Inc 5765 (B)

2787 **Corona Beatae Mariae Virginis.** 1497?

16°. [16] leaves; ill.; 110 x 80 mm.

Half 19th-century leather and tan boards. Booklabels of Philip and Frances Hofer. Imperfect: sheet [a]1 wanting; leaf [a]1 supplied in photocopy from the Prince d'Essling copy.

Pr 5764; BMC 6:613 (IA.25756); GW 7579; IGI 3223-A; Goff C-928; Sander 4263

14 September 1972—Gift of Philip Hofer. Typ Inc 5764

Padua

PRELIMINARY NOTE TO PADUA

The Printer of the 1471 Mesue has traditionally been described as the first printer in Florence, and five of his productions are recorded in BMC 6:615–16, with a sixth described by Dr. Dennis E. Rhodes in an article, "Ancora per lo stampatore del Mesue," in *Studi offerti a Roberto Ridolfi* (Firenze, 1973, p.[407]–12). Ridolfi, in his article "Lo 'Stampatore del Mesue' e l'introduzione della stampa in Firenze" (*La Bibliofilia* 56 (1954): [1]–20) shows convincingly that the Printer of the 1471 Mesue was Laurentius Canozius in Padua, which town therefore takes precedence of Florence in the annals of printing.

LAURENTIUS CANOZIUS

2788 **Pseudo-Phalaris:** Epistolae [Italian]. 1471.

4°. [64] leaves; 234 x 160 mm.

One of the works formerly assigned to the Printer of the 1471 Mesue at Florence. Italian translation by Bartholomaeus Fontius from the Latin translation of Franciscus Griffolinus.

Initials added in red or blue. 19th-century maroon morocco, spine and edges gilt. Monogram booklabel of Sir John H. Thorold with his Syston Park bookplate (no. 1511 in the Sotheby sale catalogue, December 1884); from the library of Richard Ashhurst Bowie.

H 12903*; Pr 7347 (Italian adespota); BMC 6:616 (IA.27005); IGI 7705; Goff P-566; CIBN P-297.

9 November 1908—Gift of Mrs. E. D. Brandegee. Inc 6767.10

2789   Aristoteles: De anima. 22 November 1472.

f°. [90] leaves; 397 x 266 mm.

Includes two Latin versions of Aristotle's text, one new and one old, with the commentary of Averroes on the latter. Printed by Canozius for Johannes Philippus Aurelianus et fratres.

Large initial with white vine stem and floral bud extension illuminated in gold and colors on [a]1r; smaller illuminated initials on [c]3r and [g]5r; paragraph marks added in red or blue. Half old pigskin and vellum. Autograph of Michelangelo Lanci on front flyleaf; bookplate of James Frothingham Hunnewell.

HCR 1709; BMC 7:907 (IC.29844); GW 2349; IGI 800; Goff A-969.

January 1919—Deposited by James M. Hunnewell. Inc 6767.15

2790   Aristoteles: Physica. ca. 1472/75.

f°. [238] leaves; 430 x 280 mm.

Includes two Latin versions of Aristotle's text, one new and one old, with the commentary of Averroes on the latter.

Initials illuminated in gold and colors; paragraph marks added in red or blue. Contemporary blind-stamped leather over wooden boards, repaired; one brass latch remains on back cover, plates, clasps, and thongs gone. Bookstamp of Walter Ashburner (not in the Galerie Fischer sale catalogue of his library, Lucerne, August 1938). Imperfect: leaves [a]2, [q]9-10, [s]9-10, and [t]1 wanting; [a]1, 3-4, and [g]9-10 mutilated.

HC 1683; Pell 1192; GW 2443; IGI 839; Goff A-1021.

Countway Library (William Norton Bullard Collection)

2791   Andreae, Antonius: Quaestiones de tribus principiis rerum naturalium. 1475.

f°. [66] leaves; 302 x 208 mm.

Includes his *Formalitates* and Thomas Aquinas, *De ente et essentia.* Edited by Thomas Penketh.

This copy has the same error noted by BMC for IB.29855 (last two lines on [b]7r repeated on [b]7v). Initials and paragraph marks added in red and/or blue, but most of the blue has been washed away; initials "D. B." (the rubricator?) beneath the colophon. Modern vellum; bookseller's ticket of C. E. Rappaport, Rome. Bookplate of William Norton Bullard. Leaves in the final quire remargined.

HC 990; Pr 6769; BMC 7:908 (IB.29855); Pell 634; GW 1667; IGI 476; Goff A-588; BSB-Ink A-612.

Countway Library (William Norton Bullard Collection)

BARTHOLOMAEUS DE VALDEZOCCHO

2792 Boccaccio, Giovanni: La Fiammetta. 21 March 1472.

4°. [132] leaves; 202 x 143 mm.

Printed by De Valdezoccho with Martinus de Septem Arboribus.

Initials on [a]1-2 illuminated in colors, those elsewhere added in red or blue; traces of MS quiring. 19th-century blue straight-grain morocco, gilt, edges gilt. Booklabel of Adriana R. Salem. Last two leaves remargined (supplied from another copy?).

HC 3291*; Pr 6755; BMC 7:903 (IA.29802a-b); Pell 2451; GW 4456; IGI 1779; Goff B-733; BSB-Ink B-578.

30 May 1958—Gift of Ward M. Canaday. Inc 6755

2793 Turchetus, Antonius: Oratio gratulatoria apud Nicolaum Tronum. 5 May 1472.

4°. [10] leaves (10 blank); 201 x 139 mm.

Printed by De Valdezoccho with Martinus de Septem Arboribus.

Large initial on [a]2r added in red. Modern vellum.

HC 15671; Pr 6757; BMC 7:904 (IA.29807); Polain 3856; IGI 9857; Goff T-500; CIBN T-364.

26 March 1949—Gift of Imrie de Vegh. Inc 6757

2794 **Zocchis, Jacobus de:** Canon omnis utriusque sexus disputatum ac repetitum. 28 July 1472.

f°. [128] leaves (128 blank); 278 x 200 mm.

Printed by De Valdezoccho with Martinus de Septem Arboribus.

Initials on [a]1r and [o]2r added in blue and red respectively, paragraph marks in blue or red. 18th-century olive morocco, spine and edges gilt. Bookstamp of an unidentified Italian cardinal in lower margin of [a]1r; bookplate of the Duke of Sussex (not located in the 1844–45 Evans sale catalogues of his library); autograph of J. F. Russell. Blank leaf not present.

HC 16288*; Pr 6758; BMC 7:904 (IB.29809); Polain 4069; IGI 19445; Goff Z-28; Sack 3767; CIBN Z-15.

12 June 1944—Received. Law Library

2795 **Petrarca, Francesco:** Canzoniere e Trionfi. 6 November 1472.

f°. [190] leaves (184 and 190 blank); 270 x 188 mm.

Printed by De Valdezoccho with Martinus de Septem Arboribus. Includes Leonardus Brunus Aretinus's life of Petrarch.

Initials added in blue; paragraph marks in the *tabula* added in red or blue. Modern red morocco, gilt, edges gilt, signed "Binda. Milano." Booklabel of Adriana R. Salem. Blank leaves not present.

HR 12755; Pr 6759; BMC 7:904 (IB.29811a-b); IGI 7519; Goff P-373; CIBN P-176.

December 1964—Gift of Ward M. Canaday. Inc 6759

2796 **Maurocenus, Paulus:** De aeterna temporalique Christi generatione. 28 April 1473.

4°. [78] leaves; 198 x 138 mm.

There are variant colophons; see BMC; and variant settings of [k]3-6; see Polain. Printed by De Valdezoccho with Martinus de Septem Arboribus.

In this copy the colophon agrees with BMC IA.29816, with fourth line reading "In loquor hebreos perfidiasque suas"; and the setting of

[k]3–6 agrees with Polain's transcription for his 2645. Initials added in red and brown. 18th-century calf, rebacked in red morocco. Bookplate of Richard Ashhurst Bowie.

HC 10924; Pr 6761; BMC 7:905 (IA.29816); Polain 2645; IGI 6302; Goff M–380; CIBN M–244 (Rés. D.8774).

9 November 1908—Gift of Mrs. E. D. Brandegee. Inc 6761 (A)

2797   ——Another copy. 213 x 144 mm.

Colophon and [k]3–6 as above. Initials added in red, capital strokes in yellow. Contemporary vellum, stained red; mark of clasp plate on back cover, brass latch on front, clasp and thongs gone; front cover, with MS vellum label at top, detached; in a cloth case. Bound in at end is a 15th-century paper MS (29 leaves, the first blank, the last pasted down) of the *Onus mundi* of S. Birgitta of Sweden. Bookplate of James Frothingham Hunnewell.

January 1919—Deposited by James M. Hunnewell. Inc 6761 (B)

2798   Suetonius Tranquillus, Caius: De grammaticis et rhetoribus. ca. 1473.

4°. [16] leaves (16 blank); 198 x 149 mm.

Printed by De Valdezoccho with Martinus de Septem Arboribus.

Initial spaces, one with guide-letter, not filled in; without rubrication. Modern vellum. Leaves [b]6–7 remargined, 3–5 repaired.

HC 15132; Pr 6767; BMC 7:905 (IA.29833a-b); IGI 9224; Goff S–812; CIBN S–481.

28 November 1942—Bought with the Amey Richmond Sheldon fund. Inc 6767

2799   Leonicenus, Omnibonus: De octo partibus orationis. 14 January 1474.

4°. [100] leaves; 194 x 142 mm.

Includes his *De arte metrica*. Printed by De Valdezoccho with Martinus de Septem Arboribus.

Initial and 4-sided border on a1r illuminated in gold and colors; initial spaces elsewhere either added in black or not filled in. 18th-century sprinkled calf, with a crowned monogram of interlaced L's stamped in the spine panels (Louis XIV or XV?); edges sprinkled red.

From the Sunderland Library (no. 7347 in pt. 3 of the Puttick & Simpson sale catalogue, July 1882); bookplate of Leo S. Olschki. Signatures in quires f–h and k trimmed away.

HC(+Add) 10024; Pr 6762; BMC 7:906 (IA.29820); IGI 7002; Goff L–174; CIBN L–149.

2 September 1941–Bought with the Stephen Salisbury fund. Inc 6762

2800 Hierocles: In aureos versus Pythagorae opusculum. 17 April 1474.

4°. [92] leaves (92 blank); 188 x 140 mm.

Latin translation by Johannes Aurispa.

Initial on a3r added in blue and brown, including a drawing of a dog; initials elsewhere added in red. Old vellum. Bookplate of Count Ercole Silva; from the library of Richard Ashhurst Bowie, with a slip of his MS notes inserted at front; MS ownership notation erased in upper margin of a1r.

HC(+Add) 8545*; Pr 6763; BMC 7:906 (IA.29823a–b); Polain 4432; IGI 4726; Goff H–151; CIBN H–88.

9 November 1908–Gift of Mrs. E. D. Brandegee. Inc 6763 (A)

2801 ——Another copy. 194 x 140 mm.

Initial spaces not filled in; without rubrication. 19th-century dark blue straight-grain morocco, edges gilt. Autograph of Benjamin Schmolek; bookplate of James Frothingham Hunnewell. Blank leaf not present.

January 1919–Deposited by James M. Hunnewell. Inc 6763 (B)

2802 Canis, Johannes Jacobus: De modo studendi in utroque iure. 1 October 1476.

8°. [22] leaves (22 blank); 185 x 115 mm.

Initial on [a]1r illuminated in gold and colors, with marginal extension; illuminated coat of arms in lower margin; initials elsewhere and paragraph marks added in red or blue. Half 19th-century calf and marbled boards. Bookplate of Arthur Kay (no. 159 in the Sotheby sale catalogue of his library, May 1930). Blank leaf not present.

H 4321*; Pr 6766; BMC 12:65 (IA.29832); GW 5973; IGI 2405; Goff C–97; BSB-Ink C–76.

6 April 1931–Received. Law Library

LEONARDUS ACHATES

2803 Platea, Franciscus de: Opus restitutionum, usurarum, excommunicationum. Not after 28 July 1473.

f°. [174] leaves (174 blank); 276 x 203 mm.

Initials on a1r, [h]1r, and [m]2r illuminated in gold and colors, with marginal extensions; initials elsewhere added in red and/or blue, paragraph marks in red or blue. 19th-century blind-stamped leather, edges marbled. Partly obliterated MS inscription on [q]9v, "Librum hunc Donauit ... D. Petronius bononiensis ... die .4°. Aug. 1481"; bookplates of George J. R. Gordon and of James Frothingham Hunnewell. Blank leaf not present; signatures trimmed away.

H 13036*; Pr 6776; BMC 7:909 (IB.29876); IGI 7841; Goff P-753; Sack 2900; CIBN P-431.

January 1919–Deposited by James M. Hunnewell. Inc 6776

2804 ——Another copy. 301 x 209 mm.

Initials added in red and/or blue or red and green, paragraph marks and capital strokes in red. Contemporary blind-stamped leather over wooden boards; brass clasp nails on back cover, latches on front, one clasp with leather thong remains; marks of center and corner bosses, no longer present; author's name in ink on top and lower edges. MS ownership notation below colophon, "M. Bicutij de Cilia"; another in upper margin of A1r, "Ex libris Conuentus [rest erased]."

Law Library

JOHANNES DE RENO

2805 Gentilis de Fulgineo: De balneis. 24 March 1473.

4°. [12] leaves (12 blank); 201 x 143 mm.

Includes Franciscus Casini, *De balneo Petrioli*, and Bonaventura de Castello, *De utilitatibus aquae balnei de Porretta*.

Initials added in brown on the first four leaves, not thereafter. Modern decorated boards. MS marginalia.

H 7571=5492*; BMC 7:xl (for locating Reno in Padua rather than Sant'Orso in 1473); GW 10617; IGI 4207–A; Goff G–133; BSB-Ink G–73.

Countway Library (William Norton Bullard Collection)

A L B E R T U S   D E   S T E N D A L

2806 **Thomas Aquinas:** Summae theologicae pars prima. 5 October 1473.

f°. [256] leaves (1 and 251 blank); 295 x 205 mm.

Edited by Franciscus de Nerito.

Initials, paragraph marks, and capital strokes added in red, blue, or green. 15th-century blind-stamped pigskin over wooden boards; brass clasp plates on back cover, latches on front, clasps with pigskin thongs; leather tabs attached to fore-edges of the leaves to mark sections; title in ink on fore-edges; vellum lining-leaves filled with MS Latin notes. MS ownership notations on flyleaf at front, "Pertineo Joannj Lastenhoultz" and "Nunc vero Gropengeysser ex dono eiusd[em] Joannis anno 1521 die veneris 12 Mensis Julij"; another in lower margin of [a]2r, "Carthusiae In Buxheim," with "Bibl. Buxheim:" stamp (no. 3194 in the Carl Förster sale catalogue of the library, September 1883); bookplate of James Frothingham Hunnewell.

H 1440*; Pr 6781; BMC 7:911 (IB.29893); Pell 1037; IGI 9572; Goff T-197.

January 1919—Deposited by James M. Hunnewell. Inc 6781

P E T R U S   M A U F E R

2806A **Simon Genuensis:** Synonyma medicinae, siue Clavis sanationis. 20 April 1474.

[For transcriptions see Reichling; but in the colophon correct his "Simonis" to "Simõis."] f°. [a-m^{10}, n-o^8, p^{10}, q-r^8]; [162] leaves; 315 x 232 mm. 2 columns. [a]1r: 40 lines, 224 x 151 mm. Type: 1:112R. Initial spaces, some with guide-letters.

Includes a letter from Campanus canonicus Parisiensis.

Initial spaces not filled in; without rubrication. Contemporary doeskin over wooden boards, repaired; marks of clasp plates on front cover, brass latches on back, clasps and thongs gone; marks of bosses on both covers, with one remaining on each.

HR 14748; IGI 8998; Goff S-527; CIBN S-272.

Library of Economic Botany

2807   **Petrus de Abano:** De physiognomia. 1474.

4°. [50] leaves; 188 x 144 mm.

Initial on [a]1r added in red and blue, with marginal extension. Half modern brown morocco and brown cloth. MS ownership notation at end, "Questo libro sie [?] dm̄i uicētio uliacrio [?]."

HC 18; Pr 6791; BMC 7:912 (IA.29914); Pell 13; IGI 7601; Goff P-438; CIBN P-207.

Countway Library

2808   **Corpus iuris civilis. Digesta Justiniani. Digestum novum.** 1479.

f°. [356] leaves (1 blank); 430 x 285 mm.

Printed by Maufer for Zacharias de Zacharotis. With the *glossa ordinaria* of Accursius. There are variants on a2r and Q5v; see GW.

This copy has the readings of the main GW transcriptions on a2r and Q5v. Initials and paragraph marks added in red or blue. Contemporary leather over wooden boards, rebacked and repaired; one brass latch remains on front cover, clasps and thongs gone; brass center and two corner bosses on each cover. MS ownership notation on blank a1r, "Ex Libris Cigalinorū"; autograph of Vincentius Lucinus on Q6r under one of Ambrosius Brunellus crossed out; MS index on blank a1v.

HC 9582*; Pr 6797; BMC 7:913 (IC.29928); GW 7704; IGI 5451; Goff J-568; BSB-Ink C-582.

28 September 1949—Received. Law Library

2809   **Corpus iuris civilis. Digesta Justiniani. Infortiatum.** 1479.

f°. [300] leaves (1 blank); 430 x 285 mm.

According to GW, printed by Antonius de Strata and Hercules de Buscha for Maufer and others, with Maufer's types. With the *glossa ordinaria* of Accursius.

Initials and paragraph marks added in red or blue. Half modern maroon morocco and maroon cloth. MS ownership notation on blank a1r,

"Ex Libris Cigalinorũ"; autograph of Vincentius Lucinus on P6r; MS index on blank a1v. Imperfect: leaves P3–6 mutilated, with loss of text.

H 9561*; C 3397; Pr 6798; BMC 7:913 (I.29929); GW 7680; IGI 5475; Goff J-556; Sack 1135; BSB-Ink C-614.

28 September 1949—Received. Law Library

2810 Rhazes, Muhammad: Liber nonus ad Almansorem. 1 May 1480.

[For transcriptions see Reichling; but insert a colon after "solitis" in the title and a line-ending in "im ‖ presso3" in the colophon.] f°. a–b^{10}, c–d^8, e^6, f–i^8, ij^{10}, k–l^8, m^{10}, n^8, A–G^8, I-M^8, N–O^6 (a1 blank); [218] leaves (1 blank); 418 x 285 mm. 2 columns. a2r: 66 lines, 288 x 180 mm. Type: 5:87G. Initial spaces.

Includes commentary by Johannes Arculanus. Edited by Hieronymus Turianus.

Initials added in red and/or blue, paragraph marks and underlinings in red or blue. Contemporary blind-stamped leather over wooden boards; brass clasp plates on back cover, latches on front, clasps and thongs gone; metal corner bosses on both covers; in a cloth case. MS ownership notation inside front cover, "Hic liber est mei Ieronimi monetarii de feltkirchen arciũ medicineq[ue] doctoris quem mihi feci exportari ex veneciis ad Nurembergam urbem almanie anno domini 148ii." With a folder of Münzer's MS index laid in. From the Fürstlich Dietrichstein'sche Bibliothek (no. 83 [p. 6] in Rudolf Pindter's 1905–06 catalogue of the library; no. 599 in the Gilhofer and Ranschburg sale catalogue, November 1933). Lower margins badly chewed away, not affecting text.

HR 13898; IGI 8344; Goff R-179.

Countway Library (William Norton Bullard Collection)

D . S . (D O M I N I C U S
S I L I P R A N D U S)

2811 Columella, Lucius Junius Moderatus: De re rustica liber XI. ca. 1475.

4°. [10] leaves; 203 x 145 mm.

Initial space on [a]1r not filled in; without rubrication. 19th-century dark green cloth.

HC 5498*; Pr 7331 (Italian adespota); BMC 7:914 (IA.30070); GW 7181; IGI(+Suppl) 3064; Goff C–763; BSB-Ink C–475.

22 April 1922—Gift of Sarah C. Sears. Arnold Arboretum Library

2812   **Daniel:** Somnia Danielis [1st recension]. ca. 1480.

4°. [10] leaves; 189 x 138 mm.   Plate I

Initial spaces, with guide-letters, not filled in; without rubrication. Modern tan boards.

GW 7907; Goff D–7.

June 1952—Gift of Imrie de Vegh. Inc 6798.5

J O H A N N E S   H E R B O R T

2813   **Monte, Petrus de:** Repertorium utriusque iuris. 16 November 1480.

f°. 2 vols. (vol. 1: [372] leaves, 1 and 372 blank; vol. 2: [380] leaves, 1 and 380 blank); 400 x 270 mm.

Edited by Comes de Alvarotis.

Harvard has vol. 1 only. Initials added in red or blue. Unbound; in a cloth case. Four leaves of MS index inserted at front.

HC 11589*; Pr 6802; BMC 7:917 (IC.29949); Polain 2786; IGI 6724; Goff M–844; Sack 2503.

31 March 1931—Received by exchange. Inc 6802

N . T . S . P .

2814   **Suiseth, Richardus:** Opus aureum calculationum. ca. 1477.

f°. [86] leaves (1 blank); 260 x 187 mm.

Edited by Johannes de Cipro.

Initial spaces, some with guide-letters, not filled in; without rubrication. Old vellum. MS ownership notations erased from top and lower margins of a2r; bookplate of William Norton Bullard. Blank leaf not present.

HC 15136*; Pr 6805; BMC 7:919 (IB.29968); IGI 9190; Goff S–830; CIBN S–496.

Countway Library (William Norton Bullard Collection)

M A T T H A E U S   C E R D O N I S

2815 **Philelphus, Franciscus:** Invectiva in Georgium Merulam. After 4 June 1481.

4°. [2] leaves; 209 x 148 mm.

Initial spaces and spaces for Greek not filled in; without rubrication. Modern vellum. Royal Society bookstamp, "ex dono Henr. Howard Norfolciensis," with its release stamp at end.

H 12965*; BMC 7:924 (IA.30054); IGI 3883 (with facsimile); Goff P–604.

20 October 1955—Bought with the Susan A. E. Morse fund. Inc 6805.5

2816 **Passageriis, Rolandinus de:** Flos testamentorum. 13 May 1482.

4°. 69 (i.e., 70) leaves (70 misnumbered 69); 210 x 152 mm.

With additions by Petrus de Unzola.

Initials and paragraph marks added in red. Half modern brown morocco and marbled boards.

HC 12096*; Pr 6808; BMC 7:920 (IA.29984); IGI 7240; Goff R–243.

26 November 1923—Received. Law Library

2817 **Cerutus, Blancus:** Declamationes. 29 May 1482.

4°. 14 leaves; 205 x 148 mm.

Initial spaces, with guide-letters, not filled in; without rubrication. Modern paper wrappers; in a cloth case.

H 4889*=4888; Pr 6807; BMC 7:920 (IA.29986); GW 6519; IGI 2712; Goff C–407; BSB-Ink C–243.

13 February 1935—Received. Law Library

2818 **Pseudo-Pythagoras:** Ludus. 21 August 1482.

[a]1r: Ludus Pitagore. ‖ (q³)ui recreandi causa ludo in pitagoreo se exercere vo-‖luerī t. modũ hunc seruare addistant . . . ‖ [c]1v, COLO-

PHON: Finis operis. i482. Die .2i ‖ Augusti. ҭ c̄. Laus deo ‖

4°. [a^{10} (–[a]7)]; 1–6, 8–10 leaves (leaf 7 cancelled); 198 x 142 mm. [a]1r: 32 lines, 147 x 91 mm. Type: 1:90G. Initial space on [a]1r.   Plate II

As indicated, the leaves of this book are numbered in the upper margin 1–6, 8–10, with no text lacking between 6 and 8. Hain theorizes that "f. 7 vacat," but Dr. Elmar Hertrich, to whom I wrote concerning details of the Munich copy (one of the few others recorded), says "Hains Angabe ... beruhte also wohl nicht auf Autopsie eines leeren Blattes ... sondern war lediglich die Schlussfolgerung aus der Lückenlosigkeit des Textes." Dr. Hertrich informs me that the BSB-Ink collation of their copy (present shelf-mark 4°.Inc.c.a.238) will read "9 Bl. [a$^{10-1}$], gez. 1–6, 8–10"; my own examination of the Munich copy confirms Dr. Hertrich's observation that watermarks (similar to Briquet 11754) occur on leaves numbered 2/9, 4, and 3/8; in the Harvard copy they occur on leaves numbered 2/9, 3/8, 4, and 5/6. The book is too tightly bound to determine conjugacy with certainty, but the Munich copy is loosely bound and shows Dr. Hertrich's collation to be correct. Leaf 4 in both copies has half the watermark, which presumably would be continued on leaf 7 if it were present.

Initial space not filled in; without rubrication. Modern gray boards. Imperfect: leaves [a]1 and 10 wanting, supplied in photostatic reproduction.

H 13625*; Klebs 820.1; Goff P–1146; ISTC records copies at Munich, Edinburgh, and (imperfect) at Aschaffenburg.

Countway Library

2819   **Nicolaus episcopus Modrusiensis:** Oratio in funere Petri cardinalis S. Sixti. 30 August 1482.

4°. [1], 2–7, [1] leaves; 204 x 145 mm.

Initial space on [a]1v not filled in; without rubrication. Modern gray boards.

H 11774*; BMC 7:920 (IA.29989); IGI 6852; Goff N–51.

2 September 1941—Bought with the Archibald Cary Coolidge fund. Inc 6808.5

2820   **Brunus Aretinus, Leonardus:** De studiis et litteris. 2 March 1483.

4°. [8] leaves; 204 x 143 mm.

Includes Pius II's *Epitaphium* on Brunus Aretinus.

Without rubrication. Modern gray boards. A few MS marginalia.

H 1574; BMC 7:921 (IA.30000); GW 5623; IGI 2209; Goff B-1259; BSB-Ink B-939.

23 January 1935—Bought with the Charles William Eliot fund. Inc 6811.10

2821 Aegidius Corboliensis: De urinarum iudiciis. 12 July 1483.

4°. [66] leaves; 206 x 150 mm.

With the commentary of Gentilis de Fulgineo. Edited by Venantius Mutius.

Without rubrication. 19th-century vellum.

HCR 100; Pr 6813; BMC 7:921 (IA.30004); Pell 61; GW 269; IGI 56; Goff A-93; BSB-Ink A-36.

Countway Library (William Norton Bullard Collection)

2822 Aegidius Corboliensis: De pulsibus. January 1484.

4°. [48] leaves; 201 x 148 mm.

With the commentary of Gentilis de Fulgineo. Edited by Venantius Mutius.

Without rubrication. Old MS vellum. Autograph and bookplate of Paul Dudley White.

H 103*; Pr 6815; BMC 7:921 (IA.30008); Pell 64; GW 268; IGI 55; Goff A-92; BSB-Ink A-35.

Countway Library (Gift of Paul Dudley White)

2823 Oresme, Nicolaus: De latitudinibus formarum. 18 February 1486.

4°. [20] leaves (20 blank); ill.; 200 x 147 mm.

Includes the *Quaestiones* of Blasius de Pelicanis.

Without rubrication. Modern tan boards.

H 8925*; Pr 6820; BMC 7:923 (IA.30024); IGI 7030; Goff O-94; Sander 3466.

27 October 1923—Bought with the Peter Paul Francis Degrand fund. Inc 6820

2824 **Gentilis de Fulgineo:** De dosibus medicinarum. ca. 1486.

4°. 10 leaves; 200 x 140 mm.

Woodcut initials touched with red; capital strokes and underlinings added in red. Modern vellum.

HC 7569*; Pr 6828; BMC 7:924 (IA.30048); Polain 1570; GW 10622; IGI 4210; Goff G–142; BSB-Ink G–74.

Countway Library (William Norton Bullard Collection)

2825 **Montagnana, Bartholomaeus:** De urinarum iudiciis. 17 February 1487.

4°. 26, [2] leaves ([27–28] blank); 202 x 145 mm.

Without rubrication. Old vellum. MS marginalia. Last blank leaf not present.

HCR 11553; Pr 6821; BMC 7:923 (IA.30029); Polain 2783; IGI 6701; Goff M–817; CIBN M–526.

Countway Library (William Norton Bullard Collection)

2826 **Derrames, Johannes:** Carmina de conditionibus medicinarum solutivarum. After 4 July 1487.

4°. 6 leaves; 202 x 144 mm.

Without rubrication. Old vellum.

H 6095*; Pr 6825; BMC 7:924 (IA.30036); GW 8252; IGI 3405; Goff D–141; BSB-Ink D–99.

Countway Library (William Norton Bullard Collection)

2827 **Bagellardus, Paulus:** De infantium aegritudinibus et remediis. 10 November 1487.

4°. 22 leaves (6 misnumbered 2); 198 x 145 mm.

Initials and paragraph marks added in red. Modern vellum. MS ownership notation in lower margin of [a]1r, "Hieronymi Gaffurij." MS marginalia in several different hands.

HR 2245; GW 3167; IGI 1147; Goff B–11.

Countway Library (William Norton Bullard Collection)

2828 **Petrus de Abano:** De venenis. 18 December 1487.

[For transcriptions see Pellechet; but this copy has "tractaluli" for her "tractatuli" on [e]3v.] 4°. [a–d⁸, e⁴]; 34, [2] leaves (31 and 32 misnumbered 32 and 31); 198 x 135 mm. [a]2r: 30 lines, 134 x 90 mm. Type: 1:90G. Woodcut initials.

Includes Arnoldus de Villa Nova, *De arte cognoscendi venena*, and Valascus de Tarenta, *De epidemia et peste*.

Without rubrication. Half 19th-century calf and marbled boards.

H 12*; Pr 6826; Pell 10; IGI 7605; Goff P–442; CIBN P–210.

Countway Library (William Norton Bullard Collection)

2829 Articuli Parisius condemnati. ca. 1487.

4°. 10 leaves; 200 x 146 mm.

Initial space on [a]1r not filled in; without rubrication. Modern maroon morocco by Lortic; edges gilt. Monogram booklabel "D R H [?]."

HCR 1878; C 707; BMC 12:66 (IA.30046); Pell 1398; GW 2709; IGI 915; Goff A–1150.

3 May 1945–Received. Law Library

H I E R O N Y M U S   D E   D U R A N T I S

2830 Aristoteles: Parva naturalia. 24 May 1493.

f°. [100] leaves; 293 x 204 mm.

Latin translations by Guillelmus de Moerbeka and Gerardus Cremonensis, with commentary of Thomas Aquinas. Edited by Onofrius de Funtania.

Initial spaces, with guide-letters, not filled in; without rubrication. For binding description see no. 2712, Paulus Venetus, *Summulae logicae* (Venice, Otinus de Luna, 5 May 1498), with which this is bound, along with De Luna's edition of Gualtherus Burlaeus, *Expositio in artem veterem Porphyrii et Aristotelis* (11 May 1497).

HC 1719*; BMC 7:925 (IB.30062); Pell 1216; GW 2430; IGI 837; Goff A–1019; BSB-Ink A–708.

Countway Library (William Norton Bullard Collection)

2831 **Columna, Aegidius:** De materia caeli et De intellectu possibili. 25 September 1493.

f°. [12] leaves; 305 x 211 mm.

Edited by Antoninus Aegidius Canisius.

Initial spaces not filled in; without rubrication. Modern maroon morocco.

H 114*; Pr 6831; BMC 7:925 (IB.30065); GW 7213; IGI 3087; Goff A–81; BSB-Ink A–39.

10 April 1929–Gift of James Byrne. Inc 6831

Florence

PRELIMINARY NOTE TO FLORENCE

Because of the practice of Florentine printers of the 1490s and their successors to continue using types and woodblocks that began life in the fifteenth well into the sixteenth century and to fail to date their books, I may very well have included in this section a number that should properly be excluded from a catalogue of incunabula. Dr. Dennis Rhodes of the British Library has done much to clear up uncertainties of dating in many individual instances, but even he has not been able to cover the entire field of Florentine printing, and much more remains to be done than I can undertake in the limited amount of time I can devote to each printer. I have felt justified, however, in departing from my general rule of not giving detailed descriptions of post-1500 books in a number of cases where the book has been listed by many authorities as an incunable and is rare enough so that only a few copies have been recorded but never adequately described. I have, however, excluded a number of post-1500 Savonarola tracts of no great rarity. Of these a list will be found at the end of this section.

BERNARDUS AND
DOMINICUS CENNINUS

2832 **Servius Maurus, Honoratus:** Commentarii in Vergilii opera. 7 November 1471–7 October 1472.

f°. [238] leaves (238 blank); 406 x 286 mm.

This work is divided into three parts (commentaries on the *Bucolics*, *Georgics*, and the *Aeneid*), each with its own colophon; and they may have been issued separately. Edited by Petrus Cenninus.

Harvard has pt. 2 only (commentary on the *Georgics*, [c–e¹⁰, f1–5]). Initial spaces and spaces for Greek not filled in; without rubrication. Bound in a vellum leaf of 15th-century Latin liturgical MS with musical notation.

HCR 14707; BMC 6:617 (IC.27010); IGI 8945; Goff S–481; CIBN S–243; Rhodes (F) 723.

December 1964—Gift of Ward M. Canaday. Inc 6091.5

JOHANNES PETRI
(SEE ALSO
LORENZO MORGIANI)

2833   **Savonarola, Hieronymus:** Predica fatta la mattina dell'Ascensione 1497. After 4 May 1497.

4°. [8] leaves (8 blank); 198 x 137 mm.

Edited by Girolamo Cinozzi.

Without rubrication. Leaves numbered in MS 197–203. Half modern black morocco and red cloth.

C 14398=HR 14399; Pr 6372; BMC 6:618 (IA.27842); IGI 8759; Goff S–259; CIBN S–126; Rhodes (F) 667.

17 May 1921—From the Savonarola collection formed by Henry R. Newman. Bought with the Edward Henry Hall fund. Inc 6372

2834   **Savonarola, Hieronymus:** Epistola contra sententiam excommunicationis. After 19 June 1497.

4°. [6] leaves (6 blank); 199 x 136 mm.

Includes an Italian translation by Filippo Cioni.

Without rubrication. Leaves numbered in MS 218–221 (i.e., 222). Half modern black morocco and red cloth.

HR 14453; C 5299; Pr 6374; BMC 6:618 (IA.27846); Polain 3458; IGI

8697; Goff S–191; CIBN S–96; Rhodes (F) 620.

17 May 1921–From the Savonarola collection formed by Henry R. Newman. Bought with the Duplicate fund. Inc 6374

2835 **Imitatio Christi.** 10 November 1497.

8°. [128] leaves (128 blank); 135 x 100 mm.

Includes Johannes Gerson, *De meditatione cordis.*

Without rubrication. Modern vellum, gilt and colored, signed at end by the binder "I. T. R. 1905." 12 lines of MS Latin verse on q3v. Imperfect: title page mutilated and mounted.

HCR 9110; Pr 6375; BMC 6:619 (IA.27850); Polain 2067; IGI 5125; Goff I–33; Rhodes (F) 375.

22 November 1921–W. A. Copinger Imitatio Christi Collection, presented by James Byrne. Inc 6375

2836 ——Another copy. 135 x 93 mm.

Without rubrication. Half old leather and decorated boards. MS ownership inscription obliterated from title page. Monogram bookla-bel "CHMBI [?]" with motto "Plus penser que dire" inside front cover.

Countway Library

A P U D   S A N C T U M   J A C O B U M
D E   R I P O L I

2837 **Fontius, Bartholomaeus:** Commentum in Persium. De ponderibus et mensuris. Not before December 1477.

4°. [90] leaves; 196 x 137 mm.

This copy has the same MS corrections on g1r as noted by BMC. Initial spaces, most with guide-letters, not filled in; without rubrication. Modern vellum; edges gilt. Imperfect: quire n² at end wanting.

HR 7226; Pr 6098; BMC 6:621 (IA.27031); Pell 4863; GW 10170; IGI 4012; Goff F–241; Rhodes (F) 315.

13 October 1916–Gift of Mrs. E. D. Brandegee. Inc 6098

2838   Curtius Rufus, Quintus: Historiae Alexandri Magni [Italian]. 1478.

f°. [166] leaves; 268 x 187 mm.

Italian translation by Petrus Candidus Decembrius; includes his *Comparazione di Caio Julio Cesare et d'Alexandro Magno*.

Initial spaces, with guide-letters, not filled in; without rubrication. 19th-century green calf, gilt. Booklabel of Adriana R. Salem.

HCR 5888=H 5889; Pr 6100; BMC 6:622 (IB.27038); Pell 4070; GW 7877; IGI 3292; Goff C–1006; Rhodes (F) 229.

December 1957–Gift of Ward M. Canaday. Inc 6100

2839   Pseudo-Petrarca, Francesco: Vite dei pontefici ed imperatori romani. Not after 3 February 1478/9.

f°. [104] leaves (104 blank); 280 x 205 mm.

Initial spaces, with guide-letters, not filled in; without rubrication. 19th-century orange morocco; edges gilt. MS marginalia in a contemporary hand, which has written "Laurentius de Medicis" below the colophon, but the hand does not appear to be his. Leaf a8 is misbound after p6, and another copy of a8, trimmed to the edge of text and inlaid, has been inserted after a7. Blank leaf not present.

HC(+Add) 12809*; Pr 6102; BMC 6:623 (IB.27046a); IGI 7563; Goff P–420; CIBN P–197; Rhodes (F) 500.

28 April 1874–Gift of Charles Sumner. Inc 6102

2840   Ficinus, Marsilius: Consiglio contro la pestilenza. Not before 6 July 1481.

4°. [52] leaves (52 blank); 198 x 134 mm.

Initial spaces, some with guide-letters, not filled in; without rubrication. Half old vellum and marbled boards. Autograph "Robert Willard" on flyleaf at front; bookplate of the Boston Medical Library. Imperfect: leaf g1 wanting; blank g4 not present.

HR 7082; Pr 6108; BMC 6:623 (IA.27061); Pell 4790; GW 9872; IGI 3862; Goff F–153; Rhodes (F) 293.

Countway Library

2841   Maimonides, Moses, Rabbi: De regimine sanitatis ad Soldanum Babyloniae. ca. 1481.

4°. [40] leaves; 210 x 142 mm.

16th-century blind-stamped pigskin over wooden boards; brass clasp plates on back cover, latches on front, clasps with doeskin thongs; MS paper label on front cover. MS marginalia. MS ownership notation inside front cover, "Ad Archiep. Clericorum Seminar."

HC 10525*; Pr 6109; BMC 6:623 (IA.27063); IGI 6750; Goff M-80; Rhodes (F) 420.

Countway Library (Solomon M. Hyams Collection)

2842 Valerius Flaccus, Gaius: Argonautica. ca. 1481.

[For transcriptions see Reichling.] 4°. a–i⁸, l–m⁸, n⁶; [94] leaves; 220 x 158 mm. a2r: 31 lines, 157 x 91 mm. Type: 4:105(100)R. Initial spaces.

Initial spaces not filled in; without rubrication. 19th-century vellum. MS ownership notation inside front cover, "Ex libris Aloysii Cañ.ci Zappatti Vaticanae Bibl: scriptoris latini"; small booklabel mounted in lower margin of a1r reads "Ex libris [line ruled out in ink] Romae"; according to a MS note by Richard Ashhurst Bowie mounted inside front cover, "This copy belonged to Cardinal François Xavier Telada, whose ex-libris appears upon the first page."

CR 5924; Pr 6111; IGI 10051; Goff V-21; Rhodes (F) 758.

9 November 1908—Gift of Mrs. E. D. Brandegee. Inc 6111

N I C O L A U S   L A U R E N T I I

2843 Ficinus, Marsilius: De Christiana religione. Between 10 November and 10 December 1476.

4°. [135] leaves; 227 x 158 mm.

On the duplicate settings of leaves [g]1 and [g]2 see Curt F. Bühler, "The First Edition of Ficino's *De Christiana religione*: a Problem in Bibliographical Description" in his *Early Books and Manuscripts* (New York, 1973) [307]–12. Bühler records copies in which [g]1 has been cancelled, others in which [g]2 has been cancelled, and still others in which both leaves are present.

In this copy both [g]1 and [g]2, one of which should have been cancelled, are present. Initial on [a]1r added in red and blue, with marginal extension; initials elsewhere added in blue, paragraph marks in red or blue, capital strokes in yellow. Half 18th-century leather and wooden boards with beveled edges; vellum lining leaves; in a cloth case. Tipped in at front is an autograph letter, "Marsilius Ficinus Nicholao micheloctio V[eneran]do Viro: Si Laurentius meus cognosceret Antoniũ seraphicum miniatensem, cõphilosophum nostrum, uirum sanctitate doctrinaq[ue] uenerandum ... 19 octobris 1475"; another MS note (by Ficinus?) in upper margin of [a]1r, "In omnibus quę aut hic aut alibi a me tractant[ur], tantum assertum e[ss]e uolo, q[uan]tum ab ecclesia comprobatur"; MS marginalia and interlinear corrections (by the author?) throughout. From the Bibliotheca Phillippica (no. 122 in the Sotheby sale catalogue of part of the library, 25 November 1946). Imperfect: two leaves of table at end wanting.

HCR 7069; Pr 6125; BMC 6:625 (IA.27111); GW 9876; IGI 3857; Goff F-148; BSB-Ink F-112; Rhodes (F) 294.

13 March 1947—Bought with the Duplicate fund. Inc 6125

2844 **Cavalca, Domenico:** Pungi lingua. ca. 1476/77.

4°. [118] leaves (118 blank); 263 x 190 mm.

This copy varies from the BMC and GW transcriptions of q3v: "et conessa siamo dengni sẽpre ‖ ineterno cosancti angieli lui lodrre [*sic*] et ringratiare: ‖ FINIT PERNICHOLAVM FLORENTIE. ‖ DEO GRATIAS AMEN." Initials added in red or blue, but some spaces not filled in. Modern blind-stamped calf; leather thongs with brass clasps nailed to back cover, latches on front. Booklabel of Adriana R. Salem. Leaves a1-2, p8, and q1 remargined; blank leaf not present.

HC 4771; Pr 6124; BMC 6:626 (IB.27109); Pell 3444; GW 6409; IGI 2633; Goff C-338; BSB-Ink C-203; Rhodes (F) 171.

August 1959—Gift of Ward M. Canaday. Inc 6124

2845 **Antonio da Siena:** Monte santo di Dio. 10 September 1477.

4°. [131] leaves; ill.; 265 x 195 mm.

The three engravings (two full-page, one half-page) are among the first engraved book illustrations known; the designs are attributed to Sandro Botticelli and the engraving to Baccio Baldini; but the attribution rests on Vasari rather than on contemporary sources. The BMC and GW collations can be made more precise: i⁸ (i4+1).

Initials on a1r, o1r, and p7v illuminated in gold and colors, the latter two with marginal extensions; a1r illuminated with a four-sided border; initials elsewhere and paragraph marks added in red. 18th-century red straight-grain morocco, spine and edges gilt. MS ownership notation erased from lower margin of π1r; other notations in lower margins throughout the book ("Io fra alissandro Campi," "Io fra Archangelo di checsi da bologna," and "Fra Antonio da Ferrara") are probably those of readers, not owners. The two full-page illustrations show signs of brushwork restoration.

HCR 1276; Pr 6114; BMC 6:626 (IB.27074); Pell 900; GW 2204; IGI 711; Goff A–886; Schäfer 14; Rhodes (F) 54; Sander 452.

31 March 1880—Bought with the F. C. Gray fund for the Fogg Art Museum. 24 November 1953—Placed on permanent deposit in the Houghton Library by the Fogg Art Museum. Typ Inc 6114

2846 Celsus, Aulus Cornelius: De medicina. 1478.

f° and 4°. [196] leaves (196 blank); 278 x 206 mm.

Edited by Bartholomaeus Fontius with assistance of Franciscus Saxettus. There is a variation in the headline on o5r; see BMC and GW.

In this copy the headline on o5r reads correctly ".Qvintvs." Initials and paragraph marks through g3 and in the table added in red or blue; spaces thereafter, with guide-letters, not filled in. Old limp vellum. MS marginalia, with one notation on π1v heavily inked out and with the explanation "Hęc q[uae] p[er] me hic scripta erant sunt deleta . . ."; another notation in the same hand below colophon, "Petrus Michael Carbonelus Serenissimi dñi Regis Castellę & Aragonum Scriba exoluit huius Codicis precium die Veneris .xxxi°. Januarij Anno salutis .M°.CCCC.Lxxxiij°. Ferdinãdo iii. regnãte"; later notation in upper margin of A2r, "Aquest llibre, cum diis al acabament habia sigut d'esi Pere Miguel Carbonel archiveri y bibliotecari de Fernando el Catulich." Imperfect: quire e⁶ and leaves π6, a4, d5–6, f3, and A1 wanting; quire A⁸ bound at front in this copy.

HC 4835*; Pr 6116; BMC 6:627 (IB.27079); Pell 3464; GW 6456; IGI 2674; Goff C–364; BSB-Ink C–207; Rhodes (F) 179.

7 May 1913—Gift of Alain Campbell White. Inc 6116

2847 ——Another copy. 290 x 208 mm.

Headline on o5r as above. Initial spaces not filled in; without rubrication. Half 18th-century sheep and blue boards. Autograph of J. F. Fulton. Imperfect: quire A^8 (table) wanting, supplied in MS and bound at front.

Countway Library

2848   ——Another copy. 276 x 191 mm.

In this copy the headline on o5r reads incorrectly ".Qvartvs." Initial spaces not filled in; without rubrication. 18th-century diced russia, edges gilt; in a cloth case. Quire A^8 (table) bound at front.

Countway Library

2849   **Pulci, Luca:** Il Driadeo. 3 April 1479.

[For transcriptions see Reichling.] 4°. π^2, a–g^8; [58] leaves; 208 x 127 mm. π2r: 35 lines, 158 x 88 mm. Type: 3:92R. A few initial spaces.

Initial spaces not filled in; without rubrication. 18th-century red morocco, spine and edges gilt. The Gaignat copy (no. 2018 in vol. 1 of the De Bure sale catalogue of the library, 1769).

HCR 13577; IGI 8212; Goff P–1109; Rhodes (F) 557.

December 1964–Gift of Ward M. Canaday. Inc 6116.5

2850   **Samuel Maroccanus, Rabbi:** Epistola contra Iudaeorum errores [Italian]. After 25 November 1479.

4°. [54] leaves; 217 x 157 mm.

Italian translation by Sebastiano Salvini. Includes the Athanasian creed and an exposition of various texts connected with Christ's agony in the garden and the denial of Peter; also short summaries of the Psalms and various canticles, all by Salvini.

Initials and paragraph marks added in red. Half 18th-century sheep and speckled boards. Bookstamps of the Augustinian Canons, Florence (S. Michele di Campora), the Biblioteca Pubblica, Florence, and monogram "MD"; booklabel of Angelo Maria Bandini; bookplates of Giuseppe Martini (no. 322 in his incunabula catalogue, 1934) and of Lee M. Friedman.

HCR 14275=H 14276; C 5260; Pr 6117; BMC 6:628 (IA.27085); IGI 8586; Goff S–117; CIBN S–60; Rhodes (F) 599.

1957–Bequest of Lee M. Friedman. Inc 6117

2851   Dante Alighieri: La Commedia. 30 August 1481.

f°. [372] leaves (1, 14–15, 169, and 371–72 blank); ill.; 416 x 278 mm.

"As indicated by a blank space or by an engraving preceding the cantos, a complete series of illustrations must have originally been planned for this edition. Engravings are known only for the first nineteen cantos of the *Inferno*. Of these, only those for the first three cantos are found impressed on the pages of text (in some instances, the third being a repetition of the second). The remaining engravings, if any or all appear, are found on separate slips of paper pasted in at their respective places."–Goff. The designs are attributed to Sandro Botticelli and the engraving to Baccio Baldini; but the attribution rests on Vasari rather than on contemporary sources. There are variants on oo6v of the *Purgatorio* and on A1r of the *Paradiso*; see BMC and GW. With the commentary of Christophorus Landinus and additions by Marsilius Ficinus.

In this copy the last line of commentary to the *Purgatorio* (oo6v) has reading "per sua infinita misericordia"; Landino's prologue to the *Paradiso* (A1r, missigned aaa1) is set up in 47 lines, the last beginning "te ciriempie." Engravings are present for the first two cantos only. Large initials, with marginal extensions, illuminated in gold and colors on a2r of the *Inferno* and on aa2r and aa3r of the *Purgatorio*, the first including a miniature portrait of Dante; initials elsewhere added in blue in the *Inferno* and *Purgatorio*; spaces in the *Paradiso*, with guide-letters, not filled in. Bound in three volumes in half 19th-century calf and red boards. MS ownership notation on front flyleaves of vols. 1–2, "Della Libreria di Carlo Tommaso del Senatore Alessandro Strozzi 1728." Imperfect: leaf a2 has been rebacked in the lower margin where the engraving has been impressed, with some damage to the lower margin of the engraving; leaf h8 wanting; blank leaf 2π2 not present.

HC 5946*; Pr 6120; BMC 6:628 (IC.27094-96); Pell 4114-4114A; Polain 1223; GW 7966; IGI 360; Goff D-29; BSB-Ink D-9; Schäfer 115; Rhodes (F) 231; Sander 2311.

4 May 1905—From the library of Charles Eliot Norton. Inc 6120 (A)

2852   ——Another copy. 426 x 280 mm.

Leaves oo6v and A1r with readings as above; engravings present for the first two cantos of the *Inferno* only. Without rubrication or illumination. Half modern white pigskin and wooden boards; braided pigskin thongs fastened to metal pins on edge of front cover. Bookplate of George Ticknor. Last two blank leaves not present.

28 October 1896–From the library of George Ticknor. Typ Inc 6120

2853   ——Another copy. 415 x 280 mm.

In this copy leaf oo6v has reading "per sua instituta misericordia"; leaf A1r, missigned aa1, is set up in 48 lines, the last beginning "ita: ne da tempo." With engravings for the first three cantos of the *Inferno*, the third a repetition of the second. Without rubrication or illumination. 19th-century dark blue straight-grain morocco, edges gilt. Bookplates of the Duke of Sussex (no. 457 in pt. 5 of the Evans sale catalogue, April 1845), John Wyndham Bruce, and James Frothingham Hunnewell. Only the fourth blank leaf is present.

January 1919–Deposited by James M. Hunnewell. Inc 6120 (B)

2854   ——Another copy. 417 x 275 mm.

Same readings as in the copy immediately preceding. With engravings for the first two cantos of the *Inferno* only. Monochrome wash drawings have been added to 15 of the spaces left for engravings in the *Inferno* and to one each in the *Purgatorio* and *Paradiso*; these do not correspond to the originals as described by A. M. Hind, *Catalogue of Early Italian Engravings Preserved in the ... British Museum* (London, 1910) 87–93. Inserted at front is an illuminated title page with a medallion portrait of Dante at head, and mounted on the verso is an ink and wash drawing (383 x 265 mm., School of Zuccaro, late 16th-century) depicting Hell, Purgatory, and Paradise. 19th-century dark blue straight-grain morocco, edges gilt; pink silk doublures and lining-leaves. Bookplates of Charles Carmichael Lacaita (no. 68 in the Sotheby sale catalogue of his library, 20 July 1936) and of William King Richardson. Blank leaves not present.

1951–Bequest of William King Richardson. WKR 10.2.4

2855   **Alberti, Leon Battista:** De re aedificatoria. 29 December 1485.

f°. [204] leaves; 265 x 207 mm.

Edited by Angelus Politianus. Includes a poem by Baptista Siculus. Two settings of the final quire are known; see BMC and GW.

In this setting of the final quire the colophon is set in 12 lines, lines 9–12 reading "Laurentii ‖ Alamani: Anno ‖ salutis Millesimo octua‖gesimo quinto: quarto chalendas ianuarias." Initial spaces, most with guide-letters, not filled in; without rubrication. 18th-century vellum, edges stained red. MS index (2 leaves) inserted at end; MS marginalia; MS ownership notation on a1r, "Fu del quõdã S.ᵒʳ Mario Galiota." Imperfect: several quires at end remargined, affecting marginalia.

HC 419*; Pr 6131; BMC 6:630 (IB.27155a–b); Pell 266; Polain 66 and 66A; GW 579; IGI 155; Goff A–215; Sack 56; BSB-Ink A–125; Rhodes (F) 17.

17 February 1923—Bought with the Charles Eliot Norton fund. Inc 6131

2856   ——Another copy. 272 x 192 mm.

In this setting of the final quire the colophon is set in 11 lines, lines 9–11 reading "Laurentii Alamani: Anno sa‖lutis Millesimo octuage-simo ‖ quinto: quarto Kalendas Ianuarias." Initial spaces not filled in; without rubrication. Modern blind-stamped calf. Occasional MS marginalia. Booklabel of Adriana R. Salem.

1965—Gift of Ward M. Canaday. Inc 6131.1

2857   ——Another copy. 285 x 201 mm.

Setting of the final quire as in the copy immediately preceding. Initials and paragraph marks added in red in the first five quires; spaces thereafter, most with guide-letters, not filled in. Half 18th-century green morocco and speckled boards; title in ink on lower edges. MS ownership notation on a1r, "Ex libris Rᵈⁱ p[at]ris n[ost]ri m[ag-ist]ri Bap[tis]te fer[is] Sacᵉ Theologie p[ro]fesso[r]is q[ui] die 27 m[ar]tii. 1497. obijt"; MS marginalia in the first five quires.

Countway Library (William Norton Bullard Collection)

2858   ——Another copy. 258 x 198 mm.

Setting as in the two copies immediately preceding. Initial spaces not filled in; without rubrication. 18th-century mottled calf. MS margina-lia; 16-page MS index inserted.

Berenson Library, I Tatti

FRANCESCO DI DINO

2859 **Chiarini, Giorgio:** Libro che tratta di mercanzie et usanze dei paesi. 10 December 1481.

4°. [6], LXXXXVi leaves (XX, XXiii–iiii, and LVi misnumbered XXiii, XXii–iii, and XXXXVi); 213 x 142 mm.

The ascription to Chiarini is uncertain; see BMC.

Initial spaces, most with guide-letters, not filled in; without rubrication. Modern vellum. Bookplate of the Business Historical Society, Inc.

HR 4956; Pr 6135; BMC 6:633 (IA.27144); IGI 2747; Goff C–449; Rhodes (F) 193.

23 October 1938–Gift of Charles H. Taylor, Frederic H. Curtis, and Allan Forbes. Kress Library

2860 **Pulci, Luca:** Il Driadeo. 22 August 1489.

4°. [66] leaves; 200 x 131 mm.

Initial spaces, with guide-letters, not filled in; without rubrication. Limp stiffened white wrappers. Bookplate and autograph of George Benson Weston, with his date of acquisition "Florence March 18, 1901." Imperfect: leaf g8 and quire h[10] wanting.

H 13581; BMC 12:46 (IA.27704); IGI 8215; CIBN P–700; Rhodes (F) 560.

1963–Gift of Charles D. Weston. Inc 6338.5

2861 **Pseudo-Eusebius Cremonensis:** Epistola de morte Hieronymi [Italian]. 13 February 1492/3.

4°. [116] leaves; 212 x 143 mm.

There is a variant in the colophon; see GW. Some copies have a woodcut on π1v.

This copy has "fuquesso" in line 2 of the colophon and is without the woodcut. Initial spaces, with guide-letters, not filled in; without rubrication. Modern vellum.

HR 8649; Pr 6339A; Polain 3985; GW 9472; IGI 3749; Goff H–261; Rhodes (F) 285; Sander 3396.

21 October 1919–Bought with the John Harvey Treat fund. Inc 6339A

2862 Cecchi, Domenico: Riforma santa per conservazione di Firenze. 24 February 1496/7.

4°. [28] leaves; 196 x 134 mm.

The woodcut coat of arms on the title page is sometimes lacking; and there are variants in the title; see BMC and GW.

This copy has the coat of arms and has the correct readings "con ‖ seruatione" and "cõserua ‖ re" in the title. Without rubrication. Old calf, rebacked. Bookplate of George John Warren, 5th baron Vernon (no. 129 in the Sotheby sale catalogue of part of his library, 10 June 1918). Imperfect: leaves d3–4 remargined, with some mutilation of text on d4.

HCR 4822=H 4823; Pr 6342; BMC 6:635 (IA.27713); Pell 3456; GW 6443; IGI 2663; Goff C–357; Rhodes (F) 178; Sander 1881.

20 January 1919—Bought with the Bayard Cutting fund. Inc 6342

ANTONIO DI
BARTOLOMMEO MISCOMINI

2863 Ephrem Syrus: Sermones selecti [Latin]. 23 August 1481.

f°. [90] leaves (1 blank); 255 x 177 mm.

Latin translation by Ambrosius Traversarius.

A few initials added in brown, but most spaces not filled in; without rubrication. Old vellum, spine gilt. Bookseller's ticket of Maisonneuve & cie., Paris. From the library of Richard Ashhurst Bowie.

HC 6599*; Pr 6138; BMC 6:636 (IB.27152); Pell 4582; Polain 1401; GW 9331; IGI 3679; Goff E–45; Sack 1359; BSB-Ink E–69; Rhodes (F) 273.

9 November 1908—Gift of Mrs. E. D. Brandegee. Inc 6138

2864 Vergilius Maro, Publius: Bucolica [Italian]. 28 February 1481/2.

4°. [124] leaves (124 blank); 209 x 130 mm.

Italian translation by Bernardo Pulci. Includes original elegies by Pulci and eclogues by Francesco Arsocchi, Girolamo Benivieni, and Jacopo Fiorenzo de'Buoninsegni.

Initial spaces, with guide-letters, not filled in; without rubrication. 19th-century dark blue straight-grain morocco, edges gilt. Bookplates of Robert Proctor and of Murray Anthony Potter. Imperfect: sheets p1–2 wanting; blank leaf q6 not present.

C 6137; Pr 6140; BMC 6:636 (IA.27156–56a); IGI 10241; Goff V–216; CIBN V–153; Rhodes (F) 774; Davies-Goldfinch 148.

18 June 1935—From the library of Murray Anthony Potter. Inc 6140

2865 Horatius Flaccus, Quintus: Opera. 5 August 1482.

f°. [6], CCLXIIII, [2] leaves (LXXIIII and CXXXXIIII misnumbered LXIIII and CXXXIIII); 271 x 210 mm.

Edited with a commentary by Christophorus Landinus. Includes an ode by Angelus Politianus.

A few initials added in brown, but many spaces, most with guide-letters, not filled in. 19th-century blind-stamped calf, edges gilt. MS marginalia. MS ownership notation in upper margin of π2r, "Ex lib. S. Ant. Florentiae Cat. Inscript."; bookplate of William King Richardson.

HCR 8881; Pr 6142; BMC 6:637 (IB.27161); IGI 4880; Goff H–447; CIBN H–276; Rhodes (F) 374.

1951—Bequest of William King Richardson. WKR 1.2.15

2866 Ficinus, Marsilius: Platonica theologia de immortalitate animorum. 7 November 1482.

f° and 4°. [318] leaves (9 blank); 278 x 201 mm.

Initial spaces, with guide-letters, not filled in; without rubrication. 17th-century vellum, wormed, with a MS title page prefixed. MS ownership notation in lower margin of π1r, "Liber loci S^ii. Stefani Marcinę" (i.e., Cava dei Tirreni); bookplate of Giuseppe Martini (no. 163 in pt. 1 of his 1934 catalogue), with his date of acquisition "30 Maggio 1917."

HC 7075*; Pr 6143; BMC 6:637 (IB.27164); Pell 4793; Polain 1479; GW 9881; IGI 3867; Goff F–157; BSB-Ink F–121; Rhodes (F) 298.

11 July 1944—Bought with the Bennett Hubbard Nash fund. Inc 6143

2867 ——Another copy. 288 x 210 mm.

Initial spaces not filled in; without rubrication. For binding description see no. 1846 in vol. 2, Cicero's *De fato* (Venice, Antonius de

Strata, 11 July 1485), with which this is bound, along with Quintilian, *Declamationes* (Treviso, Dionysius Bononiensis and Peregrinus de Pasqualibus Bononiensis, 1482), and Laurentius Valla, *Elegantiae linguae Latinae* (Venice, Unassigned, 17 July 1483).

Countway Library (William Norton Bullard Collection)

2868 Benevolentius, Bartholomaeus: De luce et visibili paradoxon. 1482?

4° and 8°. [52] leaves (6 blank); 200 x 135 mm.

Includes, with a separate signature, his *De analogia huius nominis verbum*, which GW treats as a separate work; but the errata list in pt. 1 includes it.

Initial spaces, with guide-letters, not filled in; without rubrication. Half 19th-century calf and marbled boards; edges stained red. Bookplate of the Dean and Chapter of Chichester.

HCR 2778; C 946(1); Pr 6323 (assigned to Buonaccorsi); BMC 6:637 (IA.27244); Pell 2039(1); GW 3838-39(=1620); IGI 1471-72; Goff B-321-22; Rhodes (F) 95-96.

Countway Library

2869 Foresi, Bastiano: Libro chiamato Ambizione. 1485?

4°. [90] leaves (1 and 90 blank); 205 x 137 mm.

Includes a free Italian version of Vergil's *Georgica* in *terza rima*.

Initial spaces, with guide-letters, not filled in; without rubrication. Half 19th-century calf and marbled boards. Illegible owner's signature on front flyleaf. First blank leaf not present.

HCR 7231; Pr 6175; BMC 6:644 (IA.27232); Pell 4865; GW 10173 ("um 1481/84 oder 1489/91"); IGI 4015; Goff F-243; Rhodes (F) 317.

12 June 1940—Bought with the Bennett Hubbard Nash fund. Inc 6175

2870 Pulci, Luca: Ciriffo Calvaneo. ca. 1485?

a1r: CYRIFFO CALVANEO COMPO ‖ STO PER LVCA DEPVLCI AD ‖ PETITIONE DEL MAGNIFICO ‖ LORENZO DEMEDICI. ‖ (i⁴)O CANTERO CY ‖ riffo caluaneo ‖ Cyriffo ilquale per ‖ paesi diuersi ‖ Errando ando per farsi almondo iddeo ‖ Nuoui amori: nuoui casi: &

nuoui uersi ‖ . . . o8v, line 23: Per tanto io son disposto che su muoia ‖ Et cosi decto se chiamare ilboia ‖

4°. a–o⁸; [112] leaves; 200 x 132 mm. a2r: 24 lines, 134 x 79 mm. Type: 112R. Initial spaces, with guide-letters, on a1r and f6v.   Plate III

Initial spaces not filled in; without rubrication. 19th-century calf, gilt, edges gilt, rehinged. Armorial bookplate of Michael Tomkinson of Franche Hall, Worcestershire (no. 1809 in the Sotheby sale catalogue of his library, April 1922). Imperfect: sheets a3–4 and o1–3 wanting, the latter three supplied in type facsimile; leaves a1–2, 7–8 remargined.

HR 13574; IGI 8211; Goff P–1108; Rhodes (F) 556.

6 July 1926—Bought with the Bennett Hubbard Nash fund. Inc 6148.5

2871 Politianus, Angelus: Miscellaneorum centuria prima. 19 September 1489.

f°. [94] leaves; 257 x 197 mm.

Includes the *editio princeps* of the 5th hymn of Callimachus, *In Palladis lavacra*, with Politian's Latin translation.

Initials added in green. 18th-century spanish sheep, rehinged; edges marbled. Inscribed by the author on p3v, "Angelus Politianus Alexandro Sartio Bonoñ. Suo. dono dat: Monum̃tũ & pignus amoris: Mcccclxxxxi. Die vi. Maij. Bononię. Ego Angelus Politianus: Qm̃ vis Archetypas [illegible] nugas." MS marginalia and corrections; leaf containing autograph and MS notes of John Dillon inserted at front, including "Bot. at a Sale of Autographs at Paris Nov. 1862" (no. 472 in the Sotheby sale catalogue of Dillon's books, June 1869); engraved portrait of Politian inserted at front. The two leaves containing "Emendationes" are bound at front in this copy.

HC(+Add) 13221*; Pr 6149; BMC 6:638 (IB.27177–77a); Polain 3232; IGI 7959; Goff P–890; CIBN P–542; Rhodes (F) 518.

28 April 1874—Bequest of Charles Sumner. Inc 6149 (A)

2872 ——Another copy. 293 x 215 mm.

Initial spaces, most with guide-letters, not filled in; without rubrication. Half 19th-century sheep and marbled boards, edges untrimmed. Crown and "F S" stamped in gilt on spine; crowned armorial stamp with motto "Expecto" in lower margin of a1r; autograph of Herbert

Weir Smyth, with his date of acquisition "Florence 1915." MS marginalia. Imperfect: leaf p4 (register) and two unsigned leaves of "Emendationes" wanting; leaves p1–3 remargined.

1937—From the library of Herbert Weir Smyth. Inc 6149 (B)

2873 Maximus, Pacificus: Hecatelegium. 13 November 1489.

4°. [100] leaves (2 blank); 205 x 136 mm.

Three variants of the dedication on π1v are known; see BMC.

This copy collates π^2, a–l^8, m^6, n^4 (π2 blank), with π^2 misbound at
end. The dedication is headed "DIVO TVRCO ARSACVM ‖ ARSA-
CI." Initial spaces, with guide-letters, not filled in; without rubrication. Modern vellum. MS ownership notations on flyleaf at front, "Alberto Dinj" and "Filippo Alessio d'Alberto Dini."

HC 10934; Pr 6150; BMC 6:639 (IA.27179); IGI 6309; Goff M–399;
CIBN M–253; Rhodes (F) 437.

15 July 1942—Bought with the Bennett Hubbard Nash fund. Inc 6150

2874 Ficinus, Marsilius: De triplici vita. 3 December 1489.

f°. [90] leaves; 265 x 198 mm.

Includes a poem by Amerigus Corsinus. Printed by Miscomini for
Philippus Valorius. The first (unsigned) quire consists of either two or
four leaves, with variant settings in the heading of the table; see GW.

This copy has the 2-leaf quire at front, with the first two lines of the
heading on π1r printed in upper case. Initial spaces, with guide-
letters, not filled in; without rubrication. Old paste-paper boards; in
a cloth case. MS ownership notation on flyleaf at front, "Antonius
Suchus [?] Aduocatus"; another in lower margin of π1r, "Adscripta
Cod:° Placentino Soc: jesu a D. Carolo Anguissola [?] Bibliothecae";
MS marginalia.

HC(+Add) 7065*; Pr 6151; BMC 6:639 (IB.27180); Pell 4799; Polain
1480; GW 9882; IGI 3868; Goff F–158; BSB-Ink F–116; Rhodes (F)
299 (+Addenda).

20 October 1944—Bought with the Bennett Hubbard Nash fund. Inc
6151 (A)

2875 ——Another copy. 278 x 210 mm.

2-leaf quire as above. Initials and paragraph marks added in red or blue. Modern blind-stamped calf. MS marginalia. Ownership and "Sold" stamps of the Royal Society; booklabel of David P. Wheatland.

29 December 1986—Gift of David P. Wheatland. Inc 6151 (B)

2876 ——Another copy. 272 x 205 mm.

2-leaf quire as above. Initial spaces not filled in; without rubrication. Modern brown morocco by Chambolle-Duru; edges gilt.

Countway Library (William Norton Bullard Collection)

2877 **Beroaldus, Philippus:** Annotationes in commentarios Servii Vergilianos. 19 December 1489.

4°. [40] leaves (40 blank); 210 x 142 mm.

Initial spaces, with guide-letters, not filled in; without rubrication. 19th-century vellum.

H 2945*; Pr 6151A; BMC 6:639 (IA.27181); Pell 2208; Polain 616; GW 4117; IGI 1586; Goff B–467; BSB-Ink B–362; Rhodes (F) 121.

5 July 1918—Bought with the Constantius fund. Inc 6151A

2878 ——Another copy. 214 x 144 mm.

Initial spaces not filled in; without rubrication. Mottled spanish sheep, spine gilt. Initials "A. S." stamped inside front cover and on front flyleaf.

Countway Library (William Norton Bullard Collection)

2879 **Politianus, Angelus:** Silua cui titulus Nutricia. 26 May 1491.

4°. [18] leaves (18 blank); 200 x 138 mm.

Initial space, with guide-letters, on a2r not filled in; without rubrication. For binding description see no. 2883, the same printer's edition of Politian's *Silua cui titulus Manto* (23 February 1491/2), with which this is bound, along with his *Praelectio cui titulus Panepistemon* (20 February 1491/2) and his *Epistola de obitu Laurentii Medicis* (Bologna, Franciscus [Plato] de Benedictis, 25 July 1492). Imperfect: sheets a3–4 wanting; blank leaf not present.

HC 13236*; Pr 6152; BMC 6:639 (IA.27185); IGI 7966; Goff P–898; CIBN P–548; Rhodes (F) 523.

29 March 1918–Bought with the Charles Eliot Norton fund. Inc 6151.9

2880 Imitatio Christi [Italian]. 22 June 1491.

4°. [104] leaves; 197 x 127 mm.

Initial spaces, most with guide-letters, not filled in; without rubrication. Half 19th-century calf and marbled boards. Bookplate of Walter Arthur Copinger.

HC(+Add) 9128; Pr 6153; BMC 6:640 (IA.27186); IGI 5131; Goff I–48; CIBN T–257; Rhodes (F) 376.

22 November 1921–W. A. Copinger Imitatio Christi Collection, presented by James Byrne. Inc 6153

2881 Savonarola, Hieronymus: Dell'orazione mentale. ca. 1491.

4°. [16] leaves; 194 x 130 mm.

Initial spaces, with guide-letters, not filled in; without rubrication. Half modern vellum and marbled boards.

HC 14404; C 5289; Pr 6180; BMC 6:645 (IA.27238); IGI 8790 ("dopo il 1494"); Goff S–231; CIBN S–114; Rhodes (F) 696.

11 September 1919–From the Savonarola collection formed by Henry R. Newman. Bought with the John Harvey Treat fund. Inc 6180

2882 Politianus, Angelus: Praelectio cui titulus Panepistemon. 20 February 1491/2.

[For transcriptions see Reichling.] 4°. a–b⁸; [16] leaves; 200 x 138 mm. a2r: 26 lines, 142 x 98 mm. Type: 112(110)R. Initial space, with guide-letter, on a1r.

Initial space not filled in; without rubrication. For binding description see no. 2883, the same printer's edition of Politian's *Silua cui titulus Manto* (23 February 1491/2), with which this is bound, along with his *Silua cui titulus Nutricia* (26 May 1491) and his *Epistola de obitu Laurentii Medicis* (Bologna, Franciscus [Plato] de Benedictis, 25 July 1492).

HR 13225; IGI 7960; Goff P–894; CIBN P–544; Rhodes (F) 519.

29 March 1918–Bought with the Charles Eliot Norton fund. Inc 6151.9

2883 Politianus, Angelus: Silua cui titulus Manto. 23 February 1491/2.

[For transcriptions see Reichling.] 4°. a^{10}; [10] leaves; 200 x 138 mm. a3r: 22 lines, 120 x 87 mm. Type: 112(110)R. Initial spaces, with guide-letters.

Initial spaces not filled in; without rubrication. 18th-century mottled calf, spine gilt. From the library of Richard Heber, with his MS note of acquisition "Dec. 1813 Willetts Sale" (no. 1976 in the Sotheby sale catalogue of Ralph Willett's library, December 1813; no. 2825 in pt. 6 of the Evans sale catalogue of Heber's library, March 1835). With this are bound the same printer's editions of Politian's *Praelectio cui titulus Panepistemon* (20 February 1491/2), his *Silua cui titulus Nutricia* (26 May 1491), and his *Epistola de obitu Laurentii Medicis* (Bologna, Franciscus [Plato] de Benedictis, 25 July 1492).

HR 13232; IGI 7964; Goff P-896; CIBN P-546; Rhodes (F) 522.

29 March 1918—Bought with the Charles Eliot Norton fund. Inc 6151.9

2884 Plotinus: Opera [Latin]. 7 May 1492.

f°. [442] leaves (1 blank); 330 x 225 mm.

Translated, with a commentary, by Marsilius Ficinus. Includes a life of Plotinus by Porphyry.

Initial spaces, with guide-letters, not filled in; without rubrication. 18th-century calf, with modern rebacking. MS presentation slip inserted at front, "Presented to the Library at Harvard College.— London June 29. 1836. O. Rich."

HC 13121*; Pr 6156; BMC 6:640 (IB.27194); Polain 3207; IGI 7906; Goff P-815; CIBN P-480; Rhodes (F) 514.

19 September 1836—Gift of Obadiah Rich. Inc 6156

2885 ——Another copy. 355 x 242 mm.

Large initial on a3r illuminated in gold and colors, with marginal extension; illuminated coat of arms in lower border; one other initial added in blue on a2r, but other spaces, with guide-letters, not filled in. 16th-century blind- and gilt-stamped leather over wooden boards; marks of clasps and latches, no longer present; spine badly deteriorated; covers loose; in a cloth case. Imperfect: two leaves of errata at end wanting; blank leaf not present.

Countway Library (William Norton Bullard Collection)

2886 Panziera da Prato, Ugo: Trattati. 9 June 1492.

[For transcriptions see Reichling 3:128.] 4°. π^2, a–l^8, m^4; [2], LXXXXII leaves (XXVII, XXXVI, XXXXI, and LXV misnumbered XXVIII, XXXIV, XXXXII, and LVX); 205 x 137 mm. a2r: 27 lines, 147 x 87 mm. Type: 112(110)R. Initial spaces, with guide-letters.

Some copies contain six additional leaves with a letter to the brothers of the Compagnia del Ceppo at Prato; cf. Reichling 6:189 and BMC 6:682 (IA.27788).

Without the six additional leaves. Initial spaces not filled in; without rubrication. Contemporary blind-stamped leather over wooden boards; marks of clasps and latches, no longer present.

HR 12302; Pr 6157; IGI 7185; Goff P–25; Rhodes (F) 479.

July 1961—Bought with the Amy Lowell fund. Inc 6157

2887 Savonarola, Hieronymus: Sermone dell'orazione. 20 October 1492.

4°. [14] leaves; ill.; 185 x 122 mm.

Initial space on a2r, with guide-letter, not filled in; without rubrication. Half modern brown morocco and marbled boards. Imperfect: title page wanting, with that for Savonarola's *Operetta della oratione mentale* (Bartolommeo di Libri, ca. 1495) supplied in its place.

HC(Add) 14405; Pr 6160; BMC 6:641 (IA.27201); IGI 8773; Goff S–265; CIBN S–136; Rhodes (F) 678; Sander 6836; Kristeller 382e.

10 June 1921—From the Savonarola collection formed by Henry R. Newman. Bought with the John Harvey Treat fund. Inc 6160

2888 Savonarola, Hieronymus: Trattato del sacramento e dei misteri della messa. Before 26 June 1492.

4°. [4] leaves; ill.; 200 x 137 mm.

Includes his *Regole a tutti e religiosi molto utile*; since this occupies the inner fold of this unsigned and unfoliated quarto, these two leaves are sometimes found separately (see following entry) and have been so recorded by Hain (14362). See Peter Amelung, "Drei Inkunabeln, die es nicht gibt," *Beiträge zur Inkunabelkunde*, 3. Folge, 3 (1967): [178]–83.

Initial spaces, with guide-letters, not filled in; without rubrication. Half modern calf and marbled boards.

H 14354?=14362; Pr 6184; BMC 6:646 (IA.27249); IGI 8794; Goff S–239; CIBN S–133 ("ante 26 VI 1492"); Schäfer 308; Rhodes (F) 700; Sander 6873; Kristeller 391c.

June 1963—Bought with the Bennett Hubbard Nash fund. Inc 6184 (A)

2889   ——Another copy. 195 x 134 mm.

The inner fold, containing the *Regole*, only. Half modern black morocco and red cloth.

17 May 1921—From the Savonarola collection formed by Henry R. Newman. Bought with the Edward Henry Hall fund. Inc 6184 (B)

2890   **Ficinus, Marsilius:** De sole. De lumine. 31 January 1493.

4°. [38] leaves (38 blank); 180 x 138 mm.

Includes a catalogue of Ficinus's works by Bindaccius Recasolanus.

Initial spaces, most with guide-letters, not filled in; without rubrication. Unbound; in a board folder. Imperfect: 2-leaf quire at end (errata and blank) wanting.

HC 7079*(incl H 7078); Pr 6166; BMC 6:641 (IA.27214); Pell 4794; GW 9880; IGI 3866; Goff F–156; BSB-Ink F–115; Rhodes (F) 297.

Countway Library (William Norton Bullard Collection)

2891   **Lilius, Zacharias:** Orbis breviarium. 5 June 1493.

4°. [130] leaves; 190 x 134 mm.

BMC has note, "In this and all later books containing type 112R. is found the peculiar Œ of type 86R." It does not occur in this copy. Initial spaces, with guide-letters, not filled in; without rubrication. Half 18th-century sheep and mottled boards. Bookstamp "Bibliothecae S. Theresiae." Leaf a3 misbound before a2.

HC(+Add) 10101; Pr 6163; BMC 6:642 (IA.27207–07a); IGI 5760; Goff L–218; CIBN L–171; Rhodes (F) 412.

4 October 1830—Received. Inc 6163

2892   **Imitatio Christi** [Italian]. 22 July 1493.

4°. [78] leaves; ill.; 210 x 135 mm.

Initial spaces, with guide-letters, not filled in; without rubrication. 19th-century vellum. Autograph of Eadmond Waterton (lot 250 in the Sotheby sale catalogue of his library, 18 January 1895); bookplate of Walter Arthur Copinger. Imperfect: sheet π1 (title page and last leaf of the table) wanting.

HC(+Add) 9130*; Pr 6165; BMC 6:642 (IA.27212); IGI 5134; Goff I-52; Rhodes (F) 378; Sander 3089; Kristeller 227b.

22 November 1921—W. A. Copinger Imitatio Christi Collection, presented by James Byrne. Inc 6165

2893 Pseudo-Bonaventura: Meditationes vitae Christi [Italian]. ca. 1493.

4°. [42] leaves; ill.; 205 x 137 mm.

An excerpt, with text ending "scripto di me nelle p[ro]phetie & psalmi."

Without rubrication; woodcuts uncolored. Modern dark blue morocco by Rivière. Booklabels of Philip and Frances Hofer.

CR 1182; Pr 6183; BMC 6:646 (IA.27248); GW 4775; IGI 1922; Goff B-911; Schäfer 72; Rhodes (F) 135; Sander 1179; Kristeller 69a.

14 September 1972—Gift of Philip Hofer. Typ Inc 6183

2894 Cessolis, Jacobus de: De ludo scachorum [Italian]. 1 March 1493/4.

4°. [68] leaves; ill.; 202 x 135 mm.

Without rubrication; woodcuts uncolored. Modern maroon morocco, edges gilt, by Rivière. Booklabels of Philip and Frances Hofer. Imperfect: last four leaves mutilated at top and restored in facsimile.

HC 4900=H 4899; Pr 6162; BMC 6:642 (IA.27205); GW 6534; IGI 2717; Goff C-419; Schäfer 99; Rhodes (F) 182; Sander 1918; Kristeller 101.

14 September 1972—Gift of Philip Hofer. Typ Inc 6162

2895 Vergilius Maro, Publius: Bucolica [Italian]. 19 April 1494.

4°. [98] leaves; ill.; 214 x 140 mm.

Italian translation by Bernardo Pulci. Includes original Italian elegies by Pulci and eclogues by Francesco Arsocchi, Girolamo Benivieni, and Jacopo Fiorenzo de'Buoninsegni.

Without rubrication; woodcut uncolored. Old vellum. Imperfect: leaf f1 slightly mutilated.

C 6139; Pr 6167; BMC 6:643 (IA.27218–18a); IGI 10242; Goff V–217; CIBN V–154; Rhodes (F) 775; Davies-Goldfinch 149; Sander 7640.

December 1964–Gift of Ward M. Canaday. Inc 6167

2896 Imitatio Christi [Italian]. 1 July 1494.

4°. [76] leaves; ill.; 204 x 135 mm.

The first four leaves of the BMC copy are wanting, so BMC has transcribed the title from Reichling, whose title does not agree with the one here present: ℭ MESSER GIOVANNI GERSON ‖ Vtile & diuota operetta della imitatione di Giesu X͞po ‖ ℭ Qui uult uenire post me/ abneget semetipsum ‖ & tollat crucem suam/ & sequatur me. ‖ [Woodcut, Christ with the Cross, within border] ‖ π2r: INCO-MINCIA LATAVOLA DE ‖ CAPITOLI DE LIBRI ‖ SEQVENTI ‖ π4v: ... Chome lhuomo nõ debbe essere curio‖so inuestigatore circha elsacramento cap. xviii. ‖ F I N I S ‖

Without rubrication. Modern dark blue morocco, edges gilt, by Rivière. Ownership stamp erased from π2r.

HCR 9131; Pr 6169; BMC 6:643 (IA.27222); Polain 2077; IGI 5135; Goff I–53; Rhodes (F) 379; Sander 3090; Kristeller 227c.

2 April 1930–Bought with the John Harvey Treat fund. Inc 6169 (A)

2897 ——Another copy. 210 x 137 mm.

Without rubrication. 19th-century blue boards. Imperfect: title page and leaf a1 wanting, supplied from the Florence, Pacini, 1505 edition.

22 November 1921–W. A. Copinger Imitatio Christi Collection, presented by James Byrne. Inc 6169 (B)

2898 Hippocrates: Aphorismi, siue Sententiae. 16 October 1494.

f°. [98] leaves (1 blank); 278 x 208 mm.

Includes the commentary of Galen. Latin translation by Laurentius Laurentianus.

Initial spaces, with guide-letters, not filled in; without rubrication. Bound in a vellum leaf of Latin liturgical MS with musical notation.

HC 8672*; Pr 6171; BMC 6:644 (IB.27225); Polain 1962; IGI 4781; Goff H–273; Sack 1849; CIBN H–143; Rhodes (F) 365.

Countway Library (William Norton Bullard Collection)

B A R T O L O M M E O   D I   L I B R I

2899 Mazza, Clemente della: Vita di San Zenobio. 8 December 1487.

4°. [46] leaves; 190 x 130 mm.

Initial spaces, with guide-letters, not filled in; without rubrication. Modern calf.

HC(+Add)R 10981; Pr 6192; BMC 6:648 (IA.27268); IGI 6317; Goff M–417; CIBN M–263; Rhodes (F) 439.

29 March 1918–Bought with the John Harvey Treat fund. Inc 6192

2900 Floccus, Andreas: De Romanorum magistratibus. After 1487.

4°. [52] leaves; 197 x 133 mm.

Includes Albricus, *De imaginibus deorum.*

Without rubrication. Half modern vellum and decorated boards. Imperfect: leaf a1 slightly mutilated.

HC 6963; Pr 6279; BMC 6:663 (IA.27524); Pell 4757; GW 10044; IGI 3818; Goff F–66; Rhodes (F) 291.

16 November 1948–Received. Law Library

2901 Formularium diversorum contractuum. After 15 December 1488.

f°. [1], II–CLVI leaves (LXXXVIIII and CXXII misnumbered LXXXXVIIII and CXXVI); 280 x 206 mm.

Without rubrication. Bound in a leaf of old limp vellum lined with leaves of Latin liturgical MS on paper; title in ink on lower edges. Bound in at end are 3 leaves of contemporary MS index followed by 3 leaves of transcripts of papal and other letters, some dated 1489.

H 7268*; Pr 6194B; BMC 6:648 (IB.27279); Polain 1504; GW 10191; IGI 4019; Goff F–250; BSB-Ink F–201; Rhodes (F) 319.

21 June 1950–Received. Law Library

2902 Dati, Leonardo: La sfera. ca. 1488/90.

4°. [18] leaves; 192 x 135 mm.

Variously attributed to both Leonardo and to Gregorio Dati; but according to Paolo Viti in *Dizionario biografico degli Italiani* 33 (Roma, 1987) 43, probability would favor Leonardo, a scholar, rather than Gregorio, a business man and politician.

Initial space on a1r, with guide-letter, not filled in; without rubrication. Modern red morocco.

R 490; GW 8028; IGI 3330; Goff D–52; Rhodes (F) 254.

January 1963—Gift of Harrison D. Horblit. Inc 6245.5

2903 Picus de Mirandula, Johannes: Heptaplus de septiformi sex dierum geneseos enarratione. ca. 1490.

f°. [58] leaves (58 blank); 277 x 212 mm.

Edited by Robertus Salviatus.

Initial spaces not filled in; spaces for Greek and Hebrew filled in in MS; without rubrication. Modern marbled boards. MS marginalia in an early hand. Ownership bookstamps erased from a1r and a2r. Blank leaf not present.

HC 13001*; Pr 6284; BMC 6:662 (IB.27536); Polain 3148; IGI 7737; Goff P–641; CIBN P–348; Rhodes (F) 504.

20 June 1924—Bought with the John Harvey Treat fund. Inc 6284

2904 Pulci, Luigi: Frottole due. ca. 1490.

4°. [4] leaves; 195 x 135 mm.

Without rubrication. 19th-century vellum. Booklabel of Count Giacomo Manzoni (no. 2679 in vol. 1 of the Sangiorgi sale catalogue of his library, 1892); autograph of Giuseppe Martini (no. 312 in his incunabula catalogue, 1934, with full description).

IGI 8224–A; Goff P–1120; Rhodes (F) 576.

7 February 1955—Bought with the Bennett Hubbard Nash fund. Inc 6260.5

2905 Brunus Aretinus, Leonardus: Historiae Florentini populi [Italian]. 5 June 1492.

f°. [222] leaves; 308 x 209 mm.

Italian translation by Donatus Acciaiolus.

Initial spaces, with guide-letters, not filled in; without rubrication. Old vellum. MS marginalia. MS ownership notation in lower margin of p1r, "Zanobi di Gio[van]b[a]tt[ist]a Lippi"; the same hand has written names and birth dates of other members of the family in the lower margins of leaves u5r, y7v, &6v, and bb10v. With this is bound the same printer's edition of Poggius Florentinus, *Historia Florentina* (3 September 1492). The table is bound at front.

HC(+Add) 1563(1); Pr 6197; BMC 6:649 (IB.27292); Pell 1116; GW 5613(1); IGI 2203(1); Goff B-1248; BSB-Ink B-946(1); Rhodes (F) 149.

26 June 1924—Bought with the Bayard Cutting fund. Inc 6197

2906   ——Another copy. 325 x 215 mm.

Initial on a2r illuminated in gold and colors, with marginal extension; illuminated coat of arms in lower margin with MS notation "Mvsto-r[um] arma"; initials elsewhere added in blue. Contemporary blind-stamped leather over wooden boards, rehinged; marks of clasps and latches, no longer present. With this is bound (as in the above and in most recorded copies) the same printer's edition of Poggius Floren-tinus, *Historia Florentina* (3 September 1492). The table is bound at front.

20 December 1954—Gift of Philip Hofer. Typ Inc 6197

2907 **Poggius Florentinus:** Historia Florentina [Italian]. 3 September 1492.

f°. [116] leaves; 308 x 209 mm.

Italian translation by Jacobus Poggius.

Initial spaces, with guide-letters, not filled in; without rubrication. For binding description see no. 2905, the same printer's edition of Leonardus Brunus Aretinus, *Historiae Florentini populi* (5 June 1492), with which this is bound. MS marginalia. MS ownership notation at end, "Questo libro e di Dinollo di Zanobi di Giobatt^a di Matteo Lippi Citt^{dno} fiorentino."

HC 13173*=HC(+Add) 1563(2); Pr 6198; BMC 6:649 (IB.27293); GW 5613(2); IGI 2203(2); Goff P-874; CIBN P-532; Rhodes (F) 515.

26 June 1924—Bought with the Bayard Cutting fund. Inc 6197

2908 ——Another copy. 325 x 215 mm.

Initial on A1r illuminated in gold and colors, with marginal extension; initials elsewhere added in blue. For binding description see no. 2906, the same printer's edition of Leonardus Brunus Aretinus, *Historiae Florentini populi* (5 June 1492), with which this is bound.

20 December 1954—Gift of Philip Hofer. Typ Inc 6197

2909 Mesue, Johannes: Opera medicinalia [Italian]. ca. 1492.

f°. [228] leaves; 280 x 208 mm.

Initial spaces, with guide-letters, not filled in; without rubrication. Modern blind-stamped calf. MS notation (by the publisher?) on B4v, "Ego P. Pacinus"; BMC conjectures that this "perhaps served to authenticate the text." Imperfect: title page in facsimile.

HCR 11113; Pr 6283; BMC 6:663 (IB.27533); IGI 6396; Goff M–520; Rhodes (F) 447.

Countway Library (William Norton Bullard Collection)

2910 Josephus, Flavius: De bello Iudaico [Italian]. 6 July 1493.

f°. [208] leaves (1 blank); 279 x 192 mm.

Anonymous Italian translation.

Initial spaces, most with guide-letters, not filled in; without rubrication. Half modern vellum and decorated boards. MS ownership notation on front flyleaf, "A. Gandolfi. Bologna, 30 Maggio 1919." Occasional MS marginalia. Blank leaf not present.

HCR 9460; Pr 6199; BMC 6:649 (IB.27297); IGI 5391; Goff J–490; CIBN J–315; Rhodes (F) 388.

June 1965—Bought with the Lee M. Friedman fund. Inc 6199

2911 Lucidarius [Italian]. ca. 1494.

4°. [48] leaves (46 blank); ill.; 195 x 132 mm.

Without rubrication. Half 19th-century black morocco and black boards. Bookstamp of Walter Ashburner; from the library of Charles Fairfax Murray, with a note in his hand on front flyleaf; booklabel of

Tammaro De Marinis, with his inscription on another flyleaf, "offert à Monsieur Philippe Hofer en souvenir de sa charmante visite à Montalto du 30 Mai 1955"; booklabel of Frances Hofer. The 2-leaf table is bound after the title page.

Pr 6288; BMC 6:658 (IA.27549); IGI 5858; Goff H–336; Rhodes (F) 371; Sander 3433; Kristeller 244a.

24 July 1974—Gift of Philip Hofer. Typ Inc 6288

2912 **Savonarola, Hieronymus:** Predica fatta addì 8 di giugno 1495. After 8 June 1495.

4°. [8] leaves; 199 x 136 mm.

Without rubrication. Half modern black morocco and red cloth.

HCR 14387; Pr 6201; BMC 6:661 (IA.27307); IGI 8752; Goff S–245; Rhodes (F) 660.

17 May 1921—From the Savonarola collection formed by Henry R. Newman. Bought with the Edward Henry Hall fund. Inc 6201

2913 **Florence. Concilium generale:** Decretum, 13 August 1495. After 13 August 1495.

4°. [4] leaves; 198 x 130 mm.

Without rubrication. Modern dark green cloth.

CR 5896; Pr 6202; BMC 6:661 (IA.27309); GW 10050; IGI 3973; Goff F–207; Rhodes (F) 310.

17 May 1921—From the Savonarola collection formed by Henry R. Newman. Bought with the Duplicate fund. Inc 6202

2914 **Burchiello:** Sonetti. Before September 1495.

4°. [76] leaves; 190 x 119 mm.

Without rubrication. Old vellum. Imperfect: title page wanting and supplied in type facsimile; three lines at bottom of a5r and two at bottom of a5v also supplied in type facsimile; several leaves remargined.

C 1375; Pr 6245; BMC 6:655 (IA.27425); Polain 4258; GW 5748; IGI 2242; Goff B–1292; Rhodes (F) 152.

2 April 1936—Bought with the Bennett Hubbard Nash fund. Inc 6245

2915 Savonarola, Hieronymus: Dell'amore di Gesù. Before September 1495.

4°. [22] leaves; ill.; 209 x 135 mm.

Without rubrication. Half modern dark gray morocco and gray cloth.

C 5279; Pr 6292; BMC 6:658 (IA.27559); IGI 8784; Goff S-169; CIBN S-76; Rhodes (F) 689; Sander 6851; Kristeller 374c.

17 May 1921—From the Savonarola collection formed by Henry R. Newman. Gift of J. P. Morgan. Inc 6292

2916 Savonarola, Hieronymus: Dell'umiltà. Before September 1495.

4°. [10] leaves; ill.; 195 x 139 mm.

Without rubrication; woodcuts uncolored. Half modern brown morocco and tan cloth. Leaves numbered in MS 115–124.

HR 14373; Pr 6272; BMC 6:657 (IA.27506); IGI 8800; Goff S-279; CIBN S-147; Rhodes (F) 706; Sander 6863.

17 May 1921—From the Savonarola collection formed by Henry R. Newman. Bought with the Edward Henry Hall fund. Typ Inc 6272

2917 Savonarola, Hieronymus: Dell'umiltà. Before September 1495.

4°. [10] leaves; ill.; 205 x 132 mm.

Without rubrication; woodcuts uncolored. Half 19th-century calf and marbled boards. Autograph of Charles Fairfax Murray.

H 14374; C 5284; Pr 6294; BMC 6:659 (IA.27564); Polain 4713; IGI 8799; Goff S-278; CIBN S-148; Rhodes (F) 705; Sander 6862; Kristeller 394b.

17 May 1921—From the Savonarola collection formed by Henry R. Newman. Bought with the Edward Henry Hall fund. Typ Inc 6294

2918 Savonarola, Hieronymus: Expositio Orationis Dominicae [Italian]. Before September 1495.

4°. [24] leaves; ill.; 207 x 131 mm.

Includes his *Epistola della communione.*

Initial on a2r added in brown; spaces elsewhere not filled in; without rubrication. Modern red cloth. Leaves numbered in MS 76–99.

HCR 14445; Pr 6290; BMC 6:659 (IA.27555); IGI 8712; Goff S–199; CIBN S–112; Rhodes (F) 634; Sander 6780; Kristeller 384b.

17 May 1921—From the Savonarola collection formed by Henry R. Newman. Bought with the Duplicate fund. Inc 6290

2919 **Savonarola, Hieronymus:** Libro della vita viduale. Before September 1495.

4°. [22] leaves (22 blank); ill.; 206 x 135 mm.

Without rubrication. Half modern calf and marbled boards. From the library of Imrie de Vegh.

HC 14368; Pr 6293; BMC 6:659 (IA.27562); IGI 8746; Goff S–287; CIBN S–149; Schäfer 303; Rhodes (F) 653; Sander 6886; Kristeller 396b.

March 1964—Gift of Mrs. Imrie de Vegh. Inc 6293

2920 **Savonarola, Hieronymus:** Dell'orazione mentale. ca. 1495.

4°. [12] leaves; ill.; 209 x 135 mm.

Without rubrication. Half modern black morocco and blue cloth.

CR 5291; Pr 6296; BMC 6:658 (IA.27569); IGI 8791; Goff S–232; CIBN S–115; Rhodes (F) 697; Sander 6808; Kristeller 383a.

17 May 1921—From the Savonarola collection formed by Henry R. Newman. Bought with the Edward Henry Hall fund. Typ Inc 6296

2921 **Savonarola, Hieronymus:** Epistola alla contessa della Mirandola. ca. 1495.

4°. [4] leaves; ill.; 208 x 138 mm.

Without rubrication. Half modern black morocco and red cloth.

HC 14465; Pr 6301; BMC 6:664 (IA.27589); IGI 8698; Goff S–188; Rhodes (F) 622; Sander 6775; Kristeller 378.

17 May 1921—From the Savonarola collection formed by Henry R. Newman. Bought with the Duplicate fund. Inc 6301

2922 **Savonarola, Hieronymus:** Expositio in psalmum LXXIX: Qui regis Israel [Italian]. ca. 1495.

4°. [10] leaves; ill.; 194 x 140 mm.

Without rubrication. Half modern dark brown morocco and brown cloth. With this is bound Savonarola's *Expositio Orationis Dominicae* (Florence, Giovanni Stefano di Carlo, ca. 1510). Imperfect: leaf a1 repaired, affecting line 1 on verso.

HCR 14435; Pr 6302; BMC 6:664 (IA.27593); IGI 8741; Goff S-221; CIBN S-109; Rhodes (F) 647; Sander 6791; Kristeller 388a.

17 May 1921—From the Savonarola collection formed by Henry R. Newman. Bought with the Duplicate fund. Inc 6302

2923 Savonarola, Hieronymus: Sermone dell'orazione. ca. 1495.

4°. [14] leaves; ill.; 209 x 135 mm.

Without rubrication; woodcuts uncolored. Half modern maroon morocco and orange boards. Bookstamp of Giovanni Andrea Barotti in lower margin of a1r.

C 5307; R 317; Pr 6295; BMC 6:659 (IA.26566); IGI 8774; Goff S-266; CIBN S-138; Rhodes (F) 679; Sander 6839; Kristeller 382c.

17 May 1921—From the Savonarola collection formed by Henry R. Newman. Bought with the Edward Henry Hall fund. Typ Inc 6295

2924 Savonarola, Hieronymus: Esposizione sopra l'Ave Maria. After April 1496.

4°. [12] leaves; 213 x 140 mm.

On dating see Roberto Ridolfi, "Incunabuli contrastampati," *La Bibliofilia* 51 (1949): 142.

Without rubrication. Half modern red morocco and red cloth.

HCR 14449; Pr 6286; BMC 6:663 (IA.27542); IGI 8709; Goff S-197; CIBN S-98; Rhodes (F) 633.

17 May 1921—From the Savonarola collection formed by Henry R. Newman. Bought with the Duplicate fund. Inc 6286

2925 Savonarola, Hieronymus: Introductorium confessorum. ca. 1496.

[For transcriptions see Reichling; but Reichling wrongly assigns this work to Angelus and Jacobus Britannicus in Brescia and is followed by IGI.] 8°. a-p⁴; [60] leaves; 140 x 100 mm. a2r: 29 lines, 112 x 74 mm. Type: 5:77R. Woodcut initials.

Without rubrication. For binding description see no. 2503 in vol. 2, Antoninus Florentinus, *Confessionale "Defecerunt"* (Venice, Petrus de Quarengiis, 21 November 1499), with which this is bound and which has the bookstamp of the Convent of St. Paul, Florence, on its title page.

R 1387; IGI 8688; Goff S-226; CIBN S-117; Rhodes (F) 648.

17 May 1921—From the Savonarola collection formed by Henry R. Newman. Bought with the Duplicate fund. Inc 6300.5

2926 **Savonarola, Hieronymus:** Epistola a tutti gli eletti di Dio. After 8 May 1497.

4°. [4] leaves; 198 x 136 mm.

Without rubrication. Half modern red morocco and orange cloth.

H 14458?; C 5300; Pr 6213; BMC 6:651 (IA.27335); IGI 8705; Goff S-195; CIBN S-90; Rhodes (F) 629.

17 May 1921—From the Savonarola collection formed by Henry R. Newman. Bought with the Duplicate fund. Inc 6213

2927 **Savonarola, Hieronymus:** Predica dell'arte del ben morire. After June 1497.

4°. [18] leaves; ill.; 207 x 137 mm.

Sermon preached 2 November 1496 "& racolta da Ser Lorenzo Violi [i.e., Vivoli] dalla uiua uoce del predecto padre mentre che predicaua." On the various editions of this work see Frederick R. Goff, "The Four Florentine Editions of Savonarola's *Predica dellarte del ben morire,*" *The New Colophon* 3 (1950): 286–301.

Without rubrication; woodcuts uncolored. Modern limp vellum.

H 14390; R 1380; Pr 6206; BMC 6:662 (IA.27320); IGI 8756; Goff S-250; CIBN S-123; Schäfer 305; Rhodes (F) 664; Sander 6813; Kristeller 375c.

17 May 1921—From the Savonarola collection formed by Henry R. Newman. Gift of J. P. Morgan. Typ Inc 6206

2928 **Savonarola, Hieronymus:** Epistola a suoi diletti fratelli in Cristo Gesù. After 15 July 1497.

4°. [2] leaves; 196 x 133 mm.

Without rubrication. 19th-century limp vellum. Bookplate of Holland House.

HR 14371; C 5306; Pr 6217; BMC 6:651 (IA.27343); IGI 8701; Goff S-193; CIBN S-94; Rhodes (F) 625.

June 1963—Bought with the Bennett Hubbard Nash fund. Inc 6217

2929 **Riposta per le medesime parole a una epistola di frate Angelo Anachorita [i.e., Angelo da Vallombrosa].** After 20 July 1497.

4°. [2] leaves; 200 x 131 mm.

GW transcribes "assere" in line 3 of the caption on [a]1r; this copy has "essere." Without rubrication. Half modern dark gray morocco and gray cloth.

GW 1919; IGI 8380; Goff R-199; Rhodes (F) 592.

17 May 1921—From the Savonarola collection formed by Henry R. Newman. Bought with the Duplicate fund. Inc 6217.5

2930 **Savonarola, Hieronymus:** Epistole a diversi. After 14 August 1497.

4°. [40] leaves; ill.; 208 x 138 mm.

For contents see IGI.

Without rubrication; woodcuts uncolored. Half modern black morocco and blue cloth.

HCR 14451; Pr 6218; BMC 6:651 (IA.27345); Polain 3453; IGI 8708; Goff S-196; CIBN S-91; Schäfer 302; Rhodes (F) 632; Sander 6778; Kristeller 381a.

17 May 1921—From the Savonarola collection formed by Henry R. Newman. Bought with the Duplicate fund. Typ Inc 6218 (A)

2931 ——Another copy. 195 x 135 mm.

Without rubrication; woodcuts uncolored. Modern vellum. Bookplate of Paul Schmidt; booklabels of Charles Bain Hoyt and of Philip Hofer. Imperfect: all after b6 wanting.

28 February 1942—Gift of Philip Hofer. Typ Inc 6218 (B)

2932 **Domenico da Pescia:** Epistola ai fanciulli fiorentini. After 3 September 1497.

4°. [4] leaves; 196 x 136 mm.

Without rubrication. Half modern brown morocco and tan cloth.

CR 2034; Pr 6219; BMC 6:652 (IA.27347); GW 8636; IGI 3528; Goff D-304; Rhodes (F) 266.

17 May 1921—From the Savonarola collection formed by Henry R. Newman. Bought with the Duplicate fund. Inc 6219

2933 **Savonarola, Hieronymus:** Epistola alle suore del terzo ordine di San Domenico. After 17 October 1497.

4°. [4] leaves; 196 x 134 mm.

Without rubrication. Half modern black morocco and green cloth. Leaves numbered in MS 195–98.

HC 14468; Pr 6220; BMC 6:652 (IA.27349); IGI 8702; Goff S-194; CIBN S-95; Rhodes (F) 626.

17 May 1921—From the Savonarola collection formed by Henry R. Newman. Bought with the Duplicate fund. Inc 6220

2934 **Savonarola, Hieronymus:** Apologia fratrum congregationis S. Marci [Italian]. 1497?

4°. [12] leaves; 212 x 137 mm.

Without rubrication. Half modern brown morocco and rust cloth.

CR 5304; Pr 6222; BMC 6:652 (IA.27357); Polain 3456; IGI 8675; Goff S-174; Rhodes (F) 603.

17 May 1921—From the Savonarola collection formed by Henry R. Newman. Bought with the Edward Henry Hall fund. Inc 6222

2935 **Savonarola, Hieronymus:** De veritate prophetica. 1497?

f°. [44] leaves; 275 x 208 mm.

Initial spaces, with guide-letters, not filled in; without rubrication. Modern vellum. In this copy the erratum listed for the headline on f3r ("NONVS") has been corrected in type by the printer to "OC-TAVVS"; the other errata have been corrected in ink by an early owner.

HC 14339; Pr 6226; BMC 6:652 (IB.27369); IGI 8689; Goff S-282; CIBN S-85; Rhodes (F) 612.

August 1970–Gift of Lathrop C. Harper, Inc., and Goodspeed's Book Shop. Inc 6226

2936 Savonarola, Hieronymus: Triumphus crucis. 1497?

f°. [98] leaves; 258 x 190 mm.

One initial on a2r added in brown; other spaces, with guide-letters, not filled in; without rubrication. Old limp vellum, with title in ink on front cover.

HC 14342*; Pr 6225; BMC 6:652 (IB.27366); Polain 3464; IGI 8801; Goff S-274; CIBN S-143; Rhodes (F) 708.

December 1964–Gift of Ward M. Canaday. Inc 6225

2937 Savonarola, Hieronymus: Triumphus crucis [Italian]. 1497?

f°. [84] leaves; 284 x 200 mm.

Includes a preface by Domenico Benivieni.

Initial spaces, some with guide-letters, not filled in; without rubrication. Half modern brown morocco and brown cloth.

HC 14345*; Pr 6224; BMC 6:652 (IB.27363); IGI 8803; Goff S-275; CIBN S-145; Rhodes (F) 710.

17 May 1921–From the Savonarola collection formed by Henry R. Newman. Bought with the Duplicate fund. Inc 6224 (A)

2938 ——Another copy. 274 x 209 mm.

Initial spaces not filled in; without rubrication. Half modern tan morocco and gray boards. MS ownership notation, "D. Aless:° Callir." Imperfect: first leaf slightly mutilated.

December 1964–Gift of Ward M. Canaday. Inc 6224 (B)

2939 Cataldus, Saint: Prophetia [Latin and Italian]. ca. 1497.

4°. [2] leaves; 199 x 127 mm.

Without rubrication. Half 19th-century maroon morocco and marbled boards.

CR 1498; Pr 6214; BMC 6:660 (IA.27337); GW 6211; IGI 2572; Goff C-273; Rhodes (F) 162.

17 May 1921–From the Savonarola collection formed by Henry R. Newman. Bought with the Duplicate fund. Inc 6214

2940 Savonarola, Hieronymus: Contro gli astrologi. ca. 1497.

4°. [36] leaves; ill.; 200 x 136 mm.

Without rubrication; woodcut uncolored. Half modern brown morocco and rust cloth.

HC 14378*; Pr 6274; BMC 6:661 (IA.27512); IGI 8788; Goff S–175; CIBN S–84; Rhodes (F) 694; Sander 6857; Kristeller 376.

17 May 1921–From the Savonarola collection formed by Henry R. Newman. Gift of J. P. Morgan. Typ Inc 6274

2941 ——Another copy. 203 x 135 mm.

Without rubrication; woodcut uncolored. 19th-century red sheep; hinges split. Imperfect: two leaves of errata at end wanting.

Countway Library (William Norton Bullard Collection)

2942 ——Another copy. 202 x 134 mm.

Without rubrication; woodcut uncolored. Leaves numbered in MS 139–72; a few MS marginalia. Half 19th-century calf and marbled boards. Imperfect: two leaves of errata at end wanting.

May 1890–Bought with the F. C. Gray fund. Fogg Art Museum (Print Room)

2943 Savonarola, Hieronymus: Circa il reggimento della città di Firenze. Not before January 1498.

4°. [20] leaves (20 blank); 199 x 135 mm.

Without rubrication. Half modern dark gray morocco and gray cloth.

CR 5305; Pr 6227; BMC 6:653 (IA.27372); IGI 8793; Goff S–236; CIBN S–79; Rhodes (F) 699.

17 May 1921–From the Savonarola collection formed by Henry R. Newman. Bought with the Edward Henry Hall fund. Inc 6227

2944 Savonarola, Hieronymus: Vita spirituale, vel Expositio in septem gradus Bonaventurae. Not before February 1498.

4°. [8] leaves; 203 x 138 mm.

Includes an Italian translation by Filippo Cioni.

Without rubrication. Half modern black morocco and blue cloth.

HC 14450; C 5283?; Pr 6228; BMC 6:653 (IA.27374); IGI 8742; Goff S-284; CIBN S-110; Rhodes (F) 650.

17 May 1921—From the Savonarola collection formed by Henry R. Newman. Bought with the Duplicate fund. Inc 6228

2945 **Savonarola, Hieronymus:** Predica fatta addì 11 de febbraio 1497. After 11 February 1497/8.

4°. [12] leaves; 198 x 135 mm.

Edited by Lorenzo Vivoli.

Without rubrication. Half modern brown morocco and tan boards.

HR 14392; Pr 6229; BMC 6:653 (IA.27376); IGI 8761; Goff S-253; CIBN S-127; Rhodes (F) 669.

17 May 1921—From the Savonarola collection formed by Henry R. Newman. Bought with the Edward Henry Hall fund. Inc 6229

2946 **Savonarola, Hieronymus:** Predica fatta addì 18 de febbraio 1497. After 18 February 1497/8.

a1r: ℭ Predica del Reuerendo padre frate Hieronymo da Ferrara racol ‖ ta da Ser Lorenzo Viuuoli adi .xviii. di febbraio. Mcccclxxxxvii. ‖ (E³)Ssendo noi dal Signore posti ī questo grã mare/ dilectissi ‖ mi in xp̄o Iesu: ... ‖ b6v: AMEN ‖

4°. a⁴, b⁶; [10] leaves; 208 x 136 mm. a3r: 35 lines, 168 x 104 mm. Type: 97R³. Woodcut initial on a1r.

Without rubrication. Half modern green morocco and green cloth.

HR 14394; IGI 8762; Goff S-255; CIBN S-129; Rhodes (F) 670.

17 May 1921—From the Savonarola collection formed by Henry R. Newman. Bought with the Edward Henry Hall fund. Inc 6229.5

2947 **Savonarola, Hieronymus:** Predica fatta addì 25 di febbraio 1497. After 25 February 1497/8.

4°. [20] leaves; 212 x 140 mm.

Edited by Lorenzo Vivoli.

Without rubrication. Half modern brown morocco and rust cloth.

HR 14395; Pr 6230; BMC 6:653 (IA.27378); IGI 8763; Goff S-256; Rhodes (F) 671.

17 May 1921—From the Savonarola collection formed by Henry R. Newman. Bought with the Edward Henry Hall fund. Inc 6230

2948 Savonarola, Hieronymus: Predica fatta il sabbato dopo la seconda domenica di Quaresima l'anno 1497. After 17 March 1497/8.

4°. [14] leaves; 208 x 136 mm.

Without rubrication. Half modern dark gray morocco and gray cloth.

HC(+Add)R 14396; Pr 6212; BMC 6:653 (IA.27333); IGI 8764; Goff S-257; CIBN S-130; Rhodes (F) 672.

17 May 1921—From the Savonarola collection formed by Henry R. Newman. Bought with the Edward Henry Hall fund. Inc 6230.4

2949 Savonarola, Hieronymus: Conclusiones rationibus ac signis supernaturalibus probandae. Between 2 and 5 April 1498.

4°. [6] leaves; 199 x 135 mm.

The main part of this work consists of Savonarola's "Risposta a certe obiectioni facte circa lo experimento dello entrare nel fuocho per la uerità da lui predicata." Includes statements of support for him by Domenico da Pescia and others of his friends and colleagues.

This copy varies slightly from the BMC transcription: a1r, line 13, insert line-ending after "ordine"; line 15, "つclusione" rather than "conclusione"; line 17, "en-‖" rather than "en‖"; a6r, line 3, "bene-‖" rather than "bene‖." Without rubrication. Half modern black morocco and blue cloth.

H 13012=14476; BMC 12:47 (IA.27379); IGI 8677; Goff S-182; Rhodes (F) 611.

17 May 1921—From the Savonarola collection formed by Henry R. Newman. Bought with the Duplicate fund. Inc 6267.5

2950 Savonarola, Hieronymus: Processo. After 19 April 1498.

[For transcriptions see Reichling; but he has mistakenly indicated a line-ending after "Amen." in line 1 on a1r.] 4°. a-b⁴, c⁶; [14] leaves; 196 x 128 mm. a2r: 35 lines, 168 x 93 mm. Type: 97R³.

Includes at end two letters in Latin of Pope Alexander VI. On the several editions of this work see Roberto Ridolfi, "Il processi del Savonarola," *La Bibliofilia* 46 (1944): [3]–41, with reproductions; and "Ancora i processi del Savonarola," *La Bibliofilia* 47 (1945): [41]–47. Ridolfi considers the Di Libri edition to be the second.

Without rubrication. Half 19th-century green sheep and marbled boards. Smudged monogram ownership stamp in lower margin of a1r. Several leaves remargined.

HR 14477; IGI 8768; Rhodes (F) 529.

August 1970—Gift of Lathrop C. Harper, Inc., and Goodspeed's Book Shop. Inc 6230.5

2951 Savonarola, Hieronymus: Expositio in psalmum XXX: In te Domine speravi [Italian]. After 23 May 1498.

4°. [20] leaves; ill.; 197 x 136 mm.

Without rubrication. Half 19th-century sheep and marbled boards.

HCR 14415; Pr 6234; BMC 6:654 (IA.27391); IGI 8722; Goff S–208; CIBN S–100; Rhodes (F) 640; Sander 6783; Kristeller 386.

17 May 1921—From the Savonarola collection formed by Henry R. Newman. Bought with the Duplicate fund. Inc 6234

2952 Savonarola, Hieronymus: Sunto e registro delle prediche fatte nel 1495. After 23 May 1498.

4°. [12] leaves (12 blank); 212 x 139 mm.

On dating see Roberto Ridolfi, "Sulla data di un'edizione di Bartolomeo de'Libri," *La Bibliofilia* 52 (1950): [38]–40. Some copies have a list of errata on b3v, others do not.

This copy is without the list of errata on b3v. Without rubrication. Half modern dark green morocco and green cloth. The blank leaf, present when the book was catalogued in 1986, was removed by a binder in Dublin.

HCR 14381; Pr 6210; BMC 6:661 (IA.27329); IGI 8780; Goff S–244; Rhodes (F) 685.

17 May 1921—From the Savonarola collection formed by Henry R. Newman. Bought with the Edward Henry Hall fund. Inc 6210

2953 Valla, Nicolaus: Seraphica sylva. 15 June 1498.

[For transcriptions see Hain; but add a line-ending between "ac" and "totius."] 4°. a–d⁸; [32] leaves; ill.; 198 x 140 mm. a2r: 26 lines, 148 x 93 mm. Type: 2:114R². Woodcut initials; woodcuts.

Without rubrication; woodcuts uncolored. Bound in part of a vellum leaf of 15th-century liturgical MS. Booklabels of Philip and Frances Hofer.

H 15832*; IGI 10102; Goff V–74; Rhodes (F) 760; Sander 7473; Kristeller 432.

24 July 1974—Gift of Philip Hofer. Typ Inc 6231.5

2954 Savonarola, Hieronymus: Regola del ben vivere. 1498.

4°. [4] leaves; ill.; 202 x 132 mm.

Without rubrication; woodcuts uncolored. Half 19th-century calf and marbled boards.

HC(Add)R 14364; Pr 6231; BMC 6:653 (IA.27381); IGI 8771; Goff S–237; Rhodes (F) 676; Sander 6835; Kristeller 389.

17 May 1921—From the Savonarola collection formed by Henry R. Newman. Bought with the Edward Henry Hall fund. Typ Inc 6231

2955 Savonarola, Hieronymus: Dichiarazione del mistero della croce. ca. 1498.

4°. [4] leaves; ill.; 200 x 140 mm.

Without rubrication. Half modern green morocco and green cloth.

H 14347; C 1937=5276; R 318; Pr 6270; BMC 6:661 (IA.27502); Polain 3457; IGI 8691; Goff S–227; CIBN S–87; Rhodes (F) 614; Sander 6768.

17 May 1921—From the Savonarola collection formed by Henry R. Newman. Bought with the Edward Henry Hall fund. Inc 6270

2956 Savonarola, Hieronymus: Expositio in psalmum L: Miserere mei Deus [Italian]. 1499.

4°. [26] leaves; ill.; 205 x 136 mm.

Without rubrication. Half modern brown morocco and green cloth.

HC(+Add)R 14431; Pr 6233; BMC 6:654 (IA.27388); IGI 8735; Goff S-217; CIBN S-103; Rhodes (F) 642; Sander 6785; Kristeller 387.

17 May 1921—From the Savonarola collection formed by Henry R. Newman. Bought with the Duplicate fund. Inc 6233 (A)

2957 ——Another copy. 188 x 128 mm.

Without rubrication. Half 19th-century gray cloth and marbled boards. Imperfect: leaf c10 wanting.

9 October 1919—Bought with the John Harvey Treat fund. Inc 6233 (B)

2958 Plenarium: Epistolae et Evangelia [Italian]. ca. 1499?

f°. cxxii, [2] (?) leaves (xxvii, xxix, xxxi, xxxvii, xxxxix, liiii, lviii, lxv, lxxvii, lxxxviii, and lxxxxiii misnumbered xxviiii, xxxi, xxx, xxxviii, xxxix, lvii, lvii, lxix, lxxvi, lxxxviiii, and lxxxxiiii); ill.; 278 x 195 mm.

I can give no transcriptions for this apparently unique fragment, since all before leaf c2 and all after q3 is wanting. However, according to Max Sander, this edition agrees page for page with that of 27 July 1495 printed by Lorenzo Morgiani and Johannes Petri, of which a type facsimile was issued by the Roxburghe Club in 1910; it is from that and from Sander's description of the 1495 edition that the above collation has been constructed. As for who printed this book and when, the type is certainly the 114G used by Jacopo di Carlo and Bartolommeo di Libri in Florence; but Di Carlo was active for only the relatively short period 1487–90, whereas Di Libri started in 1482 and went on printing through the first decade of the sixteenth century. For this reason I suggest him as the possible printer. Ten of the woodblocks used in the *Epistolae* were also used in the Italian version of Pseudo-Bonaventura *Meditationes vitae Christi* printed by Miscomini about 1493, where their state shows their precedence. Two further editions of Pseudo-Bonaventura with the same woodcuts are dated by GW ca. 1495 and ca. 1496 (though Goff dates the latter ca. 1500), in which, according to Sander, "le tirage des bois est sans doute postérieur" to the impressions in our *Epistolae*. However, Sander goes on to point out, it is not impossible that the 1495 and 1496 dates assigned by GW to the Pseudo-Bonaventura editions are too early and that they may very well have been printed at the end of the fifteenth or even the beginning of the sixteenth century, in which case our *Epistolae* would date from the same period or slightly before.

Without rubrication. 19th-century dark brown morocco, edges gilt; in a cloth case. Bought by Philip Hofer in 1932 by arrangement with the Trustees of the Whitworth Art Gallery, Manchester. Bibliographical note by J. H. Middleton, dated 2 September 1892, pasted inside front cover (not in the Sotheby sale catalogue of his library, April 1897); booklabels of Philip and Frances Hofer. Interleaved, with many leaves remargined. Imperfect: quires a^8, b^6, r^{10}, χ^2, and leaves c1, 7–8, e7, g8, h1, 6, i6, k5–6, l1, p6, and q2 wanting; q3 mutilated, with loss of text.

Goff E–96; Rhodes (F) 280; Sander (Suppl) 159.

14 September 1972—Gift of Philip Hofer. Typ Inc 6298.5

2959 Savonarola, Hieronymus: Operette. ca. 1500.

4°. [4] leaves; ill.; 204 x 137 mm.

Includes his *Regola a tutti i religiosi, Trattato del sacramento e dei misteri della messa,* and *Regola del ben vivere.*

Without rubrication. Half modern dark green morocco and green cloth.

HCR 14355; Pr 6304; BMC 6:664 (IA.27597); IGI 8750; Goff S–229; Rhodes (F) 657; Sander 6806; Kristeller 381b.

17 May 1921—From the Savonarola collection formed by Henry R. Newman. Bought with the Edward Henry Hall fund. Inc 6304

L O R E N Z O   D E   A L O P A

2960 Plato: Opera [Latin]. May 1484–before April 1485.

f°. [562] leaves (8, 9, 212, and 386 blank); 258 x 194 mm.

Latin translation by Marsilius Ficinus. Includes a poem by Naldus Nandius. There are variants in the setting and imposition of first χ^6; see below. Neither of the Harvard copies shows the stubs described by BMC as following ^{2}e8.

In this copy the leaves of first χ are correctly imposed; the second column of χ2r ends "uel tēploχ īgētia edificia/ utrũ oporterȝ cõside." Initials and paragraph marks added in red or blue. Half 17th- or 18th-century blind-stamped pigskin and tan paper over wooden boards. MS ownership notation inside front cover, "Emi

Ulmae Idibus Septembr. MDCCCXXIII Ex Bibliotheca Jesuitarum Ingolstadiensium. Frid. Creuzer"; an earlier MS notation inked out on π1r; from the library of Richard Ashhurst Bowie. Blank leaves 8 and 9 not present.

HC 13062*=H 13068?=H 7077; Pr 6405; BMC 6:666 (IB.27995); Polain 3189; IGI 7860; Goff P-771; CIBN P-446; Rhodes (F) 512.

9 November 1908—Gift of Mrs. E. D. Brandegee. Inc 6405

2961 ——Another copy. 278 x 202 and 260 x 200 mm.

In this copy the leaves of first 𝞫 are incorrectly imposed in order: 1r–v, 2r, 5r, 2r–v, 3r–v, 4r–v, 5r–v, followed by a proof-sheet of another setting of 2v and 5v; the second column of 𝞫2r ends "ingentia edificia/ utrum oporteret considerare." Bound in two volumes, divided after first 𝞫, the volumes of different binding and provenance. Volume 1, initials on the first few leaves added in red or blue, not thereafter; half 19th-century calf and tan boards. Volume 2, initials added in red or blue; 18th-century calf, edges speckled red. In volume 1, π1–5 mutilated and restored in MS; in volume 2, sheet t4 wanting, supplied in MS facsimile; sheets ꝑ1–4 bound in reverse order; blank leaf 212 not present.

Countway Library (William Norton Bullard Collection)

2962 Anthologia Graeca [Greek]. 11 August 1494.

4°. [280] leaves (280 blank); 220 x 153 mm.

The Planudean anthology. Edited by Janus Lascaris, who also designed the type. BMC has note, "The last quire is not found in all copies, probably because of the flight and proscription of Piero de'Medici shortly after the publication of the book caused the dedication to be suppressed."

The last quire is not present in this copy but has been supplied in MS facsimile; a note inserted at front states "The Letter of Lascaris at the end is in MS. copied by Mr Foss, Bookseller of Pall Mall of the Firm of Payne & Foss." Initial spaces not filled in; without rubrication. 18th-century red straight-grain morocco, blind- and gilt-stamped; edges gilt. "Mvsevm Britannicvm" and "Duplicate 1804" stamps on A1r; from the library of Sir Mark Masterman Sykes (no. 258 in pt. 1 of the Evans sale catalogue of his library, May 1824); booklabel of Edward Craven Hawtrey (no. 33 in pt. 1 of the Sotheby sale catalogue, July 1853); from the library of Richard Ashhurst Bowie.

HC 1145*; Pr 6406; BMC 6:666 (IB.28003); Pell 802; Polain 4146; GW 2048; IGI 599; Goff A–765; BSB-Ink A–557; Rhodes (F) 40.

9 November 1908—Gift of Mrs. E. D. Brandegee. Inc 6406

2963 Ficinus, Marsilius: Commentaria V perpetua in Platonem. 2 December 1496.

f°. [158] leaves; 273 x 202 mm.

Includes Ficinus's Latin translation of book 8 of Plato's *Republic.*

Initial spaces, with guide-letters, not filled in; without rubrication. Shabby old limp vellum; in a cloth case. MS ownership notation on a1r, "Angelus Beuilacqua hunc possidet librum"; bookstamp with initials "G L" several times repeated. MS marginalia. Imperfect: two leaves of errata, which should be inserted between A7 and 8 at end, wanting.

H 7076*; Pr 6409; BMC 6:669 (IB.28029); GW 9871; IGI 3861; Goff F–152; Sack 1442; BSB-Ink F–111; Rhodes (F) 292.

Countway Library

2964 Apollonius Rhodius: Argonautica [Greek]. 1496.

4°. [172] leaves (172 blank); 224 x 171 mm.

With the scholia of Lucillus, Sophocleius, and Theon. Edited by Janus Lascaris.

Initials and paragraph marks added in red. Old vellum. MS marginalia. Leaf [alpha]1 remargined at top.

HC 1292*; Pr 6407; BMC 6:667 (IB.28023); Pell 912; Polain 283; GW 2271; IGI 753; Goff A–924; BSB-Ink A–650; Rhodes (F) 59.

1937—From the library of Herbert Weir Smyth. Inc 6407

2965 ——Another copy. 235 x 171 mm.

Initial spaces not filled in; without rubrication. 19th-century red morocco, edges gilt. Booklabel of Ambroise Firmin Didot (no. 100 in pt. 1 of the Hôtel Drouot sale catalogue of his library, June 1878); bookplate of Sir Thomas Brooke (p. 23 in vol. 1 of his 1891 catalogue; no. 32 in the Sotheby sale catalogue of his brother, J. S. Brooke, who inherited his books, May 1921); bookplate of William King Richardson. Blank leaf not present.

1951—Bequest of William King Richardson. WKR 1.1.4

2966 Lucianus Samosatensis: Dialogi [Greek]. 1496.

f°. [264] leaves (1 and 264 blank); 328 x 231 mm.

On a later reissue with a title added to blank A1r, see BMC. Edited by Janus Lascaris.

Initial spaces not filled in; without rubrication. Half 19th-century brown morocco and speckled boards; edges stained blue. Oval library stamp on A2r, a lily plant with three flowers, initials "D S A," i.e., Domus Sanctissimae Annuntiatae (or Domus Annuntiatae Servitorum?; since the S is much larger than the other two letters and is twined around the stem of the lily, it is perhaps unlikely that "Sanctissimae" would be thus emphasized); see Dennis E. Rhodes, "Lilies and a Library," *The Book Collector* 24 (1975): 417–20. MS notation at foot of A2r erased but visible under ultraviolet light, "Ex munere R^{di} D^{ni} Ludouici Martelli canonici flor^i et conseruatoris huius conuentus 1574 5. iunij." Imperfect: lower third of [gamma gamma]3 cut away; [gamma gamma]4–6 and [eta eta]1–2 wanting; blank leaves not present.

HC(+Add) 10258; Pr 6408; BMC 6:667 (IB.28025); Polain 2522; IGI 5823; Goff L–320; CIBN L–245; Rhodes (F) 416.

1937—From the library of Herbert Weir Smyth. Inc 6408

2967 Callimachus: Hymni [Greek]. ca. 1496.

4°. [34] leaves; 222 x 148 mm.

With the *scholia vetusta*. Edited by Janus Lascaris.

Initial spaces, one with guide-letter, not filled in; without rubrication. Unbound quires, laid into a vellum leaf of a Latin legal document dated 1476 folded as a wrapper; in a half brown morocco case.

H 4266; Pr 6412; BMC 6:668 (IA.28019); Pell 3167; GW 5917; IGI 2373; Goff C–61; Rhodes (F) 156.

May 1960—Bought with the Amy Lowell fund. Inc 6412

2968 Pseudo-Cebes: Tabula [Greek]. ca. 1496.

8°. [74] leaves (1 blank); 159 x 112 mm.

Includes (in Greek): Basilius Magnus, *De legendis libris gentilium.*—

Pseudo-Plutarchus, *De liberis educandis.*–Xenophon, *Hiero.* There are variant endings to the text of Cebes on [beta]8v; see BMC and GW.

The ending to the text of Cebes in this copy agrees with BMC IA.28036. Initial spaces not filled in; without rubrication. Old vellum; edges stained red. Liechtenstein bookplate.

H 4820=HCR 4821; R 117; Pr 6414; BMC 6:668 (IA.28036); GW 6442; IGI 2662; Goff C-356; BSB-Ink C-205; Rhodes (F) 177.

11 April 1952–Gift of Donald F. and Mary C. Hyde. Inc 6414

FRANCESCO BONACCORSI

2969 Compagnia del Rosario: Statuti. After 4 May 1485.

[For transcriptions see Reichling.] 4°. a¹²; [12] leaves; ill.; 191 x 132 mm. a3: 25 lines, 138 x 90 mm. Type: 1:112(110)R. Initial spaces, with guide-letters, on a2v and a8v; woodcuts on a1v and a2r.

IGI and Rhodes assign this to Miscomini; but Reichling says "Typi sunt 'Jo. Nesii orationis de charitate,'" which is signed by Bonaccorsi and printed about the same time (after 23 March 1485); see R 1005 and Rhodes 466.

Initial spaces not filled in; without rubrication. Unbound; in a cloth case. Booklabel of Philip Hofer.

R 883; IGI 3112; Goff S-758; Rhodes (F) 213; Sander 6574.

9 November 1984–Bequest of Philip Hofer. Typ Inc 6305.5

2970 Laude facte et composte da piu persone spirituali. 1 March 1485/6.

4°. [9], ii–cxxxviii leaves (lxxi misnumbered lxxii); 165 x 115 mm.

A collection of poems, many of them in *ottava rima*, by Feo Belcari, Francesco Dalbizo, and others. Edited by Jacopo de'Morsi.

Initial spaces, with guide-letters, not filled in; without rubrication. Modern leatherized cloth over paste-paper boards. Occasional MS marginalia in Italian. Imperfect: sheets ᵏa1 (title page and end of table), a3, [d]1–2, [l]1, and [t]1 wanting; leaves [n]8 and [q]1 wanting; quire ᵏa misbound in order 2, 7, 3–6.

HC 11617=HCR 2752; Pr 6306; BMC 6:670 (IA.27603); IGI 5698; Goff L-76; Rhodes (F) 404.

15 November 1990—Gift of Felix de Marez Oyens. Inc 6306

2971 Petrarca, Francesco: Trionfi. ca. 1488.

4°. [42] leaves (42 blank); 209 x 136 mm.

Printed by Bonaccorsi with Antonius Francisci.

Printed on vellum. Initials on a1r, b6r, c2r, d1r, e4r, and e6v illuminated in gold and colors, with marginal extensions; initials elsewhere added in blue or gold, but some spaces, with guide-letters, not filled in; arms of the Guicciardini family illuminated in lower margin of a1r. 19th-century red straight-grain morocco, gilt. Booklabel of Adriana R. Salem.

HR 12780; C 4705; Pr 6178 (assigned to Miscomini); BMC 6:671 (IA.27736); IGI 7550; Goff P–396; Rhodes (F) 496; Amelung (Trionfi) 5.

December 1965—Gift of Ward M. Canaday. Inc 6345.5

2972 Dante Alighieri: Convivio. 20 September 1490.

4°. [90] leaves; 203 x 134 mm.

Initial on a1r added in red; spaces elsewhere, with guide-letters, not filled in. 19th-century vellum, gilt; edges stained red. Booklabel of Adriana R. Salem.

HC 5954; Pr 6309; BMC 6:673 (IA.27611); Pell 4120; Polain 1228; GW 7973; IGI 367; Goff D–36; BSB-Ink D–12; Rhodes (F) 232.

December 1965—Gift of Ward M. Canaday. Inc 6309 (A)

2973 ——Another copy. 209 x 138 mm.

Initial spaces not filled in; without rubrication. Half 19th-century calf and decorated boards. Autographed, "Charles Eliot Norton 1865." Imperfect: sheets d1–2 wanting, duplicates of e1–2 bound in their place.

4 May 1905—From the library of Charles Eliot Norton. Inc 6309 (B)

2974 Jacopone da Todi: Laude. 28 September 1490.

4°. [142] leaves; ill.; 173 x 122 mm.

Initial spaces, some with guide-letters, not filled in; without rubrication; woodcut uncolored. Bound in a vellum leaf of 15th-century MS containing a legal work; in a cloth case. MS ownership notation on title page, "Del Sacro Eremo di Montecenatio [?]"; book- and release stamps of the Metropolitan Museum of Art, New York; booklabel of Philip Hofer.

HC(+Add) 9355; Pr 6310; BMC 6:673 (IA.27615); IGI 5087; Goff J–214; CIBN J–145; Rhodes (F) 384; Sander 3549; Kristeller 220.

24 July 1974—Gift of Philip Hofer. Typ Inc 6310

2975 Bossus, Matthaeus: De veris ac salutaribus animi gaudiis. 8 February 1491.

4°. [90] leaves (1 and 90 blank); 192 x 138 mm.

Includes letters by Angelus Politianus and Timotheius Maffeius.

This copy lacks the first blank, for which has been substituted an elaborate (18th-century?) ink-and-wash title page with a scroll border; ink-and-wash initials in the same style have been added on a3r and a5r. 18th-century red morocco, gilt, edges mottled red and green. Bookplate of Paul Girardot de Préfond (no. 271 in the De Bure sale catalogue of his library, 1757). With this is bound the same author's *Sermo in Jesu Christi passionem* (Bologna, Franciscus de Benedictis, 11 November 1495).

HC(+Add) 3672*; Pr 6312; BMC 6:674 (IA.27621); Pell 2785; GW 4955; IGI 2026; Goff B–1041; BSB-Ink B–760; Rhodes (F) 139.

28 April 1874—Bequest of Charles Sumner. Inc 6312

2976 ——Another copy. 202 x 138 mm.

Initial spaces, with guide-letters, not filled in; without rubrication. Old paste-paper boards. Bookstamp "Ex libr. Fr. Franc. Raim. Adami" in lower margin of a2r. Blank leaves not present.

Countway Library (William Norton Bullard Collection)

2977 Savonarola, Hieronymus: Libro della vita viduale. 1491.

4°. [30] leaves; 196 x 137 mm.

Initials added in red and/or blue. Modern red cloth. In this copy the "M." in the colophon date has failed to print.

H 14369; BMC 12:48 (IA.27620); IGI 8744; Goff S–286; Rhodes (F) 652.

17 May 1921—From the Savonarola collection formed by Henry R. Newman. Bought with the Duplicate fund. Inc 6311.5

2978 Medici, Lorenzo de': Rappresentazione dei Santi Giovanni e Paolo. ca. 1491?

[For transcriptions see Reichling; but this copy has "RAPRESENTA-TIONE" for his "RAPPRESENTATIONE" in line 1 on a1r.] 4°. a–d^8; [32] leaves; ill.; 190 x 125 mm. a3r: 28 lines, 152 x 79 mm. Type: 1:112(110)R. Initial space on a2r; Lombard on a1r; woodcut of the Medici arms on a1r.

Initial space not filled in; woodcut colored green, blue, and orange. 19th-century maroon morocco, gilt, edges gilt. Bookstamp of Gustavo Camillo Galletti on a1r; bookplate of Baron Horace de Landau (described in vol. 1, p. 320, of his 1885–90 catalogue); autograph of Tammaro De Marinis; booklabel of Philip Hofer. Imperfect: final quire (d^8) wanting.

H 10988; R 1573; IGI 6321; Goff M–427; Rhodes (F) 442; Sander 6270; Kristeller 285c.

April 1956—Gift of Philip Hofer. Typ Inc 6315.5

2979 Savonarola, Hieronymus: Compendio di rivelazioni. 18 August 1495.

4°. [54] leaves; 198 x 133 mm.

There are two issues of this edition; see BMC. Some copies include a full-page copper engraving of the triple crown of the Virgin Mary, described on d8v of the book.

In this issue a1r has 32 lines, with line 32 ending "per non hauere" and with a space left between the 6th and 7th lines. Initial spaces not filled in; without rubrication. Modern red morocco; edges stained blue. MS marginalia. The copper engraving is not present.

HC(+Add) 14334; Pr 6313; BMC 6:674 (IA.27625); IGI 8678; Goff S–179(a); Rhodes (F) 605.

December 1965—Gift of Ward M. Canaday. Inc 6313

2980 ——Another issue. 203 x 133 mm.

In this issue a1r has 33 lines, with line 33 ending "seminato nel popu" and with no space left between the 6th and 7th lines. Initial spaces not filled in; without rubrication. Half 19th-century calf and marbled boards; edges stained red. MS ownership notation in lower margin of a1r, "Est Conuentus S.S. Cosme et Damiani [illegible word] Ff. Erem. Discal. S. P. Augustini." The copper engraving is not present.

Pr 6314; BMC 6:674 (IA.27626); IGI 8679; Goff S–179(b).

17 May 1921—From the Savonarola collection formed by Henry R. Newman. Bought with the Duplicate fund. Inc 6314

2981 Lilius, Zacharias: De origine et laudibus scientiarum. 7 April 1496.

4°. [72] leaves; ill.; 194 x 130 mm.

Printed by Bonaccorsi for Piero Pacini. Includes Lilius's *Contra Antipodes, De miseria hominis et contemptu mundi, De generibus ventorum*, and *Vita Caroli Magni.*

Without rubrication. Bound in 18th-century decorated paste-paper boards.

HC 10103; Pr 6316; BMC 6:675 (IA.27630); IGI 5762; Goff L–221; CIBN L–172; Rhodes (F) 413; Sander 3978.

Countway Library

2982 Savonarola, Hieronymus: Compendio di rivelazioni. 23 April 1496.

a1r: ℂ COMPENDIO DI REVELATIONE DELLO ‖ INVTILE SER-VO DI IESV CHRISTO ‖ FRATE HIERONYMO DA FERRA‖RA DELLORDINE DE FRA‖TI PREDICATORI ‖ ℂ IESVS MARIA ‖ [woodcut, Savonarola preaching] ‖ (B⁴)ENCHE Lungo tempo in molti modi per ‖ inspiratione Diuina ... ‖ f8v, COLOPHON: FINIS. ‖ DEO GRATIAS. ‖ ℂ Impresso in Firenze ad instantia di ser Piero pacini da ‖ Pescia Nel anno M.cccclxxxxvi. Adi .xxiii. Daprile. ‖ [Pacini devices]

4°. a–f⁸; [48] leaves; ill.; 198 x 131 mm. a2r: 37 lines, 162 x 92 mm. Type: 3:88R. Woodcut initials; woodcuts.

The publisher's devices are not present in all copies.

Without rubrication. Modern red cloth. Imperfect: the left side of the illustration on d5v is too closely trimmed.

C 5274; Goff S–181; IGI 8682; Schäfer 298; Rhodes (F) 608; Sander 6761; Kristeller 390d.

17 May 1921—From the Savonarola collection formed by Henry R. Newman. Bought with the Duplicate fund. Inc 6316.10 (A)

2983 ——Another copy. 213 x 138 mm.

This copy is without the publisher's devices on f8v. Without rubrication. Half modern black morocco and red cloth. The first three leaves are remargined.

17 May 1921—From the Savonarola collection formed by Henry R. Newman. Bought with the Duplicate fund. Inc 6316.10 (B)

2984 Savonarola, Hieronymus: Expositio in psalmum LXXIX: Qui regis Israel. 28 April 1496.

a1r: FRATER HIERONYMVS FERRARIENSIS ‖ ORDINIS PRAEDI-CATORVM SER ‖ VVS INVTILIS IESV CHRISTI ‖ FRATRI .N. CON-SERVO SVO ‖ SALVTEM ‖ PRAEFATIO ‖ (S³)ALVET Te dominus Iesus Fili Charissime. ‖ b6r, COLOPHON: ⁑ Impressum Florẽtiae per ser Franciscum de Bonaccur‖siis impensis Ser Petri Pacini de Piscia ‖ Anno salutis .M.CCCCLXXXXVI ‖ Quarto kalen. Maias. ‖ [publisher's device]

4°. a⁸, b⁶; [14] leaves; ill.; 207 x 136 mm. a3r: 36 lines, 157 x 91 mm. Type: 3:88R. Woodcut on a2r; woodcut initials on a1r and a2r.

Without rubrication. Modern red cloth.

HR 14433; IGI 8738; Goff S–220; CIBN S–106; Rhodes (F) 644; Sander 6789; Kristeller 388b.

17 May 1921—From the Savonarola collection formed by Henry R. Newman. Gift of John Pierpont Morgan. Inc 6316.5

2985 Benivieni, Domenico: Trattato in defensione e probazione della dottrina di Savonarola. 28 May 1496.

4°. [50] leaves; ill.; 212 x 143 mm.

Printed by Bonaccorsi for Piero Pacini.

Without rubrication. Half modern gray morocco and gray cloth.

HC 2784; Pr 6317; BMC 6:675 (IA.27632); Pell 2044; Polain 556; GW 3849; IGI 1480; Goff B–327; Schäfer 39; Rhodes (F) 105; Sander 896; Kristeller 52.

17 May 1921—From the Savonarola collection formed by Henry R.

Newman. Bought with the Duplicate fund. Typ Inc 6317

2986 Savonarola, Hieronymus: Prediche quadragesimali dell'anno 1495. 8 February 1496/7.

f°. [220] leaves; 278 x 206 mm.

I follow BMC in placing this with the output of Bonaccorsi because the sheet containing the date is printed with his type; but it is a cooperative work, for quires π–t are printed with the types of Bartolommeo di Libri and quires A–F with the types of Lorenzo Morgiani. Edited by Lorenzo Vivoli.

Without rubrication. Modern brown morocco, edges gilt.

HC 14382*; Pr 6209, 6320, 6369; BMC 6:651, 675, 686 (IB.27636); IGI 8766; Goff S–243; CIBN S–131; Rhodes (F) 674.

17 May 1921—From the Savonarola collection formed by Henry R. Newman. Bought with the Duplicate fund. Inc 6209

J A C O P O   D I   C A R L O

2987 Diogenes Laertius: Vitae et sententiae philosophorum [Italian]. 24 October 1489.

4°. [52] leaves; 201 x 145 mm.

An abbreviated paraphrase of the original. Printed by Di Carlo with Petrus de Bonaccursis.

Without rubrication. Half 18th- or 19th-century sheep and marbled boards; in a cloth case. Booklabel of Adriana R. Salem. This copy is copiously illustrated in the margins with ink-and-wash drawings closely related to the text. Imperfect: title page wanting, with a trimmed title from a 16th-century edition mounted in its place; leaf b6 remargined, probably removing one of the drawings.

H 6209*; BMC 6:677 (IA.27960); Pell 4282; Polain 1295; GW 8390; IGI 3468; Goff D–232; Rhodes (F) 263.

December 1959—Gift of Ward M. Canaday. Typ Inc 6334.5

2988 Cherubino da Siena: Regola della vita spirituale. ca. 1490.

4°. [80] leaves; 190 x 130 mm.

Includes his *Regola di vita matrimoniale*.

Initial spaces not filled in; without rubrication. Modern dark blue morocco, edges gilt.

C 1584; Pr 6298 (assigned to Di Libri); BMC 6:676 (IA.27685); GW 6606; IGI 2736; Goff C-443; Rhodes (F) 188.

Countway Library (William Norton Bullard Collection)

A N T O N I U S   F R A N C I S C I

2989 Pseudo-Diogenes Sinopensis: Epistolae. 22 June 1487.

4°. [54] leaves; 219 x 143 mm.

Includes the Pseudo-Brutus and Pseudo-Hippocrates collections of letters, translated by Franciscus Griffolinus and Rinucius Aretinus.

Initial spaces, with guide-letters, not filled in; without rubrication. 19th-century calf, rebacked; edges gilt. "Libro Lier" booklabel.

HC 6194; HR 12897 (Hippocrates); Pr 6329A; BMC 6:677 (IA.27672); Pell 4272; GW 8396; IGI 3456; Goff D-217; Rhodes (F) 261.

Countway Library (William Norton Bullard Collection)

B E R N A R D U S   N E R L I U S

2990 Homerus: Opera [Greek]. "8 December 1488" [i.e., not before 13 January 1489].

f°. 2 vols. (vol. 1: [250] leaves, 42 blank; vol. 2: [190] leaves, 190 blank); 322 x 224 and 327 x 200 mm.

Edited by Demetrius Chalcondylas, with lives of Homer by Herodotus and Plutarch and an essay on Homer by Dio Chrysostomus. Volume 1 contains the *Iliad*, volume 2 the *Odyssey*, *Batrachomyomachia*, and *Hymns*. Roberto Ridolfi does not believe that Bernardus and Nerius Nerlius were printers and prefers to assign this work to Demetrius Damilas, the Printer of Vergilius C 6061, and Bartolommeo di Libri. See his *La stampa in Firenze nel secolo XV* (Firenze, 1958): [95]-111.

Initials added in brown, but many spaces not filled in. Volumes of different provenance with different bindings: vol. 1, 16th-century olive morocco, rebacked, edges gilt; bookplate of Albert May Todd (not in the American Art Association-Anderson Galleries sale catalogue of part of his library, October 1929); vol. 2, 19th-century dark blue morocco, gilt, edges gilt, by Zaehnsdorf; bookplates of M. A. Elton (not in the Sotheby sale catalogue of her library, May 1916) and of Albert May Todd; MS note on front flyleaf, "H. R. Luard 28 June 1886. This copy of the Odyssey I bought at E. Cheney's sale at Sotheby's [no. 926 in the catalogue, where it is described as "oak boards covered in leather, with clasps"] bound by Zaehnsdorf, June 1889" (no. 678 in the Sotheby sale catalogue of his library, 16 November 1891). Imperfect: in vol. 1, leaves A1–2, N4–5, and V8 wanting; all supplied in positive photostat from a copy in the New York Public Library; in vol. 2, blank leaf ETET6 not present; ET4–5 from a copy of vol. 1 inserted between leaves ETET3 and 4.

HCR 8772; Pr 6194 (assigned to Bartolommeo di Libri); BMC 6:678 (IB.27657a–c); Polain 1893; IGI 4795; Goff H–300; CIBN H–173; Rhodes (F) 366.

3 November 1952—Gift of Thomas Yost Cooper. Inc 6343.5

2991   ——Another copy. 330 x 227 mm.

Initials at beginning of books illuminated in colors, probably in the 17th or early 18th century; first leaf in each volume has an illuminated border in the inner margin. 18th-century red straight-grain morocco, gilt, edges gilt; in cloth slip-cases. MS ownership notation in lower margin of AA1 in vol. 2, "Monasterio Sãcti Saluatoris Bononę"; MS note on vellum flyleaf at front of vol. 1, "Editio Princeps Homeri. This is one of the most beautiful copies of Homers Works extant; It is particularly described by de Bure in his Bibliographie Instructive N°. 2493. The Latin Dedication to Peter de Medicis by Bernard Nerlius, as well as the five sheets of a greek preface are omitted in this copy probably in order probably [sic] to make it more correspondant in appearance to the earliest printed Latin Classicks. There is a copy of this Edition of Homer in the Advocates Library Edinburgh, but without Illuminations & very inferior to this in point of Preservation. Four Hundred guineas were offered for a copy of it in Vellum. Edinburgh 25 December 1793. David Steuart"; with Steuart's armorial bookplate in both volumes, overpasted with the armorial plate of a member of the Preston family. Imperfect: 42 leaves at beginning of vol. 1 (A–D^8, E^{10}) wanting; blank leaf ETET6 at the end of vol. 2 not present.

1951—Bequest of William King Richardson. WKR 1.2.14

LORENZO MORGIANI, IN PART WITH JOHANNES PETRI

2992 Cavalca, Domenico: Pungi lingua. 8 October 1490.

f°. [72] leaves; 282 x 206 mm.

Printed by Morgiani with Johannes Petri.

Initial spaces on a2r and a2v, with guide-letters, not filled in; without rubrication. Half 19th-century sheep and blue boards. Booklabel of Adriana R. Salem.

HCR 4774; Pr 6349; BMC 6:681 (IB.27773); Pell 3446; Polain 1050; GW 6410; IGI 2634; Goff C–339; Rhodes (F) 172.

August 1959—Gift of Ward M. Canaday. Inc 6349

2993 Antonio da Siena: Monte santo di Dio. 20 March 1491.

f°. [92] leaves; ill.; 269 x 202 mm.

Printed by Morgiani with Johannes Petri.

Capital spaces not filled in; without rubrication; woodcuts uncolored. 19th-century red straight-grain morocco, gilt; in a cloth case. Book-plate of Count Dmitri Petrovitch Boutourlin (no. 462 in his 1831 catalogue); booklabels of Philip and Frances Hofer.

HR 1277; Pr 6350; BMC 6:681 (IB.27776); Pell 901; GW 2205; IGI 712; Goff A–887; Rhodes (F) 55; Sander 453; Kristeller 60.

14 September 1972—Gift of Philip Hofer. Typ Inc 6350

2994 Granollachs, Bernardus de: Lunarium, 1491–1550 [Italian]. 1 September 1491.

[For transcriptions see Reichling.] 4°. a–c⁸, d⁶, e⁴ (e4 blank); [34] leaves (34 blank); ill.; 203 x 140 mm. a4r: 37 lines and headline, 161 x 93 mm. Type: 2:130G, headings; 4:85R, text. Woodcut on title page; woodcut initial on a2r.

Printed by Morgiani with Johannes Petri.

Without rubrication. Modern decorated boards. Imperfect: title page wanting; leaves remargined, a few with slight loss of text; blank leaf not present.

H 10334; R 539; IGI 4370; Goff G–340; Rhodes (F) 353; Sander 3226; Kristeller 210a.

Countway Library

2995 **Pseudo-Augustinus:** Soliloquia (Agnoscam te . . .) [Italian]. 10 November 1491.

4°. [44] leaves; ill.; 211 x 138 mm.

Includes *Dieci gradi al perfezione*. Printed by Morgiani with Johannes Petri.

Without rubrication. Old vellum, badly wormed, lined with vellum leaves of 15th-century Latin MS; in a cloth case. MS ownership notation on f4v, "F. Gabriello Maria Lagèt Agostiniano. 1756." Imperfect: leaf f4 slightly mutilated; sheets b1–2 misbound after sheet b4.

HCR 2018; Pr 6351; BMC 6:681 (IA.27779); Pell 1523; GW 3017; IGI 1047; Goff A–1329; Rhodes (F) 76; Sander 692; Kristeller 10.

16 December 1920—Bought with the John Harvey Treat fund. Inc 6351

2996 **Calandri, Filippo:** Aritmetica. 1 January 1491/2.

8°. [104] leaves; ill.; 136 x 102 mm.

Printed by Morgiani with Johannes Petri.

Initial spaces, with guide-letters, not filled in; without rubrication. Modern tan morocco by Sangorski & Sutcliffe.

HCR 4234; Pr 6352; BMC 6:681 (IA.27782); Pell 3156; GW 5884; IGI 2352; Goff C–34; Schäfer 89; Rhodes (F) 155; Sander 1523; Kristeller 77a.

9 November 1984—Bequest of Philip Hofer. Typ Inc 6352

2997 **Contrasto di Carnesciale e della Quaresima.** ca. 1492/95.

4°. [8] leaves; ill.; 189 x 144 mm.

Without rubrication. Modern brown morocco. Booklabels of Count Giacomo Manzoni (no. 2961 in pt. 1 of the Sangiorgi sale catalogue of his library, May–June 1893) and of Philip Hofer.

C 1761; Pr 6388; BMC 6:687 (IA.27918); GW 7460; Goff C-874; Rhodes (F) 223; Sander 2128; Kristeller 85a.

April 1956—Gift of Philip Hofer. Typ Inc 6388

2998 Antoninus Florentinus: Confessionale "Curam illius habe" [Italian]. 23 May 1493.

4°. [82] leaves; ill.; 168 x 115 mm.

Printed by Morgiani with Johannes Petri.

Without rubrication. Half 19th-century black morocco and black cloth. Booklabels of Philip and Frances Hofer. Quire h misbound after quire i.

HC 1214; Pr 6355; BMC 6:682 (IA.27792); Pell 868; GW 2079; IGI 615; Goff A-785; Rhodes (F) 43; Sander 427; Kristeller 25.

14 September 1972—Gift of Philip Hofer. Typ Inc 6355

2999 Cavalca, Domenico: Frutti della lingua. 4 September 1493.

f°. [90] leaves; ill.; 278 x 210 mm.

Printed by Morgiani with Johannes Petri.

Without rubrication. Modern limp vellum. Bookplate of Leo S. Olschki; booklabels of Philip and Frances Hofer.

HCR 4779; Pr 6356; BMC 6:682 (IB.27795); Pell 3450; Polain 1051; GW 6400; IGI 2624; Goff C-331; Rhodes (F) 168; Sander 1848; Kristeller 96b.

14 September 1972—Gift of Philip Hofer. Typ Inc 6356

3000 Aegidius Assisiensis: Aurea verba [Italian]. ca. 1493.

4°. [20] leaves; ill.; 210 x 140 mm.

Includes Aurelius Augustinus, *Sermone del vivere religiosamente*. Printed by Morgiani with Johannes Petri.

Without rubrication. Old limp vellum. Booklabels of Philip and Frances Hofer.

HR 104; GW 266; IGI 54-A; Goff A-63; Rhodes (F) 5; Sander 48; Kristeller 132.

14 September 1972—Gift of Philip Hofer. Typ Inc 6383.5

3001 Savonarola, Hieronymus: Dell'amore di Gesù. Before 17 February 1493.

4°. [22] leaves; ill.; 195 x 139 mm.

Printed by Morgiani with Johannes Petri.

Without rubrication. Half modern dark green morocco and green cloth. Leaves numbered in MS 89–104. Imperfect: quire c⁶ wanting.

CR 5280; Pr 6378; BMC 6:682 (IA.27876); IGI 8786; Goff S–168; Schäfer 307; Rhodes (F) 691.

17 May 1921—From the Savonarola collection formed by Henry R. Newman. Gift of J. P. Morgan. Inc 6378

3002 Pulci, Luigi: La confessione. ca. 1494?

[a]1r, TITLE: La confessione di Luigi Pulci ‖ [woodcut, confessor with penitent, within architectural border] ‖ [a]1v, CONFESSIO ALOISII DE ‖ PVLCI .M.V. ‖ (A²)Ve uirgo Maria di gratia piena ‖ salue regina ... ‖ [a]4v, col. 2, line 28: al sommo & uero bene ‖ che dhabitare in noi sie dichinato ‖ Finis ‖

4°. [a]⁴; [4] leaves; ill.; 201 x 139 mm. 2 columns. [a]2r: 33 lines, 137 x 122 mm. Type: 4:85(81)R. Lombards; woodcut, 98 x 73 mm., border, 162 x 105 mm.

For reproductions of the title and a page of text see Tammaro De Marinis, *Appunti e ricerche bibliografiche* (Milano, 1940): plates LI–LII. De Marinis describes the work as printed "con i caratteri tondi del tipo 85R di Lorenzo Morgiani"; but a Qu not found elsewhere with that type is here used. I accept his assignment and dating with some hesitation.

19th-century blue boards. Booklabel of Philip Hofer, with his note "Bot of De Marinis, Florence, April '57."

Goff P–1119; CIBN P–704; Sander 6014bis.

April 1957—Gift of Philip Hofer. Typ Inc 6393.5

3003 Savonarola, Hieronymus: Epistola alla Christianissima Maestà del Re di Francia. After 26 May 1495.

4°. [2] leaves; 208 x 136 mm.

Printed by Morgiani with Johannes Petri?

Without rubrication. Half modern brown morocco and rust cloth.

HR 14461; BMC 12:48 (IA.27803); IGI 8695; Goff S–187; Rhodes (F) 618.

17 May 1921—From the Savonarola collection formed by Henry R. Newman. Bought with the Edward Henry Hall fund. Inc 6357.5

3004   **Savonarola, Hieronymus:** Compendio di rivelazioni. 1 September 1495.

4°. [48] leaves; ill.; 201 x 130 mm.

Printed by Morgiani with Johannes Petri.

Without rubrication. Old vellum. With this is bound his *De omnium scientiarum divisione* (Pescia, Unassigned, ca. 1492). Woodcut on d5v slightly trimmed at left edge.

HC(Add)R 14335; Pr 6358; BMC 6:683 (IA.27805); IGI 8680; Goff S–180; Schäfer 297; Rhodes (F) 606; Sander 6758.

17 May 1921—From the Savonarola collection formed by Henry R. Newman. Gift of J. P. Morgan. Typ Inc 6358

3005   **Savonarola, Hieronymus:** Epistola a uno amico. ca. 1495?

4°. [6] leaves; ill.; 207 x 128 mm.

Printed by Morgiani with Johannes Petri?

Without rubrication. Modern red cloth. Leaves numbered in MS 100–105.

CR 5302; Pr 6395; BMC 6:689 (IA.27947); IGI 8693; Goff S–183; Schäfer 300 ("vor dem 31. Oktober 1496?"); Rhodes (F) 616; Sander 6773; Kristeller 380c.

17 May 1921—From the Savonarola collection formed by Henry R. Newman. Bought with the Duplicate fund. Inc 6395

3006   **Savonarola, Hieronymus:** Epistola a uno amico. ca. 1495?

4°. [6] leaves; ill.; 195 x 135 mm.

Printed by Morgiani with Johannes Petri?

Without rubrication. Half modern dark blue morocco and gray cloth. Leaves numbered in MS 189–94.

CR 5301; Pr 6396; BMC 6:689 (IA.27950); IGI 8692; Goff S–184; CIBN S–92?; Rhodes (F) 615; Sander 6772; Kristeller 380b.

17 May 1921—From the Savonarola collection formed by Henry R. Newman. Bought with the Duplicate fund. Inc 6396

3007 Savonarola, Hieronymus: Expositio Orationis Dominicae [Italian]. ca. 1495?

4°. [24] leaves; ill.; 207 x 134 mm.

Includes his *Epistola della communione.* Printed by Morgiani with Johannes Petri.

Without rubrication. Modern red cloth. Ownership notation obliterated on a1r.

HCR 14446; Pr 6397; BMC 6:684 (IA.27953); IGI 8711; Goff S-201; CIBN S-113; Rhodes (F) 636; Sander 6781; Kristeller 384a.

17 May 1921—From the Savonarola collection formed by Henry R. Newman. Gift of J. P. Morgan. Typ Inc 6397

3008 Savonarola, Hieronymus: Operetta sopra i dieci comandamenti di Dio. ca. 1495?

4°. [28] leaves; ill.; 195 x 137 mm.

Printed by Morgiani with Johannes Petri.

Without rubrication. Half modern dark green morocco and green cloth.

HR 14442; Pr 6396A; BMC 6:684 (IA.27952); IGI 8749; Goff S-225; CIBN S-142; Schäfer 304; Rhodes (F) 656; Sander 6804; Kristeller 377a.

17 May 1921—From the Savonarola collection formed by Henry R. Newman. Bought with the Edward Henry Hall fund. Typ Inc 6396A

3009 Pseudo-Bernardus Claravallensis: Modus bene vivendi [Italian]. 27 January 1495/6.

4°. [4], CXX leaves (XXVI, CXVI, and CXVIII misnumbered XXV, CXV, and CXVII); ill.; 207 x 139 mm.

Printed by Morgiani with Johannes Petri for Piero Pacini. Includes *Sermone composto dal traductore di questa op[er]a in uulgare a Laura sua figliuola religiosa.*

Without rubrication. 16th-century blind- and gilt-stamped calf over pastepaper boards; edges gauffered and gilt; marks of ties, no longer present.

H 2898*; C 960; Pr 6359; BMC 6:683 (IA.27810); Pell 2142; Polain 596; GW 4053; IGI 1544; Goff B–418; Rhodes (F) 119; Sander 956; Kristeller 56.

21 October 1941–Bought with the Bennett Hubbard Nash fund. Inc 6359

3010 Antoninus Florentinus: Confessionale "Defecerunt" [Italian]. 22 February 1496.

4°. [114] leaves; ill.; 212 x 140 mm.

Printed by Morgiani with Johannes Petri for Piero Pacini.

Without rubrication. Half 19th-century calf and marbled boards. In MS on verso of title page is an "Ordo absoluendi omnibus fidelibus christianis ab excommunicatione." Booklabel of Philip Hofer.

HCR 1211; Pr 6370; BMC 6:683 (IA.27837); Pell 869; GW 2142; IGI 657; Goff A–836; Rhodes (F) 45; Sander 428; Kristeller 26.

28 February 1942–Gift of Philip Hofer. Typ Inc 6370

3011 Savonarola, Hieronymus: Expositio in psalmum LXXIX: Qui regis Israel [Italian]. 8 June 1496.

4°. [16] leaves (16 blank); 212 x 141 mm.

Printed by Morgiani with Johannes Petri.

Without rubrication. Half modern black morocco and black boards.

H 14436=HC(+Add) 14439; Pr 6361; BMC 6:684 (IA.27813); IGI 8739; Goff S–222; CIBN S–107; Rhodes (F) 645.

17 May 1921–From the Savonarola collection formed by Henry R. Newman. Bought with the Duplicate fund. Inc 6361

3012 Savonarola, Hieronymus: De simplicitate vitae Christianae. 28 August 1496.

4°. [48] leaves; ill.; 202 x 140 mm.

Printed by Morgiani with Johannes Petri for Piero Pacini.

Without rubrication. Modern vellum, with the arms of Victor Mas-séna, prince d'Essling, stamped in gilt on covers, edges gilt (not in the Galerie Fischer sale catalogue of his library, May 1939).

HCR 14357; Pr 6363; BMC 6:685 (IA.27818); IGI 8778; Goff S-271; CIBN S-139; Schäfer 301; Rhodes (F) 683; Sander 6841; Kristeller 392a.

25 November 1949—Gift of Imrie de Vegh. Inc 6363

3013 Savonarola, Hieronymus: Dell'orazione mentale. Before 31 October 1496.

4°. [10] leaves; ill.; 211 x 140 mm.

Printed by Morgiani with Johannes Petri?

Without rubrication. Half modern brown morocco and marbled boards.

CR 5290; Pr 6399; BMC 6:689 (IA.27959); IGI 8789; Goff S-234; CIBN S-116; Rhodes (F) 695; Sander 6810; Kristeller 383b.

17 May 1921—From the Savonarola collection formed by Henry R. Newman. Bought with the Edward Henry Hall fund. Typ Inc 6399

3014 Savonarola, Hieronymus: De simplicitate vitae Christianae [Italian]. 31 October 1496.

4°. [60] leaves; ill.; 202 x 130 mm.

For collation see BMC; but in this copy leaf f xi is signed; leaves f i, f v, f vi (missigned f ii), and f xii are mounted on stubs. Italian translation by Girolamo Benivieni.

Without rubrication. Old limp vellum.

HCR 14358; Pr 6364; BMC 6:685 (IA.27821); IGI 8779; Goff S-272; CIBN S-140; Rhodes (F) 684; Sander 6842; Kristeller 392b.

17 May 1921—From the Savonarola collection formed by Henry R. Newman. Bought with the Edward Henry Hall fund. Inc 6364

3015 Savonarola, Hieronymus: Libro della vita viduale. 26 November 1496.

[For transcriptions see Reichling; but insert a line-ending after "IMPRESSO" in the colophon on c3v.] 4°. a–b^8, c^4; [20] leaves; ill.; 207 x 134 mm. a3r: 38 lines, 161 x 88 mm. Type: 4:85R. Woodcut initials; woodcuts.

Without rubrication. Modern gray boards.

HR 14370; IGI 8747; Goff S-288; CIBN S-150; Rhodes (F) 654; Sander 6884; Kristeller 396c.

28 February 1942—Gift of Philip Hofer. Typ Inc 6365.5

3016 Savonarola, Hieronymus: Sermone dell'orazione. ca. 1496?

4°. [14] leaves; ill.; 205 x 131 mm.

Without rubrication. Half 19th-century polished calf and marbled boards.

CR 5288; Pr 6398; BMC 6:686 (IA.27956); IGI 8777; Goff S–267; Rhodes (F) 682; Sander 6838; Kristeller 382b.

17 May 1921—From the Savonarola collection formed by Henry R. Newman. Bought with the Edward Henry Hall fund. Typ Inc 6398

3017 Cerchiis, Raphael de: Il Birracino. 20 April 1497.

4°. [42] leaves; 194 x 135 mm.

Printed by Morgiani for Piero Pacini.

Without rubrication. Unbound; in a cloth case.

HR 4882; BMC 6:686 (IA.27840); GW 6513; IGI 2707; Rhodes (F) 181; Sander 1914; Kristeller 100.

26 October 1949—Received. Law Library

3018 Paolo da Fucecchio: Responsioni nelle conclusioni pubblicati contro a frate Girolamo in nome di frate Leonardo. After April 1497.

4°. [8] leaves; 199 x 135 mm.

Italian translation by Filippo Cioni.

Without rubrication. Half modern maroon morocco and brown cloth.

HR 5361; Pr 6385; BMC 6:686 (IA.27910); Pell 3793; IGI 7198; Goff P–75; CIBN P–19; Rhodes (F) 482.

17 May 1921—From the Savonarola collection formed by Henry R. Newman. Bought with the Duplicate fund. Inc 6385

3019 Benivieni, Domenico: Epistola responsiva alle calumnie contro Savonarola. 1497.

4°. [8] leaves; 204 x 135 mm.

Without rubrication. Modern vellum.

HCR 2785; Pr 6384; BMC 6:686 (IA.27906); Pell 2045; GW 3847; IGI 1478; Goff B-325; Rhodes (F) 103.

17 May 1921–From the Savonarola collection formed by Henry R. Newman. Bought with the Duplicate fund. Inc 6384

3020 **Savonarola, Hieronymus:** Predica dell'arte del ben morire. ca. 1497.

a1r: ℂ Predica dellarte del bene morire facta dal Reuerēdo ‖ padre frate Hieronymo da Ferrara adi .ii. di Nouēbre ‖ M.CCCCLXXXXVI. Et raccolta da Ser Lo‖renzo Violi dalla uiua uoce del predecto pa‖dre mentre che predicaua ‖ [woodcut, 135 x 115 mm.] c4v, line 33: ... & in ogni puncto ‖ che lamorte uiene lhuomo sitruoui preparato. ‖ LAVS DEO ‖ ET ‖ BEATE VIRGINI ‖

4°. a⁸, b–c⁴; [16] leaves; ill.; 195 x 130 mm. a2r: 38 lines, 161 x 89 mm. Type: 4:85R. Woodcut initial on a1v; woodcuts.

See reference under no. 2927.

Without rubrication. Modern dark blue cloth.

IGI 8757; Goff S-251; CIBN S-124; Rhodes (F) 665; Sander 6812; Kristeller 375a.

17 May 1921–From the Savonarola collection formed by Henry R. Newman. Bought with the Duplicate fund. Typ Inc 6397.5

3021 **Pseudo-Bonaventura:** Meditationes vitae Christi [Italian]. ca. 1500?

4°. [42] leaves; ill.; 203 x 137 mm.

An excerpt, with text ending "scripto di me nelle prophetie & psalmi."

Without rubrication. 16th-century blind-stamped calf, rebacked, with the arms of Benoît Le Court stamped on covers.

CR 1180; R 1149; Pell 2704; GW 4780; IGI 1926; Goff B-915; Rhodes (F) 136; Sander 1184; Kristeller 69b.

Fogg Art Museum (Print Room)

B E N E D I C T U S   R I C A R D I N U S

3022 **Orpheus:** Argonautica [Greek]. 19 September 1500.

4°. [52] leaves (52 blank); 225 x 167 mm.

Includes the Orphic hymns and the hymns of Proclus. Printed by Ricardinus for Filippo Giunta.

Initial spaces not filled in; without MS rubrication. Stiffened cream wrappers; in a cloth case.

HC 12106*; Pr 6236 (assigned to Di Libri); BMC 6:690 (IB.28063); IGI 7039; Goff O–103; CIBN O–65; Rhodes (F) 473; Sander 5229; Kristeller 307.

18 March 1955—Bought with the S. A. E. Morse fund. Inc 6402.5

S O C I E T A S   C O L U B R I S
(C O M P A G N I A   D E L   D R A G O)

3023 **Marullus, Michael:** Hymni et epigrammata. 26 November 1497.

4°. [96] leaves; 205 x 138 mm.

Initials added in brown, but some spaces, with guide-letters, not filled in. Half 19th-century vellum and marbled boards. From the library of Richard Ashhurst Bowie, with a slip of his MS notes inserted at front. On g8r is a MS biographical note about Marullus, and on g8v a 14-line poem "In morte Marulli Tarchaniotae" signed "Pierij."

HC(+Add) 10880; Pr 6415; BMC 6:691 (IA.28045); Polain 2636; IGI 6263; Goff M–342; Sack 2380; CIBN M–201; Rhodes (F) 432.

9 November 1908—Gift of Mrs. E. D. Brandegee. Inc 6415

3024 **Savonarola, Hieronymus:** Circa il reggimento della città di Firenze. Not before January 1498.

4°. [28] leaves; 197 x 135 mm.

There is a variant on a2r; see below.

This copy has an initial space on a2r but is without the woodcut initial. Without rubrication. Modern maroon calf; edges stained green. Leaves numbered in MS 1272-99. MS marginalia, closely trimmed.

HR 14471; Pr 6417; BMC 6:692 (IA.28052); IGI 8792; Goff S–235; CIBN S–78; Rhodes (F) 698.

December 1964—Gift of Ward M. Canaday. Inc 6417 (A)

3025 ——Another copy. 198 x 132 mm.

This copy has a woodcut initial on a2r. Without rubrication. Modern blue cloth.

17 May 1921—From the Savonarola collection formed by Henry R. Newman. Bought with the Duplicate fund. Inc 6417 (B)

3026 Psalterium abbreviatum Sancti Hieronymi. ca. 1498.

8°. [60] leaves; ill.; 135 x 93 mm.

The introduction is in Italian and Latin, the psalms in Latin. The type is Jacopo di Carlo's 114G, similar to that used by Bartolommeo di Libri but without the small Lombardic capitals employed by Di Carlo at the beginning of sentences; cf. BMC 6:646. At the end are the initials "A. M. A." found in other books printed by the Societas Colubris, along with the device of the publisher Piero Pacini.

Without rubrication. Modern red morocco, edges gilt, by Lortic, with the arms of the Prince d'Essling stamped on covers (not in the Galerie Fischer sale catalogue of his library, May 1939). Booklabel of Philip Hofer. Imperfect: sheets a3-4 wanting.

R 1337; IGI 8168; Goff P–1078; Rhodes (F) 533; Bohatta (LB) 1030; Sander 5948; Kristeller 339a.

April 1956—Gift of Philip Hofer. Typ Inc 6417.5

GERARDUS   DE   HARLEM

3027 Bellantius, Lucius: De astrologica veritate. 9 May 1498 [i.e., 1499?].

f°. [128] leaves (128 blank); 277 x 207 mm.

Includes his *In disputationes Ioannis Pici adversus astrologos responsiones*. Reference is made in the text to Savonarola's execution, which took place on 28 May 1498; the date in the colophon is probably an error.

Initial spaces, with guide-letters, not filled in; without rubrication. 16th-century blind-stamped sheep; marks of ties, no longer present. MS corrections, including the one in the colophon described by BMC. MS ownership notation on title page, "Ex libris Conuentus Carmel. Discal. Lugd."; booklabel of George Dunn, with his MS date of acquisition "Oct. 1902" (not in any of the three Sotheby sale catalogues of his library, 1913-17).

H 2758*; Pr 6420; BMC 6:692 (IB.28068); Pell 2027; Polain 553; GW 3802; IGI 1443; Goff B-300; BSB-Ink B-266; Rhodes (F) 93.

22 March 1919—Bought with the Charles Eliot Norton fund. Inc 6420

3028 ——Another copy. 273 x 205 mm.

Initial spaces not filled in; without rubrication. Old vellum. Book-stamp of Count Donato Silva; bookplate of William Norton Bullard. MS correction in the colophon as in the above copy. Imperfect: leaf of corrections at end and final blank wanting.

Countway Library (William Norton Bullard Collection)

ANTONIO TUBINI,
LORENZO DE ALOPA,
AND ANDREA GHIRLANDI

3029 Savonarola, Hieronymus: Predica fatta il 28 ottobre 1496. After 28 October 1496.

4°. [14] leaves (14 blank); 208 x 136 mm.

Without rubrication. Half modern black morocco and red cloth.

HCR 14389; Pr 6429; BMC 6:694 (IA.28097); IGI 8754; Goff S-248; CIBN S-121; Rhodes (F) 662.

17 May 1921—From the Savonarola collection formed by Henry R. Newman. Bought with the Edward Henry Hall fund. Inc 6429

3030 Savonarola, Hieronymus: Prediche dalla pasqua al avvento dell'anno 1496. ca. 1499.

f°. [166] leaves; 268 x 196 mm.

Edited by Lorenzo Vivoli.

Initial space on a1r, with guide-letter, not filled in; without rubrication. Half 19th-century sheep and speckled boards. MS ownership notation in upper margin of a1r, "Q°. libro e dela Signora Laudomia Ricasoli Ridolfi"; Liechtenstein bookplate. With this is bound the same printers' edition of Savonarola's *Prediche sopra l'Esodo* (Florence, ca. 1505).

HC 14384; Pr 6369A (assigned to Morgiani and Petri); BMC 6:694 (IB.28091); IGI 8767; Goff S-247; CIBN S-132; Rhodes (F) 675.

11 February 1954—Bought with the Bennett Hubbard Nash fund. Inc 6429.5

3031 Benivieni, Girolamo: Canzoni e sonetti con commento. 7 September 1500.

f°. [4], CL leaves (XIIII, XXXVIII, LVIII, LXXVIII, LXXXXVI, CXIII, CXVIII–XX, CXXIII, CXXVIIII, CXLIII, and CXLVII misnumbered XIII, XXXIII, VLIII, LXXVIIII, LXXXVI, CXII, CXVI–XVIII, CXXIIII, CXXVIII, CXLII, and CXLVI); 277 x 202 mm.

Some copies have the colophon dated 7, others 8, September; and some copies lack lines 24–25 of the table on π3r.

This copy has the colophon dated 7 September and has lines 24–25 of the table. Initial spaces, with guide-letters, not filled in; without rubrication. Half 19th-century vellum and marbled boards. Unidentified booklabel (dog with a bone in his mouth); bookplates of Giovanni Marchetti, of Turin, and of Leo S. Olschki.

H 2788*; Pr 6424; BMC 6:693 (IB.28083); Pell 2047; GW 3850; IGI 1481; Goff B-328; Sack 542; BSB-Ink B-279; Rhodes (F) 106.

1 August 1902—Gift of Alain C. White. Inc 6424

3032 Savonarola, Hieronymus: Dialogus de veritate prophetica [Italian]. ca. 1500.

4°. [58] leaves; ill.; 199 x 132 mm.

Without rubrication. Modern red cloth. 16th-century MS note on π2v, "Nota ch[e] q[uest]o libro della verità Prophetica, nel primo indice fu [e]xhibito, ma nell'indice del Co[n]cilio di Tre[n]to no[n] è posto in alcun modo tra libri prohibiti . . ."

HR 14341; Pr 6430; BMC 6:694 (IA.28098); IGI 8690; Goff S-283; CIBN S-86; Rhodes (F) 613; Sander 6771; Kristeller 395.

17 May 1921—From the Savonarola collection formed by Henry R. Newman. Bought with the Duplicate fund. Inc 6430

3033 Savonarola, Hieronymus: Predica fatta il 15 febbraio 1497/8. ca. 1500.

4°. [18] leaves (18 blank); 208 x 138 mm.

Without rubrication. Half modern black morocco and red cloth.

HCR 14393; Pr 6454 (not seen by Proctor and assigned by him to his Miscellaneous group); BMC 6:694 (IA.28094); IGI 8772; Goff S-254; CIBN S-128; Rhodes (F) 677.

17 May 1921—From the Savonarola collection formed by Henry R. Newman. Bought with the Edward Henry Hall fund. Inc 6430.5

UNASSIGNED

3034 **Floccus, Andreas:** De potestatibus Romanis. ca. 1485?

8°. [56] leaves; 193 x 133 mm.

Variously assigned to Rome, Silber, and to Milan, Pachel and Scinzenzeler or Philippus de Lavagnia; GW (describing the book as 4°) leaves unassigned and questions Florence and the date. Includes Albericus, *De imaginibus deorum.*

Initial on a1r added in red and blue; initials elsewhere and paragraph marks added in red or blue. Modern gray boards; in a cloth case.

H 6962; CR 6959; Pell 4755; GW 10042; IGI 3815; Goff F-63; not in Rhodes (F); Rogledi Manni 418.

26 April 1944—Received. Law Library

3035 **Savonarola, Hieronymus:** Expositio in psalmum L: Miserere mei Deus [Italian]. ca. (or after?) 1500.

4°. [14] leaves (14 blank); 200 x 137 mm.

Without rubrication. Half modern maroon morocco and black cloth.

HR 14428=HC 14429?; C 5295; R 1386; Pr 6305 (assigned to Bartolommeo di Libri); BMC 6:695 (IA.28128); IGI 8737; Goff S-216; CIBN S-104; Rhodes (F) 643.

17 May 1921—From the Savonarola collection formed by Henry R. Newman. Bought with the Duplicate fund. Inc 6454.5

(3035a) **Contrasto del Vivo e del Morto.** ca. 1505?

a1r: Io sono il gran capitano della morte ‖ Che tengo le chiaue de tutte le porte ‖ [woodcut, skeletal Death carrying a scythe and mounted on a winged horse] ‖ col. 1: ℂ Che uuol ditãta gloria poter dire ‖ La doue sta latrinita gioconda ‖ ... a4v, COLOPHON: ℂ Finito il ꝑtrasto del uiuo & morto ‖

4°. a⁴; [4] leaves; ill.; 197 x 141 mm. 2 columns. a2r: 40 lines, 163 x 120 mm. Type: 81R. Woodcut, 113 x 120 mm.

This edition is assigned by Goff and Rhodes to Lorenzo Morgiani and dated "ca. 1495?"; but the type (Qu with almost flat tail) is not one used by Morgiani; the woodcut, however, is certainly of the Florentine school.

Modern dark brown morocco, with the arms of Victor Masséna, prince d'Essling, stamped in gilt on covers (not in the Galerie Fischer sale catalogue of his library, May 1939). Booklabel of Philip Hofer.

Goff C–873; Rhodes (F) 225; Sander 2160; Kristeller 112c.

April 1956—Gift of Philip Hofer. Typ Inc 525.05.298

(3035b) **Medici, Lorenzo de':** Canzone per andare in maschera per carnevale. ca. 1505?

a1r, TITLE: ℂ Canzone per andare in maschera ꝑ carnesciale facte dapiu persone ‖ [woodcut within border] ‖ a2r: ℂ Lacãzona delle Nimphe & ‖ delle Cicale facta dal .M.L. ‖ Incomīciono le Nimphe ‖ (D³)Onne sian come uedete ‖ ... b1r: No habbiam pectini & chardi ‖ b8v, col. 2, line 33: non uiuale guardie tenere ‖ guardi pur chi ha sospecto ‖ [all thereafter wanting]

4°. a–b⁸, [c]⁸?; [24?] leaves; ill.; 196 x 140 mm. 2 columns. a2v: 34 lines, 145 x 93 mm. Type: 1:86R. Lombard on a2r. Indented text.   Plate IV

I am unable to give a complete description of this imperfect copy, which differs from copies described by Reichling, BMC, and Sander, assigned to Bartolommeo di Libri, Johannes Petri, and Lorenzo Morgiani and Petri respectively. Rhodes (*La Bibliofilia* 84 [1982]: 157–59) is in error in identifying the Harvard copy with Reichling 1157 and Sander 4459. The type is that described by BMC as Unassigned A (first group) 86R; see BMC plate XLIX*. Includes *canzone* by Bernardo Giambullari and others.

Without rubrication; woodcut clumsily touched with brown. Modern decorated boards. Imperfect: eight (?) leaves at end wanting.

Not Goff G–302 or any of the references there cited.

9 November 1984—Bequest of Philip Hofer. Typ 525.05.424

(3035c) Uberto e Filomena. ca. 1515?

a1r, TITLE: ℂ Vberto & Philomena Ttracta [sic] damore ‖ [woodcut within border, young woman giving a flower to a young man] ‖ a1v: ℂ Incomincia una nobilissima operet ‖ ta decta Philomena. nella qual si tracta ‖ Prio Duberto & Philomena & poi des ‖ so Vberto & alba figlia del Duca di bor ‖ gogna. ‖ ℂ Prologo. ‖ (P²)Oi che mia fortuna o uer destino ‖ uuol che ogni mio parlare sia pur ‖ damore . . . ‖ a2r: (A²)Mor misforza & credo p̄ mia pace ‖ uuol pur che sospirãdo renouelle ‖ . . . c2v: ℂ Incomincia ilsecondo libro di Vber ‖ to & Philomẽa & Alba come p̄ amo ‖ re finirno la lor uita. ‖ e8r: ℂ Finito Vberto & Philomena & Al ‖ ba che tracta damore. ‖ e8v blank.

4°. a–e⁸; [40] leaves; ill.; 204 x 137 mm. 2 columns of 4 octrains each. a2r: 32 lines, 152 x 111 mm. Type: BMC Unassigned A.§.1, 86R. Lombards.

For a summary of the contents of this poem see Hermann Varnhagen, *Ueber eine Sammlung alter italienischer Drucke der Erlanger Universitätsbibliothek* (Erlangen, 1892): 56–60. For a possible ascription to one Andrea di Simone see BMC 5:200 (IA.19918). And see Dennis E. Rhodes, "Notes on Early Florentine Printing," *La Bibliofilia* 84 (1982): 160, whose conclusion about the dating I accept.

Without rubrication. Early 19th-century red straight-grain morocco by C. Hering, London; edges gilt; in a cloth case. The blank escutcheon in the lower panel of the title page border has been filled in with the arms of a member of the Malipiero family; autograph of Richard Heber, with his MS note "Apr. 1808. Dents Sale of Heathcotes books" (no. 833 in the Sotheby sale catalogue of Robert Heathcote's books, April 1808; no. 6160 in pt. 2 of the Sotheby sale catalogue of Heber's library, June 1834); booklabel of Philip Hofer.

H 15907; Goff U–56; Rhodes (F), App.II, 42; Sander 7416; Kristeller 421a.

9 November 1984—Bequest of Philip Hofer. Typ 525.15.857

(3035d) Alberti, Leon Battista: Della repubblica, della vita civile e rusticana, e della fortuna. ca. 1525.

4°. [40] leaves; 193 x 128 mm.

On dating see Dennis E. Rhodes, "Notes on Early Florentine Printing," *La Bibliofilia* 84 (1982): [143]–55.

HCR 418; BMC 6:697 (IA.28130); GW 580 (assigned to Milan, Leonardus Pachel?, ca. 1492?); IGI 156 (same assignment); Goff A–216 (same assignment); Rhodes (F), App.II, 1; Rogledi Manni 37 (Milan?, Pachel?, ca. 1492?).

1952–Gift of Curt H. Reisinger. *IC.A1147.525o

(3035e) The following group of Florentine Savonarola tracts are wrongly assigned to the 15th century by Hain, Proctor, and Goff, as well as others. Rather than give them individual entries I list here the numbers of these works as found in the above authorities, so that reference can be made to them in my concordances:

HAIN	PROCTOR	GOFF
14348	6427	S–172
14375	6444	S–198
14386	6445	S–202
14397	6446	S–203
14402	6447	S–242
14403	6448	S–258
14410	6451	S–263
14444	6452	S–264
	6453	S–269
		S–281

Milan

P A M F I L O   C A S T A L D I

3036 Mela, Pomponius: Cosmographia, siue De situ orbis. 25 September 1471.

4°. [61] leaves (60–61 blank); 202 x 142 mm.

Collation: [a–c^8, d^{10}, e–g^8, h^4] (–[d]1; [h]3–4 blank). According to BMC, "In some copies the fourth quire, in others the fifth quire contains nine leaves"; but judging from the BMC collation, it is the sixth quire that contains nine leaves in their copy.

Initial spaces and spaces for Greek not filled in; without rubrication; leaves numbered in MS 83–141, with [d]10 and [g]8 skipped in the numbering. 19th-century paste-paper boards; in a half green morocco solander case. Blank leaf [h]4 pasted down.

HCR 11014; Pr 5768; BMC 6:699 (IA.25906); Polain 2661; IGI 6339; Goff M-447; CIBN M-279; Rogledi Manni 643.

1948–Gift of Harrison D. Horblit. Inc 5768

P H I L I P P U S   D E   L A V A G N I A

3037 Eusebius Caesariensis: Chronicon. ca. 1474/76.

4°. [209] leaves (209 blank); 278 x 195 mm.

Latin translation by St. Jerome, with the continuations of Prosper Aquitanus and Matthaeus Palmerius Florentinus. Includes a poem by Boninus Mombritius. The BMC and GW collations can be made more precise: [a]^{10} ([a]4+1).

Initials added in red or blue. 17th-century blind-stamped pigskin; edges speckled red. Bookplate of James Frothingham Hunnewell. Imperfect: leaf [a]2 wanting; blank leaf not present.

HCR 6716; Pr 5851; BMC 6:703 (IB.26129); Pell 4633; Polain 1426; GW 9432; IGI 3752; Goff E-116; Rogledi Manni 415.

January 1919–Deposited by James M. Hunnewell. Inc 5851

3038 Scriptores historiae Augustae. 20 July–22 December 1475.

f°. [304] leaves (1, 110–11, 254, and 303–04 blank); 322 x 230 mm.

Includes the *Vitae XII Caesarum* of Suetonius and individual lives by Aelius Spartianus, Julius Capitolinus, Aelius Lampridius, Vulcatius Gallicanus, Trebellius Pollio, Flavius Vopiscus, as well as the *Romanae historiae libri* of Eutropius and Paulus Diaconus. Edited by Bonus Accursius. The collation of this copy varies from that given by BMC: ^{2}A^{6} (^{2}A1 blank), B^{8}.

Leaf A5v in pt. 1 is illuminated with a wreath in purple and green; A6r has a large initial illuminated in gold and colors with marginal extension and an illuminated coat of arms of the Fortiguerra family of Pistoia in the lower margin; this copy originally had initials and paragraph marks elsewhere added in red or blue, but a washing removed most of them, as well as MS marginalia; initials and paragraph marks have been added in blue after the washing. 18th-century calf, spine gilt; edges speckled red. MS index on three leaves inserted at front. MS ownership notation near the coat of arms, "Pyrrhi

Gentilis Fortiguerrae I. C. P."; bookplate of Moncure Biddle (no. 702 in the Parke-Bernet Galleries sale catalogue of his library, April 1952). Imperfect: quire $^2O^8$ wanting; some signatures (which are placed very low down on the leaf) trimmed away.

HC 14561*; Pr 5845; BMC 6:702 (IB.26112); IGI 8847; Goff S–340; CIBN S–487; Rogledi Manni 904.

9 July 1952–Bought with the Frank Brewer Bemis fund. Inc 5845 (A)

3039 ——Another copy. 295 x 208 mm.

Pt. 4, Eutropius and Paulus Diaconus, only. Initials added in red or blue. 18th-century calf, gilt, edges gilt, repaired, with the arms of Michael Wodhull stamped in gilt on front cover and with his MS note of acquisition, "Leigh's Auct. Libr. Dr. Chauncy. Apr. 29ᵗʰ 1790" (no. 2737 in the Sotheby sale catalogue of the library of Charles and Nathaniel Chauncy, April 1790; no. 1055 in the Sotheby sale catalogue of Wodhull's library, January 1886); from the library of Richard Ashhurst Bowie.

9 November 1908–Gift of Mrs. E. D. Brandegee. Inc 5845 (B)

3040 Tibullus, Albius: Elegiae. 1475.

4 pts. (pt. 1: [32] leaves, 32 blank; pt. 2: [60] leaves; pt. 3: [36] leaves, 36 blank; pt. 4: [60] leaves, 60 blank); 228 x 179 and 254 x 185 mm.

Includes: pt. 1, Tibullus.–pt. 2, Propertius, *Elegiae.*–pt. 3, Catullus, *Carmina.*–pt. 4, Statius, *Silvae.* Printed by De Lavagnia for Johannes de Colonia and Johannes Manthen in Venice.

Parts 1–3 are here bound together in order: Tibullus, Catullus, Propertius; pt. 4, Statius, is bound separately. Initial spaces, with guide-letters, not filled in; without rubrication. Both vols. in old vellum, vol. 1 with MS marginalia. Vol. 1 has MS ownership notation "Giulio Domᶜᵒ. Gerini"; vol. 2 has "Bibl: Buxheim" stamp; both vols. from the library of Richard Ashhurst Bowie. Imperfect: leaf [a]1 in pt. 1 and leaf H6 in pt. 2 slightly mutilated; signatures trimmed away; blank leaf [d]8 in pt. 1 not present.

HC 4759; R 334 (Statius only, assigned to Florence, Apud Sanctum Jacobum de Ripoli, ca. 1476); Pr 4303 (assigned to Johannes de Colonia and Johannes Manthen in Venice); BMC 6:702 (IB.26118a–c); GW 6387; IGI 2614; Goff C–322 and S–699 (Statius); Rhodes (F) 741 (Statius only, assigned to Florence, Apud Sanctum Jacobum de Ripoli, ca. 1476); Rogledi Manni 263.

9 November 1908–Gift of Mrs. E. D. Brandegee. Inc 5846.5

3041 Pseudo-Victor, Sextus Aurelius: De viris illustribus. ca. 1475.

[For transcriptions see Pellechet; but insert a line-ending between GESTIS and ROMANORVM on (a)3r.] 8°. [a–d⁸, e⁴] ([e]4 blank); [36] leaves (36 blank); 177 x 123 mm. [a]1r: 24 lines, 127 x 73 mm. Type: 3:108R. Initial spaces.

Ascribed in the text to Suetonius. Edited by Petrus Melleus. Wrongly described by Hain, Pellechet, and Oates as a quarto.

Initial spaces not filled in; without rubrication. 18th-century sprinkled calf, rehinged. Autograph of Michael Wodhull, with his date of acquisition "May 11th 1792" and his note "Ld Spencer's Duplicates" (no. 272 in the Sotheby sale catalogue of books from Wodhull's library, January 1886); from the library of Richard Ashhurst Bowie. Blank leaf not present.

H 2133; Pell 1604; IGI 1091+Correzioni; Goff A–1385; Rogledi Manni 114.

9 November 1908–Gift of Mrs. E. D. Brandegee. Inc 5846.10

3042 Juvenalis, Decimus Junius: Satirae. 23 October 1476.

4°. [66] leaves; 216 x 152 mm.

Includes the satires of Persius.

Initials, paragraph marks, and capital strokes added in red. 19th-century red morocco, spine and edges gilt. From the library of Richard Ashhurst Bowie. Imperfect: top quarter of leaf a1 torn away, removing caption title and beginning of text; quire h¹⁰ (the satires of Persius) wanting.

HR 9682; Pr 5852; BMC 12:50 (IB.26132); IGI 5577; Goff J–636a (originally wrongly entered as J–631); CIBN J–354; Rogledi Manni 544.

9 November 1908–Gift of Mrs. E. D. Brandegee. Inc 5852

3043 Cicero: Epistolae ad familiares. 19 March 1477.

4°. [202] leaves (1 blank); 274 x 198 mm.

BMC quotes line 33 on [BB]5v as reading "ẽt sii ueniẽs"; this copy reads correctly "ẽt si inueniẽs." Initials and paragraph marks added in red; spaces for Greek not filled in. Modern red morocco, edges gilt. Bookplate of William King Richardson. Blank leaf not present.

HC 5179; Pr 5855; BMC 6:704 (IB.26139); GW 6824; IGI 2826; Goff C-518; Rogledi Manni 298.

1951–Bequest of William King Richardson. WKR 1.2.1

3044 Valerius Maximus, Gaius: Facta et dicta memorabilia. 4 February 1478.

f°. [130] leaves; 325 x 238 mm.

Initial spaces, with guide-letters, and spaces for Greek not filled in; without rubrication. Half 18th-century sheep and tan boards. MS marginalia. From the library of Richard Ashhurst Bowie.

HCR 15780; Pr 5859; BMC 6:705 (IB.26147); IGI 10061; Goff V-29; CIBN V-21; Rogledi Manni 1060.

9 November 1908–Gift of Mrs. E. D. Brandegee. Inc 5859

3045 Plinius Secundus, Gaius Caecilius: Epistolae. 26 February 1478.

4°. [92] leaves (92 blank); 280 x 200 mm.

Initial spaces, with guide-letters, and spaces for Greek not filled in; without rubrication. Old limp vellum. From the library of Richard Ashhurst Bowie.

HC 13112*; Pr 5860; BMC 6:706 (IB.26149); IGI 7899; Goff P-807; Sack 2924; CIBN P-474; Rogledi Manni 818.

9 November 1908–Gift of Mrs. E. D. Brandegee. Inc 5860

3046 Caesar, Caius Julius: Commentarii. 8 April 1478.

f°. [152] leaves (132 blank); 323 x 230 mm.

Includes the index of Raimundus Marlianus.

Initials, paragraph marks, capital strokes, and book numbers added in red. 18th-century mottled sheep over wooden boards. Old MS ownership notation blotted out on a1r; another on front flyleaf, "E libris Henrici Norris 1830," with Norris's MS note "This Book was given to the Monastery at Arnspurg in August 1511"; bookplates of Charles Thomas-Stanford and of Boies Penrose II. Blank leaf not present.

HC 4216*; Pr 5861; BMC 6:706 (IB.26152); Pell 3143; GW 5867; IGI 2324; Goff C-20; BSB-Ink C-26; Rogledi Manni 231.

20 November 1952—Gift of Boies Penrose II. Inc 5861

3047 Juvenalis, Decimus Junius: Satirae. 27 May 1478.

a1r: D. IVNII IVVENALIS AQVINATIS ‖ SATYRA PRIMA. ‖ (s⁷)EM- PER EGO AVDITOR ‖ tantum? . . . ‖ g8v: D. IVNII IVVVENALIS [sic] AQVINATIS ‖ SATYRARVM FINIS. ‖ h1r: AVLI PERSII FLAC- CI SATYRARVM ‖ LIBER. ‖ (n⁷)EC fonte labra prolui caballino: ‖ h10v, COLOPHON: FINIS. ‖ D. Iunii Iuuenalis: & A. Persii Flacci satyras ‖ impressit Philippus Lauagnius mediolanensis sexto ‖ kalen- das Iunii. MccccLxxviii. ‖ χ1r: PRINCIPIA CHARTARum PRIMI QVA‖TERNIONIS ‖ . . . Callidus ‖ χ2 blank.

4°. a–g⁸, h¹⁰, χ² (χ2 blank); [68] leaves (68 blank); 282 x 198 mm. a2r: 35 lines, 194 x 99 mm. Type: 3:108R. Initial spaces, with guide-letters.

Initial spaces not filled in; without rubrication. 18th-century red morocco, gilt. Quaritch's Sunderland Library bookplate (no. 7029 in pt. 3 of the Puttick & Simpson sale catalogue, July 1882); bookplate of Daniel B. Fearing.

HC 9684; IGI 5578; Goff J-638; Rogledi Manni 545.

31 May 1910—Added to the Persius Collection of Morris Hicky Morgan by Daniel B. Fearing. Inc 5861.5

3048 Aesopus: Vita et Fabulae [Latin]. 4 September 1480.

4°. [52] leaves (1 and 52 blank); 200 x 130 mm.

Latin prose translation by Rinucius Aretinus.

Initial spaces, with guide-letters, and spaces for Greek not filled in; without rubrication. 19th-century mottled calf, gilt. Autograph "Hen- ry de Cestole [?]"; booklabel and MS notes of George Dunn, with his date of acquisition "Nov. 1900" (no. 1742 in pt. 3 of the Sotheby sale catalogue of his library, November 1917). Blank leaves not present.

HC 277; Pr 5873; BMC 6:708 (IA.26185); Pell 207; GW 339; IGI 71; Goff A-101; Rogledi Manni 18.

20 January 1919—Bought with the Constantius fund. Inc 5873

A N T O N I U S   Z A R O T U S

3049 **Pius II, Pope:** Epistolae in pontificatu editae. 25 May 1473.

f°. [184] leaves (1 and 184 blank); 278 x 204 mm.

Large initial on [a]2r illuminated in gold and colors, with a coat of arms in the lower panel (the latter illumination later than that in the rest of the book); initials elsewhere illuminated in gold and colors in white vine stem style; MS quiring, partly cut away. 18th-century vellum. Hopetoun bookplate (no. 203 in the Sotheby sale catalogue of the Hopetoun library, February 1889); booklabel of Frances Hofer. As in the BMC copy, the table is bound at the beginning.

H 168*; Pr 5773; BMC 6:709 (IB.25916); Pell 104; Polain 3164; IGI 7787; Goff P–724; Rogledi Manni 804; Ganda 13.

24 January 1955—Gift of Philip Hofer in memory of Mrs. Winthrop Chanler. Typ Inc 5773

3050 **Serapion, Johannes, the Younger:** Liber aggregatus in medicinis simplicibus. 4 August 1473.

[a]1r: LIBER SERAPIONIS AGRE‖gatus ī medicīis simplicib9 Trãsla-‖tõ Symõis Ianuēsis interp̃te Abraã ‖ iudeo tortuosiēsi de arabico ī latinū ‖ Inquit Serapion. ‖ [t]8r, col. 2: INCIPIT Liber Galieni ad Papiam ‖ De Virtute Centauree. Cap✝m Pri‖mum De Intētione Eius in Hoc LI‖bro. ‖ [u]2r, col. 2, COLOPHON: Opus Impressum M✝i Per Antõium ‖ Zarotum Parmēsem Anno domini ‖ Mcccclxxiii Die Mercuꝝi .iiii. August. ‖ EXPLICIT LIBER GLIENI [*sic*] DE ‖ CENTAVREA. ‖

f°. [a¹⁰, b⁶, c–f¹⁰, g⁸, h¹⁰, i¹² (–i8), k–s¹⁰, t⁸, u²]; [185] leaves; 318 x 237 mm. 2 columns. [a]2r: 41 lines, 227 x 152 mm. Type: 2:111Rᴬ. Initial spaces.

Translated from the Arabic by Simon Genuensis and Abraham Tortuosiensis.

Initial on [a]1r, with marginal extension, illuminated in gold and colors; illuminated coat of arms in lower margin with initials "L K" and date "1477"; initials elsewhere added in red minuscules. Contemporary half leather and wooden boards, rebacked; fragments of leather thongs nailed to back cover, brass latches on front, clasps and thongs gone; title in ink on front cover; leaves numbered in MS. Two leaves of contemporary MS index inserted at front. Date and monogram in upper margin of [a]1r, "J 5 IMRDT 9 0"; MS ownership notation on vellum flyleaf at front, "S:ᵃᵉ Mariae in Sÿluis 1687." With this is bound the same printer's edition of Johannes Marlianus, *Quaestio de caliditate corporum humanorum* (27 August 1474).

HC 14691*; Pr 5775; IGI 8925; Goff S-467; CIBN S-226; Rogledi Manni 908; Ganda 15.

Countway Library (Solomon M. Hyams Collection)

3051 Marlianus, Johannes, Mediolanensis: Quaestio de caliditate corporum humanorum. 27 August 1474.

f°. [62] leaves (1 blank); 318 x 237 mm.

According to BMC, in their copy "the first leaf and the last leaf of quire [f] consist of separate half-sheets"; there is no such irregularity in this copy. Initial spaces on [a]2r not filled in; without rubrication. For binding description see preceding entry, with which this is bound.

HC 10771; Pr 5784; BMC 6:711 (IB.25942); IGI 6189; Goff M-274; Rogledi Manni 624; Ganda 27.

Countway Library (Solomon M. Hyams Collection)

3052 Victorinus, Marius Fabius: Commentaria in Rhetoricam Ciceronis. 9 December 1474.

4°. [114] leaves (1 and 114 blank); 258 x 188 mm.

Initial spaces and spaces for Greek not filled in; without rubrication. 18th-century red morocco, gilt. Blank leaves not present.

R 123=1653; Pr 5788; BMC 6:712 (IB.25950); IGI 10267; Goff V-273; Rogledi Manni 1105; Ganda 29.

1918—Bequest of George Vasmer Leverett. Hilles Library, Radcliffe College

3053 Juvenalis, Decimus Junius: Satirae. 1474.

4°. [72] leaves (1 and 61 blank); 282 x 196 mm.

Includes the satires of Persius. The Harvard copy collates: [a-g⁸, h⁴, i¹²] ([a]1 and [i]1 blank).

Initials added in red. MS marginalia. 18th-century diced russia, with the arms of Michael Wodhull stamped in gilt on cover and with his date of acquisition "Mar: 17th 1794"; from the library of Richard Ashhurst Bowie. Blank leaves not present.

HC 9680; Pr 5785; BMC 6:712 (IB.25944); IGI 5572; Goff J-636; CIBN J-351; Rogledi Manni 542; Ganda 32.

9 November 1908—Gift of Mrs. E. D. Brandegee. Inc 5785

3054 Mombritius, Boninus: De dominica Passione. 1474.

4°. [74] leaves (1 blank); 216 x 156 mm.

Initial spaces not filled in; without rubrication. Modern vellum. MS inscription on flyleaf at front, "Rm̄o P. Atanasio Peristiani Pub. Bibliothecę Patavinę Pręfecto D.C.M.M.A.S.S. 25. Octobr. 1768"; booklabel of Adriana R. Salem. Last two leaves remargined.

HCR 11542; Pr 5789; BMC 6:712 (IA.25952); IGI 6689; Goff M-808; CIBN M-520; Rogledi Manni 688; Ganda 35.

29 May 1962—Gift of Ward M. Canaday. Inc 5789

3055 Quintilianus, Marcus Fabius: Institutiones oratoriae. 9 June 1476.

f°. [206] leaves; 294 x 202 mm.

Initial spaces, with guide-letters, and spaces for Greek not filled in; without rubrication. Old vellum, edges mottled red. Autographs on front flyleaf, "W. S. Cruft. Turin Octr. 2, 1850" and "Dr John O Stone." Lower margin of a1 trimmed away, probably to remove an ownership notation.

HCR 13648; Pr 5794; BMC 6:713 (IB.25963); Polain 4678; IGI 8261; Goff Q-27; CIBN Q-17; Rogledi Manni 857; Ganda 48.

7 February 1870—Gift of John O. Stone. Inc 5794 (A)

3056 ——Another copy. 319 x 225 mm.

Initial spaces and spaces for Greek not filled in; without rubrication. 18th-century mottled calf, spine and edges gilt. Bookplate of James Frothingham Hunnewell. Imperfect: a1 slightly mutilated, affecting text.

January 1919—Deposited by James M. Hunnewell. Inc 5794 (B)

3057 Juvenalis, Decimus Junius: Satirae. 1476.

[For transcriptions see Hain.] 4°. a–h⁸, I⁴; [68] leaves; 272 x 197 mm. a5r: 34 lines, 185 x 100 mm. Type: 5:111R^B. Initial spaces, most with guide-letters.

Includes the satires of Persius.

Initial spaces not filled in; without rubrication. 18th-century calf, spine gilt. Hopetoun bookplate (no. 857 in the Sotheby sale catalogue, February 1889); bookplate of Morris H. Morgan.

H 9683*; IGI 5576; Goff J–637; Rogledi Manni 543; Ganda 54.

1 January 1910–Gift of Morris H. Morgan. Inc 5797.5

3058 Bonaventura, Saint: Legenda maior S. Francisci [Italian]. 6 February 1477.

4°. [120] leaves; 258 x 185 mm.

Includes Franciscus de Assisi, *Regula* in Italian.

Initial on a1r illuminated in gold and colors, with white vine stem extension in left and upper margins and with an illuminated coat of arms (erased) in the lower margin; initials elsewhere added in red or blue; paragraph marks in the table added in red or blue. Old vellum. Autographs on front flyleaf, "F. T. Washburn, Boston. Florence, Feb. 1869" and "W. S. Thayer, 1904"; bookplate of W. S. Thayer. Imperfect: leaf 18 slightly mutilated; the table is bound at end.

HR 3574; Pr 5798; BMC 6:714 (IB.25971); Pell 2708; GW 4662; IGI 1893; Goff B–890; Rogledi Manni 178; Ganda 56.

18 January 1933–Bequest of William S. Thayer. Inc 5798

3059 Livius, Titus: Historiae Romanae decades. 23 October 1480.

f°. [394] leaves (1, 162, and 394 blank); 402 x 266 mm.

Edited by Petrus Justinus Philelphus. Reprints the preface of Johannes Andreae from the 1469 edition. Printed by Zarotus for Johannes de Legnano.

Initial spaces not filled in; without rubrication. 19th-century citron morocco, gilt, edges gilt. MS ownership notation in upper margin of A2r, "Ex libris frīs Iacobi philippi de forestis," and beneath, "Con^{tus} Sct^i Aug^{ni} Berg^{mi}"; from the Sunderland library (no. 7452 in pt. 3 of the Puttick & Simpson sale catalogue, July 1882); bookplate of William King Richardson.

HC 10133; Pr 5805; BMC 6:716 (IB.25997); IGI 5774; Goff L–241; CIBN L–181; Rogledi Manni 573; Ganda 75.

1951–Bequest of William King Richardson. WKR 11.2.5

3060 **Suetonius Tranquillus, Caius:** Vitae XII Caesarum. 16 November 1480.

f°. [126] leaves (1 and 126 blank); 284 x 197 mm.

With introductory matter by Domitius Calderinus and Sicco Polentonus and verses by Ausonius. Printed by Zarotus for Johannes de Legnano.

Initial on a2r illuminated in colors, with marginal extension; initials elsewhere added in red or blue. Old vellum; edges speckled blue. MS initials in lower margin of a2r on either side of a patch (where a coat of arms has been excised?), "A. G."; autograph and bookstamp of Albert A. Howard. Blank leaves not present.

HCR 15120; Pr 5806; BMC 6:716 (IB.25999); IGI 9233; Goff S–821; Rogledi Manni 945; Ganda 77.

24 November 1925–From the library of Albert A. Howard. Inc 5806

3061 **Curtius Rufus, Quintus:** Historiae Alexandri Magni. 26 March 1481.

4°. [126] leaves (1 and 126 blank); 276 x 193 mm.

Printed by Zarotus for Johannes de Legnano.

Initial spaces not filled in; without rubrication. 18th-century vellum. Booklabel of Cardinal Francesco Saverio de Zelada in lower margin of a2r, though his name has been scored through in ink; MS ownership notation "Ex Libris Josephi Rossatti Camertis" on blank a1r; from the library of Richard Ashhurst Bowie, with a slip of his MS notes inserted at front, including "The edition is a rare one, and seldom to be found. My order for it remained unfilled for nearly five years. Finally a copy was found in Berlin. RAB 1881."

HCR 5882=H 5881?; Pr 5808; BMC 6:717 (IB.26003); Pell 4065; GW 7873; IGI 3288; Goff C–1000; Rogledi Manni 361; Ganda 85.

9 November 1908–Gift of Mrs. E. D. Brandegee. Inc 5808

3062 **Juvenalis, Decimus Junius:** Satirae. 11 July 1481.

a1r: IVNII IVVENALIS AQVINATIS SATYRA ‖ PRIMA. ‖ [⁷]EMPER

EGO AVDITOR TAN ‖ tum: nunquam ne reponam ‖ ... h2v: AVLI
PERSII FLACCI SATYRARVM LIBER. ‖ i4v, COLOPHON: D. Iunii
Iuuenalis Et. A. persii Flacci Satyras q̄di‖ligentissime castigatas per
Petrum augustinum ‖ Philelfum Antonius Zarothus parmensis
im‖pressit Mediolani ī pendio Iohānis legnani An‖no salutis
.M.cccclxxxi. die xi Iulii.

4°. a–h⁸, i⁴; [68] leaves; 235 x 169 mm. a2r: 34 lines, 184 x 98 mm.
Type: 5ᴬ:111Rᴮ². Initial spaces.

Initial spaces not filled in; without rubrication. 18th-century gilt- and
blind-stamped sheep, rehinged. Circular stamp with the letters "S M
A V" in the four quarters on a1r and i3v; in volume 1 (no. 53) I identified this stamp as that of the Franciscans at Augsburg, but I have
since then seen a note by Andrew G. Watson in *The Library*, 5th ser.,
28 (1973): 147–48, in which he suggests that the letters stand for
Sancta Maria Annuntiata in Varese; booklabel of Charles Butler (no.
618 in pt. 1 of the Sotheby sale catalogue of his library, April 1911).

HR 9686; IGI 5582; Goff J–640; Rogledi Manni 547; Ganda 88.

2 June 1911—Added to the Persius Collection of Morris H. Morgan
by Daniel B. Fearing. Inc 5809.5

3063 Simoneta, Johannes: Commentarii rerum gestarum Francisci Sfortiae.
23 January [1482?].

f°. [292] leaves (291–92 blank); 315 x 216 mm.

Edited by Franciscus Puteolanus. On dating see CIBN.

Initial spaces not filled in; without rubrication. Half 19th-century calf
and marbled boards, rehinged; edges stained blue. Blank leaves not
present.

HC 14753=HR 14754; Pr 5804; BMC 6:718 (IB.25995); Polain 3549;
IGI 9013; Goff S–532; CIBN S–278; Rogledi Manni 920; Ganda 96.

23 September 1921—Gift of Mrs. E. D. Brandegee. Inc 5804

3064 Panegyrici veteres Latini. ca. 1482.

4°. [169] leaves; 223 x 160 mm.

The BMC collation can be made more precise: f⁶ (f3+'f4'). Includes:
Gaius Caecilius Plinius Secundus, *Panegyricus Trajani. Panegyricus Maxi-
miniani et Constantini.*—Latinius Drepanius Pacatus, *Panegyricus Theodosii.*

Panegyricus Constantini Constantii filii.—Claudius Mamertinus, *Gratiarum actio Iuliano de consulatu suo.*—Nazarius, *Panegyrici. Oratio pro restaurandis scholis.*—C. Cornelius Tacitus, *Vita Agricolae.*—Petronius Arbiter, *Satyrici fragmenta quae extant.* Edited by Franciscus Puteolanus.

Initial spaces, with guide-letters, not filled in; without rubrication. Half 16th-century blind-stamped leather and wooden boards; leather thongs with brass clasps nailed to back cover, latches on front. MS ownership notation at end, "Est Pbri' Joannis Baptae Raynate [?]"; bookplate of Boies Penrose II.

HR 13119; Pr 5837; BMC 6:718 (IA.26084); IGI 7179; Goff P–813; CIBN P–15; Rogledi Manni 742; Ganda 104.

9 October 1945—Gift of Boies Penrose II. Inc 5837

3065 Ovidius Naso, Publius: Fasti. 5 June 1483.

f°. [192] leaves; 273 x 195 mm.

Edited with a commentary by Paulus Marsus. Includes a poem by Robertus Ursus. Printed by Zarotus for Johannes de Legnano.

Initials and paragraph marks added in red on a3–4; spaces elsewhere not filled in. Half modern black morocco and decorated boards; edges stained red. MS ownership notation on a1r, "domus oratorij aquensis"; MS marginalia.

HC 12239; BMC 12:50 (IB.26027); Polain 2951; IGI 7069; Goff O–171; CIBN O–108; Rogledi Manni 720; Ganda 109.

23 October 1920—Bought with the Constantius fund. Inc 5816.5

3066 Pius II, Pope: Epistolae in pontificatu editae. October 1487.

4°. [146] leaves (1 blank); 263 x 198 mm.

Printed by Zarotus for Johannes Petrus Novariensis.

Initial spaces not filled in; without rubrication. 19th-century vellum. Booklabel of Count Paul Riant. Imperfect: q7–8, r–u^8, χ^2 wanting.

HC 170; Pr 5823; BMC 6:719 (IB.26045); Pell 106; Polain 3174; IGI 7789; Goff P–726; CIBN P–408; Rogledi Manni 806; Ganda 144.

28 December 1899—Gift of J. Randolph Coolidge and Archibald Cary Coolidge. Inc 5823

3067 Tacitus, C. Cornelius: Opera. ca. 1487.

f°. [188] leaves (160, 176, and 188 blank); 280 x 194 mm.

Edited by Franciscus Puteolanus with the assistance of Bernardinus Lanterius.

Initials added in blue or red. Old vellum, rebacked; edges gilt. Syston Park bookplate and monogram label of Sir John H. Thorold (no. 1869 in the Sotheby sale catalogue of his library, December 1884); bookplate of James Frothingham Hunnewell. Last blank leaf not present.

HC 15219; Pr 5838; BMC 6:719 (IB.26090); Polain 3653; IGI 9256; Goff T-7; CIBN T-5; Rogledi Manni 951; Ganda 171.

January 1919–Deposited by James M. Hunnewell. Inc 5838 (A)

3068 ——Another copy. 295 x 206 mm.

Initial spaces not filled in; without rubrication. Half 19th-century leather and decorated boards. MS ownership notation in upper margin of a1r, "Johannes Protzer I. V. lice[ntia]t[us] MccccXciij Conp[ar]-a[ui]t In Italia" (cf. no. 2159 in vol. 2).

20 November 1952–Gift of Boies Penrose II. Inc 5838 (B)

3069 Manilius, Marcus: Astronomicon. 9 November 1489.

f°. [60] leaves; 299 x 211 mm.

The BMC copy lacks the first quire, which is signed A⁴; line 2 of the caption on A1r reads: NICVS .M. ROLANDO: PALAVICINO: MAR ‖. Edited by Stephanus Dulcinius.

Initial spaces, most with guide-letters, not filled in; without rubrication. 19th-century red morocco, edges gilt. From the library of Richard Ashhurst Bowie.

HC 10705; Pr 5827; BMC 6:721 (IB.26056); IGI 6129; Goff M-205; CIBN M-89; Rogledi Manni 619; Ganda 158.

9 November 1908–Gift of Mrs. E. D. Brandegee. Inc 5827

3070 Ambrosius, Saint: Epistolae [and other works]. 1 February 1491.

f°. [192] leaves; 297 x 200 mm.

Includes: Ambrosius, *De Isaac et anima. De fuga saeculi.*—Prosper Aquitanus, *De vocatione omnium gentium.*—*De situ civitatis Mediolani* [excerpt: *De aedificatione Mediolani*]. Edited by Stephanus Dulcinius.

Initial spaces, with guide-letters, not filled in; without rubrication. Half 19th-century sheep and marbled boards, rehinged. Bookplate of Richard Ashhurst Bowie.

HC(Add) 899*; Pr 5829; BMC 6:722 (IB.26062); Pell 583; GW 1601; IGI 425; Goff A–553; BSB-Ink A–479; Rogledi Manni 61; Ganda 173.

9 November 1908–Gift of Mrs. E. D. Brandegee. Inc 5829

3071 Bossius, Donatus: Chronica. 1 March 1492.

f°. [168] leaves; 324 x 230 mm.

Includes *Omnes episcopi & archiepiscopi Mediolani* (4 leaves at end).

Leaf a1v contains a genealogical table printed in red. Initial spaces, with guide-letters, not filled in. Old mottled sheep, spine gilt, edges stained red; stamped in gilt on front cover, "Bibliothecae Regiae Parmensis"; bookseller's ticket of the Libreria Loescher, Roma. Imperfect: sheet n4 wanting; leaf a1 slightly mutilated and mounted.

HC 3667*; Pr 5831; BMC 6:722 (IB.26067); Pell 2779; Polain 844; GW 4952; IGI 2017; Goff B–1040; BSB-Ink B–758; Rogledi Manni 197; Ganda 175; Sander 1238.

14 October 1914–Bought with the Bayard Cutting fund. Inc 5831

3072 ——Another copy. 324 x 228 mm.

Ruled in red throughout; initials on a2r added in gold, but spaces elsewhere not filled in. 19th-century green morocco, gilt, edges gilt; in a cloth case. Two MS ownership notations on a1r, the earlier not recoverable but a later legible under ultraviolet light, "Ex Libris Ill^{mi} M^{ri} Petri de Villari Archiep^i Viennen."; from the MacCarthy-Reagh collection (no. 3935 in vol. 2 of the De Bure catalogue, 1815), bought by George Hibbert (no. 1441 in the Evans sale catalogue of his library, March–May 1829); from the Hamilton Palace sale (no. 1105 in the Sotheby catalogue, July 1882); bookplate of Francis Hopkinson of Malvern Wells with a long note in his hand on front flyleaf.

Countway Library (William Norton Bullard Collection)

3073 Missale Romanum. 1 August 1492.

[For transcriptions see Reichling.] f°. π^8, A–I^8, k^8, L–R^8, S^{10} (π1 and

S10 blank); [154] leaves (1 and 154 blank); ill.; 305 x 216 mm. 2 columns. B4r: 44 lines, 244 x 169 mm. Types: 3:110G^a, text; 4:110G^b, versicles and responses. Initial spaces on A1r and I5r; red printed Lombards; black printed initials; musical notes on red printed staves; woodcuts on A1r and I4v.

Initial spaces not filled in. Modern red morocco by Lortic with the arms of Victor Masséna, prince d'Essling, stamped in gilt on covers and with his monogram repeated four times on the spine; edges gilt; in a cloth case (no. 184 in the Galerie Fischer sale of his library, May 1939); booklabels of Philip and Frances Hofer. Imperfect: leaf π8 wanting; blank leaves not present.

CR 4206; IGI 6628; Goff M–705; Weale-Bohatta 920; Meyer-Baer 147; Rogledi Manni 685; Ganda 179; Sander 4759.

7 December 1953–Gift of Philip Hofer. Typ Inc 5831.5

3074 Montis, Petrus de: De dinoscendis hominibus. 17 December 1492.

f°. [228] leaves; 279 x 193 mm.

Translated from the Spanish by Gundisalvus Ayora.

Initial spaces, with guide-letters, not filled in; without rubrication; title in ink on lower edges. Modern vellum. Imperfect: title page torn and mounted.

HC 11608*; Pr 5832; BMC 6:722 (IB.26070); IGI 6731; Goff M–857; CIBN M–545; Rogledi Manni 691; Ganda 180.

Countway Library (William Norton Bullard Collection)

C H R I S T O P H O R U S   V A L D A R F E R

3075 Bartholomaeus de Chaimis: Confessionale. 29 September 1474.

8°. [174] leaves; 147 x 108 mm.

Initial on [a]1r added in red and blue, with marginal extension; initials elsewhere and paragraph marks added in red or blue; traces of MS quiring, mostly trimmed away; leaves numbered in MS. 19th-century maroon morocco, edges gilt. Bookplate of James Frothingham Hunnewell.

H 2481*; Pr 5875; BMC 6:725 (IA.26207); Pell 1859; GW 6540; IGI

2718; Goff B-153; BSB-Ink C-244; Rogledi Manni 282.

January 1919—Deposited by James M. Hunnewell. Inc 5875

3076 **Arnoldus de Villa Nova:** De arte cognoscendi venena. 1475.

4°. [28] leaves (1 blank); 189 x 142 mm.

Includes: Valascus de Tarenta, *De epidemia et peste.*—Petrus de Abano, *De venenis eorumque remediis.*—*De lapide begaar ex pandectis.*

Initial spaces not filled in; without rubrication. Half modern brown cloth and marbled boards. Bookstamp of Bernardo Eloy, Flores. Imperfect: quires [c–d⁸] wanting.

H 10+1806; BMC 12:52 (IB.26213); Pell 1308; GW 2524; IGI 863; Goff A-1069; Rogledi Manni 99.

1 July 1967—Bought. Countway Library

3077 **Justinus, Marcus Junianus:** Epitome in Trogi Pompeii historias. 1 June 1476.

4°. [108] leaves; 264 x 187 mm.

CIBN points out a variant in the colophon.

This copy has the reading of the colophon as transcribed by BMC. Initial on [a]1r added in red and blue, with marginal extension; initials elsewhere and paragraph marks added in red. Half 18th-century red morocco and sheep. MS ownership notation in lower margin of [a]1r, "Con[uentus] S. [–]ricj de Cosentia"; from the library of Richard Ashhurst Bowie, with a slip of his MS notes inserted at front: "This was Heber's copy, and there is a memorandum in his handwriting, on the flyleaf, from which it appears that he bought the book at Vienna, in 1819, and paid for it 171 Austrian florins, and ten kreuzers. At his own sale, some years later, it sold for £4.8 [no. 2564 in pt. 5 of the Wheatley sale catalogue, January 1835]."

HC 9650; Pr 5879; BMC 6:726 (IB.26223); IGI 5555; Goff J-617; CIBN J-339; Rogledi Manni 540.

9 November 1908—Gift of Mrs. E. D. Brandegee. Inc 5879

3078 **Philelphus, Franciscus:** Satirae. 13 November 1476.

4°. [150] leaves (150 blank); 285 x 205 mm.

Includes a poem by Calliphilus Bernardinus Robiatinus.

Initial spaces, with guide-letters, not filled in; without rubrication. Half old vellum and white boards. Autograph of Michael Wodhull, dated 6 May 1789, with his note, "Pinelli Auction by comm:" (no. 10362 in the London sale catalogue of the Pinelli library, March–May 1789; no. 1974 in the Sotheby sale catalogue of Wodhull's library, January 1886); bookplate of Murray Anthony Potter.

H 12917*; Pr 5881; BMC 6:726 (IB.26233); IGI 3913; Goff P–615; Sack 2862; CIBN P–329; Rogledi Manni 435.

18 June 1935—From the library of Murray Anthony Potter. Inc 5881

3079 Poggius Florentinus: Facetiae. 10 February 1477.

8° and 4°. [80] leaves; 232 x 154 mm.

Printed by Valdarfer for Petrus Antonius de Castelliono.

The first leaf has been ruled in red; initial spaces, with guide-letters, not filled in. 18th-century red straight-grain morocco, with the arms of Michael Wodhull stamped in gilt on front cover, his autograph dated 19 May 1789, and his note "Pinelli Auction comm:" (no. 12706 in the London sale catalogue of the Pinelli library, March–May 1789; no. 2076 in the Sotheby sale catalogue of Wodhull's library, January 1886); booklabel of Charles Butler (no. 1901 in pt. 1 of the Sotheby sale catalogue of his library, April 1911).

H 13189*; Pr 5882; BMC 6:727 (IA.26237); IGI 7933; Goff P–861; CIBN P–521; BSB-Ink B–783; Rogledi Manni 819.

27 November 1911—Gift of Mrs. E. D. Brandegee. Inc 5882

3080 Cermisonus, Antonius: Ricette contro la pestilenza. ca. 1483–84.

8°. [6] leaves; 171 x 124 mm.

Without rubrication. Modern red morocco, hinges weak. Bookplate of H. Destailleur (no. 802 in the Paris sale catalogue of his library, April 1891, where it is described as bound with *L'assedio e la presa di Caffa* [Vicenza, Leonardus Achates, after 7 June 1475]).

C 1565; Pr 5975; BMC 6:727 (IA.26613); GW 6518; IGI 2711–A; Goff C–405; Rogledi Manni 280.

Countway Library (William Norton Bullard Collection)

3081 Thomas Aquinas: Opuscula. 1 March 1488.

4°. [66] leaves (66 blank); 191 x 131 mm.

Includes: Thomas Aquinas, *Expositio Orationis dominicae. Expositio Salutatis angelicae. Expositio Symbolum Apostolorum. De rationibus fidei. De duobus praeceptis caritatis et expositio Decem Praeceptorum.—Tractatus de tribus votis et statu religiosorum editus a quibusdam praeclaris sacrae theologiae professoribus ordinis Praedicatorum.*—Bernardus Claravallensis, *Expositio super antiphonam Salve regina. Expositio super illud Evangelii: Simile est regnum caelorum homini quaerenti bonas margaritas.*

Initial spaces, some with guide-letters, not filled in; without rubrication. Old vellum. Sheets c3–4 reversed in binding; blank leaf not present.

HC 1543; Pr 5977B; BMC 6:728 (IA.26620); IGI 9550; Goff T–262; Rogledi Manni 1007.

7 May 1913—Gift of Alain Campbell White. Inc 5977.5

J O H A N N E S   B O N U S

3082 Augustinus, Aurelius, Saint: Confessiones. 21 July 1475.

4°. [164] leaves; 201 x 142 mm.

BMC notes that a line appears to have been added after printing off at the end of [b]6r but does not mention another line added at the top of [b]6v.

Initial spaces, some with guide-letters, not filled in; without rubrication. 18th-century calf, edges speckled red. Autograph of Michael Wodhull, dated 8 April 1789, with his note "Pinelli Auction" (no. 5455 in the London sale catalogue of the Pinelli library, March–May 1789; no. 257 in the Sotheby sale catalogue of Wodhull's library, January 1886); bookplate of James Frothingham Hunnewell.

HC 2031; Pr 5883; BMC 6:728 (IA.26253); Pell 1537; GW 2894; IGI 984; Goff A–1251; Rogledi Manni 105.

January 1919—Deposited by James M. Hunnewell. Inc 5883

3083 Amadeus Derthonensis: Ratio dierum et mensium. After 26 October 1475.

4°. [32] leaves; 208 x 148 mm.

There is a variant on [a]6v; see BMC.

In this copy the last line on [a]6v agrees with the BMC transcription for IA.26256. Initial spaces, with guide-letters, and spaces for Greek not filled in; without rubrication. Half modern dark green morocco and marbled boards. Booklabel of Count Paul Riant. Two omitted lines of text added in MS at foot of [b]7r.

HCR 893; Pr 5884; BMC 6:729 (IA.26256); GW 1594; IGI 418; Goff A-548; Rogledi Manni 57.

28 December 1899–Gift of J. Randolph Coolidge and Archibald Cary Coolidge. Inc 5884

3084 Solinus, Caius Julius: Polyhistor, siue De mirabilibus mundi. 1475?

8°. [122] leaves; 201 x 135 mm.

Edited by Boninus Mombritius. The signatures, where present, are hand-stamped far down in the lower right-hand corners. On errors of imposition see BMC.

Initial spaces, a few with guide-letters, not filled in; without rubrication. Old blind-stamped sheep. MS ownership notation in upper margin of π1r, "Scтi Aug^{ni} ad Vsuʒ frīs Aurelij Aug^{ni}. de Spor [?].   Fr̄ Jo. maria asten[sis?]"; printed label inside front cover, "From the famous Pesaro Library, formerly at Venice, and after 1805 in the possession of Thomas Johnes, at Hafod, Cardiganshire, Pesaro Library catalogue, page [in MS] 48." A leaf of MS inserted at front contains a different recension of Solinus's dedication to Adventus from that found in this edition and reproduces the one in the Schurener edition (Rome, ca. 1474/75; see no. 1351 in vol. 2 of this catalogue); a MS leaf in the same hand inserted at end contains an unidentified text beginning "Relinquere est superare . . ."

HC 14873*=H 14875; Pr 5885; BMC 6:728 (IA.26258); IGI 9086; Goff S-618; CIBN S-305; Rogledi Manni 936.

November 1957–Gift of Harrison D. Horblit. Inc 5885

P R I N T E R   O F   T H E
1 4 7 5   S E R V I U S   (H   1 4 7 0 8)

3085 **Servius Maurus, Honoratus:** Commentarii in Vergilii opera. 1 December 1475.

f°. [319] leaves (319 blank); 320 x 230 mm.

The signatures are hand-stamped far down in the right-hand corner of the page; catchwords are usually centered below the text but in some quires run vertically; for details see BMC. The BMC collation can be made more precise: C^8 (–C8).

Initials added in red or blue, occasional paragraph marks in red; spaces for Greek not filled in. In this copy the catchword "Ventos" is printed out on leaf bb8v. Half 18th-century sheep and tan boards. Large armorial bookplate of Franz Karl, prince of Auersperg; from the library of Richard Ashhurst Bowie, with a slip of his MS notes inserted at front. Blank leaf not present; some signatures trimmed away.

HC 14708; Pr 5886; BMC 6:730 (IB.26262a); IGI 8946; Goff S–482; CIBN S–244; Rogledi Manni 910.

9 November 1908–Gift of Mrs. E. D. Brandegee. Inc 5886

D O M I N I C U S   D E   V E S P O L A T E

3086 **Boccaccio, Giovanni:** Il Filocolo. 14 June 1476.

f°. [184] leaves (1 and 184 blank); 280 x 204 mm.

The signatures are hand-stamped far down in the lower right-hand corners. Includes the *Vita* of Boccaccio by Hieronymus Squarzaficus and a poem by Boninus Mombritius.

Initial spaces, with guide-letters, not filled in; without rubrication. Modern blind-stamped calf by Rivière, edges gilt. Monogram bookplate "EBV" surmounted by the coronet of a baron. Signatures trimmed away; blank leaves not present.

HR 3297; Pr 5890; BMC 6:732 (IB.26283); GW 4464; IGI 1786; Goff B–741; Rogledi Manni 172.

8 June 1932–Bought with the Bennett Hubbard Nash fund. Inc 5890

3087 Bartholomaeus de Chaimis: Confessionale. 21 November 1478.

8°. [174] leaves (174 blank); 157 x 116 mm.

Printed by De Vespolate with Jacobus de Marliano.

Initial on A1r illuminated in colors, with marginal extension; initials and paragraph marks elsewhere added in red. Old vellum, edges mottled red. Circular bookstamp with initials "S B A M" and a cross in the center; from the library of Richard Ashhurst Bowie. BMC states that there are errors in the printed signatures in quires L, N, Q, and R; there are none in this copy.

H 2484*; Pr 5894; BMC 6:733 (IA.26296); Pell 1862; Polain 4189; GW 6545; IGI 2720; Goff B–158; BSB-Ink C–248; Rogledi Manni 283.

9 November 1908–Gift of Mrs. E. D. Brandegee. Inc 5894

A R C H A N G E L U S   U N G A R D U S

3088 Xenophon: Cyropaedia. Before 18 February 1477.

4°. [146] leaves; 268 x 193 mm.

Latin translation by Franciscus Philelphus. Includes a poem by Calliphilus Bernardus Robiatinus. Some copies have a colophon stating falsely that the book was printed 10 March 1474 in Rome by a nonexistent printer "Arnoldus de Villa," while others are without a colophon.

This copy is without a colophon. Initial spaces, with guide-letters, not filled in; without rubrication. 18th-century sheep. MS note by Richard Heber on front flyleaf, "March 1821 Ld Sp.ˢ Dupl. Sale" (no. 336 in the Evans sale catalogue of Earl Spencer's duplicates; no. 3956 in pt. 6 of the Sotheby sale catalogue of Heber's library, April 1835); autograph "Geo: T. Strong 1841" on front flyleaf; from the library of Richard Ashhurst Bowie, with a slip of his MS notes inserted at front. Imperfect: wormed, affecting text.

HCR 16227; Pr 3461 (assigned to "Arnoldus de Villa" in Rome); BMC 4:52 (IB.17673) corrected by 6:734 (IB.26933a–b); IGI 10404; Goff X–5; CIBN X–1; Rogledi Manni 1120.

9 November 1908–Gift of Mrs. E. D. Brandegee. Inc 5894.5

PRINTER FOR
BONINUS MOMBRITIUS

3089 **Mombritius, Boninus:** Sanctuarium, siue Vitae sanctorum. Before 14 September 1478.

f°. 2 vols. (vol. 1: [350] leaves, 1, 5, 216, 256, 282, and 350 blank; vol. 2: [365] leaves, 3 and 347 blank); 362 x 257 mm.

On dating see Tino Foffano, "Per la data dell'edizione del 'Sanctuarium' di Bonino Mombrizio," *Italia medioevale e umanistica* 22 (1979): [509]–11. Foffano records a purchase date of 14 September 1478 in a copy of volume 2 at the Biblioteca dell'Università cattolica di Milano. BMC does not include blank leaf 216 in the collation of vol. 1.

Initial spaces, most with guide-letters, not filled in; without rubrication. Half modern vellum and gray boards. MS ownership notation at beginning of vol. 1, "P. Guarini"; smudged and illegible bookstamp in both volumes; booklabel of Count Paul Riant. Imperfect: leaf nnnn4 wanting in vol. 2, as in many copies, in some of which it is replaced by an 18th-century facsimile reprint; see BMC. Blank leaves 1, 282, and 350 in vol. 1 not present; quires F–FF⁸, FFF⁶ bound after quire ff⁶.

HC 11544*; Pr 6081 (Milanese adespota); BMC 6:736 (IC.26952); Polain 2769; IGI 6690; Goff M–810; CIBN M–522; Rogledi Manni 689.

28 December 1899—Gift of J. Randolph Coolidge and Archibald Cary Coolidge. Inc 5894.10

LUDOVICUS AND
ALBERTUS PEDEMONTANI

3090 **Dante Alighieri:** La Commedia. 27 September 1477–1 March 1478.

f°. [250] leaves (6 blank); 375 x 269 mm.

Includes Dante's *Credo.* GW suggests that the Guido Terzago mentioned in the editor's foreword is the publisher. With commentary of Martinus Paulus Nidobeatus, based on that of Jacobus de Lana. According to BMC, there are two settings of sheet [b]4, but no distinguishing readings are given; there is also a variant on [b]3r; see below.

In this copy the last line of text on [b]3r has incorrect reading "elege." Initial spaces, some with guide-letters, not filled in; leaf [N]2v (beginning of the final canto of the *Paradiso*) has two initials illuminated in gold and colors, with marginal extensions; this illumination is not contemporary. Old vellum. MS ownership notation erased from lower margin of [a]2r; other ownership notations in pencil inside front cover signed with initials "CJS" and "M.J.H." Imperfect: first and last leaves wanting, the last supplied in 19th-century MS.

HR 5943; Pr 5896; BMC 6:738 (IC.26315) and 12:52 (IC.26313); Pell 4113; Polain 1222; GW 7965; IGI 359; Goff D–28; Rogledi Manni 55.

2 May 1919–Gift of the Dante Society of Cambridge. Inc 5896

JOHANNES ANTONIUS AND BENINUS DE HONATE

3091 Bartolus de Saxoferrato: Super authenticis. After 7 March 1480.

f°. [74] leaves (1 blank); 378 x 250 mm.

Initials and paragraph marks added in red or blue, occasional capital strokes in red. Spine covered with a vellum strip of 15th-century Latin MS, the covers with paper leaves from Koberger's 1478 Latin Bible, containing the end of Ephesians and beginning of Philippians on one and end of 1 Timothy and beginning of 2 Timothy on the other. With this is bound the same author's *Super tribus ultimis libris Codicis* (Venice, Nicolas Jenson, 1477). Bookplate of Christian Ernst, Graf zu Stolberg; bookstamp of the Gräfliche Stolbergische Bibliothek zu Wernigerode.

HC 2623*; Pr 5902; Pell 1951; GW 3477; IGI 1281; Goff B–186; Sack 474; BSB-Ink B–203 (Pseudo-Bartolus); Rogledi Manni 132.

21 April 1932–From the Fürstliche Stolberg zu Wernigerode Bibliothek. Law Library

3092 Bonifacius VIII, Pope: Liber sextus Decretalium. 23 July 1482.

f°. [122] leaves (1 and 122 blank); 429 x 290 mm.

Includes the commentary of Johannes Andreae and his *Super arboribus consanguinitatis et affinitatis*. Printed by De Honate for Petrus Antonius de Castelliono and Ambrosius de Chaimis.

Initial spaces, with guide-letters, not filled in; without rubrication. Half modern vellum and marbled boards. Leaves numbered in MS; MS indices on blank leaves at front and back; MS marginalia.

H 3602*; Pr 5904; Pell 2747(1); GW 4870; Goff B–994; BSB-Ink B–714; Rogledi Manni 191.

4 October 1946—Received. Law Library

3093 **Corpus iuris civilis. Digesta Justiniani. Digestum novum.** 25 July 1482.

f°. [356] leaves; 430 x 290 mm.

Includes the *glossa ordinaria* of Accursius. Edited by Matthaeus Barlasina. Printed by De Honate for Petrus Antonius de Castelliono and Ambrosius de Chaimis.

Leaf a2r with a miniature in gold and colors (kneeling author presenting his work to a mitered bishop or abbot) and an illuminated initial with marginal extension between the two columns; another miniature in lower border (seated abbot with dog at his feet, two armorial shields, one with monogram "AG"); initials elsewhere added in red or blue, paragraph marks in red; book numbers and chapter headings added in red in upper margins. Contemporary blind-stamped leather over wooden boards; brass clasp plates on back cover, latches on front, clasps and thongs gone; brass corner bosses on both covers. MS index on leaf inserted at front. Pasted down inside both covers are leaves from one of the legal works printed by Michael Wenssler in Basel (his types 121^A and 92^A). MS ownership notation in upper margin of a2r, "S. Magni in Füssen."

H 9583*; GW 7706; BSB-Ink C–584; Rogledi Manni 531.

8 June 1953—Received. Law Library

3094 **Statuta civitatis Mediolani: Tabula.** 30 November 1482.

f°. [14] leaves; 281 x 200 mm.

Intended as an index to the Milan statutes printed by Paulus de Suardis, 20 December 1480; see no. 3106.

Without rubrication. For binding description see no. 3106, *Statuta civitatis Mediolani* (Milan, Paulus de Suardis, 20 December 1480), with which this is bound.

HC(+Add) 15009(2)=HR 15010; Pr 5906; BMC 6:741 (IB.26351); IGI 6326; Goff S-717; Rogledi Manni 641.

May 1963—Gift of Ward M. Canaday. Inc 5971 (A)

3095 Thomas Aquinas: Opuscula. 1488.

f°. [314] leaves (1 blank); 305 x 218 mm.

Edited by Paulus Soncinas. For contents see Goff under the 1498 edition printed by Bonetus Locatellus, but with the works in a different order and without nos. 38, 39, 46, 48, 53–68, and 71–73 there listed.

Initial spaces, most with guide-letters, not filled in; without rubrication. 16th-century brown morocco over wooden boards, probably Spanish, stamped with knotwork borders on either side of a border made up of a small tool of a pelican in its piety; center filled with massed knotwork tooling; brass latch plates on back cover, clasps and thongs gone; in a cloth case. Bookplate of J. R. Abbey (no. 2193 in pt. 3 of the Sotheby sale catalogue of his library, June 1967).

HC(+Add) 1540; Pr 5908; BMC 6:742 (IB.26365); Pell 1092; Polain 4753; IGI 9551; Goff T-259; CIBN T-111; Rogledi Manni 1008.

August 1967—Bought with the Carl T. Keller fund. Inc 5908

3096 Cepolla, Bartholomaeus: De simulatione contractuum. 20 April 1492.

f°. [18] leaves (18 blank); 395 x 265 mm.

Printed by De Honate for Petrus Antonius de Castelliono.

Initial spaces, with guide-letters, not filled in; without rubrication. Half modern brown morocco and marbled boards. Blank leaf not present.

HC 4872; Pell 3489; GW 6510; IGI 2704; Goff C-398; Rogledi Manni 278.

14 January 1931—Received. Law Library

LEONARDUS PACHEL AND ULDERICUS SCINZENZELER

3097 Paulus Florentinus: Breviarium totius iuris canonici, siue Decretorum breviarium. 28 August 1479.

f° and 4°. [4], CXVI, [2], 119–27, [1] leaves (VIIII, XI, XXXIII, XXXVIII, LXI, and LXVIII–VIIII misnumbered VIII, X, XXXXIIII, XXXVII, LX, and LVIII–VIIII); ill.; 279 x 195 mm.

Initials on a2r added in red; spaces elsewhere, with guide-letters, not filled in. Old vellum, with green silk ties. MS ownership notation at front, "Capucinorum Bergomi"; bookstamp of Count Ercole Silva.

H 7159*; Pr 5924; BMC 6:746 (IB.26434); IGI 7189; Goff P–178; CIBN P–56; Rogledi Manni 743; Sander 651.

26 May 1944—Received. Law Library

3098 **Paulus Florentinus:** Quadragesimale de reditu peccatoris ad Deum. 10 September 1479.

f°. [296] leaves (3 and 296 blank); ill.; 260 x 191 mm.

Initial spaces, with guide-letters, not filled in; without rubrication. Old limp vellum. Blank leaf a1r covered with MS notes in Italian; blank a1v contains a 14-line Latin poem; blank oo5v–6r contains a MS list of doges of Venice from 706 to 1486. Imperfect: quire π² wanting.

HC 7166*; Pr 5926; BMC 6:747 (IB.26438); IGI 7196; Goff P–182; Schäfer 263; Rogledi Manni 746; Sander 654.

28 August 1903—Gift of Alain Campbell White. Inc 5926

3099 **Nepos, Cornelius:** Vitae imperatorum, siue De vita illustrium virorum. 1480?

4°. [58] leaves (1 blank); 198 x 135 mm.

Edited by Petrus Cornerus. Includes letters by Franciscus Philelphus and Jacobus Bechetus.

Initial spaces not filled in; without rubrication. For binding description see no. 3347, Caius Julius Solinus, *Polyhistor, siue De mirabilibus mundi* (Parma, Andreas Portilia, 20 December 1480), with which this is bound, along with Lucius Annaeus Florus, *Epitome de Tito Livio* (Siena, Sigismundus Rodt, 1486 or 7).

HR 5731; Pr 5953; BMC 6:748 (IA.26524); Pell 3984; IGI 3212; Goff C–916; Rogledi Manni 349.

January 1919—Deposited by James M. Hunnewell. Inc 6850 (B)

3100 **Brasca, Santo:** Itinerario alla santissima città di Gerusalemme. 25 February 1481.

4°. [64] leaves (64 blank); ill.; 195 x 140 mm.

Printed by Pachel and Scinzenzeler for Ambrosius Archintus.

This copy has at the beginning the two unsigned leaves described by Reichling (but he omits transcribing "grosse" after "terre" in line 1); GW describes these leaves as bound at end. Initial space on a1r not filled in; without rubrication. Modern vellum.

HCR 3763; Pr 5934; BMC 6:749 (IA.26460); GW 5073; IGI 2052; Goff B–1101; Rogledi Manni 200; Sander 1261.

8 November 1893—Bought with the Charles Minot fund. Inc 5934

3101 **Pseudo-Victor, Sextus Aurelius:** De viris illustribus. ca. 1484.

4°. [18] leaves; 193 x 140 mm.

Edited by Gaspar Lampugnanus. Ascribed in the text to Suetonius.

Initial spaces, with guide-letters, not filled in; without rubrication. Modern decorated boards. Imperfect: quire π^2 wanting.

HC 15134*=H 2132; Pr 5955; BMC 6:752 (IA.26529); IGI 1086–A; Goff A–1388; Rogledi Manni 116.

2 August 1911—Gift of Mrs. E. D. Brandegee. Inc 5955

3102 **Ubaldis, Nicolaus de:** De successionibus ab intestato. 5 May 1487.

[For transcriptions see Copinger; but this copy has "sVscepto" on a2r.] f°. a⁸, b–d⁶ (d6 blank); [26] leaves (26 blank); 388 x 263 mm. 2 columns. a4r: 65 lines, 280 x 188 mm. Type: 11:128G^B, headings; 12:86G^B, text. Initial spaces, with guide-letters.

Initial spaces not filled in; without rubrication. Half modern blue and orange boards.

HC 15894; IGI 10004; Goff U–45; Rogledi Manni 1054.

19 September 1947—Received. Law Library

3103 **Cavalca, Domenico:** Specchio di croce. 22 August 1487.

4°. [76] leaves; 188 x 134 mm.

Without rubrication. Old white paste-paper boards. 19th-century MS ownership notation inside front cover, "Del Collegio."

R 470; Pr 5957A; GW 6420; IGI 2644; Goff C–347; Rogledi Manni 269.

9 December 1920—Bought with the John Harvey Treat fund. Inc 5957A

B O N U S   A C C U R S I U S

3104 Accursius, Bonus: Plautina dicta memoratu digna. ca. 1478.

4°. [102] leaves (101–02 blank); 185 x 130 mm.

Single lines and phrases from the plays of Plautus.

Initial spaces, one with guide-letter, not filled in; without rubrication. Half modern vellum and decorated boards; edges marbled. Booklabel of Adriana R. Salem. Quire π^2 bound at end in this copy.

HC 57; Pr 5899A (assigned to Johannes Antonius and Benignus de Honate); BMC 6:755 (IA.26570); GW 185 (assigned to Johannes Antonius de Honate); Goff A-33; BSB-Ink B-752; Rogledi Manni 11.

1965—Gift of Ward M. Canaday. Inc 5962.5

3105 Marlianus, Raimundus: Index locorum in commentario Caesaris Belli Gallici descriptorum. ca. 1478.

4°. [60] leaves; 210 x 138 mm.

With minor revisions and additions by Bonus Accursius.

Large initial on a1r added in red and brown; initials elsewhere added in red through d2v, only occasionally thereafter. 19th-century dark green morocco, gilt, edges gilt. Armorial bookplate (owner's name scraped away) with motto "Viam aut inveniam aut faciam"; autograph and booklabel of George Dunn, with his date of acquisition "Dec. 1903" (no. 3445 in pt. 3 of the Sotheby sale catalogue, November 1917).

HR 10776; BMC 6:755 (IB.26558); IGI 6193; Goff M-276; CIBN M-136; Rogledi Manni 625.

17 June 1920—Bought with the Constantius fund. Inc 5961.5

P A U L U S   D E   S U A R D I S

3106 Statuta civitatis Mediolani. 20 December 1480.

f°. [240] leaves (1, 32–33, and 105 blank); 281 x 200 mm.

Initial spaces at beginning of sections, some with guide-letters, not filled in. Modern blind-stamped calf over wooden boards. Leaves numbered in MS; MS marginalia in the *Statuta mercatorum* section. Bound in at front is the *Tabula* printed for this edition by Johannes Antonius de Honate (30 November 1482; see no. 3094). Bookstamps "Ex Biblioth. Margaritis" and of Count Ercole Silva.

HC(+Add) 15009(1); Pr 5971; BMC 6:758 (IB.26574); IGI 6324; Goff S–716; Rogledi Manni 639.

May 1963—Gift of Ward M. Canaday. Inc 5971 (A)

3107 ——Another copy. 287 x 200 mm.

Initial spaces not filled in. Half 18th-century red straight-grain morocco and brown boards, spine gilt. MS marginalia. Booklabel "Justice of the Peace. T. B. Cooper, Esq. Mansion House, Bengeworth"; autograph "Florence A. Green de Woolfson" inside front cover. 4-page MS index laid in at front. First 4 quires misbound in order: a2–7, c8, d1, b1–6, c1–7, d5–6, 2–4, 7–9. Imperfect: leaf a8 (first quire) and quires ^{6}a–d^8 and ^{7}a^6, b^8 wanting; blank leaves not present.

7 December 1928—Bought with the Susan Green Dexter fund. Inc 5971 (B)

3108 ——Another copy. 280 x 205 mm.

The *Statuta datiorum* section only (^{5}a–c^6, d^8). Initial on a1r added in blue and red, paragraph marks in blue. Half modern vellum and decorated boards.

30 December 1920—Bought with the Bayard Cutting Fellowship fund. Inc 5971 (C)

3109 ——Another copy. 280 x 197 mm.

Initial on a2r illuminated in gold and colors, with marginal extension; initials elsewhere and paragraph marks added in blue. Modern vellum. MS index to the first section on 2 leaves at front. MS ownership notation on blank a1v, "J. C. Julii Cȩsaris Butrij."

20 August 1946—Received. Law Library

P E T R U S   D E   C O R N E N O

3110 Hugo Senensis: Trattato circa la conservazione della sanità. 31 May 1481.

8°. [54] leaves; 194 x 138 mm.

Initial spaces, with guide-letters, not filled in; without rubrication. Half 19th-century calf and marbled boards. Bookplate of J. Cigertia. A few leaves remargined.

HCR 9021; Pr 5973; BMC 6:759 (IA.26585); IGI 4943; Goff H–548; CIBN H–329; Rogledi Manni 512.

Countway Library

S I M O N   M A G N I A G U S

3111 Diedus, Franciscus: Vita S. Rochi. After 1 June 1479.

4°. [22] leaves; 199 x 147 mm.

Includes a letter to the author by Petrus Ludovicus Maldura.

Initials crudely added in brown. Half 19th-century calf and marbled boards. Bookplate of Thomas Gaisford.

C 1973; Pr 7269 (assigned to Antonio de Corsiono in Casal di San Vaso); BMC 6:760 (IA.26597); GW 8329; IGI 3425; Goff D–188; Rogledi Manni 377.

Countway Library

3112 Philelphus, Franciscus: Mediolanensia convivia duo. ca. 1483/84.

4°. [96] leaves; 194 x 140 mm.

There is a variant on b3r; see BMC. Includes letters from Johannes Franciscus Marlianus and Leonardus Justinianus.

This copy has the reading of BMC IA.26605 on b3r. Initial spaces, with guide-letters, not filled in; without rubrication. Half 19th-century sheep and marbled boards, rehinged. Booklabel of Georg Kloss (no. 2821 in the Sotheby sale catalogue, May 1835). Sheets d3–4 misbound before d1–2.

HC(+Add) 12956; Pr 7268 (assigned to Antonio de Corsiono in Casal de San Vaso); BMC 6:760 (IA.26605); Polain 4653; IGI 3881; Goff P–605; CIBN P–321; Rogledi Manni 429.

22 August 1856—Gift of Winslow Lewis. Inc 5974.10

U L D E R I C U S   S C I N Z E N Z E L E R

3113 Ambrosius, Saint: De officiis [and other works]. 17 January 1488.

4°. [140] leaves; 205 x 144 mm.

Includes: Paulinus Mediolanensis, *Vita Ambrosii.*—Ambrosius, *De officiis. De obitu fratris sui Satyri. De bono mortis.*—Pseudo-Ambrosius, *Vita gloriosae virginis Agnetis. Passio sanctorum martyrum Vitalis et Agricolae. Passio sanctorum martyrum Protasii et Gervasii. De cruce Domini. De resurrectione Domini.* Printed by Scinzenzeler for Philippus de Lavagnia.

Initial spaces, with guide-letters, not filled in; without rubrication. Half modern white pigskin and gray boards.

HC 911 (incl HC 908*); Pr 6006; BMC 6:762 (IA.26705); Pell 594; GW 1612; IGI 432; Goff A–561; BSB-Ink A–473; Rogledi Manni 64.

13 November 1916—Bought with the John Harvey Treat fund. Inc 6006

3114 Ferrerius, Vincentius: Sermones de sanctis. 3 March 1488.

4°. [176] leaves (176 blank); 185 x 135 mm.

Edited by Nicolaus de Serazonibus. With additions by Paulus Soncinas. Printed by Scinzenzeler for Aloysius de Serazonibus.

Initial on a2r added in red and blue; initials elsewhere and paragraph marks added in red or blue. Old vellum. MS ownership notation on a1r obliterated; bookstamp "N. C. S. Poyntz, Dorchester, Oxon." Blank leaf not present.

HC 7003; Pr 6007; BMC 6:763 (IA.26707); GW 9834; IGI 10276; Goff F–127; Rogledi Manni 1106.

20 July 1922—Bought with the John Harvey Treat fund. Inc 6007

3115 Pseudo-Albertus Magnus: Mariale. 17 April 1488.

4°. [112] leaves (112 blank); 192 x 138 mm.

Edited by Augustinus de Pavia. Printed by Scinzenzeler for Aloysius de Serazonibus.

Initial on a4r added in red and blue, with marginal extension; initials elsewhere and paragraph marks added in red or blue. Old mottled calf, rebacked. MS ownership notation on 07v, "Est Conuentus scṫi Antonij de Morbinio."

HC(+Add) 464; Pr 6008; BMC 6:763 (IA.26709); Pell 301; GW 682; IGI 183; Goff A–275; BSB-Ink A–189; Rogledi Manni 38.

17 February 1923—Bought with the John Harvey Treat fund. Inc 6008 (A)

3116 ——Another copy. 178 x 135 mm.

Contemporary (?) blind-stamped leather over paste-paper boards; marks of leather ties, no longer present; in a cloth case. Engraved bookplate of Sebastian Denich, titular bishop of Almira (Leiningen-Westerburg p. 331). Vellum leaves of 15th-century Latin MS pasted down inside covers, that in front mostly covered by the bookplate. Booklabel of David P. Wheatland.

1 January 1991—Gift of David P. Wheatland. Inc 6008 (B)

3117 Ovidius Naso, Publius: Fasti. 10 November 1489.

f°. [168] leaves; 305 x 215 mm.

Edited with a commentary by Paulus Marsus. Includes a poem by Robertus Ursus. Printed by Scinzenzeler for Gabriel Conagi.

Initial spaces, some with guide-letters, not filled in; without rubrication. Half old vellum and marbled boards. Waterstained.

HCR 12241=H 12243 (with error in year date); Pr 6012; BMC 6:763 (IB.26718); IGI 7072; Goff O–173; Rogledi Manni 721.

20 June 1924—Bought with the Stephen Salisbury fund. Inc 6012

3118 Martialis, Marcus Valerius: Epigrammata. 20 September 1490.

f°. [172] leaves; 293 x 210 mm.

With the commentary of Domitius Calderinus. Includes a poem by Lucius Phosphorus.

Initial spaces not filled in; without rubrication. Modern vellum. By errors of imposition, q8r and q1v have been misimposed upside-down on q1v and q8r respectively; and u6r and u3v have been misimposed upside-down on u3v and u6r.

HC(Add) 10820; Pr 6015; BMC 6:764 (IB.26724); IGI 6228; Goff M–309; CIBN M–171; Rogledi Manni 631.

9 November 1923–Bought with the Constantius fund. Inc 6015

3119 Plautus, Titus Maccius: Comoediae. 1 December 1490.

f°. [236] leaves (1 blank); 303 x 206 mm.

Edited by Georgius Merula; revised by Eusebius Scutarius. Printed by Scinzenzeler for Johannes de Legnano.

Initial spaces, with guide-letters, not filled in; without rubrication. Contemporary blind-stamped leather over wooden boards, repaired. MS ownership notation inside front cover, "Del Conte Vgo di Prepoli [?] et de li amici"; MS marginalia. Bookseller's ticket of B. Westermann & Co., New York. Visiting card of Kenneth G. T. Webster inserted at front with MS notation "Happy New Year to Will Thayer! Jan. 10, 1926."

HCR 13077; Pr 6016; BMC 6:765 (IB.26726); IGI 7872; Goff P–781; CIBN P–453; Rogledi Manni 815.

16 January 1933–Bequest of William S. Thayer. Inc 6016 (A)

3120 ——Another copy. 305 x 210 mm.

Initial spaces not filled in; without rubrication. Old vellum. MS ownership notation on a2r, "Monasterii Olivensis Ordinis Cisterciorum in [illegible]"; another on a4r, "Beatae Mariae de Oliua Ordinis Cisterciorum in [illegible]." MS marginalia. From the library of Richard Ashhurst Bowie. Several leaves at front and back remargined.

9 November 1908–Gift of Mrs. E. D. Brandegee. Inc 6016 (B)

3121 Persius Flaccus, Aulus: Satirae. 1490.

f°. [28] leaves; 271 x 184 mm.   Plate V

With the commentary of Bartholomaeus Fontius.

Initial spaces, some with guide-letters, not filled in; without rubrication. Half old vellum and marbled boards. Autograph "Jules Tarlier 1864" inside front cover; from the library of Richard Ashhurst Bowie;

leaf of MS notes by Morris H. Morgan inserted at front, "The important thing about this copy is that it has the date M.CCCC.L.XXXx, with the last x *small*, & *still to be seen*. In the Br. Mus & Bodl. copies this x is erased, so that the book has been attributed to 1480. But the Ambrosian Library copy, wh. I have seen, has the date as in this book. It was an inquiry wh. I made from Mr Bowie about the state of the date in this copy that eventually led to the coming of the Bowie Library here [i.e., to the Harvard College Library]. M.H.M." Imperfect: leaf a1 wanting; leaf b6 slightly mutilated.

HR 12726; Pr 6018; BMC 6:765 (IB.26730); IGI 7502; Goff P-349; Rogledi Manni 786.

9 November 1908—Gift of Mrs. E. D. Brandegee. Inc 6018

3122 Suetonius Tranquillus, Caius: Vitae XII Caesarum. 19 November 1491.

f°. [2], iii–cxxxvii, [1] leaves ([i] and [cxxxviii] blank; xxiiii and xxxvii misnumbered xiiii and xxxviii); 303 x 214 mm.

With the commentary of Marcus Antonius Sabellicus. Includes verses of Ausonius on Suetonius and an excerpt from Sicco Polentonus.

Without rubrication. Original wooden boards, rebacked with 19th-century red morocco; fragments of leather thongs nailed to back cover, brass latches on front, clasps gone. From the library of Richard Ashhurst Bowie.

HC 15123; Pr 6021; BMC 6:766 (IB.26736); Polain 3628; IGI 9236; Goff S-823; Rogledi Manni 946.

9 November 1908—Gift of Mrs. E. D. Brandegee. Inc 6021

3123 Poggius Florentinus: India recognita. After 15 February 1492.

4°. [14] leaves; 204 x 147 mm.

Edited by Christophorus Bullatus. Containing the report of Niccolò de'Conti's travels in the Far East, this tract constitutes the fourth book of Poggius's *De varietate fortunae*.

Without rubrication. Modern limp vellum; in a half morocco case.

H 13208; Pr 6022; BMC 6:766 (IA.26738); Goff P-875; Rogledi Manni 822.

10 January 1954—Gift of Harrison D. Horblit. Inc 6022

3124 Albericus de Rosate: Lectura super Codice. 1 March–28 July 1492.

f°. 3 pts. in 1 vol. (pt. 1: [190] leaves, 1 blank; pt. 2: [108] leaves, 1 blank; pt. 3: [222] leaves, 1 blank); 381 x 277 mm.

In pt. 3, GW mistakenly calls for ff⁸ rather than ff⁴.

Initial spaces, with guide-letters, not filled in; without rubrication. Bound in two vellum leaves of 15th-century Latin theological MS dealing with baptism; rebacked in vellum; edges stained red. Bookplate of Christian Ernst, Graf zu Stolberg; bookstamp of the Gräfliche Stolbergische Bibliothek zu Wernigerode. In pt. 1, leaf G6 has not been printed; quire l is misbound after quire D; and blank a1 is not present.

H 14008*; GW 522; IGI 134; Goff A–190; BSB-Ink A–105; Rogledi Manni 32.

21 April 1932–From the Fürstliche Stolberg zu Wernigerode Bibliothek. Law Library

3124A Angelus de Clavasio: Correctorium Summae angelicae. Before 4 June 1492.

a1r: (q⁷)Vi vult habere sūmaჳ an ‖ gelicam correctissimā que ‖ ret primo impressā claua ‖ sii et postea attēdat ad cor ‖ rectoriū infrascriptuჳ in ‖ quo ī ueniet multa que ui ‖ tio transcriptoꝣ ꞇ ī presso ‖ rū corrupta sūt uel ommissa ... ‖ b8r: Lector humanissime ne ī erratis labores ‖ Recognito opusculo ... ‖ b8v blank.

4°. a–b⁸; [16] leaves; 202 x 144 mm. 2 columns. a1r: 51 lines, 158 x 108 mm. Type: 2:63G. Initial space, with guide-letter, on a1r.   Plate VI

Since these corrections and additions are described as "factum cum exemplari proprio ipsius fratris Angeli" and since they have been made in the Venice edition of Georgius Arrivabenus dated 4 June 1492 (see no. 2129 in vol. 2), which is stated to be "correcta secundum primum exemplar ipsius Angeli," it is clear that the printing of these 16 leaves must antedate that edition. The corrections are keyed to the first edition (Chivasso, Jacobinus Suigus, 13 May 1486; see no. 3584) but could be used for other editions as well ("Vel si non habes predictam summam impressam clauasij sed aliam impressam uenetiis vel alibi," etc.). None of the editions recorded in GW make any mention of these leaves, and I am told by the office of the Gesamtkatalog, "dem GW waren diese 16 Blätter Korrekturen und Ergänzungen zur Summa angelica völlig unbekannt." Why these corrections should have been printed by Scinzenzeler in Milan, who is not recorded with an edition of the *Summa*, is unclear, nor do we know whether or not Angelus himself had anything to do with the printing.

Initial space not filled in; without rubrication. For binding description see no. 3584, the Chivasso edition of the *Summa*, at front of which these 16 leaves are bound. Imperfect: a1 wormed, slightly affecting text.

Unrecorded.

January 1919–Deposited by James M. Hunnewell. Inc 7323

3125 Isocrates: Orationes [Greek]. 24 January 1493.

f°. [200] leaves (1, 16, and 34 blank); 290 x 202 mm.

Edited by Demetrius Chalcondylas. While the colophon states that this book was printed by "Henricus" Scinzenzeler along with an otherwise unknown Sebastianus de Ponte Tremulo, "Henricus" appears to be simply a linguistic variant of "Uldericus" and not another individual with a separate press, as set up by Proctor; see BMC 6:xxvii. There are variant settings of quires A and B; see BMC.

In this copy the setting of quire A agrees with BMC IB.26855 and quire B with BMC IB.26856. Initial spaces, most with guide-letters, not filled in; without rubrication. 19th-century calf, gilt, edges gilt, by Lewis, with the arms and initials of Sir Mark Masterman Sykes stamped on covers (no. 1653 in the Evans sale catalogue, May 1824); Syston Park bookplate and monogram booklabel of Sir J. H. Thorold (no. 1026 in the Sotheby sale catalogue, December 1884); monogram bookstamp "MD" within a circle in lower margin of α2r. First two blank leaves not present.

HC 9312; Pr 6065; BMC 6:767 (IB.26855-57); IGI 5421; Goff I-210; CIBN I-88; Rogledi Manni 528.

14 October 1918–Bought with the Constantius fund. Inc 6024.10

3126 ——Another copy. 275 x 192 mm.

In this copy the setting of quire A agrees with BMC IB.26855 and quire B with BMC IB.26857. Initial spaces not filled in; without rubrication. 19th-century diced calf, gilt, edges gilt. Bookplate of William King Richardson. First blank leaf not present.

1951–Bequest of William King Richardson. WKR 1.3.2

3127 Demetrius Chalcondylas: Erotemata [Greek]. ca. 1493.

f° and 4°. [148] leaves (60 blank); 279 x 194 mm.

On sixteen lines of type used as furniture but wrongly inked and printed on (eta)7r, see BMC; in this copy an early owner has crossed them out in red ink. Includes, each with separate signatures, Manuel Moschopulus, *Erotemata* [Greek], and Gregorius Corinthius, *De dialectis* [Greek].

Initial spaces, with guide-letters, not filled in; without rubrication. 19th-century olive morocco, edges gilt. Booklabel of Henry Huth (no. 1448 in pt. 2 of the Sotheby sale catalogue, June 1912).

HCR 6093; Pr 5968–70 (the 3 pts. listed separately and assigned to Bonus Accursius); BMC 6:767 (IB.26861) and 12:54 (IB.26860); Pell 4189; Polain 1256; GW 8250; IGI 3404; Goff D–139; Rogledi Manni 374.

7 October 1912—Gift of Mrs. E. D. Brandegee. Inc 6024.5

3128 Petrarca, Francesco: Canzoniere e Trionfi. 10 February–26 March 1494.

f°. 2 pts. in 1 vol. (pt. 1: [8], 128 leaves, [1] blank, 24, 27, 29, 33, 35, 36–39, 100, 109, and 120 misnumbered 14, 29, 39, 55, 54, 56–59, 10, 119, and 129; pt. 2: 102 [i.e., 101], [1] leaves, 97 omitted and 16 misnumbered 10); ill.; 300 x 205 mm.

Edited by Franciscus Tantius Corniger. Includes the commentaries of Bernardo Lapini, Franciscus Philelphus, and Hieronymus Squarzaficus. The *Trionfi* precede.

Woodcut initials; without rubrication. Modern blind-stamped leather. MS ownership notation on N6v of pt. 2, "Iste petrarca est Lucretię Imperialis"; booklabels of P. Brunet and of Adriana R. Salem. Blank leaf not present.

HCR 12775; Polain 3068; IGI 7556 and 7537; Goff P–389; CIBN P–191; Rogledi Manni 789 and 791; Sander 5603.

December 1965—Gift of Ward M. Canaday. Inc 6025.5

3129 ——Another copy. 284 x 198 mm.

Without rubrication. 19th-century mottled calf, edges stained red. MS ownership notation on N5v of pt. 2, "Est mei Bassiani de bursis." Imperfect: in pt. 2, sheets A1 and N1 wanting; blank leaf not present.

28 February 1942–Gift of Philip Hofer. Typ Inc 6025.5

3130 Sancto Georgio, Johannes Antonius de: Commentaria super Decreto. 18 June 1494.

f°. [270] leaves; 402 x 282 mm.

Initial spaces, with guide-letters, not filled in; without rubrication. Half old blind-stamped pigskin and modern plywood (!) boards. Bookstamp of the Stuttgart Landesbibliothek, with MS notation "Als Dublette abgegeben 11.7.1967."

HC 7583*; Pr 6026; BMC 6:768 (IC.26748); Polain 3449; IGI 8600; Sack 3153; Rogledi Manni 881.

Law Library

3131 Brudzewo, Albertus de: Commentum in theoricas planetarum Georgii Purbachii. 30 March 1495.

4°. [40] leaves; ill.; 209 x 154 mm.

Includes a letter by Johannes Otto.

A few woodcut initials; spaces elsewhere, with guide-letters, not filled in; without rubrication. Modern vellum. Bookstamp erased from title page.

HC 3999*; Pr 6028; BMC 6:769 (IA.26752); Pell 3027; GW 5577; IGI 241; Goff B–1218; BSB-Ink B–928; Rogledi Manni 42; Sander 1407.

1948–Gift of Harrison D. Horblit. Inc 6028

3132 ——Another copy. 200 x 140 mm.

Initial spaces not filled in; without rubrication. Modern gray boards.

Countway Library (William Norton Bullard Collection)

3133 Carcano, Michael de: Sermonarium de commendatione virtutum et reprobatione vitiorum. 11 July 1495.

4°. [266] leaves (266 blank); 195 x 143 mm.

Printed by Scinzenzeler for Raphael Peragallus, who appends a letter at end.

Initial spaces, most with guide-letters, not filled in; without rubrication. Modern vellum, with vellum thongs that slip into clasps on front cover. Leaves numbered in red MS; contemporary MS alphabetical index of the sermons on blank H6 and 8 additional leaves at end; MS ownership notations on flyleaf at front, "Pauli ab Aldringen" and "Collegii S. Petri junioris Argentinae."

HC 4505*; Pr 6030; BMC 6:770 (IA.26758); Pell 3298; Polain 1007; GW 6128; IGI 2517; Goff C-198; BSB-Ink C-144; Rogledi Manni 252.

29 May 1931–Bought with the John Harvey Treat fund. Inc 6030

3134 Pseudo-Bernardus Claravallensis: Meditationes de interiori homine. ca. 1495.

4°. [62] leaves; 188 x 140 mm.

Includes Pseudo-Bernardus, *De conscientia aedificanda, Epistola de gubernatione rei familiaris, Orationes devotissimae, De ordine vitae et morum institutione, Speculum de honestate vitae,* and *Octo puncta perfectionis assequendae.*

Woodcut initials; without rubrication. For binding description see no. 3423, the author's *Sermones super Cantica canticorum* (Brescia, Angelus Britannicus, 28 January 1500), with which this is bound. Imperfect: quires f-g^8, h^6 wanting.

HR 2919; C 970; GW 4035; IGI 1538; Goff B-407; Rogledi Manni 160.

August 1973–Gift of Philip Hofer. Typ Inc 7002

3135 Pius II, Pope: Epistolae familiares. 10 December 1496.

f°. [188] leaves; 300 x 216 mm.

Edited by Ambrosius Archintus and Johannes Vinzalius.

Initial spaces not filled in; without rubrication. Half modern calf and marbled boards. MS marginalia. Bookplate of Murray Anthony Potter. Bound in at front is a Latin letter dated "Rome. 4 Febr 1501."

HC 157*; Pr 6032; BMC 6:770 (IB.26762); Pell 96; IGI 7779; Goff P-721; Sack 2890; CIBN P-416; Rogledi Manni 803.

16 June 1935–From the library of Murray Anthony Potter. Inc 6032

3136 ——Another copy. 282 x 200 mm.

Initial spaces not filled in; without rubrication. Old limp vellum.

Countway Library (William Norton Bullard Collection)

3137 Plautus, Titus Maccius: Comoediae. ca. 1497?

f°. [234] leaves; ill.; 295 x 198 mm.

Edited by Sebastianus Ducius and Georgius Galbiatus. Includes the commentaries of Hermolaus Barbarus, Georgius Merula, Angelus Politianus, and Philippus Beroaldus.

BMC notes that the first sheet of quire G is missigned Fiiii; it is correctly signed in this copy. Initial spaces, with guide-letters, not filled in; without rubrication. Half 19th-century red morocco, top edges gilt. Two MS ownership notations obliterated on title page; from the library of Richard Ashhurst Bowie, with a slip of his MS notes inserted at front, "The extraordinary lettering on the back of this book ['Ald. Edit. 1472'], is an emanation of genius on the part of Mr Richard Grant White, to whom it formerly belonged, and at whose sale it was bought [no. 1818 in the Bangs catalogue, October 1870]. No ordinary ingenuity must have been needed to discover a production of the Aldine press dated more than twenty years before that press was in operation. It is an evidence of 'culture' of which he may well be proud."

H 13085*; Pr 6031; BMC 6:773 (IB.26760); IGI 7874; Goff P-783; Rogledi Manni 816; Sander 5746.

9 November 1908—Gift of Mrs. E. D. Brandegee. Inc 6031

3138 ——Another copy. 303 x 205 mm.

First sheet of quire G correctly signed. Initial spaces not filled in; without rubrication. 18th-century calf, spine gilt; hinges split. MS ownership notation on H4r, "Pbr Donatus di Carchasolis possidet hunc librum." Imperfect: a1 wanting; H4 slightly mutilated; a4 misbound before a2.

Countway Library (William Norton Bullard Collection)

3139 Fulgentius Planciades, Fabius: Enarrationes allegoricae fabularum. 23 April 1498.

f°. [48] leaves (42 blank); 277 x 190 mm.

Edited with a commentary by Johannes Baptista Pius.

Woodcut initials; without rubrication. 18th-century red morocco, edges gilt, with the arms of Carlos III, king of Spain, stamped in gilt on covers; beneath them, within a wreath, the letters "S.D.S.I.D.A."; blue moiré silk lining leaves. From the library of Richard Ashhurst Bowie. Leaves mounted on 1-inch guards at inner margin; blank leaf not present.

HC 7392*; Pr 6037; BMC 6:773 (IB.26776); Pell 4936; Polain 1523; GW 10423; IGI 4106; Goff F–326; BSB-Ink F–280; Rogledi Manni 450.

9 November 1908—Gift of Mrs. E. D. Brandegee. Inc 6037

3140 ——Another copy. 290 x 210 mm.

Without rubrication. Occasional MS marginalia. For binding description see no. 3142, Scinzenzeler's edition of Caius Sollius Sidonius Apollinaris, *Epistolae et carmina* (4 May 1498), with which this is bound, along with Aulus Cornelius Celsus, *De medicina* (Venice, Johannes Rubeus, 8 July 1493). Blank leaf not present.

7 May 1901—Bought with the Henry Lillie Pierce fund. Inc 6038

3141 ——Another copy. 293 x 197 mm.

Without rubrication. Old calf; front cover loose, back cover gone. Autograph "John Jones" on front flyleaf and inscription on title page, "From Col. James H. Jones. U.S. Marine Corps Feb 1876"; ownership stamp "Historical Society of [town erased]."

Countway Library (William Norton Bullard Collection)

3142 Sidonius Apollinaris, Caius Sollius: Epistolae et carmina. 4 May 1498.

f°. [144] leaves; 290 x 210 mm.

Edited, with a commentary, by Johannes Baptista Pius. Includes poems by Baldassarre Taccone and Sebastianus Ducius. Printed by Scinzenzeler for Hieronymus de Asula and Johannes de Abbatibus. There are variants on A4r, c8r, and s8r; see BMC.

In this copy the readings on A4r and c8r agree with BMC IB.26778, that on s8r with IB.26778a. Woodcut initials; without rubrication. 18th-century vellum stained green, with the arms of Louis II, prince de Bourbon-Condé, stamped in gilt on covers; rehinged. Bookplates of William Horatio Crawford (no. 2917 in the Sotheby sale catalogue,

March 1891) and of Aubrey St. John Mildmay; autograph on front fly-leaf, "Geo. H. Powell Lond. a.c. 1897." Occasional MS marginalia. With this are bound Scinzenzeler's edition of Fabius Fulgentius Plan-ciades, *Enarrationes allegoricae fabularum* (23 April 1498) and Aulus Cornelius Celsus, *De medicina* (Venice, Johannes Rubeus, 8 July 1493). Title page, with scribbles in French and Latin, partly remargined.

HC 1287*; Pr 6038; BMC 6:773 (IB.26778–78a); Pell 910; Polain 282; IGI 8967; Goff S–494; CIBN S–250; Rogledi Manni 916.

7 May 1901—Bought with the Henry Lillie Pierce fund. Inc 6038

3143 Petrarca, Francesco: De vita solitaria. 13 August 1498.

f°. [62] leaves; 274 x 188 mm.

Edited by Franciscus Caymus. Includes Pseudo-Petrarca, *Epistola de dispositione vitae suae.*

Initial on A2r added in brown but spaces elsewhere, with guide-let-ters, not filled in; without rubrication. Old vellum. MS ownership notation in upper margin of A2r, "Est conuentus casalensis ordinis predicatorum"; another in lower margin of H5v, "Est Conuentus Sancti Dominicj de Casalj Prouinciae ... Lombardiae."

HCR 12797; Pr 6039; BMC 6:774 (IB.26782); Polain 3070; IGI 7587; Goff P–419; CIBN P–172; Rogledi Manni 793.

5 May 1914—Gift of the Saturday Club of Boston. Inc 6039

3144 Bartholomaeus Pisanus: Quadragesimale de contemptu mundi. 1498.

4°. [154] leaves (18 blank); 186 x 130 mm.

Edited by Johannes Maria Mapellus.

Initial spaces, with guide-letters, not filled in; without rubrication. Half modern morocco and gray cloth. Originally bound with Nicolaus de Lyra, *Postilla super epistolas et evangelia quadragesimalia* (Venice, Johannes Hamann, 13 December 1494); see no. 2235 in vol. 2. MS ownership notation on front flyleaf, "Sum Judocj Ezigerj Minoritae Lucernatis"; another on title page, "F Min: Con: S. Francisci Lucer-nae"; bookplate of George D. Dutton.

HC 2530*; Pr 6042; BMC 6:775 (IA.26787); Pell 1895; GW 3449; IGI 1266; Goff B–168; BSB-Ink B–110; Rogledi Manni 128.

1983—Bequest of Marjorie S. Dutton. Inc 6042

L E O N A R D U S   P A C H E L
(A L O N E)

3145 Imitatio Christi. July 1488.

8°. [76] leaves (76 blank); 158 x 107 mm.

Includes Johannes Gerson, *De meditatione cordis*.

Woodcut and Lombard initials; a few spaces, with guide-letters, not filled in. 19th-century red morocco, gilt. Bookplate of Walter Arthur Copinger. Imperfect: sheet k2 wanting.

HC(Add) 9096*; Pr 5978; BMC 6:777 (IA.26623); Polain 2057; IGI 5116; Goff I–18; CIBN T–236; Rogledi Manni 515.

22 November 1921–W. A. Copinger Imitatio Christi Collection, presented by James Byrne. Inc 5978

3146 Visconti, Girolamo: Lamiarum siue striarum opuscula. 13 September 1490.

4°. [24] leaves; 196 x 146 mm.

Edited by Alvisius de la Cruce.

Initial spaces, with guide-letters, not filled in; without rubrication. Old vellum. Bookplate of Sebastian Evans.

C 6200=3210; Pr 5986; BMC 6:778 (IA.26646); IGI 10263; Goff V–272; Rogledi Manni 1104.

29 April 1921–Bought with the George Lyman Kittredge fund. Inc 5986

3147 ——Another copy. 204 x 146 mm.

Initial spaces not filled in; without rubrication. Old vellum. Booklabel of Count Giacomo Manzoni (no. 3607 in pt. 2 of the Sangiorgi sale catalogue, May–June 1893); MS inscription on flyleaf at front, "Presented to Boston Medical Library. February 29. 1916 by William N. Bullard, M.D."

Countway Library (William Norton Bullard Collection)

3148 Persius Flaccus, Aulus: Satirae. 22 April 1494.

[For transcriptions see Copinger; but correct his colophon to "Im-

pressum Vennetiis [*sic*] ‖ anno .M.cccc.Lxxxxiiii. die .xxii. Aprilis."]
f°. a⁸, b–g⁶, h⁴; [48] leaves; 294 x 200 mm. Text bordered by commentary, with side-notes. a4r: 60 lines, 249 x 162 mm. Types: 3:111R, text; 10:83R, commentary. Woodcut initials.

The colophon is false. Includes the commentaries of Johannes Britannicus and Bartholomaeus Fontius.

Without rubrication. Half 19th-century sheep and speckled boards; edges speckled red. MS ownership notation on title page, "Coll. Ven. Soc. Jesu." Bound with Decimus Junius Juvenalis, *Satirae* (Reggio Emilia, Franciscus de Mazalibus, 1503).

C 4703; IGI 7506; Goff P–355 (assigned to Johannes Tacuinus in Venice) corrected by Suppl P–355; Rogledi Manni 787.

7 July 1926—Bought with the Charles Eliot Norton fund. Inc 5996.5

3149 Bernardus Claravallensis: Sermones de tempore et de sanctis et de diversis. 5 October 1495.

4°. [4], 237, [1] leaves ([238] blank; 33, 41, 42, 124, 127, 129, 130, 186, 191, 199, 210, and 215 misnumbered 36, 31, 41, 131, 128, 130, 120, 176, 194, 201, 200, and 218); ill.; 215 x 157 mm.

Without rubrication; woodcuts uncolored. 16th-century blind-stamped pigskin over wooden boards; brass clasp plates on back cover, latches on front, clasps with pigskin thongs. MS ownership notation on π1v, "FF: B. V. in Salem."; another inside back cover, "Johannes Schnell," with his MS note of purchase as a duplicate from the Heidelberg Library on 22 April 1876. With this is bound the same printer's edition of Bernard's *Epistolae* (15 December 1495).

HC 2850; Pr 5997; BMC 6:781 (IA.26679); Pell 2092; GW 3946; IGI 1561; Goff B–441; BSB-Ink B–319; Rogledi Manni 162; Sander 966.

3 December 1907—From the library of Charles Eliot Norton. Inc 5997

3150 Bernardus Claravallensis: Epistolae. 15 December 1495.

4°. [164] leaves (1 blank); ill.; 215 x 157 mm.

Includes: Bernardus Claravallensis, *Ad milites templi de laude novae militiae, De diligendo Deo, De gratia et libero arbitrio,* and *De praecepto et dispensatione.*—Johannes Homo Dei, *De ordine vitae et morum institutione.*—Guillelmus de Sancto Theodorico, *Epistola ad fratres de Monte Dei.*—Pseudo-Bernardus Claravallensis, *Meditationes de interiori homine* (excerpt, *De miseria et brevitate vitae*), *De temptationibus et otio, De bona et mala voluntate, Speculum super emendatione vitae hominis religiosi.*

Without rubrication; woodcut uncolored. For binding description see preceding entry, the same printer's edition of Bernard's *Sermones de tempore et de sanctis et de diversis* (9 October 1495), with which this is bound.

HR 2873; Pr 5998; BMC 6:781 (IA.26680); Pell 2107; GW 3927; IGI 1525; Goff B-387; BSB-Ink B-312; Rogledi Manni 159; Sander 953.

3 December 1907—From the library of Charles Eliot Norton. Inc 5997

3151 ——Another copy. 210 x 151 mm.

Without rubrication; woodcut uncolored. Half modern morocco and cloth. Booklabel of Philip Hofer.

28 February 1942—Gift of Philip Hofer. Typ Inc 5998

3152 Fulgosius, Baptista: Anteros. 10 May 1496.

4°. [80] leaves (80 blank); ill.; 214 x 151 mm.

Includes a poem by Piatino Piati.

This copy varies from the BMC and GW transcriptions of the caption on a2r: "PLATINVS IN ANTEROTA ILLVSTRIS ‖ BAPTITAE. C. FVLGOSI AD LECTOREM." Woodcut initials; space, with guide-letter, on a3v not filled in; woodcut uncolored. Contemporary half blind-tooled leather and wooden boards, front board split and spine damaged; fragments of leather thongs nailed to front cover, brass latches on back; clasps and thongs gone. MS ownership notation on title page, "Domus Auariciorum [illegible word]." Blank leaf not present.

HCR 7393; Pr 5999; BMC 6:781 (IA.26682); Pell 4937; GW 10424; IGI 4107; Goff F-329; Schäfer 135; Rogledi Manni 451; Sander 2946.

Countway Library (William Norton Bullard Collection)

3153 Lucanus, Marcus Annaeus: Pharsalia. 4 May 1499.

f°. [218] leaves; 304 x 208 mm.

Includes the commentaries of Omnibonus Leonicenus and Johannes Sulpitius, revised by Johannes Taberius.

Initial spaces, some with guide-letters, not filled in; without rubrication. Removed from a binding, with headband, cords, and sewing visible on spine; in a cloth case. MS ownership notation on title page, "Ex lib. Philippi [illegible] Nouocomensis." MS marginalia. Imperfect: title page mounted; aa2-3 mutilated, affecting text; half of A6 cut away.

H 10243; Oates 2304 (with collation and transcriptions); IGI 5824; Goff L-308; CIBN L-242; Rogledi Manni 578.

31 March 1931—Received by exchange. Inc 6003.5

3154 Melchior de Parma: Dialogi de anima. 29 August 1499.

a1v: (L³)Vdouicus Maria Sfortia Anglus Dux Mediolani ⳇc. Papie Angle ‖ rieq₃ Comes ... Cõposuit vt accepimus ‖ Veneᷓ. Frater Melchion [sic] Parmeñ. ordinis Diui Francisci librum de ‖ anima quem Dyalogum appellauit: ... a3r, col. 1: (I²)Ncipit liber primus Dyalo ‖ gorum de anima editus a fra ‖ tre parmense ordinis minorum ... n5v, col. 2, COLOPHON: Impressu₃. Mediolani ꝑ. Magistru₃ ‖ Leonardum pacchel anno domini. ‖ M.cccc.lxxxxix die .xxix. augusti. ‖ n6r, col. 1: ⳏ Incipit tabula totius libri. ‖ o5v, col. 2, line 7: dergli libro secũdo .329. vsque ad .336. ‖

f°. a-l⁸, m-o⁶ (o6 blank); [1], 2-105, [1] leaves ([106] blank; 6 and 68 misnumbered 4 and 60); ill.; 272 x 194 mm. 2 columns. a3r: 38 lines and headline, 177 x 142 mm. Type: 94G. Woodcuts; woodcut initials; one Lombard on a3r.

Text in Italian.

Without rubrication; woodcuts uncolored. Modern brown morocco, edges gilt, by Lortic, with the arms of Victor Masséna, prince d'Essling, stamped in gilt on covers and with his monogram in the spine panels (no. 177 in the Galerie Fischer sale catalogue, May 1939). Booklabel of Philip Hofer. Blank leaf not present.

HR 11045; Pr 6003; IGI 6351; Goff M-473; Rogledi Manni 644; Sander 4486.

28 February 1942—Gift of Philip Hofer. Typ Inc 6003

P R I N T E R   O F   B A R B A T I A ,
C O N S I L I A   (H   2 4 2 6)

3155 Accoltis, Franciscus de: Super secunda parte Infortiati. 29 October 1492.

f°. [64] leaves (1 and 64 blank); 396 x 282 mm.

Edited by Thomas de Pontremolo. Printed for Petrus Antonius de Castelliono.

Initial spaces, with guide-letters, not filled in; without rubrication. Occasional MS. marginalia. Old vellum.

H 55*; GW 152 (corrected by insert); Goff A-20; BSB-Ink A-17; Rogledi Manni 3.

26 September 1946—Received. Law Library

P H I L I P P U S   D E   M A N T E G A T I I S

3156 Galeottus, Martius: Liber de homine. 19 November 1490.

f°. [88] leaves; 231 x 187 mm.

Includes Georgius Merula, *In librum De homine Martii Galeotti* and Galeottus's *Refutatio obiectorum in librum De homine a Georgio Merula.* Printed by De Mantegatiis for Andreas Lelius and Franciscus Tantius.

Harvard has quires h–o^6 only, the *Refutatio.* Initial spaces, with guide-letters, not filled in; without rubrication. Half modern vellum and orange boards. Occasional MS marginalia.

HC 7434*; Pr 6051; BMC 6:784 (IB.26823); Pell 4978; IGI 4132; Goff G-43; CIBN M-187; Rogledi Manni 457.

Countway Library (William Norton Bullard Collection)

3157 Gafurius, Franchinus: Theorica musicae. 15 December 1492.

f°. [68] leaves; ill.; 268 x 198 mm.

Includes a poem by Lancinus Curtius. Printed by De Mantegatiis for Johannes Petrus de Lomatio.

Initial spaces, with guide-letters, not filled in; without rubrication. Leaves numbered in MS, with book numbers added in MS in the upper margins and MS catchwords on the verso of the last leaf of each quire. Old limp vellum. MS ownership notations on title page, "Est [illegible] Ioannis Gaibelij" and "Gio. Agostino Carrocio"; book-label of Adriana R. Salem. MS poem (5 distichs in Carrocio's hand) on k8v. Lower edge of title page remargined.

HCR 7406; Pr 6055; BMC 6:785 (IB.26831); Polain 1528; GW 10437; IGI 4115; Goff G–6; Hirsch I:191; Rogledi Manni 454; Sander 2982.

December 1959—Gift of Ward M. Canaday. Inc 6055

3158 Honorius Augustodunensis: Elucidarius. 22 March 1493.

4°. [52] leaves; 216 x 150 mm.

Printed by De Mantegatiis for Bernardinus de Scharliono. Edited by Pantaleo Cusanus.

Initial spaces, with guide-letters, not filled in; without rubrication. Bound in a vellum leaf of 15th-century Latin MS. MS ownership notations blotted out on title page and f8v; another on f8v, "Est Jo. Antonij Rouerini et Amicorum." Occasional MS marginalia; leaves numbered in MS.

HCR 6139; Pr 6056; BMC 6:786 (IA.26833); IGI 5854; Goff H–324; Rogledi Manni 584.

18 February 1890—Gift of the Massachusetts Historical Society. Inc 6056

3159 ——Another copy. 204 x 142 mm.

Initial spaces not filled in; without rubrication. Half modern vellum and marbled boards; edges stained green. In MS in lower margin of f1r, "frater deodatus di Pisauro ord^s. Seruo[rum]."

Countway Library

3160 Judicium cum tractatibus planetariis. 20 December 1496.

[For transcriptions see Reichling.] 4°. a–e⁴; [2], 2–19 leaves; ill.; 172 x 127 mm. a4r: 32 lines, 137 x 86 mm. Type: 5:87G. Black-ground woodcut initial on a2r, Lombards elsewhere.

Without rubrication. Modern brown morocco, edges gilt.

HR 9469; IGI 5427; Goff J–496; CIBN J–321; Rogledi Manni 529; Sander 3676.

November 1958—Gift of Harrison D. Horblit. Inc 6063.5

GUILLAUME LE SIGNERRE

3161 Gafurius, Franchinus: Practica musicae. 30 September 1496.

f°. [112] leaves (112 blank); ill.; 282 x 202 mm.

Includes a poem by Lucinus Conagus. Printed by Le Signerre for Johannes Petrus de Lomatio.

Woodcut initial at beginning of dedication and of each book; spaces elsewhere, with guide-letters, not filled in; without rubrication; woodcuts uncolored. Modern blind-stamped vellum, rehinged; edges stencilled red. MS ownership notation "Erhardvs Satheerg [?]" dated 1533 on verso of blank leaf at end; monogram bookstamp "T" with other indecipherable letters on same leaf; bookplate "Bibliothek des musikhistorischen Museums von Wilhelm Heyer in Cöln"; booklabel of Philip Hofer.

HC 7407; Pr 6067; BMC 6:789 (IB.26883); Pell 4949; Polain 1529; GW 10434; IGI 4112; Goff G-3; Hirsch I:192; Rogledi Manni 453; Sander 2983.

28 February 1942–Gift of Philip Hofer. Typ Inc 6067

AMBROSIUS DE CAPONAGO

3162 Statuta civilia Mediolanensia reformata a Ludovico Maria Sfortia duce. 10 November 1498.

f°. [16], 144, [2] leaves ([1] and [16] blank); 283 x 207 mm.

Printed by De Caponago for Alexander Minutianus.

Initial on a1r added in brown. Half modern brown morocco and marbled boards. Heavily annotated in the margins in several hands; some of the marginalia slightly trimmed. Blank leaves not present.

HR 15011; IGI 6325-A (with collation and transcriptions); Goff S-718; CIBN S-399; Rogledi Manni 640.

2 June 1913–Bought with the Bayard Cutting fund. Inc 6074.5

JOHANNES BISSOLUS AND BENEDICTUS MANGIUS

3163 Suidas: Lexicon Graecum. 15 November 1499.

f°. [516] leaves; 343 x 241 mm.

Suidas (more properly, Suda) is the name of the lexicon, not the author. Edited by Demetrius Chalcondylas. Includes verses by Antonius Motta and Johannes Salandus, a dialogue by Stephanus Niger, and a dedicatory letter by Johannes Maria Cataneus. There are variants on ZZ6r; see BMC.

This copy has the misprints recorded by BMC on ZZ6r. Initial spaces, some with guide-letters, not filled in; without rubrication. 16th-century blind-stamped pigskin over wooden boards; brass clasp plates on back cover, latches on front, clasps with pigskin thongs; brass corner bosses on both covers. MS note in a 16th-century hand on ZZ6r, "Emptus est iste liber & ligatur pretio 5 florinorum." Bookplate of William Horatio Crawford (no. 3039 in the Sotheby sale catalogue, March 1891); MS notes of Herbert Weir Smyth. Blank lower third of the first leaf cut away and replaced.

HC 15135*; Pr 6077; BMC 6:792 (IC.26913); Polain 3631; IGI 9189; Goff S–829; CIBN S–495; Rogledi Manni 942.

1937–From the library of Herbert Weir Smyth. Inc 6077 (A)

3164 ——Another copy. 341 x 235 mm.

In this copy the misprints on ZZ6r have been corrected, as in BMC IC.26914–15. Initial spaces not filled in; without rubrication. 18th-century calf, rebacked. MS ownership notations on first leaf, "M Bochart" and "Dr. Henry's Library Linlithgow."

6 December 1909–Bought with the Charles Eliot Norton fund. Inc 6077 (B)

3165 ——Another copy.

Not located.

Countway Library (William Norton Bullard Collection)

JOHANNES   ANGELUS
SCINZENZELER

3166 Tudeschis, Nicolaus de: Lectura super quinque libris Decretalium. 20 June–12 November 1500.

[For transcriptions see Reichling; but his title page for vol. 3 should read "Abbas super secun ‖ da secundi."] f°. 5 pts. in 8 vols. (vol. 1, pt. 1: a–r^8; [136] leaves; pt. 2: AA–SS^8; [1], 2–144 leaves; vol. 2: a–t^8, v–x^6; [1], 2–164 leaves; vol. 3, pt. 1: aa–qq^8, rr^6, rr6 blank; [134] leaves; pt. 2: aaa–nnn^8; [1], 2–104 leaves, 60 misnumbered 50; vol. 4: A–Z^8; [1], 2–184 leaves, 101 and 116 misnumbered 100 and 119; vol. 5, pt. 1: AA^6, BB–DD^8, EE^6, FF^4; [40] leaves; pt. 2: AAA–OOO^8; [1], 2–111, [1] leaves); 433 x 292 mm. 2 columns. vol. 2, a3r: 78 lines, 317 x 189 mm. (with side-notes, 244 mm.). Types: 1:160G, headings; 2:82G, text. Initial spaces, with guide-letters.

Edited by Bernardinus Landrianus, with additions by Antonius de Butrio, Bartholomaeus de Bellincinis, Antonius Corsettus, and Bernardus Parmensis. Printed by Scinzenzeler for Johannes de Legnano.

The Harvard set lacks the two parts of vol. 1, for the collation of which I rely on Reichling. Initial spaces not filled in; without rubrication. The six volumes present are bound in half modern vellum and decorated boards. Two of them have MS note, "Pertinet ad locum Sancti Francisci [illegible word]." Imperfect: besides the two lacking volumes the title page of vol. 5, pt. 1, is wanting.

CR 4589; IGI 9763, 9769, 9787, 9819, 9836, and 9852; Goff P-55.

Law Library

3167 Nonius Marcellus: De proprietate Latini sermonis. 1500.

[For transcriptions see Copinger.] f°. a^4, b–i^8, k^4, l–m^6, n^8, o^6, oo^8, p–r^6, s^4 (s4 blank); [4], LII, [34], xix, [3] leaves ([xxii] blank); 280 x 203 mm. 2 columns (6 in the *tabula*). b2r: 62 lines, 248 x 159 mm. Types: 10:80R; occasional Gk. Initial spaces, with guide-letters.

Includes Sextus Pompeius Festus, *De verborum significatione*, Marcus Terentius Varro, *De lingua Latina*, and a prefatory letter by Johannes Baptista Pius. Both Copinger and Balsamo are in error in giving the number of leaves as 112. Copinger gives an inadequate signature collation ("a–o, oo, p–s"), while Balsamo gives none at all. I extrapolate the final four quires of this imperfect copy, which is a more or less page-for-page reprint of the Venice, Antonius de Gusago, 1498 edition (see no. 2736 in vol. 2), as p–r⁶, s⁴, in which case the number of leaves is 128, with the final blank.

Initial spaces not filled in; without rubrication. Half 19th-century dark green straight-grain morocco and marbled boards. MS ownership notation on title page partly erased ("Joannes" still visible); bookplate of the Duke of Sussex (not located in the Evans sale catalogues, 1844–45); autograph "J. A. Jeremie 1847" on flyleaf at front; from the library of Richard Ashhurst Bowie. Imperfect: quires p–s (Varro's *De lingua Latina*) wanting.

HC 11909; IGI 6938; Goff N–274; CIBN N–160; Rogledi Manni 703; Balsamo 9.

9 November 1908—Gift of Mrs. E. D. Brandegee. Inc 6078.5

(3167a) Socinus, Bartholomaeus: Scripta super varios titulos iuris. ca. 1503.

f°. 7 pts.; 396 x 276 mm.

For a description see Sack. Harvard has 4 of the 7 pts., now each bound separately but showing by the consecutive MS numbering of the leaves that they were once bound together. These pts., which are found separately, are assigned by various catalogues to printers in Pavia or Milan and are dated conjecturally between 1496 and 1500. Printed by Johannes Angelus Scinzenzeler and Alexander Minutianus for Johannes Jacobus de Legnano, whose publisher's device in its first state (1503) appears in one of the parts not present here.

Initial spaces, with guide-letters, not filled in; without rubrication. Each part bound in half modern vellum and gray boards. MS ownership notation in pt. 1, "Seb: Franc: Grezinger."

H 14842; Goff S–590, 593, 601, and 603; Sack (3245a); Rogledi Manni 925–28 (citing Goff only).

10 May 1946—Received. Law Library

ALEXANDER MINUTIANUS

3168 Juvenalis, Decimus Junius: Satirae. 1500?

[For transcriptions see Reichling.] f°. a–i⁶, k⁸ (a1 and k8 blank); [62] leaves (1 and 62 blank); 287 x 199 mm. a3r: 38 lines, 215 x 90 mm.

Type: 2:111R. Woodcut initial on a2r; spaces elsewhere.

Includes the satires of Persius.

Initial spaces not filled in; without rubrication. Half 19th-century dark green morocco and marbled boards. Blank leaves not present.

R 578; Pr 6080; IGI 5604; Goff J-641; Rogledi Manni 552.

13 October 1916—Bought with the Constantius fund. Inc 6080

UNASSIGNED

3169 Ubaldis, Baldus de: Super I-IX Codicis. 10 May-15 November 1487.

vol. 1, a2r: Quemadmodum Baldus perusinus conspicue Iuris prudentie vir. cũ in humanis vitam ageret ... ‖ line 16: Incipit nouissima ᴛ emendatissima impressio com‖mentariorum summi vtriusqȝ iuris interpretis Baldi d' ‖ Perusia super libro codicis Iustiniani cum additõibus ‖ siue apostillis iurisconsulti clarissimi Alexandri Tarta‖gnini de Imola. ‖ cc5v, col. 1, line 45: Baldi pusini iuriscõsulti clarissimi ĩ primũ ƀm ᴛ terti‖um librum Codicis Iustĩaniani [sic]. lectura diligenti studio ‖ ac cura emendata correctaqȝ. feliciter explicit. ‖ Impressuȝ Mli. ‖ col. 2: Registrum ... ‖ col. 3: ... sideat scd'o ‖

vol. 2, a2r: Quemadmodum. Baldus perusinus conspicue Iuris prudentie vir: cum in humanis vitam ageret ... ‖ line 16: Opus domini Baldi de perusio iuris vtriusqȝ doc‖toris super quarto libro Codicis. ‖ z6r, col. 1, line 48: Digna perusini lectura nouissima Baldi. ‖ Codicis in quinto clauditur arte noua. ‖ [Impressuȝ Mli. (? hole in the paper)] col. 2: Registrum ... ‖ col. 3: ... tibus sufficit ‖

vol. 3, a2r: Opus domini bal. d'Perusio iuris vtriusqȝ docto‖ris super sexto libro Codicis. ‖ z5v, line 61: in ‖ glo. que incipit sed quid de statu liberis   diligenter no. ‖ Finis. ‖ z6r: Registrum ... ‖ col. 4: ... quid tenet iudiciuȝ ‖

vol. 4, a2r: Lectura petie noue iuris utriusqȝ interp̄tis. d. Baldi ‖ de perusio suꝑ septimo. C. Que cũ trãscriptoruȝ ĩperitia ‖ aut veteris petie exẽplari aut nulla a doctis ĩ erroribus ‖ corrigendis Retroactis tẽporibus adhibita diligentia. ‖ ee9r, COLOPHON: Baldi Perusini iurisconsulti clarissimi ĩ septimuȝ. ‖ octauum. ᴛ nonum. libruȝ Codicis. Iustiniani lectura di‖ligẽti studio ac cura emendata correctaqȝ feliciter expli‖cit. Opus quidẽ utile immo necessarium o ĩbus. Tam põ‖tifici   ciuil' iuris professoribus. Impressũ Ml'i. Anno ‖

salutis. M.cccc.lxxvij [*sic*]. Regnante Ilustrissimo ꝗ excel‖lētissimo Duce Joh'e. Galleazio. Decī o septī o kal'. d'cēb'. ‖ ee9v: Registrum ... ‖ col. 3: ... In tex. ‖

f°. 4 vols. in 2 (vol. 1: a^8, $B-S^8$, $T-X^6$, $y-z^8$, τ^8, ρ^8, $\not{z}^8$, aa^8, $bb-cc^6$, a1 and cc6 blank; [222] leaves, 1 and 222 blank; vol. 2: $a-p^8$, q^{10}, $r-y^8$, z^6, a1 and q10 blank; [184] leaves, 1 and 130 blank; vol. 3: $a-e^8$, $f-g^6$, h-n^8, o^6, p^8, q^6, $r-y^8$, z^6, a1 blank; [174] leaves, 1 blank; vol. 4: $a-i^8$, k^6, $l-n^8$, o^6, p^4, $A-F^{10}$, $aa-bb^8$, cc^{10}, dd^8, ee^{10}, a1 and ee10 blank; [216] leaves, 1 and 216 blank); 419 x 285 mm.

I give transcriptions and collations for all 4 volumes, since according to the BMC transcriptions for vols. 3–4 (they lack vols. 1–2) there are variant settings. BMC has note: "The edition of Baldus on the Code of which part is catalogued below was printed at Milan for the chief publishing firm at Venice, De Colonia, Jenson & Co., with Jenson's types, in 1487 ... The book was possibly executed in the office of Pachel and Scinzenzeler."

Initials and paragraph marks added in red or blue. Half 16th-century blind-stamped pigskin and wooden boards; fragments of leather thongs nailed to back cover, latches on front, clasps and thongs gone.

H 2284+2289; Pell 1724; BMC 6:796 (IC.26980); IGI 9946, 9950, 9959, and 9962; Goff U–13; Rogledi Manni 1035, 1036, and 1040.

15 July 1938–Received. Law Library

Bologna

BALTHASAR AZOGUIDUS

3170 Antoninus Florentinus: Confessionale "Curam illius habe" [Italian]. 1472.

4°. [96] leaves (1 blank); 237 x 165 mm.

Includes: *Trattato dell'excomunicazione.*–Thomas Aquinas, *Orazione laquale diceva quando andava a celebrare.*–*Orazione che se fa dopo la comunione.*–*Li Dieci Comandamenti volgare fatti in rima.*–*Credo volgare fatto in rima.* There is a variant setting on [a]2r; see BMC and GW.

This copy has the main BMC and GW transcription for [a]2r. Initials and paragraph marks added in red or blue. Vertical catchwords on the inner margin of the last page of most quires. Half 19th-century red morocco and marbled boards. Bookplate of James Frothingham Hunnewell, with his note "From the Hastie-Tracy library" (no. 2945 in the Leavitt sale catalogue of the library of Peter Hastie and Edward H. Tracy, January 1877). Leaf [k]10 misbound after [m]7; quires [l-m] misbound after [e]6. Imperfect: leaf [m]8 wanting; blank leaf not present.

HCR 1229; Pr 6515; BMC 6:799 (IA.28515); GW 2075; IGI 611; Goff A-782.

January 1919—Deposited by James M. Hunnewell. Inc 6515

3171 Diodorus Siculus: Bibliothecae historicae libri VI. 1472.

f° and 4°. [102] leaves (94, 101-02 blank); 282 x 215 mm.

Latin translation by Johannes Franciscus Poggius Bracciolinus. Includes the *Germania* of Tacitus. BMC and GW give variant collations for this book.

The collation of this copy, which has MS quiring, agrees with that of the BMC. Initials on [a]2 illuminated in gold and colors, with an illuminated coat of arms within a wreath with initials "I. B." in the lower margin; initials and paragraph marks elsewhere added in red or blue. Half 18th-century vellum and cream boards. MS marginalia. MS note by Michael Wodhull inside front cover (no. 910 in the Sotheby sale catalogue of books from his library, January 1886). Imperfect: leaf [a]1 misbound after [m]5; leaf [a]2 remargined; quire [n] inserted from another copy and remargined; blank leaves [n]7-8 not present.

HCR 6188; Pr 6516; BMC 6:799 (IB.28518); Pell 4266; GW 8374; IGI 3451; Goff D-210; Sack 1252.

30 December 1955—Gift of Mrs. Charles W. Clark. Inc 6516

3172 Statuta civilia civitatis Bononiae. After 28 February 1475.

f°. [126] leaves (126 blank); 331 x 237 mm.

Large initial on [a]1r illuminated in gold and colors; illuminated coat of arms within a wreath in the lower margin, but with the charges obliterated; initials elsewhere and paragraph marks added in red or blue. Old vellum, backed in paper. Circular bookstamp with motto "Omnia pondere et mensvra" on [a]1r, along with two other smudged and illegible bookstamps. Title in ink on lower edges. Heavily annotated in the margins throughout. Inserted at end are four leaves of MS "Comentum Statuti de Successionibus Ab intestato."

HR 14998; BMC 12:58 (IB.28526); IGI 1997; Goff S-707; CIBN S-392 ("Ugo Ruggeri ou Annibale Malpigli?, circa 1476").

27 November 1945–Received. Law Library

SCIPIO MALPIGLIUS

3173 Conti, Giusto de': La bella mano. 1472.

8°. [74] leaves (see below); 210 x 145 mm.

Both BMC and GW describe leaf [k]1 as blank, but both BMC copies lack that leaf, as do many of the copies recorded by GW. In the first Harvard copy described below [k]1 would seem to be a cancellans prepared to replace [a]6, though the cancellation has not been carried out ([a]5–6 are conjugate in both Harvard copies, as they are in both British Library copies). Leaf [a]6r contains 25 lines of text, with line 20 reading "De mie fortune e di passati affanni"; [k]1r contains the normal 24 lines of text, without the above-quoted line 20; [a]6r, line 10 ends "mi cõdãna"; on [k]1r that line ends "mi conforta." Includes a poem by Johannes Baptista de Refrigeriis.

On [a]1r an initial has been added in brown in a vine stem and floral bud design with marginal extension; a few other initials added in red, blue, or gold, but many in brown. 19th-century dark green morocco, gilt, edges gilt, by C. Lewis. Birth and death records in MS, dated between 1526 and 1561, on blank [a]1r. Armorial bookplate of Alexander Hamilton Douglas, 10th duke of Hamilton (no. 600 in the Sotheby sale catalogue, May 1884); bookplate of James Frothingham Hunnewell.

HC 5543; Pr 6524; BMC 6:802 (IA.28554); Pell 3885; GW 7454; IGI 3183; Goff C-786.

January 1919–Deposited by James M. Hunnewell. Inc 6524 (A)

3174 ——Another copy. 204 x 129 mm.

Initial on [a]2r illuminated in gold and colors, with marginal extension; initials elsewhere added in gold, red, or blue. In this copy, "cõdãna" in line 10 on [a]6r has been scraped away and "cõforta" written in. Modern brown morocco. Leaf [k]1 not present.

1965–Gift of Ward M. Canaday. Inc 6524 (B)

JOHANNES VURSTER

3174A Silvaticus, Matthaeus: Liber pandectarum medicinae. July 1474.

f°. [356] leaves (1, 7, and 356 blank); 358 x 238 mm.

Edited by Matthaeus Moretus. Printed by Vurster with Dominicus de Lapis. For a collation varying from that given by BMC see Sack.

This copy agrees with Sack's collation ([xx^{12}, yy^{2}]). A few initials added in brown, but most spaces not filled in; without rubrication. Half modern leather and paste-paper boards. Bookplate of James Frothingham Hunnewell. Imperfect: leaves [tt]8 and [xx]3 wanting; blank leaves not present; top margins of leaves mouse-eaten.

H 15195*; Pr 7189 (assigned to Vurster's press at Modena); BMC 6:803 (IC.28603); IGI 8980; Goff S–511; Sack 3235.

January 1919–Deposited by James M. Hunnewell. Inc 6524.5

PRINTER OF BARBATIA, *REPETITIO* (H 2438)

3175 Barbatia, Andreas: Repetitio rubricae: De fide instrumentorum. 1 February 1474.

f°. [32] leaves (32 blank); 437 x 282 mm.

Initial on [a]1r illuminated in gold and colors; paragraph marks added in red. MS quiring; leaves foliated in MS 144–76. Occasional MS marginalia. Half modern white pigskin and maroon cloth.

HC 2438; Pr 6525; BMC 6:804 (IC.28574); Pell 1833; GW 3357; IGI 1226; Goff B–111.

1 November 1949–Received. Law Library

UGO RUGERIUS

3176 Manilius, Marcus: Astronomicon. 20 March [i.e., May?] 1474.

f°. [88] leaves (1 and 30 blank); 302 x 207 mm.   Plate VII

The date in the colophon (20 March) is called into question by the fact that at least two copies are known in which the text on leaf 2v of Rugerius's edition of Valerius Flaccus (7 May 1474) appears on the verso of [h]8 of Manilius, blank in most copies, having been used as furniture and accidentally inked. Quires [i-k⁸, l⁶] contain the *Phaeno-mena* of Aratus in the Latin translation of Germanicus Caesar; the lower margins of most of these leaves are left blank for the insertion of pictures of the signs of the zodiac and the constellations referred to in the text, a guide to their order being printed on [h]8r. Printed by Rugerius with Doninus Bertochus.

Initial spaces not filled in; without rubrication. Modern calf, blind- and gilt-stamped; edges gilt. This work was originally bound with a copy of the 1482 Euclid printed by Ratdolt at Venice, both belonging to the 16th-century Italian humanist Sebastiano Serico; the volume was later in the library of Antaldo Antaldi of Pesaro, but sometime in the 20th century the two works were separated and bound individually. The Manilius is heavily annotated by Serico and contains his collation of variant readings found in a "codex vetustissimus" (cf. his MS note on verso of blank [a]1). For a description of the volume in its original form, see L. S. Olschki, "Un volume con postille autografe ed inedite dell'umanista Sebastiano Serico," *La Bibliofilia* 1 (1899): 12–17.

HCR 10707; Pr 6526; BMC 6:805 (IB.28583); IGI 6126; Goff M–203; CIBN M–86.

7 April 1958—Gift of Harrison D. Horblit. Inc 6526

3177 Burchiello: Sonetti. 3 October 1475.

4°. [90] leaves; 185 x 135 mm.

Initials added in red or blue (by a modern hand?) over initials originally added in brown; text ruled in red throughout. 19th-century red straight-grain morocco, gilt, edges gilt; blue moiré silk lining leaves. Booklabel of Adriana R. Salem. First two and last two leaves remargined.

H 4096; GW 5739; Goff B–1287.

August 1959—Gift of Ward M. Canaday. Inc 6530.5

3178 Aristoteles: Ethica ad Nicomachum. ca. 1475.

4°. [90] leaves (90 blank); 228 x 155 mm.

Latin translation by Leonardus Brunus Aretinus. BMC has note, "This tract has been retained under Rugerius, where Proctor placed it ... but it may belong rather to H. Malpiglius."

Initial spaces not filled in; without rubrication. MS quiring. Old vellum. First few leaves heavily annotated in the margins but only occasionally thereafter. Booklabels of Walter Sneyd (no. 53 in the Sotheby sale catalogue, December 1903) and of George Dunn (no. 762 in pt. 2 of the Sotheby sale catalogue, February 1914).

HCR 1742; H 1744?; Pr 6532; BMC 6:806 (IA.28598); GW 2369; IGI 819; Goff A–986.

13 October 1916–Gift of Mrs. E. D. Brandegee. Inc 6532

3179 Sandeus, Ludovicus: Sonetti. After 1 July 1485.

4°. [24] leaves; 193 x 133 mm.

Edited by Alexander Sandeus, the author's son; includes poems by Antonius Tebaldeus. BMC has note, "This book was catalogued among the Italian adespota by Proctor (no. 7416), with the note: 'perhaps printed at Pisa'. The type differs slightly from that in the signed work of Rugerius."

Initial space on a2r, with guide-letter, not filled in; without rubrication. Old vellum.

R 1622; Pr 7416; BMC 6:807 (IA.28793); IGI 8620; Goff S–160a.

April 1962–Bought with the Amy Lowell fund. Inc 6563.5

3180 Bologninus, Ludovicus: Syllogianthon. 10 January 1486.

f°. [152] leaves; 270 x 195 mm.

Initial spaces, most with guide-letters, not filled in; without rubrication. For binding description see no. 426 in vol. 1, Goffredus de Trano, *Summa super titulos Decretalium* (Cologne, Ludwig von Renchen, ca. 1488), which is bound with this.

HC 3439*; Pr 6564; BMC 6:807 (IB.28794); Pell 2569; Polain 752; GW 4637; IGI 1875; Goff B–842; BSB-Ink B–635.

21 April 1932–From the Fürstliche Stolberg zu Wernigerode Bibliothek. Law Library

3181 Auctoritates Aristotelis et aliorum philosophorum. 15 April 1488.

4°. [68] leaves (1 blank); 215 x 150 mm.

This recension has title *Propositiones universales Aristotelis*, begins "Alexander magnus rex," and ends with the two propositions "Empedocles in libro suo."

Initial spaces not filled in; without rubrication; leaves numbered in MS. Modern blind-stamped sheep. Occasional MS marginalia. Bookplate of William Norton Bullard.

HC 1930*; Pr 6567A; BMC 6:808 (IA.28805); Pell 1268; GW 2834; IGI 947; Goff A–1200; BSB-Ink A–831.

Countway Library (William Norton Bullard Collection)

3182 **Samuel Maroccanus, Rabbi:** Epistola contra Iudaeorum errores. 13 May 1496.

4°. [28] leaves; 185 x 133 mm.

Translated by Alphonsus Boni Hominis. Includes a letter from Fridericus de Manfredis and the *De sacerdotio Iesu Christi* of Ambrosius Traversarius.

Initials added in brown. Half 19th-century red cloth and marbled boards. Smudged and illegible bookstamp on a1r; bookplate of Lee M. Friedman.

H 14269*; Pr 6655; BMC 6:809 (IA.29174); IGI 8582; Goff S–112; CIBN S–58.

1957—Bequest of Lee M. Friedman. Inc 6655

3183 **Manfredis, Hieronymus de:** Liber de homine [Italian]. 4 March 1497.

f°. [56] leaves; 290 x 200 mm.

Initial spaces, most with guide-letters, not filled in; without rubrication. Half modern brown morocco and marbled boards. Autograph on flyleaf at front, "Ammi Brown 1852"; tipped in at front is an A.L.s. (Winslow Lewis) to J. L. Sibley, Librarian, Harvard College; Boston, 11 February 1857; 1 sheet (2 leaves); 'I send you another "incunable" and it is rather a rare work ...' Imperfect: leaves i4–6 mutilated, with some loss of text; sheet h2 misbound after b3.

HCR 10691; Pr 6657; BMC 6:810 (IB.29179); IGI 6113; Goff M–193; CIBN M–75.

16 February 1857—Gift of Winslow Lewis. Inc 6657

P R I N T E R   O F   B A R B A T I A ,
J O H A N N I N A   (H   2 4 2 9)

3184 Barbatia, Andreas: Johannina. Not before 1475.

f°. [100] leaves (1 blank); 436 x 282 mm.

There is a variant setting of the first few lines on [a]2r; cf. BMC and GW.

This copy has the readings of the main BMC and GW transcriptions on [a]2r. The first three quires have cropped fragments of printed signatures very low down in the lower margins, but if they were present elsewhere they have been trimmed away. Initial on [a]2r illuminated in gold and colors; columns numbered in MS. Occasional MS marginalia. Half modern white calf and maroon cloth. Blank leaf not present.

H 2429*=2430; Pr 6669; BMC 6:813 (IC.29272); Pell 1828; GW 3379; IGI 1219; Goff B–107; BSB-Ink B–67.

1 November 1949–Received. Law Library

D O M I N I C U S   D E   L A P I S

3185 Benedictus de Nursia: De conservatione sanitatis. 1477.

4°. [140] leaves; 205 x 148 mm.

Includes Thaddaeus Florentinus, *De regimine sanitatis*. Printed by De Lapis for Sigismundus de Libris.

Initial spaces, most with guide-letters, not filled in; without rubrication. Half 17th- or 18th-century pigskin and marbled boards; leather label on spine.

HC 11920*; Pr 6536; BMC 6:814 (IA.28617); GW 3819; IGI 1463; Goff B–314.

Countway Library (Solomon M. Hyams Collection)

H E N R I C U S   D E   C O L O N I A

3186 Lignano, Johannes de: De bello, repraesaliis, et duello. 17 December 1477.

[For transcriptions see Reichling.] f°. a⁸, b⁶, c⁸, d–f⁴, g⁶ (a1 and g6 blank); [40] leaves (1 and 40 blank); 392 x 273 mm. 2 columns. a2r: 62 lines, 280 x 160 mm. Type: 91G. Initial spaces.

With additions by Paulus de Lignano. Printed by Henricus for Sigismundus de Libris.

Initial spaces not filled in; without rubrication. Old limp vellum. Blank leaves not present.

HR 10092; IGI 5305; Goff L–215.

5 April 1929–Received. Law Library

3187 Manfredis, Hieronymus de: Tractatus de peste. After 31 December 1479.

a1r: Tractatus vtilis valde de peste compositus per magistrum ‖ Hieronimū de manfredis ciuem Bononiensem phisicū. ac astro ‖ logum dignissimum. ‖ f6v, COLOPHON: Per me Hieronimum de manfredis artium ꝛ ‖ medicine doctorem compositum hoc opuscu-‖sculum [*sic*] litterali sermone Bononie ‖ M.CCCC.LXXVIIII. ‖ die vltima decembris.

4°. a–f⁶; [36] leaves; 200 x 140 mm. a3r: 32 lines, 144 x 85 mm. Type: 91G. Initial spaces.

Several words have been omitted at the end of the last line on e4v and have been added in MS. Initials, paragraph marks, underlinings, and capital strokes added in red. Modern vellum. MS marginalia.

HR 10696*; IGI 6118; Goff M–196 (assigned to Johannes Walbeck).

Countway Library (William Norton Bullard Collection)

3188 Johannes de Anania: Commentaria super prima et secunda parte quinti Decretalium. 7 December 1479–5 January 1480.

[For transcriptions see Hain.] f°. 2 vols. (vol. 1, pt. 1: a⁸, b⁶, c¹⁰, d⁶, e⁸, f⁴, g⁸, a1 and g8 blank; pt. 2: a¹⁰, b–i⁸, k⁶, l–m⁸, n–o⁶, p–q⁸, r–s¹⁰, a1 blank; [194] leaves, 1, 50–51 blank; vol. 2: [210] leaves?); 443 x 288 mm. 3 columns. vol. 1, a3r: 62 lines, 280 x 170 mm. Type: 91G. Initial spaces.

Harvard has vol. 1 only. Initials, paragraph marks, and capital strokes added in red. 17th-century pigskin, backed in white doeskin with leather labels on spine; device stamped on front cover (crowned lion

passant guardant in upper half, three stars in lower); marks of clasps
and latches, no longer present; title in ink on lower edges. MS ownership notation in upper margin of a2r in vol. 1, "Monasterij S. Petri
Salisburgi, tt°. Legati Henricj Knoll, I.V.D. Anno Dñj 1639."

H 938*; IGI 5245 (vol. 1 only).

7 March 1955—Received. Law Library

J O H A N N E S   S C H R I B E R

3189 Soldus, Jacobus: Opus de peste. 1478.

4°. [36] leaves; 200 x 142 mm.

Includes a letter to the author by Jacobus Burgensis. Printed by
Schriber for Thomas de Bononia.

Initial spaces not filled in; without rubrication. Half 19th-century
sheep and blue boards.

HC 14870*; Pr 6548; BMC 6:818 (IA.28672); Polain 3558; IGI 9082;
Goff S–613; CIBN S–300.

Countway Library (William Norton Bullard Collection)

J O H A N N E S   D E   N Ö R D L I N G E N

3190 Zerbus, Gabriel: Quaestiones metaphysicae. 1 December 1482.

f°. [512] leaves; 302 x 205 mm.

Printed by Johannes de Nördlingen with Henricus de Harlem.

Initial spaces, some with guide-letters, not filled in; without rubrication. Old vellum.

H 16285*; Pr 6556A; BMC 6:820 (IB.28727); Polain 4067; IGI 10443;
Goff Z–27; CIBN Z–13.

29 December 1919—Bought with the John Harvey Treat fund. Inc 6556.5

3191 ——Another copy. 300 x 205 mm.

Initial spaces not filled in; without rubrication. Contemporary half
blind-stamped leather and wooden boards; leather thongs with brass

clasps nailed to back cover, latches on front; paper labels on spine and front cover. Monogram in ink on ᵏA1r, "CLN [?]."

Countway Library (William Norton Bullard Collection)

3192 Martinus Polonus: Margarita Decreti. 1482?

f°. [124] leaves; 297 x 205 mm.

Printed by Johannes de Nördlingen with Henricus de Harlem.

Initials added in red or blue; two small colored coats of arms in lower margin of leaves π2v and a1r. Modern red morocco.

HC 10836; Pr 6563 (assigned to Henricus de Harlem); BMC 6:820 (IB.28729); IGI 6238; Goff M–321; CIBN M–180.

18 August 1955—Received. Law Library

B A Z A L E R I U S   D E   B A Z A L E R I I S

3193 Istoria d'un mercadante Pisano. ca. 1490.

4°. [4] leaves; 207 x 154 mm.

For full description, with facsimile, see Giuseppe Martini, *Catalogo della libreria* I (Milano, 1934): 177–79. Without rubrication. Half 19th-century red straight-grain morocco and red boards. Bookplate of Giuseppe Martini.

Goff H–565.

24 January 1951—Bought with the Bennett Hubbard Nash fund. Inc 6578.5

3194 Petrus Ravennas: Phoenix. "10 January 1491[/2]" [i.e., after 10 January 1492].

4°. [16] leaves; 200 x 142 mm.

A piracy, reprinting the genuine edition of Bernardinus de Choris at Venice, with the colophon unaltered.

Initial space on b3r, with guide-letter, not filled in; without rubrication. Bound with Baldovinus Sabaudiensis, *Ars memoriae* (Paris, Antoine Caillaut, ca. 1482/84).

R 707; Pr 7420 (Italian adespota); BMC 7:1151 (IA.28860); IGI 7667; Goff P–532; CIBN P–268.

Countway Library

B A L T H A S A R   D E   H Y R B E R I A

3195 Ariostis, Alexander de: De usuris. 8–15 April 1486.

4°. [74] leaves (1 and 74 blank); 195 x 140 mm.

Printed by De Hyrberia for Jacobus de Peregrino.

Initial spaces not filled in; without rubrication. Old vellum. Blank leaves not present.

HC 1653; Pr 6573; BMC 6:821 (IA.28823); Pell 1172; GW 2329; IGI 788; Goff A–956; BSB-Ink A–671.

17 December 1919—Bought with the John Harvey Treat fund. Inc 6573

F R A N C I S C U S   (P L A T O)
D E   B E N E D I C T I S

3196 Baptista Mantuanus: Parthenice prima siue Mariana. 17 October 1488.

4°. [70] leaves; 194 x 147 mm.

Includes his *Ad Beatam Virginem votum*. Edited by Caesar de Nappis. Printed by De Benedictis for himself and Benedictus Hectoris Faelli. According to GW there are variant settings of a3–4, c1r, c2v, c7r, and c8v, but variant readings are given for a3r and c1r only.

This copy has the readings of the GW *Anmerkung* on a3r and c1r. Initial spaces, with guide-letters, not filled in; without rubrication. For binding description see no. 3198, the same printer's edition of Baptista's *De suorum temporum calamitatibus* (1 April 1489), with which this is bound, along with his *Parthenice secunda* (9 February 1489) and *In Robertum Severinatem panegyricum carmen* (21 July 1489).

H 2364*; Pr 6585; BMC 6:823 (IA.28869a); Pell 1760; Polain 4182; GW 3276; IGI 1179; Goff B–58; BSB-Ink B–52.

9 November 1908—Gift of Mrs. E. D. Brandegee. Inc 6587

3197 Baptista Mantuanus: Parthenice secunda siue Catharinaria. 9 February 1489.

4°. [44] leaves; 194 x 147 mm.

Edited by Franciscus Ceretus. Printed by De Benedictis for himself and Benedictus Hectoris Faelli. There are variants in the colophon on g6v; cf. GW.

This copy has the readings of the main GW transcription on g6v. Initial spaces, with guide-letters, not filled in; without rubrication. For binding description see next entry, the same printer's edition of Baptista's *De suorum temporum calamitatibus* (1 April 1489), with which this is bound, along with his *Parthenice prima* (17 October 1488) and *In Robertum Severinatem panegyricum carmen* (21 July 1489).

H 2371*; Pr 6586; BMC 6:823 (IA.28872a); Pell 1772; GW 3290; IGI 1184; Goff B–66; BSB-Ink B–56.

9 November 1908—Gift of Mrs. E. D. Brandegee. Inc 6587

3198 Baptista Mantuanus: De suorum temporum calamitatibus. 1 April 1489.

4°. [64] leaves; 194 x 147 mm.

Prefixed is his *Contra poetas impudice loquentes carmen*. Edited by Franciscus Ceretus. Printed by De Benedictis for himself and Benedictus Hectoris Faelli.

Initial spaces, with guide-letters, not filled in; without rubrication. Half 19th-century calf and marbled boards, rebacked; leather labels on spine. Table of contents in a 16th-century hand on blank a1r. MS ownership notation in upper margin of a2r, "Ad Bibl PP. Francis. Ingol."; circular bookstamp with initials "S M A I" (i.e., S. Maria Assumpta Ingolstadii) on lower edges; bookplate of Richard Ashhurst Bowie. With this are bound the same printer's editions of Baptista's *Parthenice prima* (17 October 1488), *Parthenice secunda* (9 February 1489), and *In Robertum Severinatem panegyricum carmen* (21 July 1489).

H 2386*; C 846; R 56; Pr 6587; BMC 6:823 (IA.28875a); Pell 1805; Polain 484; GW 3246; IGI 1197; Goff B–89; BSB-Ink B–38.

9 November 1908—Gift of Mrs. E. D. Brandegee. Inc 6587

3199 Maimonides, Moses, Rabbi: Aphorismi secundum doctrinam Galeni [Latin]. 29 May 1489.

4°. [158] leaves (134 blank); 205 x 145 mm.

Includes: Johannes Damascenus, *Aphorismi* [Latin].—Muhammad Rhazes, *De secretis in medicina* [Latin].—Hippocrates, *Capsula eburnea* [Latin translation by Gerardus Cremonensis]. Printed by De Benedictis for Benedictus Hectoris Faelli.

Initial on a1r added in red, blue, and brown; initials elsewhere added in red or blue. 18th-century red morocco, spine and edges gilt. Autograph on r5v, "Jacobus Pelerinus M.D. . . . 1614"; nautilus bookplate of Oliver Wendell Holmes; bookstamp of the Boston Medical Library dated 8 August 1908.

HC 10524*; Pr 6588; BMC 6:824 (IA.28878); IGI 6744; Goff M–77; Sack 2309.

Countway Library

3200   ——Another copy. 192 x 140 mm.

Initial spaces, with guide-letters, not filled in; without rubrication. Modern vellum. MS ownership notation washed away from lower margin of a1r but partly visible under ultraviolet light, "A° M.D. Joannis Antonij Barbar[ini?]."

Countway Library (Solomon M. Hyams Collection)

3201   **Baptista Mantuanus:** In Robertum Severinatem panegyricum carmen. 21 July 1489.

4°. [50] leaves; 194 x 147 mm.

Includes his *Somnium Romanum* and *Epigrammata ad Falconem*. Printed by De Benedictis for himself and Benedictus Hectoris Faelli.

Initial spaces, with guide-letters, not filled in; without rubrication. For binding description see no. 3198, the same printer's edition of Baptista's *De suorum temporum calamitatibus* (1 April 1489), with which this is bound, along with his *Parthenice prima* (17 October 1488) and *Parthenice secunda* (9 February 1489).

H 2394*; BMC 5:824 (IA.28881); Pell 1784; GW 3256; IGI 1194; Goff B–85; BSB-Ink B–48.

9 November 1908–Gift of Mrs. E. D. Brandegee. Inc 6587

3202   **Baveriis, Baverius de:** Consilia medica. 5 November 1489.

f°. [2], CLIX, [1] leaves ([CLX] blank; XVII–XVIII and CXXXXVI misnumbered XVI–XVII and CXXXVI); 309 x 210 mm.

With additions by Marcus Antonius and Ludovicus de Baveriis, sons of the author, and Philippus Beroaldus.

Initial spaces, some with guide-letters, not filled in; without rubrication. Half 18th-century calf and speckled boards; leather labels on spine. Bookplate of William Norton Bullard. Blank leaf not present.

HC 2712; Pr 6589; BMC 6:824 (IB.28882); Pell 2010; GW 3739; IGI 1423; Goff B–283; BSB-Ink B–242.

Countway Library (William Norton Bullard Collection)

3203 **Pseudo-Boccaccio, Giovanni:** Urbano. ca. 1490.

4°. [34] leaves; 214 x 145 mm.

Authorship variously attributed to Giovanni Buonsignori, Buonaccorsi da Ginestrata, and Cambio di Stefano. See Verdun L. Saulnier, "Boccace et la nouvelle française de la renaissance," *Revue de littérature comparée* 21 (1947): 404–13.

Initial spaces, with guide-letters, not filled in; without rubrication. Modern green calf, blind- and gilt-stamped. Booklabel of Adriana R. Salem.

HCR 3312; C 1076; Pr 6611; BMC 6:826 (IA.28939); Pell 2462; GW 4502; IGI 1812; Goff B–762.

August 1959—Gift of Ward M. Canaday. Inc 6611

3204 **Alberti, Johannes Michael:** De omnibus ingeniis augendae memoriae. 24 January 1491.

4°. [12] leaves; 201 x 147 mm.

Initial spaces, most with guide-letters, not filled in; without rubrication. 19th-century marbled boards. Bookplate of William Norton Bullard.

HC 426*; Pr 6591; BMC 6:824 (IA.28887); Pell 270; GW 570; IGI 48; Goff A–210; BSB-Ink C–155.

Countway Library (William Norton Bullard Collection)

3205 **Beroaldus, Philippus:** Orationes et carmina. 1491.

4°. [76] leaves; 204 x 151 mm.

Printed by De Benedictis for himself and Benedictus Hectoris Faelli.

Initial spaces, most with guide-letters, not filled in; without rubrication. Half 19th-century sheep and marbled boards, rehinged. Booklabel of Georg Kloss (no. 626 in the Sotheby sale catalogue, May 1835).

H 2949*; Pr 6594; BMC 6:825 (IA.28897); Pell 2210; Polain 4204; GW 4144; IGI 1602; Goff B-491; BSB-Ink B-380.

22 August 1856—Gift of Winslow Lewis. Inc 6594

3206   ——Another copy. 189 x 137 mm.

Initials on a1r added in brown; spaces elsewhere not filled in. Old limp vellum. The Vollbehr copy.

Countway Library (William Norton Bullard Collection)

3207 Politianus, Angelus: Epistola de obitu Laurentii Medicis. 25 July 1492.

4°. [6] leaves; 200 x 138 mm.

Without rubrication. For binding description see no. 2883, Politianus's *Silua cui titulus Manto* (Florence, Antonio di Bartolommeo Miscomini, 23 February 1491/2), with which this is bound, along with the same printer's editions of Politianus's *Praelectio cui titulus Panepistemon* (20 February 1491/2) and *Silua cui titulus Nutricia* (26 May 1491).

Accurti (1930) 131; IGI 7957; Goff P-888.

29 March 1918—Bought with the Charles Eliot Norton fund. Inc 6151.9

3208 Bossus, Matthaeus: Recuperationes Faesulanae. 20 July 1493.

f°. [184] leaves; 296 x 208 mm.

Includes a letter to the reader by Philippus Beroaldus.

Initial spaces, with guide-letters, not filled in; without rubrication. Modern vellum.

HC 3669*; Pr 6597; BMC 6:826 (IB.28906); Pell 2782; Polain 845; GW 4958; IGI 2022; Goff B-1045; BSB-Ink B-762.

14 September 1920—Bought with the Charles Eliot Norton fund. Inc 6597

3209   ——Another copy. 285 x 210 mm.

Initial spaces not filled in; without rubrication. 17th-century calf, hinges broken, edges stained red, with the name of Edward Gwynn stamped in gilt on front cover and with his initials on back; autograph and MS marginalia of Étienne Baluze (no. 1933 in vol. 1 of the Paris sale catalogue of his library, May 1719); autographs of Richard Bordes (in Greek) and of E. W. Skinner, dated 1892, on title page; engraved bookplate of Joseph Knight inside front cover; shelfmark of the Sunderland library (no. 1843 in pt. 1 of the Puttick & Simpson sale catalogue, December 1881). Imperfect: leaf O8 slightly mutilated.

Countway Library (William Norton Bullard Collection)

3210 Herodianus: Historia de imperio post Marcum Aurelium. 31 August 1493.

f°. [68] leaves; 307 x 204 mm.

Translated by Angelus Politianus.

Initial spaces, with guide-letters, not filled in; without rubrication. Modern vellum, with doeskin ties. MS inscription by the translator on blank aa1r (partly washed but still legible), "Mitto herodianū tibi qua forma estimaui minus mendosū. Ter enim pauculis diebus ī diuersis officinis impressus. Sed vero hūc quidem satis arbitror rectum. Quare iudicio interdū tuo mi Cesar erit elimandus. Vale. Politianus tuus." According to an A.L.s. by Maria Pisani laid in, "La persona cui è indirizzata la dedica sembra potersi identificare con Cesare Carmento, corrispondente del Poliziano." Quire ii⁴ wrongly folded.

HC 8467*; Pr 6598; BMC 6:827 (IB.28909); IGI 4690; Goff H–86; Sack 1799; CIBN H–52.

29 December 1958—Gift of Ward M. Canaday. Inc 6598

3211 Beroaldus, Philippus: De felicitate. 1 April 1495.

4°. [36] leaves (4 blank); 191 x 137 mm.

Initial spaces, with guide-letters, not filled in; without rubrication. 19th-century dark green morocco, edges gilt. From the library of Richard Ashhurst Bowie. Imperfect: printer's device cut away from last leaf.

HC 2969; Pr 6606; BMC 6:828 (IA.28928); Pell 2224; Polain 620; GW 4132; IGI 1594; Goff B–482; Sack 594; BSB-Ink B–365.

9 November 1908—Gift of Mrs. E. D. Brandegee. Inc 6606

3212 ——Another copy. 205 x 150 mm.

Initial spaces not filled in; without rubrication. Modern vellum. MS ownership notation washed away on title page but legible under ultra-violet light, "Ex libris Joannis Condulmarij."

Countway Library (William Norton Bullard Collection)

3213 Bossus, Matthaeus: De instituendo sapientia animo. 6 November 1495.

4°. [128] leaves; 193 x 146 mm.

Includes a poem by Antonius Aldegatus.

Initial spaces, most with guide-letters, not filled in; without rubrication. Half 19th-century calf and marbled boards, hinges weak; in a cloth case.

HC 3675=3677*; Pr 6609; BMC 6:828 (IA.28934); Pell 2781; Polain 4240; GW 4954; IGI 2020; Goff B–1043; Sack 789; BSB-Ink B–759.

Countway Library (William Norton Bullard Collection)

3214 Bossus, Matthaeus: Sermo in Jesu Christi passionem. 11 November 1495.

4°. [12] leaves; 192 x 140 mm.

Initial on a1r added in red, paragraph mark in blue. For binding description see no. 2975, the same author's *Dialogus de veris et salutaribus animi gaudiis* (Florence, Francesco Bonaccorsi, 8 February 1491), with which this is bound.

HC 3678*; Pr 6610; BMC 6:828 (IA.28937); Pell 2784; GW 4960; IGI 2025; Goff B–1047; BSB-Ink B–764.

28 April 1874—Bequest of Charles Sumner. Inc 6312

3215 Scriptores rei militaris. 10 July 1495–17 January 1496.

f°. [98] leaves; 270 x 195 mm.

In this edition the signatures are continuous. Edited by Philippus Beroaldus. Includes: Sextus Julius Frontinus, *Strategemata*.—Flavius Vegetius Renatus, *De re militari*, with the preface of Johannes Sulpitius reprinted from the 1487 edition.—Aelianus Tacticus, *De instruendis aciebus*, translated from the Greek by Theodorus Gaza.—Modestus, *De vocabulis rei militaris*.

Initials on AA2r and GG2r added in red, blue, and purple; initials elsewhere and paragraph marks added in red or blue. 18th-century calf, spine gilt, edges speckled red. From the library of Richard Ashhurst Bowie, with his note, "From the library of the University of Leyden." Imperfect: leaf RR1 mutilated, with some loss of text.

C 5330=2594; Pr 6607; BMC 6:828 (IB.28930); Pell 4933; Polain 3477; GW 10410; IGI 8852; Goff S-345; Sack 1488; CIBN S-173; BSB-Ink D-48.

9 November 1908—Gift of Mrs. E. D. Brandegee. Inc 6607

H E N R I C U S   D E   H A R L E M

3216 **Orbellis, Nicolaus de:** Compendium in mathematicam, physicam, et metaphysicam. 1485; 31 March 1485.

4°. 2 vols. (vol. 1: [104] leaves, 104 blank; vol. 2: [94] leaves, 1 blank); 197 x 145 mm.

Printed by Henricus with Matthaeus Crescentinus. Includes poems by Petrus Almadianus.

Harvard has vol. 1 only. Initial spaces, some with guide-letters, not filled in; without rubrication. Half 19th-century vellum and marbled boards. Several MS ownership notations obliterated on title page; bookplate of Raimondo Ambrosini, with his name scraped away, inside front cover; MS marginalia in the first four quires.

HR 12050 (incl H 12042 and H 12049); Pr 6558A and 6558C; BMC 6:830 (IA.28765); IGI 7016; Goff O-73; CIBN O-39.

11 September 1919—Bought with the Peter Paul Francis Degrand fund. Inc 6558.5

3217 **Savonarola, Michael:** De pulsibus, urinis, et egestionibus. 8 May 1487.

f°. [64] leaves (1 blank); 253 x 185 mm.

Printed by Henricus with Johannes Walbeck.

Initial spaces not filled in; without rubrication. Modern vellum.

HC 14490*; Pr 6559; BMC 6:830 (IB.28772); Polain 3468; IGI 8814; Goff S-299.

Countway Library (William Norton Bullard Collection)

3218 **Bernardus Parmensis:** Casus longi super quinque libros Decretalium. 29 November 1487.

f°. [220] leaves (1 blank); 301 x 210 mm.

Edited by Antonius Corsettus. Printed by Henricus with Johannes Walbeck. There is a variant on a2r; cf. GW.

This copy has the reading of the main GW transcription on a2r. Initials crudely added in brown. Half modern vellum and tan boards. MS marginalia. Imperfect: leaf C6, containing register and colophon, wanting.

HC 2934*; Pr 6560; BMC 6:830 (IB.28775); Pell 2196; GW 4099; IGI 1577; Goff B–459; Sack 587; BSB-Ink B–345.

12 January 1946—Received. Law Library

3219 **Saladinus de Asculo:** Compendium aromatariorum. 12 March 1488.

f°. [30] leaves (30 blank); 302 x 195 mm.

Printed by Henricus with Johannes Walbeck for Benedictus Hectoris Faelli.

Initial spaces, some with guide-letters, not filled in; without rubrication. Bound in a leaf of 15th-century Latin liturgical MS. Blank leaf not present.

HCR 14131; Pr 6561; BMC 6:831 (IB.28778); IGI 8500; Goff S–19; CIBN S–13.

Countway Library (William Norton Bullard Collection)

D I O N Y S I U S   B E R T O C H U S

3220 **Savonarola, Michael:** De febribus. 8 March 1487.

f°. [124] leaves (1 and 124 blank); 297 x 205 mm.

Initial spaces, some with guide-letters, not filled in; without rubrication. Contemporary boards, crudely backed in leather; marks of clasp plate and latch, no longer present. MS marginalia. Bookplate of William Norton Bullard. Imperfect: leaf l8 torn down the middle and crudely patched back together with sealing wax.

H 14487; Pr 6574; BMC 6:832 (IB.28833); Polain 3466; IGI 8808; Goff S-293; CIBN S-154.

Countway Library (William Norton Bullard Collection)

CALIGULA DE BAZALERIIS

3221 Beroaldus, Philippus: De felicitate. "1 April 1495" [i.e., ca. 1496?].

4°. [20] leaves; 210 x 152 mm.

A reprint of the Franciscus de Benedictis edition, with unaltered date.

Initial spaces, with guide-letters, not filled in; without rubrication. Half 19th-century calf and brown boards. Smudged bookstamp on title page; the Vollbehr copy.

HC 2968*; Pr 6615; BMC 6:836 (IA.28985); Pell 2223; GW 4133; IGI 1595; Goff B-483; BSB-Ink B-366.

Countway Library

3222 Statuta et decreta communis Genuae. 30 June [i.e., 4 July] 1498.

f°. [6], 87, [1], 29, [1] leaves ([88] blank); 303 x 203 mm.

Colophon dated 30 June but dedicatory letter dated 4 July 1498. Edited by Antonius Maria Viscominus. There is a variant on l6r; cf. BMC.

In this copy the last line on l6r reads as in BMC IB.28996a. Initial spaces, with guide-letters, not filled in; without rubrication. Modern vellum. MS marginalia. MS ownership notation on title page, "Dominici Cepollini J.C." Bound in at end are 27 leaves of Latin MS, the first 5 headed "Decreta criminalia nouiter cedita Anno M.D.xxxxviij," the rest in a later hand headed "Repertoriũ capitulorũ ordinariorum." Sheet h3 bound in upside-down.

HC 15007*; Pr 6619; BMC 6:837 (IB.28996–96a); Polain 3593; IGI 4211; Goff S-714; CIBN S-398.

20 September 1920—Bought with the Bayard Cutting fund. Inc 6619 (A)

3223 ——Another copy. 302 x 208 mm.

In this copy the last line on l6r reads as in BMC IB.28996. Initial spaces not filled in; without rubrication. Modern vellum, with old limp vellum covers bound in. Strip cut away at top of A1, probably to remove an ownership notation.

May 1963—Gift of Ward M. Canaday. Inc 6619 (B)

3224   ——Another copy. 270 x 190 mm.

In this copy the last line on 16r reads as in BMC IB.28996. Initial spaces not filled in; without rubrication. Old vellum.

Countway Library (William Norton Bullard Collection)

3225   **Cicero:** De finibus bonorum et malorum. 20 June 1499.

f°. [46] leaves; 298 x 195 mm.

This forms the fifth part of a collection of Cicero's philosophical works, the first four parts of which were printed by Bazalerius de Bazaleriis at Reggio Emilia, 1498–10 April 1499; the signatures of this part continue those of the other parts; see no. 3551. Includes Cicero's *Timaeus*, the *Somnium Scipionis*, and Quintus Tullius Cicero's *De petitione consulatus*.

Initial spaces, with guide-letters, not filled in; without rubrication. For binding description see no. 3551, the collection of Cicero's philosophical works referred to above, with which this is bound.

H 5331 and 5344*; Pr 6619A and 7258A; BMC 6:837 (IB.28998); GW 6903; IGI 2883; Goff C–573; BSB-Ink C–378.

9 November 1908—Gift of Mrs. E. D. Brandegee. Inc 7258A

BENEDICTUS HECTORIS FAELLI

3226   **Suetonius Tranquillus, Caius:** Vitae XII Caesarum. 5 April 1493.

f°. [7], ii–xvii, 18–326, [2] leaves ([328] blank; 149, 187–88, and 310 misnumbered 159, 186–87, and 301); 300 x 202 mm.

Edited with commentary by Philippus Beroaldus. Includes epigrams by Johannes Baptista Pius and Bartholomaeus Ugerius.

Initial spaces, with guide-letters, not filled in; without rubrication. From the library of Richard Ashhurst Bowie. Imperfect: preliminary quire A⁶ wanting; blank leaf not present.

HC 15126*; Pr 6623; BMC 6:840 (IB.29045); Polain 4736; IGI 9238; Goff S-825; CIBN S-493.

9 November 1908—Gift of Mrs. E. D. Brandegee. Inc 6623 (A)

3227 ——Another copy. 295 x 200 mm.

A total of 12 initials illuminated in gold and colors; other initials added in red or blue. 17th-century calf, rebacked. Autographs of Henry, John, and Josias White and of William Poulton on V2v; autograph of Herbert Weir Smyth on flyleaf at front. Imperfect: preliminary quire A⁶ and leaf V3 wanting; blank leaf not present.

1937—From the library of Herbert Weir Smyth. Inc 6623 (B)

3228 **Achillinus, Alexander:** Quodlibeta de intelligentiis. After 1 June 1494.

f°. [36] leaves (36 blank); 300 x 210 mm.

This copy varies slightly from the GW transcription of the title page: "Alexãdri achillini bono ‖ niensis de intelligentiis ‖ quolibeta. in quib9 quid Cõmenta. ꞇ Ari ‖ stotiles senserint ꞇ in quo a veritate deui ‖ ent [*sic*] continentur." In addition, a line-ending should be inserted after "vniformiter" in line 4 on A2r. Types: 3:135G, headings; 7:93G, text.

Initial spaces not filled in; occasional paragraph marks added in red. Modern vellum. Blank leaf not present.

HR 70; Pell 42; GW 192; IGI 46; Goff A-38.

Countway Library

3229 **Scriptores rei rusticae.** 19 September 1494.

f°. [274] leaves; 293 x 208 mm.

Edited after Georgius Merula and Franciscus Colucia by Philippus Beroaldus. Includes: Marcus Porcius Cato, *De re rustica.*—Marcus Terentius Varro, *De re rustica.*—Lucius Junius Moderatus Columella, *De re rustica* (with commentary of Pomponius Laetus).—Rutilius Taurus Palladius, *De re rustica* (with commentary of Antonius Urceus Codrus).—Poems by Bartholomaeus Ugerius.

Initial on a1r illuminated in gold and colors, with marginal extension; illuminated coat of arms in lower margin, with MS ownership notation "Est Conuentus Sancti Dominici de Casali"; initial spaces elsewhere, with guide-letters, not filled in. 18th-century paste-paper boards, rebacked in leather; edges speckled blue. Bookplate of Richard Ashhurst Bowie.

HC 14568*; Pr 6626; BMC 6:841 (IB.29054); IGI 8855; Goff S-348; CIBN S-176.

9 November 1908—Gift of Mrs. E. D. Brandegee. Inc 6626 (A)

3230 ——Another copy. 307 x 210 mm.

Initial spaces not filled in; without rubrication. Half 19th-century sheep and brown boards; leather label on spine. Bookplate of Daniel B. Fearing.

30 June 1915—Gift of Daniel B. Fearing. Inc 6626 (B)

3231 **Cicero:** De natura deorum; De finibus bonorum et malorum; De legibus. 10 December 1494.

f°. [100] leaves (1 blank); 308 x 210 mm.

Includes a poem by Cornelius Severus on the death of Cicero.

Initial spaces, with guide-letters, not filled in; without rubrication. Half 18th-century sheep and marbled boards, spine repaired. From the library of Richard Ashhurst Bowie. Blank leaf not present.

HC 5335*; Pr 6628; BMC 6:842 (IB.29057); Pell 3672; GW 6906; IGI 2881; Goff C-571; BSB-Ink C-372.

9 November 1908—Gift of Mrs. E. D. Brandegee. Inc 6628

3232 ——Another copy. 307 x 210 mm.

Initial spaces not filled in; without rubrication. Modern vellum.

Countway Library

3233 **Picus de Mirandula, Johannes:** Opera. 20 March–16 July 1496.

f°. 2 pts. in 1 vol. (pt. 1: [176] leaves, 176 blank; pt. 2: [144] leaves, 142 blank); 297 x 202 mm.

Edited by Johannes Franciscus Picus. On dating see BMC.

Initial spaces, with guide-letters, not filled in; without rubrication. Old vellum. Imperfect: 2 unsigned leaves at end of pt. 2, containing errata, wanting; blank leaves not present.

HC(Add) 12992*; Pr 6630–31; BMC 6:843 (IB.29063–64); Polain 3146(2); IGI 7731; Goff P–632; CIBN P–344.

Andover-Harvard Theological Library

3234 Censorinus: De die natali [and other works]. 12 May 1497.

f°. [38] leaves; 287 x 200 mm.

Edited by Philippus Beroaldus. Includes: Pseudo-Cebes, *Tabula* (Latin translation by Ludovicus Odaxius).—Leon Battista Alberti, *Dialogus de virtute conquerente cum Mercurio.*—Epictetus, *Enchiridion* (Latin translation by Angelus Politianus).—Basilius Magnus, *De liberalibus studiis et ingenuis moribus* (Latin translation by Leonardus Brunus Aretinus). *Oratio de inuidia* (Latin translation by Nicolaus Perottus).—Plutarchus, *Libellus de differentia inter odium et inuidiam* (anonymous Latin translation).

Large initials at beginning of individual works added in red, blue, or green; other initial spaces, with guide-letters, not filled in. Half 18th-century diced russia, rebacked. From the library of Richard Ashhurst Bowie, with his MS note, "This edition is very uncommon. I sent a general order for it to Germany in 1875, but nearly five years elapsed before a copy was offered for sale."

HC 4847*; Pr 6633; BMC 6:843 (IB.29070a–b); Pell 3471; GW 6471; IGI 2682; Goff C–376; BSB-Ink C–219.

9 November 1908—Gift of Mrs. E. D. Brandegee. Inc 6633

3235 ——Another copy. 290 x 197 mm.

Initial spaces not filled in; without rubrication. 19th-century green boards; in a cloth case.

Countway Library (William Norton Bullard Collection)

3236 Beroaldus, Philippus: Declamatio philosophi, medici, oratoris de excellentia disceptantium. 13 December 1497.

4°. [38] leaves; 210 x 149 mm.

Includes his *De optimo statu et principe.*

Initial spaces, with guide-letters, not filled in; without rubrication. Bound as no. 1 in a 17th-century vellum tract volume containing 5 works of Beroaldus, printed between 1497 and 1499.

HC 2963*; Pr 6635; BMC 6:844 (IA.29076); Pell 2218; Polain 4203; GW 4126; IGI 1591; Goff B-473; Sack 592; BSB-Ink B-371.

Countway Library (William Norton Bullard Collection)

3236A Laetus, Pomponius: De Romanorum magistratibus. After 1497.

4°. [16] leaves; 203 x 141 mm.

For transcriptions, collation, and type identification see IGI.

Initial spaces, with guide-letters, not filled in; without rubrication. Unbound; in a cloth case.

H(not R) 9832; not Pr 7431; IGI 7989; not Goff L-28.

28 May 1945—Received. Law Library

3237 Scanarolus, Antonius: Disputatio de morbo Gallico. 26 March 1498.

4°. [16] leaves; 205 x 140 mm.

Initial spaces, with guide-letters, not filled in; without rubrication. Old vellum; red leather label on spine; in a cloth case.

H 14505*; Pr 6636; BMC 6:844 (IA.29079); IGI 8826; Goff S-304; CIBN S-160.

Countway Library

3238 Achillinus, Alexander: De orbibus. 7 August 1498.

f°. [1], 2-51, [1] leaves (2 and 15 misnumbered 1 and 14); 302 x 212 mm.

Initial spaces, most with guide-letters, not filled in; without rubrication. Modern marbled paste-paper boards.

HCR 72; Pr 6638; BMC 12:60 (IB.29085); GW 191; IGI 45; Goff A-37.

Countway Library (William Norton Bullard Collection)

3239 Plinius Secundus, Gaius Caecilius: Epistolae. 19 October 1498.

4°. [140] leaves; 209 x 150 mm.

Edited by Philippus Beroaldus.

Initial on a1v added in blue and red; initials elsewhere, with guide-letters, not filled in. Old vellum, edges speckled blue; leather label on spine. MS marginalia.

HC 13115*; Pr 6639; BMC 6:844 (IA.29087); Polain 3206; IGI 7902; Goff P-810; CIBN P-478.

16 December 1920—Bought with the Stephen Salisbury fund. Inc 6639

3240 Beroaldus, Philippus: Heptalogos, siue Septem Sapientes. 18 December 1498.

4°. [24] leaves (24 blank); 210 x 149 mm.

Initial spaces on a2-3 not filled in; without rubrication. Bound as no. 5 in a 17th-century vellum tract volume containing 5 works of Beroaldus, printed between 1497 and 1499.

HC(Add) 2974*; Pr 6640; BMC 6:844 (IA.29089); Pell 2227; Polain 4087; GW 4138; IGI 1598; Goff B-487; BSB-Ink B-375.

Countway Library (William Norton Bullard Collection)

3241 ——Another copy. 205 x 152 mm.

This copy lacks the hyphen at the end of the third line of the title. Initial spaces not filled in; without rubrication. Modern speckled orange boards. Blank leaf not present.

Countway Library (William Norton Bullard Collection)

3242 Beroaldus, Philippus: De felicitate. 13 April 1499.

4°. [28] leaves; 211 x 154 mm.

Initial spaces on A1v and A3r, with guide-letters, not filled in; without rubrication. Half modern calf and paste-paper boards. Bookplates of Raimondo Ambrosini and of William Norton Bullard.

HC(Add) 2971*; Pr 6641; BMC 6:844 (IA.29091); Pell 2225; GW 4134; IGI 1596; Goff B-484; BSB-Ink B-367.

Countway Library (William Norton Bullard Collection)

3243 Cicero: Orationes. 13 April 1499.

f°. [271] leaves; 310 x 208 mm.

Edited by Philippus Beroaldus. The *Oratio aduersus Valerium* added to this edition is a forgery attributed to Janus Cardo. The BMC and GW collations can be made more precise: F⁶ (-F4).

Initial spaces, with guide-letters, not filled in; without rubrication. Half modern brown morocco and marbled boards. From the library of Richard Ashhurst Bowie, with a slip of his MS notes inserted at front. Leaf VV6 mounted.

HC 5129*; Pr 6642; BMC 6:845 (IB.29095); Pell 3696; Polain 4285; GW 6771; IGI 2933; Goff C-549; BSB-Ink C-386.

9 November 1908—Gift of Mrs. E. D. Brandegee. Inc 6642

3244 **Formularium diversorum contractuum.** 31 August 1499.

f°. [1], 2-88 leaves; 277 x 194 mm.

Enlarged edition for Bologna.

This copy varies from the GW transcriptions: a1v, line 1, "Instrmẽtuʒ mũdualdi"; p4r, line 5 of the colophon, "Regnantte." Initial space on a3r not filled in; without rubrication. 17th-century vellum, edges speckled red; title in ink on spine. MS ownership notation on title page, "Ludouico di margoli."

H 7274*; Pr 6643; Pell 4868; GW 10196; IGI 4022; Goff F-252; BSB-Ink F-202.

12 November 1947—Received. Law Library

3245 **Beroaldus, Philippus:** Oratio prouerbiorum. 17 December 1499.

4°. [28] leaves (28 blank); 201 x 143 mm.

Initials added in brown. Pages numbered in MS 239-91. 19th-century purple boards. Blank leaf not present.

HC 2966*; Pr 6645; BMC 6:845 (IA.29101); Pell 2221; Polain 625; GW 4142; IGI 1600; Goff B-489; Sack 595; BSB-Ink B-379.

30 July 1924—Bought with the George Schünemann Jackson fund. Inc 6645

3246 ——Another copy. 210 x 149 mm.

Initial spaces, with guide-letters, not filled in; without rubrication. Bound as no. 4 in a 17th-century vellum tract volume containing 5 works of Beroaldus, printed between 1497 and 1499.

Countway Library (William Norton Bullard Collection)

3247 Beroaldus, Philippus: Declamatio ebriosi, scortatoris, et aleatoris. 1499.

4°. [20] leaves; 201 x 145 mm.

In this edition the caption title on a3r reads "ARGVMENTVM."

Initial spaces, with guide-letters, not filled in; without rubrication. Bound in part of a vellum leaf of 15th-century Latin liturgical MS.

BMC 6:845 (IA.29099); GW 4131; IGI 1590; Goff B–472.

30 July 1924—Bought with the George Schünemann Jackson fund. Inc 6644.5

3248 ——Another copy. 210 x 149 mm.

Initial spaces not filled in; without rubrication. Bound as no. 3 in a 17th-century vellum tract volume containing 5 works of Beroaldus, printed between 1497 and 1499.

Countway Library (William Norton Bullard Collection)

3249 Apuleius Madaurensis, Lucius: Asinus aureus. 1 August 1500.

f°. [4], 282 leaves (155 misnumbered 156); 310 x 214 mm.

To some copies is prefixed a *Tabula* (A–B⁶, C⁴), which BMC describes as "printed later than the body of the book, as it shows a later state of the commentary type ... while the paper is also smaller." Edited, with a commentary, by Philippus Beroaldus. Includes a poem by Coelius Calcagninus.

Without the *Tabula*. Initial spaces, with guide-letters, not filled in; without rubrication. Half 19th-century sheep and marbled boards, hinges broken. MS ownership notation washed away on title page; armorial bookplate (lion rampant on shield with lion supporters, motto "Vigor in virtute," coronet of a viscount). In quire Z an extra sheet has gone through the press with sheet Z2.

HC 1319*; Pr 6647; BMC 6:845 (IB.29107); Pell 926; GW 2305; IGI 773; Goff A–938; Sack 254; BSB-Ink A–657.

Countway Library

3250 Beroaldus, Philippus: Orationes et carmina. 1 November 1500.

4°. [128] leaves; 190 x 138 mm.

Initial spaces, with guide-letters, not filled in; without rubrication. Half modern vellum and white boards. MS ownership notation erased from title page.

H 2955*; Pr 6648; BMC 6:846 (IA.29109); Pell 2214; Polain 626; GW 4148; IGI 1605; Goff B-495; BSB-Ink B-384.

Countway Library

3251 **Beroaldus, Philippus:** Oratio prouerbiorum. 17 November 1500.

4°. [28] leaves (28 blank); 196 x 145 mm.

Initial spaces on A1v and A3r, with guide-letters, not filled in; without rubrication. Modern vellum. The Vollbehr copy.

HC(Add) 2967; Pr 6649; BMC 6:846 (IA.29111); GW 4143; IGI 1601; Goff B-490.

Countway Library

3252 **Solinus, Caius Julius:** Polyhistor, siue De mirabilibus mundi. 1500.

4°. [90] leaves (90 blank); 213 x 154 mm.

Edited by Philippus Beroaldus.

Initial spaces, with guide-letters, not filled in; without rubrication. Half 19th-century sheep and marbled boards; leather labels on spine. Booklabel of Georg Kloss (no. 3418 in the Sotheby sale catalogue, May 1835).

HC(Add) 14886; Pr 6646; BMC 6:845 (IA.29104); IGI 9093; Goff S-625.

10 March 1922—Received gratis. Inc 6646

3253 **Beroaldus, Philippus:** Declamatio philosophi, medici, oratoris de excellentia disceptantium. "13 December 1497" [i.e., ca. 1500?].

4°. [40] leaves; 203 x 150 mm.

Reprinted from Benedictus's edition of 13 December 1497 with the date unaltered; possibly later than 1500. Includes his *De optimo statu et principe*.

Initial spaces, with guide-letters, not filled in; without rubrication. Modern vellum.

C 1005; BMC 6:846 (IA.29113); GW 4127; IGI 1592; Goff B-474.

Countway Library

J O H A N N E S   W A L B E C K

3254 Caccialupis, Johannes Baptista de: Repetitio legis Si qua illustris (Cod. 6,57.5). 5 February 1493.

f°. [14] leaves (1 blank); 392 x 272 mm.

Without rubrication. Old limp vellum.

C 1400; GW 5859; IGI 2315; Goff C-11.

20 November 1936—Received. Law Library

3255 Caccialupis, Johannes Baptista de: Repetitio legis Frater a fratre (Dig. 12,6.38). 23 August 1493.

f°. [16] leaves (1 blank); 394 x 264 mm.

Edited by Johannes Franciscus Paganus.

Initial space on a2r not filled in; without rubrication. Half modern blue and orange boards. Leaves 2-16 numbered in MS 134-48.

H 4196*; GW 5851; IGI 2308; Goff C-10; BSB-Ink C-7.

19 September 1947—Received. Law Library

D A N E S I U S   H E C T O R I S
F A E L L I

3256 Bartolinus, Pius Antonius: Correctio locorum lxx iuris civilis. Not before September 1495.

4°. [26] leaves; 196 x 137 mm.

Includes his *De ordine imperatorum* and a poem by Marius Carpentarius.

Initial space on a1v not filled in; without rubrication. Sewn into modern cream wrappers; in a cloth case.

HC 2537*; Pr 6651; BMC 6:847 (IA.29135); Pell 1899; GW 3473; IGI 1277; Goff B-182; BSB-Ink B-121.

6 November 1933—Received. Law Library

3257 ——Another copy. 202 x 148 mm.

Initial space not filled in; without rubrication. Sewn into modern cream wrappers; in a cloth case.

23 December 1904—Received. Law Library

J U S T I N I A N U S   D E   R U B E R I A

3258 Michael Scotus: Expositio super auctorem Spherae. 16 September 1495.

4°. [40] leaves; 188 x 137 mm.

Includes poems by Pompilius Alcialius and Johannes Romagnisius.

Initial spaces, with guide-letters, not filled in. Half 19th-century dark brown straight-grain morocco and marbled boards. Autograph on fly-leaf at end, "George M Kendall, Lowell Mass 1877."

HC(+Add) 14555*; Pr 6661; BMC 6:849 (IA.29195); IGI 6416; Goff M–550; CIBN M–349.

15 August 1943—Gift of Aubrey H. Starke. Inc 6661

3259 Caiadus, Henricus: Eclogae. 23 July 1496.

4°. [30] leaves; 194 x 134 mm.

Includes a poem by Bartholomaeus Ugerius.

Initial spaces, with guide-letters, not filled in; without rubrication. 19th-century marbled boards. "Bibliotheca Heberiana" stamp on front flyleaf (no. 1218 in pt. 1 of the Sotheby sale catalogue, April 1834); bookplate of Fernando Palha (no. 740 in pt. 2 of the catalogue of his library, Lisbon, 1896). Imperfect: leaf d6 slightly mutilated.

CR 1403; Pr 6662; BMC 6:849 (IA.29199); GW 5883; IGI 2336; Goff C–33.

3 December 1928—Library of Fernando Palha, gift of John B. Stetson, Jr. Inc 6662

3260 Niccolò da Poggibonsi: Viaggio da Venezia alla santa Gerusalemme e al Monte Sinai. 6 March 1500.

f°. [68] leaves; ill.; 270 x 185 mm.

Edited by Johannes Cola. This work came to be attributed to Noè, a Franciscan, either through misreading of a MS or through confusion with Noè Bianchi, author of a similar work with title *Viaggio in Terra Santa*. There are variants on c6r, i1r, and i6v; see BMC.

This copy has the readings of BMC IB.29209a on i1r and i6v and the reading of IB.29209 on c6r. Initial spaces, with guide-letters, not filled in; without rubrication; woodcuts uncolored. Modern brown morocco by Lortic, edges gilt, with the arms of Victor Masséna, prince d'Essling, stamped in gilt on covers and with his monogram in the spine panels. Booklabel of Philip Hofer.

C 5965=4576; Pr 6663; BMC 6:850 (IB.29209–09a); IGI 1627; Goff V-267; Sander 4998.

31 December 1948—Gift of Philip Hofer. Typ Inc 6663

VINCENTIUS ET FRATRES DE BENEDICTIS

3261 Piperarius, Andreas: De laudibus legum oratio. After 22 October 1498.

4°. [4] leaves; 200 x 140 mm.

Initial spaces, with guide-letters, not filled in; without rubrication. Sewn into modern cream wrappers; in a cloth case. Pages numbered in MS 273–80.

C 4758; Pr 6665; BMC 6:852 (IA.29246); IGI 7748.

13 November 1945—Received. Law Library

JOHANNES ANTONIUS DE BENEDICTIS

3262 Platina, Bartholomaeus: De honesta voluptate et valetudine. 11 May 1499.

4°. [96] leaves (96 blank); 222 x 158 mm.

There are variant colophons; see Polain; some copies are dated 10 May; see IGI and Goff.

This copy has the colophon transcribed by Polain 3185A and is dated 11 May. Initial spaces, with guide-letters, not filled in; without rubrication. Half modern vellum and marbled boards. Bookplate of Daniel B. Fearing.

HC 13056*; Pr 6666; BMC 6:852 (IA.29252); Polain 3185A; IGI 7854; Goff P-766; Sack 2909.

30 June 1915—Gift of Daniel B. Fearing. Inc 6666

3263 ——Another copy. 211 x 152 mm.

Colophon as above. Initial spaces not filled in; without rubrication. Old vellum; leather labels on spine. MS ownership notation on a2r, "Ad Vsum fr'is Gabriellis de crema S: Augⁱ Creme"; bookplates of Georges Vicaire and of William Norton Bullard. Quire f misbound with the leaves in order: 1-2, 5-6, 3-4, 7-8; blank leaf not present.

Countway Library (William Norton Bullard Collection)

Naples

SIXTUS RIESSINGER

3264 Fliscus, Georgius: Eubois. ca. 1471.

8°. [20] leaves (1 blank); 208 x 139 mm.

Initial added in brown on [a]2r; spaces elsewhere not filled in; without rubrication. 19th-century vellum. Booklabel of Count Paul Riant. Blank leaf not present.

H 7132*; Pr 3471 (assigned to Rome, In domo A. and R. de Vulterris); BMC 6:855 (IA.29312); GW 9995; IGI 3977; Goff F-195; BSB-Ink F-134; Fava-Bresciano 45.

28 December 1899—Gift of J. Randolph Coolidge and Archibald Cary Coolidge. Inc 6670.5

3265 Puteo, Paris de: De re militari et de duello. ca. 1476/77.

f°. [188] leaves (188 blank); 270 x 195 mm.

Initials added in red or blue. 16th-century blind- and gilt-stamped calf over wooden boards, repaired; brass latches on back cover, marks of clasp plates on front, clasps and thongs gone; title "De re militari" stamped in gilt at top of front cover; in a cloth case. Large painted coat of arms in colors inside front cover, with motto "Comes sis Minerva" and name "Ieronumou [in Greek] Endorffers" in ink at top; MS dates on flyleaf at front, "1506 Decembr[is] 2 noctu 9 sonitu cu[m] ¼. 27 Julij 10 ho. 1. mi[nus] ¼. in Mosen"; in MS on verso of flyleaf at front, "15 V 68 Eil Mitt Weil Joachim Graue zu Ortenburg"; woodcut bookplate (Ortenburg arms) pasted to front flyleaf, with MS date "15 II 69" and motto "Lente Festina" in cartouche at head.

Pr 6680; GW (Nachtr) 266 (described as "Paralleldruck zu Hain 13615"); IGI 8236; Goff P–1140; CIBN P–712; Fava-Bresciano 41.

19 December 1955—Gift of Christian A. Zabriskie. Inc 6680

A R N A L D U S   D E   B R U X E L L A

3266 Puteoli: De mirabilibus Puteolorum et de balneis ibidem existentibus. 31 December 1475.

8°. [46] leaves (1 and 46 blank); 182 x 128 mm.

Compiled by the printer and edited by Franciscus Griffolinus. Erroneously attributed to Johannes Elysius.

Initials and paragraph marks added in red, but some initial spaces not filled in; capital strokes added in yellow; the rubricator has added "Compilatio Arnaldi de Bruxella" beneath the caption on a2r and "ex diuersis auctoribus" after "recollectum" in the colophon. 19th-century red morocco by C. Lewis; edges gilt. Syston Park bookplate and monogram booklabel of Sir J. H. Thorold (no. 177 in the Sotheby sale catalogue, December 1884); bookplate of James Frothingham Hunnewell. Blank leaves not present.

HR 6585; Pr 6690; BMC 6:858 (IA.29372); IGI 8242; Goff M–590; Fava-Bresciano 92.

January 1919—Deposited by James M. Hunnewell. Inc 6690

P R I N T E R   O F   S I L V A T I C U S ,
1 4 7 4   (H   1 5 1 9 4)

3267 Silvaticus, Matthaeus: Liber pandectarum medicinae. 1 April 1474.

f°. [342] leaves (6 and 7 blank); 423 x 282 mm.

Edited by Angelus Cato.

Initial spaces, most with guide-letters, not filled in; without rubrication. 18th-century red morocco, edges gilt, with the arms of Louis-Léon-Félicité, duc de Brancas, comte de Lauraguais, stamped in gilt on covers. MS (ownership?) notation on verso of last leaf, "Duca dasscolo"; in MS in upper margin of π1r, "Bibliothecae Colbertinae" (not located in the Paris 1728 sale catalogue of the library); Syston Park bookplate and monogram booklabel of Sir J. H. Thorold (no. 1801 in the Sotheby sale catalogue, December 1884); bookplate of John Chipman Gray. Blank leaf π6 not present.

HC 15194; BMC 6:859 (IC.29360); IGI 8979; Goff S–510; CIBN S–263; Fava-Bresciano 86 (assigned to Arnaldus de Bruxella).

12 May 1958—From the library of John Chipman Gray and his son Roland Gray, whose four children give this book in memory of their father and grandfather. Inc 6691.5

3268 Pseudo-Phalaris: Epistolae [Latin]. ca. 1474.

[For transcriptions see Reichling; but insert a period after "Malatestis" in line 3 of the caption on [a]2r, and correct his leaf count to 54.] 4°. [a–c^{10}, d–f^{8}] ([a]1 blank); [54] leaves (1 blank); 205 x 143 mm. [a]3r: 27 lines, 145 x 83 mm. Type: 109R. Initial spaces.

Latin translation by Franciscus Griffolinus.

Initial spaces not filled in; without rubrication; MS catchwords added vertically on the last leaf of each quire. Contemporary half leather (rebacked) and wooden boards; pigskin thong nailed to front cover, brass latch on back, clasp and most of thong gone. With this is bound the same printer's edition of the Italian translation of this work (ca. 1474).

HC 12882; R 285 (assigned to Bologna, Balthasar Azoguidus, ca. 1471); IGI 7689; Goff P–553; CIBN P–288; Fava-Bresciano 255 (Edizioni dubbie).

30 December 1955—Gift of Mrs. Charles W. Clark. Inc 6691.10

3269 Pseudo-Phalaris: Epistolae [Italian]. ca. 1474.

4°. [64] leaves (1 blank); 205 x 143 mm.

Italian translation by Giovanni Andrea Ferabos from the Latin version of Franciscus Griffolinus.

Initial spaces not filled in; without rubrication; MS catchwords added vertically on the last leaf of each quire. For binding description see the preceding entry (the same printer's edition of the Latin translation of this work, ca. 1474), with which this is bound.

CR 4736; Pr 6688 (assigned to Arnaldus de Bruxella); BMC 6:859 (IA.29368); IGI 7706; Goff P-570; CIBN P-298; Fava-Bresciano 93 (assigned to Arnaldus de Bruxella).

30 December 1955—Gift of Mrs. Charles W. Clark. Inc 6691.10

M A T H I A S   M O R A V U S

3270 Maius, Junianus: De priscorum proprietate verborum. 1475.

f°. [368] leaves (368 blank); 380 x 270 mm.

Printed by Moravus with Blasius Romerus.

Initial spaces not filled in; without rubrication. Old vellum, stained brown; edges stained blue. Imperfect: leaf a1 wanting; leaves a2–3 and mm9 badly mutilated, with loss of text, which has been supplied in MS; leaves a4–10, b1–2, LL1–10, and mm1–9 remargined; blank leaf mm10 not present.

H 10539*; Pr 6695; BMC 12:62 (IC.29396); IGI 6036; Goff M-95; CIBN M-37; Fava-Bresciano 108.

29 July 1949—Received. Law Library

3271 Seneca, Lucius Annaeus: Opera philosophica. 1475.

f°. [253] leaves (1 blank); 372 x 258 mm.

Includes Seneca's *Epistolae*, as well as the spurious letters supposedly exchanged between Seneca and St. Paul. Edited by Blasius Romerus. The BMC collation can be made more precise: [q]^8 (–[q]7). Colophon misdated "M.lxxiiiii."

Initials and paragraph marks added in red, blue, or green. 17th-century blind-stamped pigskin, edges stained red; pigskin thongs with brass clasps nailed to back cover, metal fasteners on edge of front cover; with the arms of Candidus Pfeiffer, abbot of the Cistercians at

Baumgartenberg, impressed on the covers. Bookplate of William King Richardson. Imperfect: leaves [a]2-3, [q]4-5, and [r]9-10 inserted from another copy, with variant rubrication; inserted leaves (except [a]3) trimmed to the edge of text and inlaid; blank leaf not present.

HC 14590; Pr 6694; BMC 6:861 (IC.29395); IGI 8867; Goff S-368; CIBN S-183; Fava-Bresciano 109.

1951—Bequest of William King Richardson. WKR 2.2.2

3272 **Augustinus, Aurelius, Saint:** De civitate Dei. 1477.

f°. [298] leaves (1, 18, and 298 blank); 285 x 210 mm.

Initial spaces, most with guide-letters, not filled in; without rubrication. Half modern brown morocco and wooden boards. Imperfect: last four digits of the colophon date scraped away and paper abraded; first and last blank leaves not present. Sheet dd4 duplicated after dd5.

HC 2053; Pr 6697; BMC 6:862 (IB.29405); Pell 1552; Polain 361; GW 2881; IGI 973; Goff A-1237; Fava-Bresciano 116.

7 May 1913—Gift of Alain Campbell White. Inc 6697

3273 **Officium Beatae Virginis Mariae.** 3 October 1487.

π1r (red): (I^2)Anuarius habet dies xxxj. ‖ a1r (red): Incipit officiū beate Marie $\tilde{v}$‖ginis secūdū cōsuetudinē Ro-‖mane curie. Ad matutinas. ‖ m7v, COLOPHON: Impressuʒ [Neapoli .p Mathiā morauum[?]] Anno a natiuitate dñi ‖ M.cccc.lxxxvij. Die tertia men‖sis Octobris.

16°. π^{10}, a-m^8 (m8 blank); [106] leaves (106 blank); ill.; 98 x 67 mm. a1r: 20 lines, 67 x 40 mm. Types: 10:63G and 9:60G* (but with capitals smaller than 8:60G). Lombards; woodcuts.   Plate VIII

Includes additional material traditionally contained in Books of Hours: Seven penitential psalms, Litany of the saints, Office of the dead, etc.

Printed on vellum. The four woodcuts present have been painted over in gold and colors; leaves a1r, f2r, h3r, l7r, and m2r have been illuminated with 4-sided borders in gold and colors, that on a1r with an owner's coat of arms in the lower panel; initials, some with miniatures, illuminated in gold and colors. Contemporary Neapolitan leather binding, richly gilt, edges gilt; marks of a clasp plate and latch, no longer present; in a cloth case. MS ownership notation scraped away on flyleaf at front; another notation below, "dato dal Dottor Martini Siena 1796"; booklabels of Léon Rattier (according to Fava-Bresciano, no. 38 in the Paris sale catalogue of books and MSS from his library, 1909) and of Philip Hofer. Bound in at end are nine vellum leaves of MS prayers with painted miniatures of Christ and various saints. Imperfect: leaf π10 (end of calendar and woodcut of the Nativity) wanting; the words in the colophon in square brackets above have been scraped away.

Bohatta(H) II.51; Meyer-Baer p. 36; Goff O-38; Fava-Bresciano 135bis (with wrong leaf count); Sander 5040 (note).

May 1984—Gift of Philip Hofer in honor of Eleanor M. Garvey. Typ Inc 6706.5

3274 Pontanus, Johannes Jovianus: De fortitudine. 15 September 1490.

4°. [100] leaves (79, 80, and 100 blank); 220 x 148 mm.

Includes his *De principe.*

Initials added in brown. 19th-century calf, spine gilt. MS note on flyleaf at front, "From the Meerman Collection" (no. 222 in vol. 2 of The Hague sale catalogue, 1824); bookplates of the Duke of Sussex (not located in the Evans sale catalogues, 1844–45) and of James Frothingham Hunnewell. Blank leaf k8 not present.

HC(+Add) 13256*; Pr 6708; BMC 6:865 (IA.29440); IGI 7994; Goff P-918; CIBN P-566; Fava-Bresciano 144.

January 1919—Deposited by James M. Hunnewell. Inc 6708

3274A Pontanus, Johannes Jovianus: De oboedientia. 25 October 1490.

4°. [104] leaves (1, 103–04 blank); 214 x 152 mm.

Initial spaces not filled in; without rubrication. Modern vellum. Bookstamp "Ignaz Lamatsch" in upper margin of a2r; bookplate of Boies Penrose II. Final blank leaf not present.

HC 13257*; Pr 6709; BMC 6:865 (IA.29442); Polain 3239; IGI 7996; Goff P-920; CIBN P-568; Fava-Bresciano 145.

9 October 1945—Gift of Boies Penrose II. Inc 6709

3275 Missale Romanum. ca. 1490.

π1r (red): ℂ Annus habet mēses .xij. septimanas .lij. ꝶ diē unuȝ. ꝶ habet ‖ dies .ccclxv. ꝶ .vi. horas. qn̄ ē bisextus habet dies .ccclxvi. ‖ (KL²) Ianuarius habet dies .xxxi. Luna .xxx.... a1r, col. 1 (red): Incipit ordo missalis scŏm ‖ ꝓsuetudineȝ Romane curie. ‖ A1r, col. 1 (red): Incipit proprium sanctoruȝ ‖ de missali in vigilia sancti an‖dree apostoli. Introitus. ‖ L7r, col. 2 (red): ℂ Hec sunt capitula seu acci‖dētia que possunt accidi ī ce‖lebratione missarum. ‖ L8r, col. 2, line 16 (red): ... aut etiā si aliter nō ualeret ‖ solidū trans-glutiret. ‖ Laus deo. ‖ [device of the publisher Antonius Gontier]

f°. π⁶, a–f⁸, g⁶, h–i⁸, k–n¹⁰, o–r⁸ (r8 blank); A–L⁸; [236] leaves (196 blank); ill.; 295 x 207 mm. 2 columns (except in the calendar). a1r: 38 lines, 210 x 130 mm. Types: 3:112G and 6:94G (leaded to 104). Printed in red and black; Lombards and initial spaces; 3 woodcuts; musical notation. Plate IX

This apparently unique book has been assigned to the press of Cristannus Preller because it contains, at end, a device identified by BMC (6:873) and Husung (no. 69) as belonging to Antonius Gontier, a Neapolitan publisher and printer. (On various interpretations of the initials found on the device see Fava-Bresciano I:103–04.) This device does occur in a Landino of 21 May 1490 printed with Preller's types for Gontier, but the types used in the present missal are clearly those of Mathias Moravus, not Preller, and so I assign the work to him, though this is contrary to the references given below, all of which (except Copinger) question Preller as the printer. I see no reason why Gontier, in his capacity as a publisher, should have restricted himself to a single printer.

Large initial on a1r illuminated in gold and colors, with marginal extension; episcopal coat of arms in lower margin; another initial illuminated on n2r, with marginal extension; initials elsewhere added in blue; woodcut of the Crucifixion on n1v colored. Modern brown morocco by Douglas Cockerell, with his monogram and date "1900" inside back cover; braided thongs fasten to pins on fore-edge of front cover. MS notation on flyleaf at end, "Q[ue]sto mesale e del R^mo Epō di rosi"; booklabels of C. W. Dyson Perrins (no. 180 in the Sotheby sale catalogue, June 1946) and of Philip Hofer.

C 4185 ("Venetiis, c. 1484"); Goff M–704; Weale-Bohatta 887; Meyer-Baer 130; Fava-Bresciano 174; Sander 4753.

20 December 1954—Gift of Philip Hofer. Typ Inc 6709.5

J O D O C U S   H O H E N S T E I N

3276 **Stephanus de Caieta:** Sacramentale Neapolitanum. 14 September 1475.

f°. [230] leaves (1, 9, and 230 blank); 405 x 275 mm.

Includes a commendation by Fuscus Severinus.

Initial spaces not filled in; without rubrication. Early 19th-century diced russia, with binder's ticket of L. Staggemeier and Welcher, London. Autograph of Michael Wodhull, with his MS date of acquisition "Apr. 17th 1793" and note "wants the contents" (i.e., table of *quaestiones* and register; no. 2418 in the Sotheby sale catalogue, January 1886). Imperfect: 9 leaves at front wanting.

HC 4232*; Pr 6711; BMC 6:866 (IC.29453); Pell 3155; Polain 957; IGI 9166; Goff S–789; CIBN S–465; Fava Bresciano 148.

January 1919—Deposited by James M. Hunnewell. Inc 6711

3277 **Cermisonus, Antonius:** Consiglio per preservar della peste. ca. 1476.

4°. [10] leaves (1 blank); 210 x 145 mm.

Without rubrication. Modern tan boards. On [a]4v is an impression of a piece of type that fell out of the forme while it was being printed.

Accurti (1936) 9 (described as "Olim apud I. B. Samonati bibliopolam romanum"); Ballard 262 (with facsimile); Klebs 263.1; Goff C–401.

Countway Library (William Norton Bullard Collection)

P R I N T E R   O F   C A R P A N I S ,
D E   N U T R I E N D A   M E M O R I A
(H   4 5 3 6)

3277A **Carpanis, Dominicus de:** De nutrienda memoria. After 16 December 1476.

4°. [8] leaves (8 blank); 198 x 145 mm.

Initial spaces not filled in; without rubrication. Modern vellum.

HR 4536; GW 6139; IGI 2529; Goff C–219; Fava-Bresciano 196.

Countway Library

PRINTER OF NICOLAUS
DE LYRA, *CONTRA HEBRAEOS*
(H 10408)

3278 Gambilionibus, Angelus de: Tractatus de maleficiis. After 15 January 1477.

f°. [86] leaves (1 and 86 blank); 405 x 280 mm.   Plate X

The assigning of this unknown printer to Naples is circumstantial but probable: of the two works known to have been printed in his type, eight copies of the Nicolaus de Lyra are located in Italy, two in Paris (both of Italian provenance), and one in London; while of the De Gambilionibus five (i.e., four) are recorded by GW, one in Naples, one in Paris (GW is wrong in recording two), one in Segovia, and another here at Harvard. The Paris copy is bound with four other works, all printed in Rome. The letter forms of this printer's type seem to have been copied after those of Mathias Moravus in Naples, though they are much cruder and indicate a less competent hand. See Dennis E. Rhodes, "Towards an Identification of Proctor 7393," *Gutenberg-Jahrbuch* 1963: 47–48, and BMC 12:82–83.

Includes additions by Hieronymus de Castellanis.

Initial spaces not filled in; without rubrication. Bound in a vellum leaf of Latin liturgical MS containing musical notation.

R 399 (assigned to Georgius Lauer in Rome); Pell 1148; GW 10522; IGI 4158; Goff G–59a.

25 October 1924—Bought with the George Lyman Kittredge fund. Inc 6716.5

FRANCESCO DI DINO

3279 Samuel Maroccanus, Rabbi: Epistola contra Iudaeorum errores. ca. 1478/80.

4°. [40] leaves (1 and 40 blank); 193 x 136 mm.

Translated by Alphonsus Boni Hominis.

Initial spaces not filled in; without rubrication. Modern japanese vellum. Bookplate of Lee M. Friedman. Imperfect: leaf [e]7 slightly mutilated; blank leaf [e]8 not present.

HC 14264*; R 721; Pr 3949 (assigned to Herolt at Rome); BMC 6:868 (IA.29499); IGI 8578; Goff S-107; CIBN S-55; Fava-Bresciano 218.

1957–Bequest of Lee M. Friedman. Inc 6722.5

FRANCESCO DEL TUPPO

3280 Manfredis, Hieronymus de: Liber de homine [Italian]. 31 August 1478.

f°. [110] leaves (110 blank); 268 x 185 mm.

Erroneously attributed in this edition to Albertus Magnus. Printed by Del Tuppo for Bernardinus de Gerardinis.

Initial spaces not filled in; without rubrication. Old vellum. Bookseller's ticket of C. E. Rappaport, Rome. Smudged bookstamp on [a]2r; bookplate of William Norton Bullard. Sheet [l]4 misbound after [h]3.

HR 10690=H 572*; Pr 6682A; BMC 6:869 (IB.29179); IGI 6112; Goff M-192; Fava-Bresciano 49.

Countway Library (William Norton Bullard Collection)

3281 Ursinis, Bartholomaeus de: Quadragesimale quod dicitur Gratia Dei. Not before 1478.

f°. [336] leaves (1, 6, and 336 blank); 287 x 207 mm.

In some copies leaf 6 is blank, in others it contains a letter of the printer to the King of Naples. Printed by Del Tuppo for Bernardinus Gerardinus.

In this copy leaf 6 (blank?) is not present. Initial spaces not filled in; without rubrication. Old vellum, with vellum thongs slipping into fasteners on front cover. MS ownership notation on blank leaf 1, "Hic Lib[er] ... est mei Petrj [illegible] Joh[ann]is de s[an]cto Chrisstano [?] ciuis & not[ar]ij pisanij"; booklabel of Adriana R. Salem. Badly wormed.

HR 2532; Pr 6676 (assigned to Riessinger and dated 1473); BMC 6:869 (IB.29320); Pell 1897; IGI 10032; Goff U-69; CIBN U-33; Fava-Bresciano 51.

May 1963–Gift of Ward M. Canaday. Inc 6723.5

3282 Ovidius Naso, Publius: Epistolae heroides [Italian]. ca. 1480.

4°. [74] leaves (74 blank); ill.; 210 x 143 mm.

Italian prose translation variously attributed to Filippo Ceffi or to Alberto della Piagentina.

Initial spaces not filled in; without rubrication; woodcuts uncolored. 19th-century blind- and gilt-stamped calf; in a cloth case. Booklabels of Philip and Frances Hofer. Imperfect: leaves [a]1, 4, 5, 8, [h]1, 10 wanting; these (except blank [h]10) have been supplied in photographic reproduction from the Vatican Library copy and are laid into the case in a separate folder. Quire [b] misbound after quire [h].

Accurti (1930) 117; IGI 7110; Goff O–151; Sander 5292.

24 July 1974—Gift of Philip Hofer. Typ Inc 6723.7

3283 Aesopus: Vita Aesopi et Aesopus moralisatus [Latin-Italian]. 13 February 1485.

f°. [168] leaves (1, 44, and 168 blank); ill.; 277 x 200 mm.

The *Vita* is in the Latin version of Rinucius; the fables are in the Latin verse version of Anonymus Neveleti (Gualtherus Anglicus?), with Italian prose translation and commentary by Del Tuppo. Printed by the "Germani fidelissimi" for Del Tuppo.

A few woodcut initials; spaces elsewhere, most with guide-letters, not filled in; woodcuts uncolored. Modern blind- and gilt-stamped brown morocco by Gruel, edges gilt. Booklabels of C. W. Dyson Perrins (no. 1 in the Sotheby sale catalogue, June 1946) and of Philip Hofer. Imperfect: many leaves inlaid and remargined; blank leaves not present.

HC(+Add)R 353; Pr 6724; BMC 6:870 (IB.29553a–b); Pell 227; GW 441; IGI 103; Goff A–155; BSB-Ink A–78; Schäfer 2; Fava-Bresciano 63.

9 November 1984—Bequest of Philip Hofer. Typ Inc 6724

3284 Picus de Mirandula, Johannes: Apologia conclusionum suorum. After 31 May 1487.

f°. [60] leaves (1 and 60 blank); 283 x 205 mm.

Woodcut initials; spaces for Greek not filled in. For binding description see no. 1451 in vol. 2, Petrus Garcia's *Determinationes magistrales contra conclusiones Johannis Pici Mirandulae* (Rome, Eucharius Silber, 15 October 1489), which is bound with this. Imperfect: slightly wormed; paper flaw in leaf [i]1 affects a few words of text.

H 13000?; Pr 6706 (assigned to Mathias Moravus); BMC 6:871 (IB.29535); IGI 7734; Goff P–635; Fava-Bresciano 69.

May 1969–Bought with the Duplicate fund. Inc 6723.10

A Y O L F U S   D E   C A N T O N O

3285 Lilius, Zacharias: Orbis breviarium. 9 November 1496.

4°. [112] leaves; 206 x 141 mm.

Includes the reply of Matthaeus Bossus to Lilius's dedicatory letter.

Initial spaces, most with guide-letters, not filled in; without rubrication. Half 19th-century calf and marbled boards. Booklabel of Count Paul Riant. Imperfect: leaf o6 slightly mutilated.

HC 10102*; Pr 6744; BMC 6:874 (IA.29559); IGI 5761; Goff L–219; Fava-Bresciano 190; Sander 3975.

28 December 1899–Gift of J. Randolph Coolidge and Archibald Cary Coolidge. Inc 6744

Perugia

P E T R U S   P E T R I   A N D
J O H A N N E S   N I C O L A I
D E   B A M B E R G A

3286 Bartolus de Saxoferrato: Super secunda parte Digesti veteris. Before 6 April 1474.

f°. [198] leaves (1 blank); 436 x 288 mm.

Initials and paragraph marks added in red. Contemporary half blind-stamped pigskin and wooden boards; brass clasp plates on back cover with fragments of leather thongs, latches on front, clasps gone. MS ownership notation in upper margin of [a]2r, "Collegii S. Petri junioris Argentinae"; Hopetoun bookplate (no. 247 in the Sotheby sale catalogue, February 1889). Imperfect: sheet 12 wanting, supplied in photographic reproduction; wormed.

H 2569(2); Pell 1918(2); GW 3593 (assigned to Vydenast, Petri, and Nicolai); IGI 1358; Veneziani 7.

30 November 1951–Received. Law Library

3287 **Cepolla, Bartholomaeus:** De servitutibus urbanorum et rusticorum praediorum. ca. 1475.

f°. [132] leaves (1 and 132 blank); 344 x 240 mm.

Initial spaces not filled in; without rubrication. Half 18th-century calf and marbled boards.

CR 1556; Pr 7367 (Italian adespota); BMC 6:876 (IC.32702); GW 6494 ("Johann Vydenast und Genossen"); IGI 2693; Goff C–388; Veneziani 14.

13 November 1945–Received. Law Library

3288 **Ubaldis, Nicolaus de:** De successionibus ab intestato. ca. 1475.

[For transcriptions see Copinger.] f°. [a–b^{10}, c^8, d^6]; [34] leaves; 417 x 287 mm. 2 columns (except on [a]1v). [a]2r: 52 lines, 280 x 177 mm. Type: 109R. Initial spaces.

Initials, paragraph marks, underlinings, and capital strokes added in red. Modern blind-stamped calf; brass clasp plates on back cover, latches on front, clasps and thongs gone.

HC 15890; IGI 10001; Goff U–43; Veneziani 19.

Law Library

J O H A N N E S   V Y D E N A S T

3289 **Corneus, Petrus Philippus:** Lectura in librum sextum Codicis. 14 June 1477.

f°. [440] leaves (390, 395, and 440 blank); 425 x 287 mm.

Some copies have a woodcut on [a]2r, others do not.

This copy is without the woodcut. Initial spaces not filled in; without rubrication. Old vellum; leather label on spine. Bookplate of Baron

Horace de Landau (not located in the 1948–49 Sotheby sale catalogues or in Landau's 1885–90 library catalogue). Imperfect: sheet [m]5 and leaves [S]10–12 wanting; blank leaf [V]1 not present.

H 5741*; GW 7565; IGI 3215; Goff C–921; Sack 1101; BSB-Ink C–537.

13 July 1951—Received. Law Library

3290 Bartolinis, Baldus de: De dotibus et dotatis mulieribus et earum iuribus et privilegiis. After 11 March 1482.

f°. [212] leaves (1 and 25 blank); 418 x 282 mm.

Printing begun by Friedrich Eber (or Ebert) and completed by Vydenast after Eber's death in October of 1479; see Giocondo Ricciarelli, "I prototipografi in Perugia," *Bollettino della Deputazione di storia patria per l'Umbria* 67,2 (1970): 140–41. Includes a letter from Cardinal Oliverius Carafa. There is a variant in the caption on [d]3r; see GW.

This copy has error "Iucipit" in the caption on [d]3r. Initials added in brown. Half 19th-century calf and brown cloth. Bookplate of Lee M. Friedman. First blank leaf not present.

H 2467*; Pr 6796 (assigned to Maufer in Padua); GW 3467; IGI 1273; Goff B–178; Sack 471; BSB-Ink B–118.

6 November 1952—Gift of Lee M. Friedman. Inc 7231.20

Treviso

GERARDUS DE LISA

3291 Hermes Trismegistus: Pimander, seu De potestate et sapientia Dei. 18 December 1471.

8°. [56] leaves; 196 x 140 mm.

Translated by Marsilius Ficinus.

A few initials, paragraph marks, and underlinings added in red, but most spaces not filled in; spaces for Greek not filled in. Modern vellum. Autograph in pencil on front flyleaf, "T. De Marinis Florence"; booklabel of Adriana R. Salem.

HR 8456; Pr 6458; BMC 6:883 (IA.28312) and 12:64 (IA.28311); Polain 1885; IGI 4684; Goff H-77; CIBN H-45; Rhodes (T) 5.

27 December 1962–Gift of Ward M. Canaday. Inc 6458 (A)

3292 ——Another copy. 198 x 137 mm.

Initial spaces and spaces for Greek not filled in; without rubrication. 19th-century dark blue straight-grain morocco, blind- and gilt-stamped, edges gilt, by Thouvenin. Booklabel of Sir Mark Masterman Sykes (no. 504 in pt. 2 of the Evans sale catalogue, May 1824); Syston Park bookplate and monogram booklabel of Sir John H. Thorold (no. 1344 in the Sotheby sale catalogue, December 1884); from the library of Richard Ashhurst Bowie. Quire [e] misbound after quire [c].

9 November 1908–Gift of Mrs. E. D. Brandegee. Inc 6458 (B)

3293 ——Another copy. 214 x 147 mm.

Initials added in red and/or blue, capital strokes in yellow; MS quiring; leaves numbered in MS. For binding description see no. 930 in vol. 1, Henricus de Gorichen, *De superstitiosis quibusdam casibus* (Esslingen, Conrad Fyner, not after 1473), with which this is bound, along with Pseudo-Victor, Sextus Aurelius, *De viris illustribus* (Venice, Nicolaus Jenson, ca. 1473), Pseudo-Seneca, *De quattuor virtutibus cardinalibus* (Venice, Printer of Juvenalis, ca. 1470), and Pseudo-Augustinus, *Manuale* (Venice, Florentius de Argentina, not after 1473). Imperfect: leaf [a]1 wanting.

January 1919–Deposited by James M. Hunnewell. Inc 6458 (C)

3294 Pseudo-Phalaris: Epistolae [Latin]. 1471.

8°. [62] leaves; 192 x 133 mm.

Translated by Franciscus Griffolinus.

Initial spaces not filled in; without rubrication. MS signatures, mostly trimmed away. 19th-century calf, edges gilt, rebacked, with the arms of Edward Vernon Utterson stamped in gilt on both covers (not located in the Sotheby sale catalogues of 19 April 1852 or 20 March 1857); autograph on [f]12v, "B. Heywood Bright" (not located in the Sotheby sale catalogues of 3 March or 7 July 1845); from the library of Richard Ashhurst Bowie.

HCR 12892; Pr 6456; BMC 6:883 (IA.28306); IGI 7684; Goff P-548; CIBN P-283; Rhodes (T) 2.

9 November 1908—Gift of Mrs. E. D. Brandegee. Inc 6456

3295 Latini, Brunetto: Il tesoro. 16 December 1474.

f°. [126] leaves (6 blank); 326 x 225 mm.

Translation from the original French attributed to Bono Giamboni.

Large initial on [b]1r illuminated in gold and colors, with extensions in side and upper margins and between the columns; illustration in lower margin (landscape with putti); at center, within a wreath supported by putti, is a coat of arms pasted in to replace an original that has been cut out; initials "F M" on either side of the wreath (?Francesco Melchiori of Oderzo, whose printed booklabel with MS date "1615" is pasted inside the front cover); 5 other initials illuminated, with others added in red or blue. Contemporary blind-stamped leather over wooden boards; leather thongs with brass clasps nailed to front cover, latches on back; inscription "TEXORO DE SER BRVNETO" in orange on lower, side, and top edges; in a half morocco case. Booklabel of George Dunn (no. 894 in pt. 2 of the Sotheby sale catalogue, February 1914); bookplate of Giuseppe Martini (no. 231 in his incunabula catalogue, 1934). Blank leaf not present.

HCR 4009; Pr 6459; BMC 6:884 (IB.28317); Pell 3033; IGI 5696; Goff L-70; CIBN L-52; Rhodes (T) 9.

10 January 1954—Gift of Harrison D. Horblit. Inc 6459

3296 Pius II, Pope: Epistola ad Mahumetem. 12 August 1475.

4°. LVI leaves (XXVIII and XXXIII misnumbered XXVIIII and XXXII); 188 x 138 mm.

Initial space, with guide-letter, on [a]1r not filled in; without rubrication. 19th-century marbled boards. Booklabel of Count Paul Riant. Imperfect: leaf [f]8 wanting.

H 177*=176; Pr 6464; BMC 6:884 (IA.28328); Pell 114; Polain 3163; IGI 7765; Goff P-700; CIBN P-393; Rhodes (T) 15.

28 December 1899—Gift of J. Randolph Coolidge and Archibald Cary Coolidge. Inc 6464

3297 Zacchia, Laudivius, Vezzanensis: Epistolae magni Turci. ca. 1476.

4°. XXII leaves (XII misnumbered IIX); 207 x 144 mm.

Includes a poem by Antonius Beccadelli.

Initial space, with guide-letter, on [a]1r not filled in; without rubrication. Half 19th-century calf and marbled boards; red leather label on front cover. Autograph "Joh Striglitzund [?]" on c6r and c8r; booklabel of Georg Kloss (no. 2301 in the Sotheby sale catalogue, May 1835).

HC 10502*; Pr 6466; BMC 6:885 (IA.28335); Polain 2562; IGI 5967; Goff M–59; Sack 3764; CIBN L–58; Rhodes (T) 21.

13 August 1856—Gift of Winslow Lewis. Inc 6466

3298 Arte dell'abbaco. 10 December 1478.

4°. [62] leaves; 185 x 122 mm.

Initial spaces, with guide-letters, not filled in; without rubrication. 17th-century vellum; edges stained blue; in a full morocco case. Unidentified bookstamp in upper margin of leaf [a]1r; bookplate and label of C. W. Dyson Perrins (no. 27 in the Sotheby sale catalogue, June 1946). Quire [a] misbound in order: 1–2, 7–8, 3–6.

HCR 1863; BMC 6:883 (note only); GW 2674 (assigned to Michael Manzolus; but see BMC 6:886, note about De Lisa's type 80G); IGI 906 (Manzolus); Goff A–1141; Rhodes (T) 25.

May 1950—Gift of Harrison D. Horblit. Inc 6466.5

3299 Purliliarum, Jacobus, comes: De generosa liberorum educatione. 11 September 1492.

4°. XVIII leaves; 200 x 135 mm.

Includes a poem by Johannes Baptista Uranius and a letter by Franciscus Niger.

Initial spaces, with guide-letters, not filled in; title page ruled in red; without other rubrication. 18th-century calf, front cover loose; in a cloth case. Autograph of Michael Wodhull, with his note "Auct: R. Hoblyn Esqr" and date of acquisition "Mar: 30th 1778" (not located in the Baker & Leigh sale catalogue of the library of Robert Hoblyn, March 1778; no. 2175 in the Sotheby sale catalogue of Wodhull's library, January 1886); bookplate of Richard A. Hoblyn.

H 13608*; Pr 6506; BMC 6:885 (IA.28463); Polain 3244; IGI 8234; Goff P–1139; CIBN P–710; Rhodes (T) 27.

Countway Library

3300 Haedus, Petrus: Anterotica, siue De amoris generibus. 13 October 1492.

4°. [6], XCVII, [1] leaves ([XCVIII] blank); 200 x 146 mm.

Includes poems by Quintius Aemilianus.

Initial spaces, some with guide-letters, not filled in; without rubrication. Old blind-stamped sheep, repaired and rebacked. Bookplate of
Boies Penrose II.

HC 8343*; Pr 6507; BMC 6:885 (IA.28466); Polain 1843; IGI 4642;
Goff H-2; CIBN H-1; Rhodes (T) 28.

9 October 1945—Gift of Boies Penrose II. Inc 6507

3301 Pallavicinus, Baptista: Historia flendae crucis et funeris Jesu Christi.
21 February 1494.

4°. [16] leaves; 180 x 130 mm.

Includes Leonardus Justinianus, *Cantilena "Maria vergine bella."*

Initial spaces, with guide-letters, not filled in; without rubrication.
Modern vellum. Bookplate of Raffaello Bertieri.

HC(+Add) 12282; Pr 6509; BMC 6:885 (IA.28474); Polain 2962; IGI
7152; Goff P-14; CIBN P-9; Rhodes (T) 31.

June 1969—Received by exchange. Inc 6509

M I C H A E L   M A N Z O L U S

3302 Plinius Secundus, Gaius: Historia naturalis. Not before 13 October
1479.

f°. [360] leaves (1 and 360 blank); 285 x 200 mm.

Edited by Philippus Beroaldus. Includes a poem by Hieronymus
Bononius dated "tertio idvs Octobres MCCCCLXXIX."

Initial spaces, most with guide-letters, not filled in; without rubrication. Half old calf and paste-paper boards; title in ink on lower edges.
MS ownership notation "Ludouici Mazentij" in lower margin of a2r;
bookplate and bookstamp of Count Ercole Silva; from the library of
Richard Ashhurst Bowie. Blank leaves not present.

HC 13092*; Pr 6472; BMC 6:888 (IB.28354); IGI 7883; Goff P-791;
CIBN P-462; Rhodes (T) 43.

9 November 1908—Gift of Mrs. E. D. Brandegee. Inc 6472

3303 ——Another copy. 301 x 210 mm.

Large initial on a5v illuminated in gold and colors, with marginal extension; initials elsewhere added in red or blue, paragraph marks, capital strokes, and underlinings in red. 19th-century brown paper wrappers.

Countway Library (William Norton Bullard Collection)

3304 Duranti, Guillelmus: Rationale divinorum officiorum. 1479.

f°. [280] leaves; 295 x 202 mm.

Includes a dedicatory letter from Johannes Aloisius Tuscanus, reprinted from the 1478 Liechtenstein edition.

Initial spaces, with guide-letters, not filled in; without rubrication. Bound in vellum leaves from a printed liturgical work. MS ownership notation on blank a1r, "Fratris Ludouici Jacobonij Interamnatis ord. min. co. anno dñi 1600 6. ap^{lis}." Imperfect: sheet q2 wanting, q4 duplicated in its place.

H 6481*; Pr 6471; BMC 6:887 (IB.28351); Pell 4500; Polain 4341; GW 9119; IGI 3628; Goff D–419; BSB-Ink D–337; Rhodes (T) 38.

30 November 1945—Received. Law Library

3305 Eusebius Caesariensis: De evangelica praeparatione. 12 January 1480.

f°. [108] leaves (1 and 108 blank); 291 x 204 mm.

Translated by Georgius Trapezuntius. Edited by Hieronymus Bononius.

Initials added in blue or red. Half old calf (rebacked) and wooden boards; marks of clasps and latches, no longer present; title in ink on top edges. MS marginalia. Bookstamp "Wm. H. Campbell"; booklabel of Georg Kloss (no. 1571 in the Sotheby sale catalogue, May 1835). Blank leaves not present.

HC 6702*; Pr 6474; BMC 6:888 (IB.28358); Pell 4644; Polain 1432; GW 9443; IGI 3757; Goff E–121; BSB-Ink E–117; Rhodes (T) 45.

20 April 1918—Bought with the Charles Eliot Norton fund. Inc 6474

3306 Caesar, Caius Julius: Commentarii. 30 June 1480.

f°. [168] leaves (1 blank); 290 x 193 mm.

Edited by Hieronymus Bononius. Includes the index of Raimundus
Marlianus.

Initials and paragraph marks added in red. Old paste-paper boards.
MS marginalia, with MS note by the annotator on blank a1r, ".C.
IVLII CAESARIS COMMENTARIORVM BELLI GALLICI LIB.
PRIMVS INCIP. IVLIVS CELSVS CONST. V. C. EMENDAVIT."
From the library of Richard Ashhurst Bowie. Sheet r2 bound in
reverse order.

HC 4217*; Pr 6476; BMC 6:889 (IB.28362); Pell 3144; Polain 4263;
GW 5868; IGI 2325; Goff C-21; BSB-Ink C-27; Rhodes (T) 52.

9 November 1908—Gift of Mrs. E. D. Brandegee. Inc 6476

3307 Juvenalis, Decimus Junius: Satirae [Italian]. Not before 31 August
1480.

f°. [88] leaves (1 blank); 267 x 184 mm.

Italian translation by Georgius Summaripa. Includes Latin and Italian
epigrams by Jacobus Juliarius and Hieronymus Bononius.

Initial spaces not filled in; without rubrication. 18th-century vellum.
Autograph of Michael Wodhull on front flyleaf, with his date of ac-
quisition "Apr: 17th 1783" and note "Paterson's Auct: lib. Rev^d M^r
Crofts" (no. 1820 in the Paterson sale catalogue of the library of
Thomas Crofts, April 1783; no. 1458 in the Sotheby sale catalogue of
books from Wodhull's library, January 1886); from the library of
Richard Ashhurst Bowie. Imperfect: leaf o4 wanting; blank leaf not
present.

HCR 9720; Pr 6477; BMC 6:889 (IB.28364); IGI 5605; Goff J-667;
CIBN J-371; Rhodes (T) 54.

9 November 1908—Gift of Mrs. E. D. Brandegee. Inc 6477

H E R M A N N U S   L I E C H T E N S T E I N

3308 Terentius Afer, Publius: Comoediae. 18 September 1477.

f°. [180] leaves (1, 92, and 180 blank); 300 x 205 mm.

With the commentaries of Aelius Donatus and Johannes Calphurnius. Includes a poem by Hieronymus Bononius. According to IGI, some copies have an extra leaf inserted after a5 to make up lacunae in the text and commentary.

This copy is without the extra leaf in quire a. Initials on A2r and a1r added in red, blue, and green, with marginal extensions; initials elsewhere and paragraph marks added in red or blue, capital strokes in red; some spaces for Greek filled in in MS, others left blank. Contemporary blind-stamped calf, rebacked; brass clasp plates on back cover, latches on front, clasps and thongs gone. MS marginalia. MS ownership notations on verso of blank leaf at end, "Henricus Pyll hunc sibi vendicat librum" and "Edward H. Hall, Heidelberg Apr. 26 [18]56"; others inside front cover, "Sum Andreae Schlick ex dono Henrici PŸlej Anno 1573" and "Ex libris Johannis Hieronymi Schlick. Anno 1663"; bookplate of Charles F. Dunbar.

HC 15408*; Pr 6481; BMC 12:64 (IB.28387); IGI 9428; Goff T-75; CIBN T-71; Rhodes (T) 71.

23 October 1896—Gift of Charles F. Dunbar. Inc 6481

3309 Bonaventura, Saint: Commentarius in secundum librum Sententiarum. 1477.

f°. [334] leaves; 280 x 200 mm.

Initial on A1r added in blue and red, with marginal extension; initials elsewhere added in red or blue. Half old calf and paste-paper boards. Bookplates of Amadeo Svajer and of James Frothingham Hunnewell.

HC 3539*; Pr 6482; BMC 6:892 (IB.28288); Pell 2713; GW 4658; IGI 1884; Goff B-872; Sack 744; BSB-Ink B-658; Rhodes (T) 68.

January 1919—Deposited by James M. Hunnewell. Inc 6482

BERNARDUS DE COLONIA

3310 Maius, Junianus: De priscorum proprietate verborum. 1477.

f°. [330] leaves; 335 x 228 mm.

Large initial on a1v added in red and brown, with marginal extension; initials elsewhere added in red and blue. Half old doeskin and marbled paste-paper boards. MS ownership notation on blank a1r,

"Joannis Zellkis [?]"; from the library of Richard Ashhurst Bowie.

H 10540*; Pr 6483; BMC 6:892 (IB.28393); Polain 2575; IGI 6037; Goff M–96; CIBN M–38; Rhodes (T) 73.

9 November 1908—Gift of Mrs. E. D. Brandegee. Inc 6483

3311 Seneca, Lucius Annaeus: Opera philosophica. 1478.

f°. [214] leaves (1 and 214 blank); 327 x 224 mm.

Includes at end Seneca's *Epistolae*, as well as the spurious letters supposedly exchanged between Seneca and St. Paul. A reprint of the Naples 1475 edition edited by Blasius Romerus.

Initials, paragraph marks, underlinings, and capital strokes added in red. Contemporary blind-stamped pigskin over wooden boards; brass clasp plates on back cover, marks of latches on front, clasps and thongs gone; vellum title label on front cover. Shelf-label of the Universitätsbibliothek Erlangen on spine, with its "doublette" stamp on a2r; from the library of Richard Ashhurst Bowie.

HC 14591*; Pr 6484; BMC 6:892 (IB.28396); Polain 3481; IGI 9969; Goff S–369; Sack 3199; CIBN S–184; Rhodes (T) 74.

9 November 1908—Gift of Mrs. E. D. Brandegee. Inc 6484

BARTHOLOMAEUS
CONFALONERIUS

3312 Merula, Georgius: Enarrationes Satirarum Juvenalis. Not before May 1478.

f°. [122] leaves (1 and 122 blank); 278 x 205 mm.

Includes his *Aduersus Domitii Calderini commentarios* and *Annotationes in orationem Ciceronis pro Ligario.*

Initial spaces, most with guide-letters, not filled in; without rubrication. Half 19th-century vellum and marbled boards. MS ownership notation on p5r, "Liber hic Pauli est Brigolinj 1528 Mart."; booklabel of George Dunn, with his MS date of acquisition "Dec. 1903" (no. 1384 in pt. 2 of the Sotheby sale catalogue, February 1914). Blank leaves not present.

HC 11091*; Pr 6486; BMC 6:893 (IB.28402); Polain 2676; IGI 6378;

Goff M–502; CIBN M–306; Rhodes (T) 75.

18 November 1920—Bought with the Stephen Salisbury fund. Inc 6486

3313 **Vergilius Maro, Publius:** Opera. 13 November 1482.

[For transcriptions see Copinger; but he describes leaf 𝜒10a as blank; in this copy it contains "REGISTRVM HVIVS VOLVMINIS" in 3 columns.] f°. a–z¹⁰, &¹⁰, ꝑ¹⁰, 𝜒¹⁰, aa⁸, bb¹⁰, cc–dd⁸, A⁸, B–C⁶; [314] leaves; 296 x 200 mm. 2 columns (except a1–5 and quires dd–C). bb5r: 42 lines of text, 53 of commentary, 234 x 152 mm. Types: 3:111R, text; Haebler 6*:87/8, commentary. Initial spaces, some with guide-letters.

On the assignment to Treviso see Piero Scapecchi, "Note sulla tipografia trevisana del secolo XV," *Studi trevisani* 2,4 (1985): 23. The book has been assigned to the press of Petrus Maufer in Verona (or Venice), but according to Scapecchi, relying on a document published by Antonio Sartori, Maufer contracted with Bartholomaeus Confalonerius in May 1482 to publish an edition of Vergil. The text type 111R is the same as that used by Confalonerius in his edition of Theophrastus in February 1483. Cf. BMC 7:951 (note on Maufer's types).

With the commentaries of Servius and Domitius Calderinus. Includes the *Appendix Vergiliana*.

Initial spaces not filled in; without rubrication. Contemporary blind-stamped leather over wooden boards; marks of clasp plates on front cover, brass latches on back, clasps and thongs gone. MS ownership notation blotted out on a1r. Imperfect: blank outer margins of leaves dd1–C5 cut away.

C 6059; IGI 10206 (Verona, Maufer); Goff V–181 (Venice, Maufer); Davies-Goldfinch 48.

17 April 1957—Gift of Mrs. Robert C. Seamans and Campbell Bosson. Inc 6488.5

3314 **Theophrastus:** De historia plantarum [Latin]. 20 February 1483.

f°. [156] leaves (1 blank); 305 x 201 mm.

Latin translation by Theodorus Gaza. Edited, with a table, by Georgius Merula.

Initial spaces, most with guide-letters, not filled in; without rubrication. 16th-century blind-stamped leather over wooden boards; marks of clasp plates on front cover, brass latches on back, clasps and thongs gone; marks of center and corner bosses, no longer present; title in ink on lower edges. MS marginalia. MS ownership notation "Antonii Fvmanelli" on k6v; from the library of Richard Ashhurst Bowie.

HC 15491*; Pr 6489; BMC 6:894 (IB.28409); IGI 9508; Goff T–155; CIBN T–108; Rhodes (T) 78.

9 November 1908–Gift of Mrs. E. D. Brandegee. Inc 6489

3315 ——Another copy. 305 x 212 mm.

Initial spaces not filled in; without rubrication. Old vellum; leather labels on spine. Blank leaf not present.

Countway Library (William Norton Bullard Collection)

B E R N A R D I N U S   C E L E R I U S

3316 **Dionysius Halicarnassensis:** Antiquitates Romanae. 24 February 1480.

f°. [300] leaves (1 blank); 291 x 202 mm.

Some copies have "DION. HALICARNA." on [a]1r, others do not; there are variants on [a]2r and [P]6r; see BMC and GW. Latin translation by Lampugninus Biragus.

This copy is without [a]1 (blank?) and has the main GW transcriptions on [a]2r and [P]6r. Initial spaces, with guide-letters, not filled in; without rubrication. Half 19th-century red morocco and marbled boards. From the library of Richard Ashhurst Bowie.

HC(+Add) 6239*; Pr 6490; BMC 6:895 (IB.28412, 28412a–b); Pell 4300, 4300A–C; Polain 1312, 1312A; GW 8423; IGI 3484; Goff D–250; BSB-Ink D–174; Rhodes (T) 79.

9 November 1908–Gift of Mrs. E. D. Brandegee. Inc 6490 (A)

3317 ——Another copy. 288 x 210 mm.

This copy is without [a]1 (blank?) and has the main GW transcriptions on [a]2r and [P]6r. Leaf [a]4r has a large initial illuminated in gold and colors and has the illuminated arms of Bilibald Pirckheimer in the lower margin; initials elsewhere not filled in. Modern black morocco over wooden boards; top edges gilt. Bookplates of Bilibald Pirckheimer and of the Royal Society, with the latter's "Sold" stamp; bookplate of James Frothingham Hunnewell.

January 1919—Deposited by James M. Hunnewell. Inc 6490 (B)

3318 ——Another copy. 294 x 210 mm.

This copy is without [a]1 (blank?) and has the main GW transcriptions on [a]2r and [P]6r. Initial spaces not filled in; without rubrication. Old vellum, with the armorial stamp of Thomas Grenville in gilt on the covers and his booklabel inside front cover. Imperfect: inner sheet of each quire (a total of 76 leaves) wanting.

August 1979—Gift of Mrs. Carl Pickhardt. Inc 6490 (C)

J O H A N N E S   R U B E U S

3319 **Strabo:** Geographia. 26 August 1480.

f°. [320] leaves (1 and 320 blank); 288 x 200 mm.

Latin translation by Guarinus Veronensis and Gregorius Tiphernas. A reprint of the Sweynheym and Pannartz edition edited by Giovanni Andrea Bussi. Includes a letter by Bartholomaeus Parthenius.

Initial spaces not filled in; without rubrication. Contemporary wormed boards, rebacked in modern leather; marks of clasp plates and latches, no longer present. MS ownership notation in upper margin of a2r, "Monasterij Baumburg."

HC 15089*; Pr 6493; BMC 6:896 (IB.28422); Polain 3625; IGI 9173; Goff S-796; Sack 3296; CIBN S-473; Rhodes (T) 84.

29 May 1962—Gift of Ward M. Canaday. Inc 6493

3320 **Plinius Secundus, Gaius Caecilius:** Epistolae. 1483.

4°. [92] leaves (1 blank); 205 x 150 mm.

A few initials added in brown, but most spaces, some with guideletters, not filled in; without rubrication. Half modern brown morocco and green cloth; vellum index tabs at beginning of books. From the library of Richard Ashhurst Bowie.

HC 13113*; Pr 6497; BMC 6:896 (IA.28433); Polain 4662; IGI 7900;

Goff P–808; CIBN P–475; Rhodes (T) 87.

9 November 1908–Gift of Mrs. E. D. Brandegee. Inc 6497

3321　——Another copy. 185 x 140 mm.

Initials added in red or blue. Old vellum. Autographs on a2r and fly-leaf at end, "Jacobus Jacquillat" and "Joseph Camusat 1748." Blank leaf not present.

Countway Library

3322 Thucydides: Historia belli Peloponnesiaci. 1483?

f°. [136] leaves (1 and 136 blank); 298 x 198 mm.

Latin translation by Laurentius Valla. Edited by Bartholomaeus Parthenius.

Initial spaces not filled in; without rubrication. Half old vellum and marbled boards. Bookseller's ticket of John Penington & Son, Philadelphia. MS ownership notations in upper margin of a2r, "Francisci Bocchij" (crossed out) and "Ludovici Torbini"; from the library of Richard Ashhurst Bowie. Blank leaf a1 not present.

HC 15511*; Pr 6500; BMC 6:896 (IB.28439); Polain 3782; IGI 9641; Goff T–359; CIBN T–263; Rhodes (T) 88.

9 November 1908–Gift of Mrs. E. D. Brandegee. Inc 6500

3323　——Another copy. 305 x 210 mm.

Initial spaces not filled in; without rubrication. Contemporary Neapolitan blind- and gilt-tooled binding, with some minor repair and regilding where clasp plates and latches have been removed; spine also repaired, probably reproducing the original tooling; edges gauffered with a small tool; in a cloth case. MS ownership notations on a2r, "S Seuerinus" and (washed) "Durand"; another on blank a1r, "Sibi et amicis emit [name blotted out] aquis Sextiis [i.e., Aix-en-Provence] 1551 18^{lb}"; and in another hand, "cet ouvrage appartenait a durand de maillane avocat au parlement d'aix"; booklabels of Philip and Frances Hofer. Blank leaf r8 not present.

7 December 1953–Gift of Philip Hofer. Typ Inc 6500

3324　——Another copy. 272 x 182 mm.

Initial spaces not filled in; without rubrication. 19th-century brown morocco by Rivière. Bookstamp of the Biblioteca municipale, Ancona, on k5r. First blank leaf not present.

Countway Library

3325 Platina, Bartholomaeus: Vitae pontificum. 10 February 1485.

f°. [136] leaves (136 blank); 281 x 195 mm.

BMC has note, "This book, which shows no internal connexion with Treviso, may conceivably be Venetian and date from 1485/6. The watermark of a crescent was in use in both Treviso and Venice about this time."

Initial spaces not filled in; without rubrication. 19th-century vellum; edges stained red. Booklabel of Count Paul Riant. Imperfect: quire q^8 wanting; blank leaf not present.

HC 13048*; Pr 6498; BMC 6:897 (IB.28435); Polain 3188; IGI 7859; Goff P-770; Sack 2907; CIBN P-445; Rhodes (T) 91.

28 December 1899—Gift of J. Randolph Coolidge and Archibald Cary Coolidge. Inc 6498

3326 Livius, Titus: Historiae Romanae decades. 1485.

f°. [256] leaves (1, 106, and 256 blank); 318 x 228 mm.

Edited by Lucas Porrus after the edition of Giovanni Andrea Bussi. There are variant settings of quire a; see below.

This copy has the following line-endings in quire a:

a2r, line 46:	praestãtius
a2v, line 45:	audiente .p
a3r, line 4:	ipse hau-
a3v, line 10:	quo cogita
a4r, line 20:	de quo
a4v, line 3:	defēderat
a5r, line 8:	aesti-
a5v, line 21:	captus est

Large initial on c2r illuminated in gold and colors, with marginal extension; initials elsewhere and capital strokes added in red. 18th-century black morocco, spine and edges gilt. Leaf a10 misbound after b6; blank leaves not present.

HC 10136*; Pr 6499; BMC 6:897 (IB.28437); Polain 2499; IGI 5777; Goff L–244; Sack 2254; CIBN L–183; Rhodes (T) 90.

28 April 1913–Gift of Mrs. E. D. Brandegee. Inc 6499 (A)

3327 ——Another copy. 326 x 222 mm.

This copy has the following line-endings in quire a:

a2r, line 46:	praestantius
a2v, line 45:	audiēte per
a3r, line 4:	ipse hause-
a3v, line 10:	quo cogi-
a4r, line 20:	de quo am-
a4v, line 3:	defenderat
a5r, line 8:	aestimatis
a5v, line 21:	captus ē

Initial spaces not filled in; without rubrication. Half modern brown morocco and brown buckram. MS ownership notation in upper margin of a2r, "Ad usum magistri Andreae [quon]dam tonelli de fiuizano"; bookplate of John S. Lawrence. Imperfect: sheet gg4 wanting; first and last blank leaves not present.

8 August 1924–Bequest of John Strachan Lawrence. Inc 6499 (B)

P A U L U S   D E   F E R R A R I A

3328 Terentius Afer, Publius: Comoediae. 5 July 1481.

f°. [158] leaves (1 and 158 blank); 285 x 196 mm.

With the commentary of Aelius Donatus. Edited by Aloisius Strazarolus.

Initials added in red or blue, paragraph marks in red. Half modern dark blue morocco and gray cloth. Partly eradicated coat of arms in lower margin of a2r; smudged bookstamp on same leaf with initials

"N B"; from the library of Richard Ashhurst Bowie. Leaf a10 misbound after b1; blank leaves not present.

HC 15393*; Pr 6501; BMC 6:898 (IB.28444); IGI 9436; Goff T-79; Rhodes (T) 94.

9 November 1908–Gift of Mrs. E. D. Brandegee. Inc 6501

3329 Persius Flaccus, Aulus: Satirae. 1481.

f°. [28] leaves; 281 x 196 mm.

With the commentary of Bartholomaeus Fontius.

Initial on a2r added in brown; spaces elsewhere, one with guide-letter, not filled in; without rubrication. Old vellum. Booklabel of George Dunn, with his MS date of acquisition "Jan. 1901" (no. 1459 in pt. 2 of the Sotheby sale catalogue, February 1914).

H 12719?=H 12720=H 12727*; Pr 6502; BMC 6:898 (IB.28445); IGI 7494; Goff P-342; CIBN P-138; Rhodes (T) 93.

23 April 1914–Bought with the Constantius fund. Inc 6502

Genoa

MATHIAS MORAVUS
AND MICHAEL DE MONACHO

3330 Nicolaus de Ausmo: Supplementum Summae Pisanellae. 22 June 1474.

f°. [370] leaves (1 and 370 blank); 290 x 210 mm.

Includes Astesanus de Ast, *Canones poenitentiales.*

Initials and paragraph marks added in red and/or blue; traces of MS quiring. Half 19th-century vellum and marbled boards; leather labels on spine. MS ownership notation erased from lower margin of [a]2r; booklabel of Adriana R. Salem.

HC 2152; Pr 7185; BMC 7:901 (IB.31913); Pell 1625; IGI 6869; Goff N-59; CIBN N-32.

30 May 1958–Gift of Ward M. Canaday. Inc 7185

Mantua

P E T R U S   A D A M
D E   M I C H A E L I B U S

3331 Gambilionibus, Angelus de: Tractatus de maleficiis. 1472.

f°. [108] leaves; 408 x 290 mm.

Initials on [a]1r, paragraph marks, capital strokes, and underlinings added in red. Contemporary blind-stamped leather over wooden boards, rebacked and repaired; brass clasp plates on back cover, latches (lettered "ONO") on front, clasps and thongs gone. Luigi Pescasio (*Pietro Adamo de'Micheli, protoeditore mantovano* [Mantova, 1972]) describes this as "la seconda opera" of De Michaelibus and reproduces the first leaf from the BMC copy.

H 1623; Pr 6880; BMC 7:927 (IC.30603); Pell 1150; GW 10517; IGI 4154; Goff G–58; Rhodes (M) 1.

23 November 1945–Received. Law Library

3332 Nuvolonus, Philippus: Oratio ad Christiernum, regem Daciae, habita Mantuae 12 Maii 1474. After 12 May 1474.

4°. [10] leaves; 202 x 142 mm.

It is uncertain whether this pamphlet was printed by Petrus Adam de Michaelibus or by Paulus de Butzbach, who, along with his brother Georgius, printed an edition of Dante (1472) in which De Michaelibus's type 106R (the type of this Nuvolonus) is used. According to BMC, "De Michaelibus had apparently abandoned printing by February, 1473" and suggests that the Nuvolonus pamphlet "is probably the work of some jobbing printer." But Dennis E. Rhodes (see "Filippo Nuvolone of Mantua" in his *Studies in Early Italian Printing* [London, 1982]: [144]–48) questions this and says "unless contemporary documents exist to prove this, it seems to me equally possible that Petrus Adam was still in charge of his press." Luigi Pescasio (see previous entry) describes the Nuvolonus as "la quarta opera" of De Michaelibus and reproduces it in facsimile.

Initial on [a]1r added in red and brown, with marginal extension. Unbound; in a half calf case. From the library of Count Paul Riant. Imperfect: last leaf (end of text and colophon) wanting, supplied in photographic reproduction from the copy in the Marciana, Venice.

R 1008; IGI 6940; Goff N–279.

28 December 1899–Gift of J. Randolph Coolidge and Archibald Cary Coolidge. Inc 6882.5

JOHANNES VURSTER

3333 Arnoldus de Villa Nova: De arte cognoscendi venena. 1473.

4°. [42] leaves (17 blank); 215 x 155 mm.

Includes: Valascus de Tarenta, *De epidemia et peste.*–Petrus de Abano, *De venenis eorumque remediis.*–Matthaeus Silvaticus, *De lapide begaar.* Printed by Vurster with Johannes Baumeister.

Harvard has the Petrus de Abano section only ([c¹⁰, d–e⁸]). Initials, paragraph marks, capital strokes, and underlinings added in red. 19th-century marbled boards. Bookplate of James Frothingham Hunnewell. Blank leaf [c]1 not present.

HC 7* and 1805*; Pr 6884; BMC 7:929 (IA.30623); Pell 6 and 1307; Polain 3075; GW 2522; IGI 861; Goff A–1067; BSB-Ink A–735; Rhodes (M) 9 and 12.

January 1919–Deposited by James M. Hunnewell. Inc 6884

**3334 ——Another copy. 220 x 165 mm.

The Petrus Abano section only. Initials on [c]3v and [c]4r added in red and blue and red and green respectively, with marginal extensions; initials elsewhere added in red or blue. Old vellum, spine and edges gilt. Stamp on [c]2r, "Bibliothecae & Conventus S. Himerij"; booklabel and autograph of George Dunn, with his MS date of acquisition "May 1898" (no. 685 in pt. 2 of the Sotheby sale catalogue, February 1914).

Countway Library

3335 Pseudo-Aristoteles: Problemata [Text beginning: Cur exuperantiae]. 1473?

4°. [96] leaves (1 blank); 258 x 175 mm.

Latin translation by Theodorus Gaza. Printed by Vurster with Johannes Baumeister.

Initial spaces not filled in; without rubrication. 18th-century olive morocco by Derôme; edges gilt. From the library of Richard Ashhurst Bowie, with his MS notes inserted at front: "This is the copy which belonged to the duc de La Vallière [no. 1231 in vol. 1 of the De Bure catalogue, 1783] ... The binding is by Derôme. The volume figured in the Didot sale (1876), and came thence to me ... RAB—1878."

HCR 1729; Pr 6886; BMC 7:929 (IB.30628); Pell 1217; GW 2452; IGI 846; Goff A–1030; Rhodes (M) 21 (dated "c. 1475"; but Vurster had moved to Bologna before the end of 1473).

9 November 1908—Gift of Mrs. E. D. Brandegee. Inc 6886

PAULUS DE BUTZBACH

3335A Thomas Aquinas: Summae theologicae secundae partis pars secunda. ca. 1473?

f°. [396] leaves (1 and 388 blank); 321 x 218 mm.

Printed by Butzbach for Ludovicus de Cremona.

Initial spaces not filled in; paragraph marks added in red. Old vellum; edges mottled red and green. MS marginalia. Booklabel of George Dunn, with his MS date of acquisition "Ap. 1897" (no. 1668 in pt. 2 of the Sotheby sale catalogue, February 1914). First blank leaf not present.

HC 1458; Pr 6888A; BMC 7:930 (IB.30633); Pell 1048; IGI 9590; Goff T–213; CIBN T–180.

22 March 1919—Bought with the John Harvey Treat fund. Inc 6888A

3336 Petrus de Abano: Expositio Problematum Aristotelis cum textu. 1475.

[For transcriptions see Pellechet; but this copy has "nutrimentū" for her "nutrimētū" on leaf 9.] f°. [π^4, a–d^{10}, e–h$^{8.10}$, i–n^{10}, o–r^8, s^{10}, t^8, v–z$^{8.10}$, A–B$^{8.10}$, C^8, D^6, E–H^8, I–K^{10}] ([π]1 and [K]9–10 blank); [300] leaves (1 and 299–300 blank); 418 x 283 mm. 2 columns (3 in the table). [a]4r: 63 lines, 246 x 175 mm. Types: 3:105G, text of Aristotle; 2:78G, commentary. Catchwords on each leaf in the first half of the book, none in the second. Initial spaces.

Edited by Stephanus Illarius. The text of Pseudo-Aristotle is in Latin translation. The Annmary Brown catalogue gives a variant arrangement of the first two lines of the colophon: Explicit expositio succinta problematum ‖ Aristo. quā Petrus edidit Paduanus ea nullo prius īterp̄tante ‖.

Initial spaces not filled in; without rubrication. 19th-century red morocco, gilt, edges gilt. Syston Park bookplate and monogram booklabel of Sir John H. Thorold (no. 173 in the Sotheby sale catalogue, December 1884); bookplate of James Frothingham Hunnewell. Blank leaves [π]1 and [K]10 not present.

H 16*; Pr 6892; Pell 11; IGI 846-A; Goff P-436; Rhodes (M) 24.

January 1919–Deposited by James M. Hunnewell. Inc 6892

3337   ——Another copy. 370 x 260 mm.

Initials and paragraph marks added in red or blue. 19th-century blind-stamped calf, with the armorial device of Ralph Sneyd stamped in gilt on covers; covers detached; in a cloth case. Occasional MS marginalia. Imperfect: leaf [a]2 in facsimile; blank leaves not present.

Countway Library (William Norton Bullard Collection)

3338   **Nicolaus de Lyra:** Postilla super quattuor evangelistas. 24 July 1477.

f°. [244] leaves (1 and 244 blank); 290 x 202 mm.

Includes additions of Paulus de Sancta Maria and the *Replicationes* of Matthaeus Doering.

Initials added in red or blue, paragraph marks and capital strokes in red. Old vellum. Bookstamp of Giuseppe Ruzzini. Quire ii^8 misbound after quire ⁊^{10}; blank leaf at end not present.

HC 10386*; Pr 6893; BMC 7:931 (IB.30640); Polain 2828; IGI 6835; Goff N-130; CIBN N-66; Rhodes (M) 30.

10 May 1943–Bought with the Subscription fund. Inc 6893

3339   **Albertus Magnus:** De animalibus. 12 January 1479.

f°. [306] leaves (5 blank); 407 x 285 mm.

Printed by Butzbach for Marcus Mazola and Antonius de Vignono.

Initial spaces, some with guide-letters, not filled in; without rubrication. Half 18th-century sheep and orange boards. Quire Z misbound in order: 4-7, 1-3, 8-10. Imperfect: quire π^4 (table) wanting.

HC(Add) 546*; Pr 6895; BMC 7:931 (IC.30645); Pell 340; GW 588; IGI 162; Goff A-224; BSB-Ink A-143; Rhodes (M) 32.

Museum of Comparative Zoology Library

J O H A N N E S   S C H A L L U S

3340 Paulus de Sancta Maria: Scrutinium scripturarum. 1475.

f°. [270] leaves (150 and 250 blank); 276 x 193 mm.

Includes Rabbi Samuel Maroccanus, *Epistola contra Iudaeorum errores* in the Latin translation of Alphonsus Boni Hominis. The first quire is unsigned; in quires b–g the signatures have been added by hand-stamping far down in the lower right-hand corner and have probably been trimmed away in many copies; in the rest of the book the signatures are in normal position immediately below the text.

Initial spaces not filled in except in quires M–N, where initials are added in red; these two quires have probably been supplied from another copy. 19th-century calf; top edges stained red. Bookplate of James Frothingham Hunnewell. Blank leaf L10 not present.

HC 10765; Pr 6898; BMC 7:933 (IB.30652); Polain 3011; IGI 7328; Goff P-204; CIBN P-73; Rhodes (M) 16.

January 1919–Deposited by James M. Hunnewell. Inc 6898

3341 Eusebius Caesariensis: Historia ecclesiastica. Not before 15 July 1479.

f°. [172] leaves (172 blank); 298 x 207 mm.

Latin translation by Rufinus Aquileiensis.

Initial spaces, some with guide-letters, not filled in; without rubrication. Half 19th-century brown morocco and marbled boards, re-hinged and repaired. Blank leaf not present.

HC 6711*; Pr 6908; BMC 7:933 (IB.30664); Pell 4638; Polain 1428; GW 9437; IGI 3762; Goff E-127; Sack 1377; BSB-Ink E-112; Rhodes (M) 33.

18 February 1890–Gift of Alfred Waites. Inc 6908

3342 ——Another copy. 289 x 200 mm.

Initial spaces not filled in; without rubrication. Old vellum. Bookplates of Arthur Kay (not in the Sotheby sale catalogue, May 1930) and of William King Richardson. MS ownership notation on [a]1v, "Ex bibli^{ca}. Altemps^{na}."

1951—Bequest of William King Richardson. WKR 1.2.5

VINCENTIUS BERTOCHUS

3343 Baptista Mantuanus: Adolescentia. 16 September 1498.

4°. [40] leaves; 208 x 154 mm.

In some copies the day-date is omitted from the colophon.

This copy has the day-date in the colophon. Initial spaces, most with guide-letters, not filled in; capital strokes added in red in the first quire only. Modern red morocco by Sangorski & Sutcliffe. Marginal annotations in quires a–d.

HC(+Add) 2401; C 857; Pr 6910; BMC 7:934 (IA.30683); Pell 1808; GW 3244; IGI 1175; Goff B-53; BSB-Ink B-37; Rhodes (M) 40.

November 1967—Gift of Mrs. Henry S. Grew. Inc 6910

3344 Bossus, Matthaeus: Epistolae familiares et secundae. 9 November 1498.

f°. [144] leaves (144 blank); 290 x 203 mm.

Includes additions by Jason Mayno and Balthasar Crassus. Quire b occurs in two settings; cf. BMC; GW points out variants on A3r, A4r, c1r, and z7v.

This copy has the readings of BMC IB.30685 in quire b, the main GW transcriptions for A3r, A4r, and z7v, and the GW *Anmerkung* reading for c1r. Blank leaf z8r shows an offset of z1v, z8v an offset of z2r. Initial spaces, most with guide-letters, not filled in; without rubrication. Old vellum, spine gilt; leather labels on spine. Two impressions of a smudged bookstamp on title page. Quire m misbound after n.

HC(+Add) 3671*; Pr 6911; BMC 7:923 (IB.30685); Pell 2780; GW 4956; IGI 2019; Goff B-1042; Sack 790; BSB-Ink B-761; Rhodes (M) 42.

Countway Library (William Norton Bullard Collection)

Parma

A N D R E A S   P O R T I L I A

3345 Ovidius Naso, Publius: Metamorphoses. 15 May 1480.

f°. [188] leaves (1 and 188 blank); 262 x 176 mm.

Includes Domitius Calderinus, *De exilio Ovidii.*

Initial spaces, with guide-letters, not filled in; without rubrication.
Half old vellum and decorated boards. Autograph of James B. Thayer
dated April 1898; bookplate and autograph of William S. Thayer
dated 1904. Imperfect: sheets a2-3 wanting; blank leaf &6 not present.

H 12160*; BMC 7:937 (IB.30263); IGI 7118; Goff O-182; CIBN O-
116.

16 January 1933—Bequest of William S. Thayer. Inc 6849.10

3346 Solinus, Caius Julius: Polyhistor, siue De mirabilibus mundi. 20
December 1480.

4°. [102] leaves (1 blank); 193 x 135 mm.

Initials added in red or blue. Old vellum; edges stained blue. MS
ownership notation below colophon, "Hic liber est Dõnj Frãciscj Bar-
barj aere p̄rno consecutus"; from the library of Richard Ashhurst
Bowie, with a slip of his MS notes inserted at front: "On the last page
is the autograph of Francesco Barbaro, a noble Venetian, to whom
the volume belonged. He was a greatgrandson of the celebrated Francesco Barbaro, who died in 1454, and father to Daniel Barbaro, patri-
arch of Aquileia. Ermolao Barbaro, the celebrated scholar, author of
the 'Castigationes Plinianae,' etc., was his uncle. The book seems to
have come to him by inheritance, for he speaks of it as 'aere paterno
consecutus.' " Quire b wrongly bound in order: 1-2, 4, 3, 6, 5, 7-8.

HC 14878; Pr 6850; BMC 7:937 (IA.30264); IGI 9088; Goff S-619;
CIBN S-306.

9 November 1908—Gift of Mrs. E. D. Brandegee. Inc 6850 (A)

3347 ——Another copy. 198 x 135 mm.

Initial spaces, with guide-letters, not filled in; without rubrication.
18th-century calf, rebacked; edges speckled blue. Bookplate of James

Frothingham Hunnewell. With this are bound Cornelius Nepos, *Vitae imperatorum* (Milan, Pachel and Scinzenzeler, 1480?), and Lucius Annaeus Florus, *Epitome de Tito Livio* (Siena, Sigismundus Rodt, 1486 or 7). Blank leaf not present.

January 1919—Deposited by James M. Hunnewell. Inc 6850 (B)

3348 Plinius Secundus, Gaius: Historia naturalis. 8 July 1481.

f°. [268] leaves (1 and 268 blank); 405 x 271 mm.

Edited by Philippus Beroaldus.

Large initial on a3r illuminated in gold and colors; illuminated coat of arms in lower margin; initials elsewhere added in red or blue. Old vellum. Bookplate of William King Richardson.

HC 13094*; Pr 6851; BMC 7:937 (IC.30266); IGI 7885; Goff P–793; CIBN P–464.

1951—Bequest of William King Richardson. WKR 10.2.3

3349 ——Another copy. 416 x 288 mm.

Initials added in red and/or blue, paragraph marks in red or blue, but the blue has been partly washed away. 17th-century calf, spine gilt; edges speckled red. MS ownership notation in top margin of a2r, "Joannes Potier"; crowned armorial bookstamp in lower margin; large aquatinted bookplate "Bibliotheca Electoralis publica," signed "C. F. Holtzmann fec. Dresde." Blank leaves not present.

Countway Library

STEPHANUS CORALLUS

3350 Plinius Secundus, Gaius: Historia naturalis. 1476.

f°. [358] leaves (1 and 358 blank); 417 x 282 mm.

Edited by Philippus Beroaldus. There is a variant on [z]9r; see BMC.

In this copy the last word on [z]9r is printed "ulcerib9." Large initial on [c]1r illuminated in red, blue, green, and gray, with marginal extension; initials elsewhere and paragraph marks added in red or blue. Old vellum. MS ownership notation in lower margin of [a]2r, "Est Bibl.ae S. Georgij M.is Venet.rum"; another in lower margin of

[P]3r, "Iste liber ẽ monachoᚱ congⁿⁱˢ. s. Justine de padua deputat9 ĩ s. Georgio Venetiaᴢ signat9 nͬo. 545"; MS notation in upper margin of [a]2r, "King's Chapel, Boston, to the Library of Harvard University, Cambridge. 1841." Blank leaves not present.

HC 13091; Pr 6842; BMC 7:939 (IC.30223-23a); IGI 7882; Goff P-790; CIBN P-461 ("Roma"[!]).

1841–Gift of the Minister, Wardens, and Vestry of King's Chapel, Boston. Inc 6842 (A)

3351   ——Another copy. 402 x 263 mm.

In this copy the last word on [z]9r is printed "ulcreib9." Initial spaces not filled in; without rubrication. 18th-century red morocco, spine and edges gilt. Bookplate of James Frothingham Hunnewell. Imperfect: leaves [a]1-3 and [P]3-4 wanting; text of [P]3 supplied in MS; [a]4 slightly mutilated.

January 1919–Deposited by James M. Hunnewell. Inc 6842 (B)

3352   ——Another copy. 430 x 280 mm.

In this copy the last word on [a]9r is printed "ulcerib9." Large initial on [a]4r illuminated in gold and colors, with an elaborate 3-sided white vine stem border, including an illuminated coat of arms in the lower panel; initials at beginning of books illuminated in gold and colors; other initials added in red or blue. Contemporary blind-stamped leather over wooden boards; marks of clasps, no longer present. Bookstamp of the Albani library on [a]2r; autograph of Henry H. Gibbs, baron Aldenham, dated 1860, with his Aldenham House bookplate (described on p. 132 of his 1888 library catalogue); booklabel of Frances Hofer.

24 July 1974–Gift of Philip Hofer. Typ Inc 6842

3353   ——Another copy. 350 x 230 mm.

In this copy the last word on [a]9r is printed "ulcreib9." Initials at beginning of books crudely added in pencil or water color, but most spaces not filled in. Half 16th-century blind-stamped pigskin and wooden boards; one brass clasp plate with leather thong and clasp remains on back cover, latch on front, the other gone. Autograph "M: G: Wichrig [?] 1639" on [a]2r; also "Carmeli Straubingani Ex Donatione D. Förgin [?]." Blank leaf [a]1 not present; quire [F] misbound after [G].

Countway Library (Warren Library)

3354 Florus, Lucius Annaeus: Epitome de Tito Livio. 1476/78.

4°. [80] leaves; 228 x 160 mm.

Edited by Philippus Beroaldus.

Initial on [a]1r added in brown; spaces elsewhere, with guide-letters, not filled in. Old vellum; leather labels on spine; edges stained blue. MS ownership (?) notation on flyleaf at front, "June 27. 1723. Collat. & perfect. J. Wright"; another on inner margin of [a]1r, "Liber Joannis Gordon de Buthlay advocati. 16.° Maij 1761. Edinburgi."; armorial bookplate "Gordon of Buthlaw"; from the library of Richard Ashhurst Bowie, with a slip of his MS notes inserted at front.

HC(Add) 7200; Pr 6845; BMC 7:939 (IB.30232); Pell 4854; GW 10097; IGI 4009; Goff F–235.

9 November 1908—Gift of Mrs. E. D. Brandegee. Inc 6845

3355 ——Another copy. 212 x 158 mm.

Initial spaces not filled in; without rubrication. For binding description see no. 1600 in vol. 2, Plutarchus, *Apophthegmata* (Venice, Printer of Basilius, *De vita solitaria*, ca. 1471/72), which is bound with this.

9 December 1920—Bought with the Stephen Salisbury fund. Inc 4142.10

D A M I A N U S   D E   M O Y L L I S

3356 Magistris, Johannes de: Quaestiones super tota philosophia naturali. 12 December 1481.

f°. [164] leaves (1 blank); 294 x 198 mm.

Initial spaces, with guide-letters, not filled in; without rubrication. Old calf over wooden boards. Occasional MS marginalia. Armorial bookplate "Bibliothèque de Sᵗ Philippe," with motto "Sans peur et sans reproche."

HC 10447*; Pr 6860; BMC 7:940 (IB.30314); Polain 4538; IGI 5939; Goff M–25; Sack 2303; CIBN M–17.

17 February 1923—Bought with the John Harvey Treat fund. Inc 6860 (A)

3357 ——Another copy. 265 x 183 mm.

Initials added in red and/or blue, paragraph marks in red or blue; ruled in red throughout. Modern green buckram. Bookplate of Francis H. Fobes. MS marginalia; inserted are three leaves of MS diagrams. Imperfect: leaves r2 and 5 wanting; blank leaf not present.

May 1957–Bequest of Francis H. Fobes. Inc 6860 (B)

3358 ——Another copy. 290 x 195 mm.

Initial spaces not filled in; without rubrication. 19th-century decorated boards. MS ownership notation in lower margin of a2r, "Pertinet ad locum santi Giorgij." MS marginalia.

Countway Library

3359 Martialis, Marcus Valerius: Epigrammata. ca. 1482?

4°. [180] leaves; 193 x 139 mm.

Initial spaces, with guide-letters, not filled in; without rubrication. Half 19th-century calf and marbled boards; edges stained red. Bookplate of Giovanni Marchetti, of Turin; booklabel of John S. Lawrence. Sheets 1–5 of quire g bound in reverse order.

HC(+Add) 10807; Pr 7405 (Italian adespota); BMC 7:941 (IA.30318a-b); IGI 6223; Goff M–303; CIBN M–166.

8 August 1924–Bequest of John Strachan Lawrence. Inc 6861.5

PRINTER OF HIERONYMUS, EPISTOLAE (H 8557)

3360 Hieronymus, Saint: Epistolae. 18 January–15 May 1480.

f°. 2 vols. (vol. 1: [254] leaves, 1 and 254 blank; vol. 2: [330] leaves, 1 blank); 400 x 265 mm.

Reprinted, with changes, from the edition of Theodorus Laelius (Venice, Miscomini, 1476).

Initial spaces, with guide-letters, not filled in; without rubrication; leaves numbered in MS. Half 19th-century vellum and marbled boards. Printed label pasted to lower margin of π2r in vol. 2, "Ex dono D. Parochi Ripaltae"; from the library of Richard Ashhurst

Bowie. Imperfect: first four leaves in vol. 2 remargined and repaired, with some loss of text; blank leaves not present.

HC 8557*; Pr 6855; BMC 7:942 (IC.30283); Polain 4434; IGI 4739; Goff H-169; CIBN H-104.

9 November 1908–Gift of Mrs. E. D. Brandegee. Inc 6855 (A)

3361 ——Another copy. 440 x 290 mm.

Initials added in red and/or blue, paragraph marks in red or blue. Half modern calf and paper boards; leaves numbered in MS. Book- and sold-stamps of the Royal Society, London; from the library of Bilibald Pirckheimer; laid into vol. 1 was found an A.L.s. (Paulus Phrygio) to Pirckheimer, dated "ex Eychstet xv Septembris Anno Etc xiiij"; with a textual question about the reading of a Greek passage in a letter of Jerome to Pammachius (r7v in vol. 1 of this edition). MS marginalia, which do not seem to be in Pirckheimer's hand. Blank leaves not present.

January 1919–Deposited by James M. Hunnewell. Inc 6855 (B)

3362 **Varro, Marcus Terentius:** De lingua Latina. 11 December 1480.

f°. [4], XLVI leaves; 290 x 198 mm.

Issued with the same printer's edition of Nonius Marcellus, *De proprietate sermonum* (1480), but apparently also available separately and so recorded by BMC and IGI. Edited by Pomponius Laetus and Franciscus Rolandellus.

Initial spaces, with guide-letters, not filled in; without rubrication. For binding description see following entry, with which this is bound.

HC 11903*(3); Pr 6858; BMC 7:942 (IB.30288); Polain 4786; IGI 10122; Goff N-267(3); CIBN N-156(3).

May 1957–Bequest of Francis H. Fobes. Inc 6857-58

3363 **Festus, Sextus Pompeius:** De verborum significatione. 1480.

f°. LIIII leaves (XXIIII misnumbered XXIIIII); 290 x 198 mm.

Issued with the same printer's edition of Nonius Marcellus, *De proprietate sermonum* (1480), but apparently also available separately and so recorded by BMC and IGI.

Initial spaces, with guide-letters, not filled in; without rubrication. Old vellum. MS inscription inside front cover, "Bought by Hon. John D. Willard of Troy, N.Y. in Europe. This property of his son Henry Willard. 1864"; bookplate of Francis H. Fobes. With this is bound the same printer's edition of Marcus Terentius Varro, *De lingua Latina* (11 December 1480).

HC 11903*(2); Pr 6857; BMC 7:942 (IB.30287); Polain 4362; IGI 3853-A; Goff N-267(2); CIBN N-156(2); BSB-Ink F-109.

May 1957—Bequest of Francis H. Fobes. Inc 6857-58

ANGELUS UGOLETUS

3364 Augustinus, Aurelius, Saint: Opuscula. 31 March 1491.

f°. [306] leaves (306 blank); 300 x 205 mm.

Edited by Eusebius Conradus and Thaddeus Ugoletus, with a prefatory letter by Severinus Chalcus. For contents see BMC.

Initial spaces, most with guide-letters, not filled in; without rubrication. Half modern brown morocco and marbled boards. Illegible ownership notation on flyleaf at front. Blank leaf not present.

HC 1952; Pr 6864; BMC 7:944 (IB.30336); Pell 1463; GW 2867; IGI 1018; Goff A-1220.

7 May 1913—Gift of Alain Campbell White. Inc 6864

3365 Statuta Parmae. 16 September 1494.

f°. [18], CCXXVI leaves; 290 x 200 mm.

Initial spaces, with guide-letters, not filled in; without rubrication. Half 19th-century vellum and marbled boards. MS marginalia.

HCR 15016; Pr 6872; BMC 7:946 (IB.30360); IGI 7231; Goff S-721; CIBN S-402.

2 June 1913—Gift of William Endicott, Jr. Inc 6872

3366 ——Another copy. 295 x 198 mm.

Initial spaces not filled in; without rubrication. Half 18th-century sheep and marbled boards; leather labels on spine. MS marginalia. Imperfect: leaves aa1-2 and D8 wanting, supplied in MS facsimile;

leaves aa7–8 and bb1 remargined; leaves 14–15 bound in reverse order.

Countway Library (William Norton Bullard Collection)

3367 ——Another copy. 288 x 202 mm.

Initial spaces not filled in; without rubrication. Half old vellum and paste-paper boards.

11 March 1912—Received. Law Library

3368 Ausonius, Decimus Magnus: Opera. 10 July 1499.

4°. [8], LXXVIII leaves; 194 x 140 mm.

Edited by Thaddeus Ugoletus, with additions by Franciscus Paxius and Antonius Securanus.

Initial spaces, with guide-letters, not filled in; without rubrication. 19th-century vellum, spine gilt; leather labels on spine. Bookplate of Count Dmitri Boutourlin (no. 610 in the "Éditions du XV siècle" section of his 1831 catalogue); from the library of Richard Ashhurst Bowie.

HC(+Add) 2181; Pr 6873; BMC 7:946 (IA.30367); Pell 1649; Polain 4178; GW 3094; IGI 1101; Goff A-1404; BSB-Ink A-948.

9 November 1908—Gift of Mrs. E. D. Brandegee. Inc 6873

Verona

J O H A N N E S   N I C O L A I
D E   V E R O N A

3369 Valturius, Robertus: De re militari. 1472.

f°. [262] leaves (5, 6, and 175 blank); ill.; 343 x 235 mm.

For a recent article on this printer see Daniela Fattori, "Per la storia della tipografia da Verona," *La Bibliofilia* 92 (1990): [269]–81.

A few initials added in brown, but most spaces not filled in; without rubrication; dedication to Sigismundus Malatesta added in calligraphic MS capitals on [a]1r; MS quiring; MS catchwords written vertically at ends of quires. Original (?) wooden boards, covered with 19th-century marbled paper; in a cloth case. Booklabel of George Dunn, with his MS date of acquisition "July 1900" (no. 1701 in pt. 2 of the Sotheby sale catalogue, February 1914); bookplate of William King Richardson.

HC 15847*; Pr 6912; BMC 7:948 (IB.30706); IGI 10114; Goff V–88; CIBN V–57; Schäfer 346; Sander 7481.

1951–Bequest of William King Richardson. WKR 2.2.8

3370   ——Another copy. 330 x 228 mm.

Large initial on [a]1r illuminated in gold and colors; original illuminated coat of arms in lower margin excised and replaced by that of a later owner; dedication to Sigismundus Malatesta added in colored MS calligraphic capitals; initials elsewhere added in blue or red, chapter summaries in red; illustrations colored. Half 18th-century red morocco and diced russia. Booklabel of Philip Hofer. Imperfect: a number of leaves remargined at foot; blank leaves not present.

9 November 1984–Bequest of Philip Hofer. Typ Inc 6912

G I O V A N N I   A N D
A L B E R T O   A L V I S E

3371 **Ars moriendi** [Italian]. 28 April 1478.

4°. [32] leaves (32 blank); 208 x 145 mm.

Initials added in red or blue. Modern vellum. Booklabel of Adriana R. Salem.

H 4397=4398; Pr 6913; BMC 7:949 (IA.30713); GW 2621; IGI 889; Goff A–1104.

30 May 1958–Gift of Ward M. Canaday. Inc 6913

3372 **Aesopus:** Fabulae [Metrical version ("Aesopus moralisatus") by Anonymus Neveleti (Gualtherus Anglicus?)]. 26 June 1479.

4°. [120] leaves; ill.; 200 x 146 mm.

Edited and with an Italian translation by Accio Zucco. Woodcuts attributed to Liberale da Verona.

This copy is printed on palimpsest vellum. Initials added in red or blue; woodcuts uncolored. Modern vellum. Booklabel of Philip Hofer. Laid in is a paper copy of the text appearing on k2r, which shows signs of having been pasted over the text on the vellum leaf; the reason for this is unclear, since there is no textual variation; the verso of the paper leaf contains the text appearing on k8v, again with no textual variation. Leaf k1r also shows signs of a paper leaf having been pasted to it, but the leaf is no longer present. Imperfect: quires a–c⁸ and p⁸ wanting; in quire h the text for h3v, h4r, h5v, and h6r has been imposed in the wrong order (h5v, h6r, h3v, and h4r).

HCR 345; Pr 6915; BMC 7:949 (IA.30721); Pell 225; GW 428; IGI 101; Goff A–148; BSB-Ink A–77; Sander 50.

10 January 1956—Gift of Philip Hofer. Typ Inc 6915

PETRUS   MAUFER

3373 Josephus, Flavius: De antiquitate Iudaica. De bello Iudaico. 25 December 1480.

f°. [214] leaves (3 blank); 295 x 195 mm.

The Latin translation is by Rufinus Aquileiensis. Edited by Ludovicus Cendrata. Printed by Maufer for Innocens Ziletus.

A large initial space on a2r has been cut out and replaced (probably in the 19th century) with an initial illuminated in gold and colors and containing a coat of arms; initials elsewhere at beginning of books added in red and blue. 18th-century red morocco, spine and edges gilt. MS ownership notation on flyleaf at front, "Tillhör Bernhard Rosenblad D.16 1820"; bookplate of James Frothingham Hunnewell. Imperfect: quire π² wanting; leaves a2 and D6 mutilated; blank a1 not present.

HC 9452*; Pr 6918; BMC 7:951 (IB.30733); Polain 2334; IGI 5388; Goff J–484; Sack 2161; CIBN J–313.

January 1919—Deposited by James M. Hunnewell. Inc 6918

3374 ——Another copy. 305 x 200 mm.

Large initial on a2r illuminated in gold and colors, with marginal extension; initials elsewhere added in red and blue, paragraph marks in red. Contemporary blind-stamped leather over wooden boards, covers detached; brass clasp plates on back cover, marks of latches on front, clasps and thongs gone. Autograph "Andreas Steynkeller" inside front cover; "Bibliotheca Pezoldiana" bookplate. Blank leaf not present.

Countway Library (Solomon M. Hyams Collection)

B O N I N U S   D E   B O N I N I S

3375 Blondus, Flavius: Roma instaurata. De origine et gestis Venetorum. Italia illustrata. 20 December 1481–7 February 1482.

f°. 2 pts. in 1 vol. (pt. 1: [58] leaves, 58 blank; pt. 2: [94] leaves, 94 blank); 285 x 203 mm.

There are two settings of the first unsigned quire, one in four leaves, the other in six, the first leaf blank and the sixth containing additional verses by Hieronymus Broianicus, a dedicatory epistle by Johannes Antonius Pantheus to Paulus Ramusius, and verses by Ramusius. The register at end of pt. 2 is for both parts and calls for a 4-leaf unsigned quire at beginning of pt. 1.

This copy contains the 4-leaf preliminary quire and agrees with the main GW transcription for the first printed leaf of that quire. Initial spaces not filled in; without rubrication. For binding description see no. 3394, the same author's *Roma triumphans* (Brescia, Bartholomaeus de Carlo, Vercellensis, 1482), with which this is bound. Blank leaf M6 not present.

HC 3243*+3247*; Pr 6920; BMC 7:951 (IB.30743); Pell 2423 and 2425; Polain 702; GW 4423; IGI 1760; Goff B–702; Sack 704; BSB-Ink B–554.

4 May 1905—From the library of Charles Eliot Norton. Inc 6952

3376 Valturius, Robertus: De re militari. 13 February 1483.

f°. [254] leaves (1 and 254 blank); ill.; 296 x 190 mm.

Includes a dedicatory letter of Paulus Ramusius to Pandolfo Malatesta.

Initial spaces, some with guide-letters, not filled in; without rubrication. 18th-century calf, spine gilt, edges speckled red. Bookplate of James Frothingham Hunnewell. Blank leaves not present.

HC 15848*; Pr 6921; BMC 7:952 (IB.30746); IGI 10115; Goff V-89; CIBN V-58; Sander 7482.

January 1919–Deposited by James M. Hunnewell. Inc 6921

3377 ——Another copy. 315 x 210 mm.

Leaf a1r contains a garish and probably not contemporary initial illuminated in gold and colors, with marginal extension; an illuminated coat of arms in the lower panel has been eradicated, with some damage to the paper; initials elsewhere added in red and purple or blue and red. Half old vellum and marbled boards, red label on spine. Bookplate of Philip Hofer. Imperfect: quire y^8 wanting, with quire D^8 of the same printer's Italian edition substituted in its place (the same woodcuts occur in both quires); blank leaf E10 not present.

28 February 1942–Gift of Philip Hofer. Typ Inc 6921

3378 **Valturius, Robertus:** De re militari [Italian]. 17 February 1483.

f°. [314] leaves (1, 7, and 314 blank); ill.; 300 x 202 mm.

Italian translation by Paulus Ramusius.

Initial spaces, a few with guide-letters, not filled in; without rubrication. Half 18th-century vellum stained green and paste-paper boards. Autograph of Michael Wodhull on front flyleaf, with his MS date of acquisition "Feb. 6th 1790" and note "Pinelli Auction" (no. 1205 in the London sale catalogue of the Pinelli library, March 1789; no. 2651 in the Sotheby sale catalogue of books from Wodhull's library, January 1886). Imperfect: many leaves inlaid and remargined; first blank leaf not present.

HC 15849; Pr 6922; BMC 7:952 (IB.30748); IGI 10116; Goff V-90; CIBN V-59; Sander 7483.

6 October 1919–Bought with the Charles Eliot Norton fund. Inc 6922

3379 **Leonicenus, Omnibonus:** De arte metrica. Before 6 June 1483.

[For transcriptions see Copinger.] 4°. A^{12}; [12] leaves; 197 x 148 mm. A1r: 25 lines, 140 x 96 mm. Type: 2:114R; crude and eccentric Greek. Initial spaces.

Initial spaces not filled in; without rubrication. For binding description see following entry, with which this is bound.

C 3545 (dated 1480); IGI 6998; Goff L–170.

27 April 1954–Bought with the Duplicate fund. Inc 6922.5

3380 Perottus, Nicolaus: De generibus metrorum. Before 6 June 1483.

4°. [30] leaves (1 blank); 197 x 148 mm.

Includes his *De Horatii et Boethii metris* and the Hippocratic oath in Latin.

Initial spaces not filled in; without rubrication. Modern vellum. With this are bound (perhaps as issued) Omnibonus Leonicenus, *De arte metrica*, and Servius Maurus, *Centimetrum*, both printed in the same type as the Perottus and without colophons.

C 4691 (assigned to Venice); R 670 (assigned to Han in Rome); Pr 6789 (assigned to Stendal in Padua); BMC 7:952 (IA.30750); IGI 7430; Goff P–298.

27 April 1954–Bought with the Duplicate fund. Inc 6922.5

3381 ——Another copy. 214 x 158 mm.

Initial spaces not filled in; without rubrication. Half japanese vellum and decorated boards. Sheets a3–4 transposed in binding.

Countway Library (William Norton Bullard Collection)

3382 Servius Maurus, Honoratus: Centimetrum. Before 6 June 1483.

4°. [6] leaves; 197 x 148 mm.

Initial spaces not filled in; without rubrication. For binding description see previous entry, with which this is bound.

C 5445 (assigned to Venice, ca. 1476); cf. BMC 7:952 (IA.30750, note); GW (Nachtr) 323; IGI 8942; Goff S–477.

27 April 1954–Bought with the Duplicate fund. Inc 6922.5

PAULUS   FRIDENPERGER

3383 Lucretius Carus, Titus: De rerum natura. 28 September 1486.

f°. [96] leaves (1 and 96 blank); 312 x 206 mm.

There are two settings of sheet c4 and quire d; see BMC and Gordon.

In this copy line 11 of d7r reads "Capitula praecedentis libri secundi." Initial spaces, one with guide-letter, not filled in; without rubri-
cation. 18th-century red morocco, gilt, rebacked; edges stained red.
Autograph of Michael Wodhull on flyleaf at front, with his MS date
of acquisition "Apr: 17th 1783" and note "Paterson's Auct. libr: Revd
Mr Crofts" (no. 1849 in the Paterson sale catalogue of Thomas
Crofts' library, April 1783; no. 1616 in the Sotheby sale catalogue of
books from Wodhull's library, January 1886); from the library of
Richard Ashhurst Bowie. With Wodhull's occasional MS marginalia.
Blank leaf a1 not present.

HCR 10282; Pr 6923; BMC 7:953 (IB.30764); IGI 5866; Goff L–333;
CIBN L–256; Gordon 2.

9 November 1908–Gift of Mrs. E. D. Brandegee. Inc 6923

3384 ——Another copy. 304 x 208 mm.

Reading on d7r as above. Initial spaces not filled in; without rubrication. 18th-century red morocco, gilt, spine gilt. Autograph of Gilbert
Wakefield dated 1795 on flyleaf at front. Imperfect: sheet m1 wanting; several leaves at end waterstained, with some retouching of letters with pen and ink.

30 June 1924–Gift of Sarah C. Sears. Arnold Arboretum Library

PRINTER   OF   AUGURELLUS

(H   1 9 4 3)

3385 **Curtius Rufus, Quintus:** Historiae Alexandri Magni. 18 August 1491.

f°. [70] leaves (70 blank); 300 x 205 mm.

Initial spaces, most with guide-letters, not filled in; without rubrication. Half modern black morocco and red boards. Autograph "Sum
Io: Angelus Aliprandus" on a1v. Blank leaf i6 pasted down.

HCR 5884=H 5883?; Pr 6925; BMC 7:954 (IB.30776); Pell 4066; GW
7874; IGI 3289; Goff C–1001; Sack 1199.

31 March 1931–Received by exchange. Inc 6925

Cremona

BERNARDINUS DE MISINTIS AND CAESAR PARMENSIS

3386 Dio Chrysostomus: De Troia non capta. 22 July 1492.

4°. [20] leaves (1 blank); 200 x 150 mm.

Latin translation by Franciscus Philelphus. Includes additions by Nicolaus Lucaris and Petrus Maria Camarinus. There is a variant in the colophon; see BMC.

In this copy the first word of the colophon reads "Ingeniossimi." Initial space on a3v, with guide-letter, not filled in; without rubrication. Modern white boards.

HC 6184*; Pr 6926; BMC 7:956 (IA.30814); Pell 4262; GW 8370; IGI 3448; Goff D-206; BSB-Ink D-169.

September 1963—Bought with the Susan A. E. Morse fund. Inc 6926

3387 Petrarca, Francesco: De remediis utriusque fortunae. 17 November 1492.

f°. [166] leaves (1 and 166 blank); 310 x 210 mm.

Edited by Nicolaus Lucaris.

Woodcut initial on a2r; initial spaces elsewhere, with guide-letters, not filled in; without rubrication. Old vellum; edges stained blue. From the library of Richard Ashhurst Bowie, with a slip of his MS notes inserted at front.

HC 12793*; Pr 6927; BMC 7:956 (IB.30816); Polain 4644; IGI 7578; Goff P-409; CIBN P-164.

9 November 1908—Gift of Mrs. E. D. Brandegee. Inc 6927

CAROLUS DE DARLERIIS

3388 Aegidii, Guillelmus: Super caelestium motuum indagatione. 14 February 1494/5.

4°. [26] leaves; 210 x 150 mm.

There are a number of variants; see BMC and GW. Edited by Boninus de Boninis.

This copy has a dedication on a2r-v and is without the printer's colophon on c10r. Without rubrication. 19th-century paste-paper boards. MS ownership notation obliterated on title page.

HC(Add) 16220; R 796; Pr 5231 (var.; assigned to Christophorus de Pensis, Venice); BMC 7:958 (IA.30841, var.); GW 264; IGI 54 (var.); Goff A-61.

Countway Library (William Norton Bullard Collection)

3389 Silvester de Prierio: Compendium in Johannem Capreolum cum additionibus. 15-28 April 1497.

4°. [320] leaves; 237 x 180 mm.

Initial spaces, a few with guide-letters, not filled in; without rubrication. Laid into a binding of vellum-covered wooden boards, probably not the original; if lifted out of this binding the stitching and cords are visible, as well as offset from a vellum MS with which the spine was covered; in a cloth case.

HC(+Add) 13346*; Pr 6932; BMC 7:959 (IB.30850); Polain 3543; IGI 8990; Goff S-519; Sack 3238; CIBN S-268.

21 November 1919–Bought with the John Harvey Treat fund. Inc 6932

3390 Barianus, Nicolaus: Causa Vitaliana de praecedentia Heremitarum et Minorum decisa. 6 April 1500.

4°. [26] leaves (26 blank); 196 x 140 mm.

Initial spaces, with guide-letters, not filled in; without rubrication. Half modern olive morocco and green boards. Quire a⁴ misbound between +2 and 3.

H 2461; Pr 6933; BMC 7:960 (IA.30854); GW 3392; IGI 1250; Goff B-123.

8 May 1922–Bought with the John Harvey Treat fund. Inc 6933

Brescia

THOMAS FERRANDUS

3391 Pseudo-Phalaris: Epistolae [Latin]. 1 September [1473?].

4°. [56] leaves (56 blank); 207 x 145 mm.

Translated by Franciscus Griffolinus. Veneziani thinks it possible that this should be dated 1472; but I am not convinced.

Initial on [a]1r illuminated in gold and colors, with marginal extension; illuminated coat of arms in the lower margin has been trimmed by the binder; initials elsewhere added in red or blue. 17th-century mottled calf. From the library of Richard Ashhurst Bowie, with a slip of his MS notes inserted at front.

HR 12890; Pr 6944; BMC 7:962 (IA.31015); IGI 7688; Goff P–551; Veneziani 3.

9 November 1908–Gift of Mrs. E. D. Brandegee. Inc 6944

HENRICUS DE COLONIA AND STATIUS GALLICUS

3392 Homerus: Ilias [Latin]. 24 November 1474.

f°. [160] leaves; 301 x 205 mm.

Latin translation by Laurentius Valla, with a dedictory epistle by Justinianus Luzagus.

In this copy the signatures a–o^8, p^{10} are hand-stamped in the lower right corner of the leaves; signatures q–s^{10}, t^8 are in MS in the same position; both have been partly cropped. Initial spaces not filled in; without rubrication. 18th-century sprinkled calf, rehinged. Ownership stamp of the Franciscan monastery of S. Maria Assumpta at Ingolstadt on top edges; bookplate of James Frothingham Hunnewell. Imperfect: sheet i3 and quire r^{10} wanting, supplied in photographic reproduction from the Württembergische Landesbibliothek copy in Stuttgart; text of quire r^{10} also supplied in contemporary MS on 11 leaves bound in at end.

HR 8774; Pr 6945; BMC 7:964 (IB.31023); IGI 4800; Goff H–311; CIBN H–176; Veneziani 19.

January 1919—Deposited by James M. Hunnewell. Inc 6945

GABRIELE DI PIETRO

3393 Britannicus, Johannes: In Persii satiras commentarii. 14 November 1481.

f°. [88] leaves (1 and 88 blank); 258 x 187 mm.

Printed by Gabriel with his son Paulus.

Initials added in blue, red, or purple, but some spaces, with guide-letters, not filled in. Modern brown morocco, edges gilt. Bookplate of Morris H. Morgan, with his MS note on front flyleaf, "M.H.M. from William R. Thayer 1895."

HC(+Add)R 3987=HC 12729; Pr 6951; BMC 7:965 (IB.31053); Polain 909; GW 5556; IGI 2171; Goff B-1213; Veneziani 39.

January 1910—Gift of Morris H. Morgan. Inc 6951

BARTHOLOMAEUS DE CARLO, VERCELLENSIS

3394 Blondus, Flavius: Roma triumphans. 1482.

f°. [182] leaves (2 blank); 285 x 203 mm.

Initial spaces, most with guide-letters, not filled in; without rubrication; woodcut initial on e8v. Old vellum. Autograph of Charles Eliot Norton inside front cover dated 1857. With this is bound the same author's *Roma instaurata* (Verona, Boninus de Boninis, 20 December 1481-7 February 1492). The 2-leaf preliminary quire is bound at end in this copy.

HC(+Add) 3245*; Pr 6952; BMC 7:966 (IB.31063); Pell 2427; Polain 703; GW 4425; IGI 1762; Goff B-704; BSB-Ink B-555; Veneziani 41.

4 May 1905—From the library of Charles Eliot Norton. Inc 6952

PRINTER FOR BONIFACIUS DE MANERVA

3395 Gerardus Odonis: Sententia et expositio cum quaestionibus super libros Ethicorum Aristotelis. 30 April 1482.

f°. [348] leaves (348 blank); 305 x 205 mm.

This work has been assigned by various authorities to the press of Boninus de Boninis on the rather shaky ground of his having in 1486 come into possession of the type here used. But in 1482 Boninus was still in Verona and did not arrive in Brescia until sometime between February and June of 1483. I follow BMC, Sack, and BSB-Ink in believing the work to have been produced by an unknown printer for Bonifacius de Manerva. Edited by Gratianus Brixianus.

Initials and paragraph marks added in red or blue. Contemporary blind-stamped pigskin over wooden boards; brass clasp plates on back cover, latches on front, clasps and thongs gone. Signed by the rubricator at end, "P: W: 1.4.88." Bookplate of Georg Kloss (no. 2883 in the Sotheby sale catalogue, 1835); MS inscription inside front cover, "Robert Troup Paine to Harvard College." Imperfect: sheet a3 wanting, supplied in contemporary MS.

H 11968*; Pr 7048 (Brescian adespota); BMC 7:966 (IB.31283); IGI 6960; Goff O–28 (Boninus de Boninis); Sack 1520; CIBN O–15 (Boninus de Boninis); BSB-Ink G–131; Veneziani 44.

9 April 1879—Bequest of Robert Troup Paine. Inc 6952.5

BONINUS DE BONINIS

3396 Macrobius, Aurelius Theodosius: In Somnium Scipionis expositio. Saturnalia. 6 June 1483.

f°. [192] leaves (1 blank); ill.; 290 x 190 mm.

Large initial on a2r illuminated in gold and colors, with marginal extension; initials at beginning of books added in red, blue, and purple; initials elsewhere and paragraph marks added in red or blue. Half 18th-century leather and paste-paper boards; edges speckled red and brown. Bookplate of Daniel B. Fearing. Blank leaf not present.

HC 10427*; Pr 6953; BMC 7:968 (IB.31072); IGI 5924; Goff M–9; CIBN M–7; Veneziani 45; Sander 4072.

30 June 1915—Gift of Daniel B. Fearing. Inc 6953

3397 Nonius Marcellus: De proprietate Latini sermonis. 17 July 1483.

[For transcriptions see Copinger; but his collation is incorrect.] f°. A⁸,
B⁴, a–c⁸, d–q⁶·⁸, r–s⁶; [12], CXXVI leaves (XLI misnumbered XL); 300
x 208 mm. a2r: 38 lines, 210 x 125 mm. Type: 3:111R. Initial spaces.

Initial spaces not filled in; without rubrication. 18th-century brown
morocco, gilt. From the library of Richard Ashhurst Bowie. Imperfect: 12 unnumbered leaves at front (A⁸, B⁴) and sheet k3 wanting.

C 4436; Pr 6956; IGI 6932; Goff N–268; Sack 2606; Veneziani 48.

9 November 1908—Gift of Mrs. E. D. Brandegee. Inc 6956

3398 Gellius, Aulus: Noctes Atticae. 3 March 1485.

f°. [192] leaves; 302 x 205 mm.

Marcus Scaramucinus is listed in the colophon as "corrector."

Initial spaces not filled in; without rubrication. Old vellum; leather
labels on spine. MS marginalia largely washed away. Autograph "R.
Trenck" inside front cover; bookplate of William King Richardson.
Quires AA–BB⁸ bound at end in this copy.

HC 7521*; Pr 6958; BMC 7:968 (IB.31080); Pell 5012; Polain 1560;
GW 10597; IGI 4190; Goff G–122; BSB-Ink G–65; Veneziani 52.

1951—Bequest of William King Richardson. WKR 1.2.10

3399 Plutarchus: De claris mulieribus. 23 March 1485.

4°. [34] leaves (1 blank); 162 x 120 mm.

Latin translation by Alamanus Rinutinus.

Initials crudely added in brown. Modern red straight-grain morocco;
edges speckled red. At one time an edition of Augustinus Datus's *Elegantiolae* was bound with this according to a MS note on a2r, "Subse-
quuntur elegantiolae Augustini Dati." Cropped MS ownership notation on a2r, "Collegij Societatis Jesu taurin[ensis]."

HC 13144*; Pr 6959; BMC 7:968 (IA.31081); Polain 4663; IGI 7910;
Goff P–819; Veneziani 53.

12 December 1946—Bought with funds provided by Friends of the
Harvard College Library. Inc 6959

3400 Macrobius, Aurelius Theodosius: In Somnium Scipionis expositio. Saturnalia. 31 May 1485.

f°. [176] leaves (1 blank); ill.; 304 x 200 mm.

Copies are dated either 15 or 31 May 1485.

This copy is dated 31 May 1485. Initials added in red or blue, paragraph marks and capital strokes in red. Half modern brown morocco and green cloth. From the library of Richard Ashhurst Bowie.

H 10428*(var.); R(Suppl) 112; Pr 6962; BMC 7:969 (IB.31085); IGI 5926; Goff M-11; Sack 2296(var.); CIBN M-8(var.); Veneziani 56; Sander 4073(var.).

9 November 1908—Gift of Mrs. E. D. Brandegee. Inc 6962

3401 Jacobus Philippus de Bergamo: Supplementum chronicarum. 1 December 1485.

f°. [23], 358, [1] leaves (1 and 20 blank, 24–381 numbered 1–358 on rectos and versos; 16v, 164r, 165r, 254r, 256r–v, 257r, 257v, 258r, 265v, 324r, and 330v misnumbered 19, 154, 155, 452, 258, 252, 259, 260, 267, 234, and 300); 294 x 204 mm.

Includes a poem by Barillus Bergomensis.

Large initial on a3v illuminated in colors, with marginal extension (this leaf is folded to avoid trimming by the binder); initials elsewhere added in red and/or blue, paragraph marks and capital strokes in red. For binding description see no. 2184 in vol. 2, the Italian translation of this work printed by Bernardinus Rizus in Venice, 8 October 1491, which is bound with this. First blank leaf not present.

HC 2806*; Pr 6965; BMC 7:969 (IB.31089); Pell 2065; Polain 1493; IGI 5076; Goff J-209; CIBN J-141; Veneziani 59.

4 May 1905—From the library of Charles Eliot Norton. Inc 6965

3402 Statuta Placentiae. ca. 1485.

AA2r: Rubrice statutorum primi libri. ‖ a1r: [for transcription see Reichling; but add a line-ending after "emendata &" in line 8.] ff4r, line 27: Publicatũ fuit ℗ Iacobũ nadalmũ tubatorē cõis placen. suprascriptũ decre‖tũ & factũ ℗ut in dictis litteris & decreto continentur. Die .xxi. mensis octo‖bris presentis ãni proxime suprascripti. ‖

f°. AA⁴, BB⁶, a⁸, b–i⁶, k⁴, l–o⁶, A–B⁶, aa–ee⁶, ff⁴ (AA1 blank); [140]

leaves (1 blank); 285 x 197 mm. 2 columns in the table, not else-where. a1r: 40 lines, 220 x 138 mm. Types: 4:81R, table; 3:111R, text. Initial spaces, most with guide-letters.

Initial spaces not filled in; without rubrication. Old vellum. "Gvarini" in MS on blank AA1 along with the record of the birth of a boy named Jacobus Antonius on 18 May 1501; another MS note on ff4r records the date 17 December 1610; MS marginalia throughout.

R 740 ("Placentiae? c.1490"); R 7:42 ("Med., Zarotus, 1485"); IGI 7837 ("Brescia, Bonino de'Bonini, c.1485"); Goff S–722 ("Brescia: Bernardinus de Misintis, about 1495"); CIBN S–403 ("Brescia, Bernardino Misinta, circa 1495?"); Veneziani 61 (assigned to De Boninis).

9 June 1931—Bought with the Archibald Cary Coolidge fund. Inc 6966.5

3403 Dante Alighieri: La Commedia. 31 May 1487.

f°. [310] leaves (310 blank); ill.; 338 x 232 mm.

Both BMC and GW transcribe "REGISRO" on &1a; this copy reads correctly "REGISTRO." Includes the commentary of Christophorus Landinus.

Initial spaces, with guide-letters, not filled in; without rubrication. Modern vellum, with wallet edges; edges gilt. Imperfect: probably a made-up copy; many leaves remargined.

HCR 5948; C 5943; Pr 6973; BMC 7:971 (IB.31103); Pell 4116; Polain 1224; GW 7968; IGI 362; Goff D–31; Schäfer 116; Veneziani 74 ("1487–31 mar."); Sander 2312.

18 December 1903—Gift of Alain Campbell White. Typ Inc 6973

3404 Ubaldis, Baldus de: Consiliorum partes prima et secunda. 15 July–1 September 1490.

f°. 2 vols. (vol. 1: [160] leaves; pt. 2: [134] leaves, 13 blank); 422 x 284 mm.

For a description of vols. 3–5 see Hain and Sack; the work was completed on 17 December 1491. Edited, with tables, by Johannes Antonius de Zanetis and Petrus de Monte.

Large initials on a2r of vol. 1 and g2r of vol. 2 added in red, blue, and purple; initials elsewhere added in red or blue, capital strokes in red. The two volumes are bound together in modern vellum with doeskin ties. Bookplate of Eugen, Freiherr von Maucler (Bibliothek Oberherrlingen), dated 1839.

HC 2330*; BMC 7:971 (IC.31109–10); Pell 1746; IGI 9931–32; Goff U–22; Sack 3574; Veneziani 83(1).

13 June 1945—Received. Law Library

A N G E L U S   A N D
J A C O B U S   B R I T A N N I C U S

3405   Imitatio Christi. 6 June 1485.

8°. [120] leaves (1, 6, and 120 blank); 138 x 98 mm.

Attributed in this edition to Bernardus Claravallensis.

Initial spaces, with guide-letters, not filled in; without rubrication. Old leather; paper labels on spine. Ownership stamp (a reversed E and an S in a square frame) on A3r. Imperfect: sheet a1 wanting; lower margin of a2 trimmed away to remove an ownership notation.

HC(Add) 9087; Pr 6978; BMC 7:974 (IA.31119); IGI 5108; Goff I–9; Veneziani 90.

22 November 1921—W. A. Copinger Imitatio Christi Collection, presented by James Byrne. Inc 6978

3406   Diogenes Laertius: Vitae et sententiae philosophorum. 23 November 1485.

f°. [124] leaves; 302 x 210 mm.

Latin translation by Ambrosius Traversarius.

Initial spaces, most with guide-letters, not filled in; without rubrication. Modern vellum. MS marginalia. Booklabel of Adriana R. Salem.

HC 6201; Pr 6979; BMC 7:974 (IB.31121); Pell 4276; GW 8380; IGI 3460; Goff D–221; Veneziani 93.

December 1959—Gift of Ward M. Canaday. Inc 6979

3407   Plutarchus: De liberis educandis. 7 December 1485.

4°. [18] leaves; 204 x 148 mm.

Latin translation by Guarinus Veronensis. Includes Pseudo-Hieronymus, *De officiis liberorum erga parentes admonitio.*

Initial spaces, with guide-letters, not filled in; without rubrication. Modern vellum, stained green. MS marginalia.

HC(Add) 13148*; Pr 6980; BMC 7:974 (IA.31123); IGI 7916; Goff P-824; Veneziani 96.

10 May 1920—Bought with the Constantius fund. Inc 6980

3408 Pseudo-Augustinus: Sermones ad heremitas. 5 January 1486.

8°. [172] leaves (1 blank); 128 x 88 mm.

Initials and paragraph marks added in red, capital strokes in yellow. Half 19th-century calf and paste-paper boards; edges stained red. MS ownership notation on [a]2r, "Sum S^{ti} Xisti plac[entiae]"; from the library of Richard Ashhurst Bowie. Blank leaf not present.

HC 2001*; Pr 6981; BMC 7:974 (IA.31124); Pell 1512; Polain 4173; GW 3001; IGI 1033; Goff A-1313; BSB-Ink A-919; Veneziani 97.

9 November 1908—Gift of Mrs. E. D. Brandegee. Inc 6981

3409 Persius Flaccus, Aulus: Satirae. 17 February 1486.

f°. [36] leaves (36 blank); 304 x 212 mm.

With the commentary of Johannes Britannicus.

Initials crudely added in brown. Half modern brown morocco and marbled boards. Bookstamp of the Prince of Ol'denburg; bookplate of Morris H. Morgan.

HC 12730; Pr 6982; BMC 7:975 (IB.31125); IGI 7501; Goff P-350; Veneziani 98.

January 1910—Gift of Morris H. Morgan. Inc 6982 (A)

3410 ——Another copy. 315 x 212 mm.

A few initials added in red, but most spaces not filled in. Autograph and painted coat of arms of Hieronymus Schenck on a2v; MS marginalia throughout in Schenck's hand; MS note on a1r, "Dis buch hatt mir Hans Friderich Schenck verehrett den 17.tn alten Mertzen 1606. Sigismund von Hanisch"; from the library of Richard Ashhurst Bowie. According to a MS note on front flyleaf, there were originally bound with this Juvenalis, *Satirae* (Venice, Bartholomaeus de Zanis, 1487), and Martialis, *Epigrammata* (Venice, Baptista de Tortis, 17 July 1485).

9 November 1908—Gift of Mrs. E. D. Brandegee. Inc 6982 (B)

3411 Rhazes, Muhammad: Liber Elhavi, seu Ars medicinae. 18 October 1486.

f°. [590] leaves (1 and 590 blank); 360 x 245 mm.

Latin translation by Feragius Salernitanus. Edited by Johannes Bugatus, with a dedicatory letter by Johannes Britannicus.

Initials added in red and/or blue, paragraph marks in red or blue, capital strokes and underlinings in red. Bound in vellum leaves of 15th-century Polish MS, rebacked in calf; in a cloth case. MS ownership notations on π2r, "Loci Capucinorum Teinitij" and "Sum Joachimj Strüppij de Gelnhausen D.M.68"; another illegible one beneath, along with an armorial seal in red wax. MS marginalia. At end is a MS leaf containing "Tabula simplicivm .XXI. XXIII. et .XXIII. librorvm." Blank leaf at end not present.

HC 13901*; Pr 6984; BMC 7:975 (IC.31128); IGI 8342; Goff R-178; Sack 3066; CIBN R-113; Veneziani 100.

Countway Library (Solomon M. Hyams Collection)

3412 Statuta Brixiae. 8 December 1490.

f°. [180] leaves (16, 20, 116, and 160 blank); ill.; 298 x 210 mm.

Initial spaces, most with guide-letters, not filled in; without rubrication. Modern blind-stamped leather over wooden boards; fragment of one leather thong nailed to back cover, two brass latches on front, clasps and thongs gone. Whoever bound this book must have been either mad or drunk, for the quires are now in the following disorder: a⁸, o⁶, [oo]⁴, p–r⁸, n⁸, m⁸, s–t⁸, [tt]², u⁸, x⁶, y⁴, d⁸, ²d⁸, e–h⁸, i⁶, b⁸, [ii]⁴, l⁸, k⁸, [c]⁴.

R 337; Pr 6985A; BMC 7:976 (IB.31134) and 12:70 (IB.31134a); IGI 2176; Goff S-710; Veneziani 106; Sander 1266.

26 June 1944—Received. Law Library

3413 Statuta Bergomi. 18 December 1491.

f°. [228] leaves (13, 17, and 228 blank); 292 x 210 mm.

Printed by Angelus and Jacobus.

Initial spaces, with guide-letters, not filled in; without rubrication. Half modern brown morocco and marbled boards. In this copy the quire designated as [*]⁴ is bound at front; blank leaf hh6 not present.

HC 14996; Pr 6987; BMC 7:976 (IB.31139); IGI 1490; Goff S-706; CIBN S-391; Veneziani 109.

2 June 1913–Gift of Archibald Cary Coolidge. Inc 6987

3414 ——Another copy. 282 x 202 mm.

Initial spaces not filled in; without rubrication. Quire [*]⁴ bound at front. Old vellum; leather label on spine. Autograph of Bernardus Baltus on recto of first leaf.

30 June 1951–Received. Law Library

3415 **Bernardus Claravallensis:** Opuscula. 18 March 1495.

8°. [348] leaves; 145 x 100 mm.

Includes 33 of the smaller works; for contents see GW. Edited by Theophilus Brixianus, with his *Carmen de vita S. Bernardi* prefixed. Printed by Angelus and Jacobus.

A few initials added in red, but most spaces, with guide-letters, not filled in. Old vellum. Ownership stamp erased from title page; MS ownership notation at foot, "Hic li[ber] pertinet ad locū [illegible]."

CR 994; Pr 6989; BMC 7:977 (IA.31147); Pell 2156; Polain 596bis; GW 3907; IGI 1547; Goff B-364; Veneziani 115.

10 May 1943–Bought with the George Schünemann Jackson fund. Inc 6989

3416 **Philelphus, Franciscus:** Odae. 4 July 1497.

4°. [94] leaves; 200 x 142 mm.

Includes a poem by Johannes Franciscus Hostianus.

A few woodcut initials; initial spaces, with guide-letters, not filled in; without rubrication. Half modern green vellum and marbled boards.

HC 12954*; Pr 6994; BMC 7:978 (IA.31157); IGI 3879; Goff P-606; CIBN P-322; Veneziani 121.

14 June 1921—Bought with the Charles Minot fund. Inc 6994

3417 Gafurius, Franchinus: Practica musicae. 23 September 1497.

f°. [112] leaves (112 blank); ill.; 272 x 194 mm.

Includes a poem by Lucinus Conagus.

Woodcut initials; spaces, with guide-letters, not filled in; without rubrication. Half 19th-century brown morocco and marbled boards by Lortic; top edges gilt. Leather booklabel of Ambroise Firmin-Didot (no. 290 in the Hôtel Drouot sale catalogue of his library, June 1882). Imperfect: leaf a1, sheets b3–4, and 111 wanting; leaf a8 misbound before b7, and sheet dd4 misbound after leaf b2.

HCR 7408; Pr 6995; BMC 7:979 (IB.31159a) and 12:70 (IB.31159b); Pell 4950; Polain 1530; GW 10435; IGI 4113; Goff G–4; Hirsch I:193; Veneziani 126.

1 July 1920—Bought with the Elkan Naumburg Fellowship fund. Inc 6995

3418 Beroaldus, Philippus: Orationes et carmina. 1497.

4°. [88] leaves; 210 x 149 mm.

Initial space, with guide-letter, not filled in on a2r; woodcut initials elsewhere. Bound as no. 2 in a 17th-century vellum tract volume containing 5 works of Beroaldus, printed between 1497 and 1499.

HC(Add) 2953*=HR 2957; BMC 7:979 (IA.31160); Pell 2212; GW 4146; IGI 1604; Goff B–493; BSB-Ink B–382; Veneziani 130.

Countway Library (William Norton Bullard Collection)

3419 Gregorius I, Pope: Moralia, siue Expositio in Job. 2 June 1498.

4°. [426] leaves (426 blank); 187 x 140 mm.

In this copy, as in Pellechet, a block of type from AA4r, used as a bearer under the second column on BB8r, has been accidentally inked and printed.

Initial spaces at beginning of books added in brown, but some spaces, with guide-letters, not filled in; woodcut initials, including Lombards, elsewhere. 19th-century paste-paper boards covered with marbled paper. MS ownership inscriptions on title page, "Est Joannis Pauli Pinelli," "Ac nunc 1591 die 26 Aprilis est P. Thomae Calligarij S. Vincentij Rectoris," "Ad usum Rdi. P. Benedicti Ruisechi," "Ex Codicibus Bp. [?] Augustini Oliuarij," and "Giuseppe Leveroni 17 Luglio 1871." Imperfect: burn hole in leaves a2-3, affecting text.

C 2780; Pr 6996; BMC 7:979 (IA.31162); Pell 5382; Polain 1718; IGI 4446; Goff G-434; Veneziani 133.

9 June 1905—Gift of George Joseph Pfeiffer. Inc 6996

3420 Turrecremata, Johannes de: Quaestiones evangeliorum de tempore et de sanctis. 2 June 1498.

4° and 8°. [166] leaves; 184 x 138 mm.

BMC describes sheets q3-4 and quire r as being octavo; in this copy sheets q3-4 are quarto, quire r octavo.

Initial spaces, most with guide-letters, not filled in; woodcut initials also. Half 19th-century leather and marbled boards. MS ownership notation erased from title page. Imperfect: sheets g1-2 wanting.

HC 15718; Pr 6997; BMC 7:980 (IA.31163); IGI 9892; Goff T-548; Sack 3550; Veneziani 134.

7 October 1912—Gift of the Graduate School of Business Administration. Inc 6997

3421 Ubaldis, Angelus de: Lectura super titulo De interdictis ff. novi. 29 August 1498.

f°. [58] leaves; 430 x 290 mm.

For transcriptions, collation, and type identification see IGI.

Initial spaces not filled in; without rubrication. For binding description see no. 2111 in vol. 2, Baldus de Ubaldis, *Super usibus feudorum* (Venice, Bernardinus Benalius, 20 March 1500), with which this is bound.

H 15880; IGI 9927; Goff U-11; Veneziani 136.

7 October 1947—Received. Law Library

3422 Nepos, Cornelius: Vitae imperatorum, siue De vita illustrium virorum. 17 September 1498.

f°. [26] leaves (1 blank); 304 x 210 mm.

Without rubrication. Modern cream boards.

HC 5736; Pr 7005; BMC 7:982 (IB.31185); Pell 3986; Polain 4305; IGI 3213; Goff C–917; Veneziani 139.

26 March 1949—Bought with the Duplicate fund. Inc 7005

3423 Bernardus Claravallensis: Sermones super Cantica canticorum. 28 January 1500.

4° and 8°. [150] leaves; 188 x 140 mm.

Edited by Gregorius Britannicus.

Initial space on a1r, with guide-letter, not filled in; woodcut initials elsewhere. At top of title page is a portrait medallion in antique style illuminated in gold and colors, surrounded by motto "Esempio sicvritate virtv"; similarly illuminated below is the coat of arms of the Capra family of Vicenza. 16th-century blind-stamped calf over wooden boards, rebacked; in a cloth case. MS ownership inscription on flyleaf at front, "Huius opusculi, cuius autorē esse perhibent Diuū Bernardum Clareuallensem abbatem, possessor est hieronymus Iulianus, qui hoc emit Regio numo. Anno dñi 1559. Scriptū hic Anno dñi 1560 die 27 aprilis." Booklabels of W. A. Harding, Madingley, and of Philip Hofer. With this is bound Pseudo-Bernardus Claravallensis, *Meditationes de interiori homine* (Milan, Uldericus Scinzenzeler, ca. 1495).

HR 2860; Pr 7002; BMC 7:981 (IA.31175); Pell 2099; GW 3938; IGI 1554; Goff B–431; Veneziani 150.

August 1973—Gift of Philip Hofer. Typ Inc 7002

3424 Persius Flaccus, Aulus: Satirae. 21 July 1500.

f°. [34] leaves; 300 x 205 mm.

Includes the commentary of Johannes Britannicus.

A few woodcut initials; initial spaces, with guide-letters, not filled in; without rubrication. Half old leather and paste-paper boards; edges speckled red. MS ownership notations on title page, "Codex Jacobi Vitudoni," "Codex Baptiste Rambstengi [?]," and "Pauli Iouij Sancti Juliani liber"; bookplate of Morris H. Morgan, with his MS date of acquisition "1894." With this is bound the Britannicus edition of Juvenal (Brescia, 1501).

HC 12732*; Pr 7011; BMC 7:983 (IB.31196); Polain 3058; IGI 7513; Goff P–351; Veneziani 154.

January 1910—Gift of Morris H. Morgan. Inc 7011

3425 ——Another copy. 288 x 200 mm.

Initial spaces not filled in; without rubrication. Half 19th-century tan cloth and gray boards. In MS on title page, "ad usum D. Hippolyti. Est Monast^i Ste Euphemie"; autograph on front flyleaf, "P. Morgan Watkins ... Nov. 30. 1890."

Countway Library (William Norton Bullard Collection)

B A P T I S T A   F A R F E N G U S

3426 Fiore di virtù. 8 February "1499" [i.e., 1489].

4°. [24] leaves; ill.; 195 x 134 mm.

On the date see Veneziani, p. 96.

Two woodcut initials on a2r; Lombards elsewhere. Modern red morocco. Autograph "W. Ashburner Firenze 1921" on title page; Ashburner's bookstamp on a1v and c8v (no. 72 in the Galerie Fischer sale catalogue, August 1928); booklabels of Philip and Frances Hofer.

H 7115; GW 9951; IGI 3966; Goff F–186; Veneziani 161; Sander 2739.

24 July 1974—Gift of Philip Hofer. Typ Inc 7012.5

3427 Bonaventura, Saint: Commentarius in primum librum Sententiarum. 20 October 1490.

4°. [204] leaves (1 and 8 blank); 212 x 150 mm.

The errors in the colophon as transcribed by BMC have been corrected in the GW transcription.

This copy has the errors in the colophon as transcribed by BMC. Initial spaces, some with guide-letters, not filled in; without rubrication. Modern black calf. Booklabel of George Dunn (no. 1942 in pt. 3 of the Sotheby sale catalogue, November 1917). Blank leaves not present.

HR 3537; BMC 12:70 (IA.31205); Pell 2711; GW 4657; IGI 1883; Goff B–871; Veneziani 166.

24 March 1919—Bought with the John Harvey Treat fund. Inc 7013.8

3428 Pseudo-Albertus Magnus: Philosophia pauperum. 13 June 1493.

4°. [50] leaves; ill.; 192 x 146 mm.

Also ascribed to Albertus de Orlamünde. Includes an excerpt from Aegidius Columna's *De regimine principum*.

Woodcut initials colored yellow; spaces, some with guide-letters, not filled in; paragraph marks and underlinings added in red, capital strokes in yellow. Old paste-paper boards. MS marginalia in red. Bookplate of William Norton Bullard.

H 505*; BMC 7:985 (IA.31213); Pell 324; GW 712; IGI 221; Goff A–297; BSB-Ink A–129; Sander 192.

Countway Library (William Norton Bullard Collection)

3429 Dominicis, Dominicus de: De reformationibus Romanae Curiae. 13 March 1495.

4°. [18] leaves; 184 x 134 mm.

Printed by Farfengus for Franciscus Laurinus.

Initial spaces on a1r and b9r not filled in; woodcut initials elsewhere; without rubrication. Modern dark blue morocco, edges gilt. Bookplate of Sidney Graves Hamilton (no. 175 in the Sotheby sale catalogue, July 1917).

HCR 6321; Pr 7019; BMC 7:986 (IA.31217); GW 8638; IGI 3532; Goff D–305; Veneziani 187.

11 May 1951—Gift of Harold T. White. Inc 7019

B E R N A R D I N U S   D E   M I S I N T I S

3430 Sallustius Crispus, Gaius: Opera. 13 January 1495.

f°. [110] leaves; 300 x 210 mm.

Includes the commentaries of Laurentius Valla and Johannes Chrysostomus Soldus. Edited by Pomponius Laetus and Johannes Britannicus. Printed by De Misintis for Angelus and Jacobus Britannicus.

Pargraph marks added in red or blue, underlinings in red. 19th-century blind- and gilt-stamped calf by J. Ford, Manchester, spine repaired; edges speckled red and blue. Bookplate of John S. Pakington, baron Hampton (no. 595 in the Sotheby sale catalogue, February 1881); booklabel of George Dunn (no. 1578 in pt. 2 of the Sotheby sale catalogue, February 1914).

H 14230*; Pr 7028; BMC 7:988 (IB.31233); Polain 3429; IGI 8557; Goff S-82; Veneziani 228.

14 December 1914—Bought with the Constantius fund. Inc 7028

3431 **Alexander Aphrodisiensis:** De anima ex Aristotelis institutione. 13 September 1495.

4°. [92] leaves (1 blank); 215 x 160 mm.

Latin translation by Hieronymus Donatus.

Woodcut initial on a2r; spaces elsewhere, with guide-letters, not filled in; without rubrication. 19th-century diced calf, with the arms of James Harris, earl of Malmesbury, stamped in gilt on covers; MS ownership notation in upper margin of a2r, "Collegii S. Petri junioris Argentinae." Blank leaf not present.

H 656*; Pr 7030; BMC 7:989 (IA.31237); Pell 441; Polain 111; GW 859; IGI 283; Goff A-386; BSB-Ink A-236; Veneziani 232.

5 February 1954—Bought with the Constantius fund. Inc 7030

3432 ——Another copy. 205 x 155 mm.

Initial spaces not filled in; without rubrication. Modern vellum with wallet edges. Leaves in the first three quires partly remargined.

Countway Library

3433 **Bonaventura, Saint:** Opuscula. 17 December 1495.

8° and 4°. [184] leaves (5 and 184 blank); 174 x 125 mm.

For contents see BMC and GW. Printed by De Misintis for Angelus Britannicus.

Initials and paragraph marks added in red in the first few quires, but only occasionally thereafter; many spaces, with guide-letters, not filled in. Half modern gray cloth and marbled boards. MS ownership notation on title page, "Pertinet ad locū Strôconii"; oval bookstamp "Libra [sic] S. Francisci. Stronconi." Imperfect: leaf i8 wanting; blank leaves not present.

HC 3467*(incl H 3481); Pr 7033; BMC 7:989 (IA.31242); Pell 2621; GW 4649; IGI 1933; Goff B-929; BSB-Ink B-672; Veneziani 235.

19 October 1916—Bought with the John Harvey Treat fund. Inc 7033

3434 Zacchia, Laudivius, Vezzanensis: Epistolae magni Turci. ca. 1495.

4°. [10] leaves; 200 x 154 mm.

Includes a poem by Antonius Panormitanus.

Without rubrication. 19th-century vellum. MS marginalia. Booklabel
of Count Paul Riant.

H 10503*; BMC 7:990 (IA.31247); IGI 5969; Goff M-64; CIBN L-61;
Veneziani 227.

28 December 1899—Gift of J. Randolph Coolidge and Archibald Cary
Coolidge. Inc 7033.5

3435 Catharina Senensis, Saint: Libro della divina dottrina [Latin]. 15
April 1496.

8°. [192] leaves (192 blank); 149 x 100 mm.

Latin translation by Raymundus Capuanus. Includes 22 *Orationes* of
Catharine, also in Latin translation, and the life of the saint by Stephanus Maconi. Edited by Marcus Civilis.

Initial spaces, most with guide-letters, not filled in; without rubrication. Top and lower panels of a 16th-century blind-stamped leather
binding preserved and mounted, rebacked and re-edged; brass clasp
plates on back cover, latches on front, clasps with leather thongs.

HC 4693*; Pr 7034; BMC 7:990 (IA.31244); Pell 3392; GW 6226; IGI
2595; Goff C-285; BSB-Ink C-194.

Countway Library (William Norton Bullard Collection)

3436 Beroaldus, Philippus: Annotationes centum. 17 December 1496.

f°. [112] leaves (38, 84, and 112 blank); 307 x 210 mm.

Includes: Beroaldus, *Annotationes in Commentarios Servii Vergilianos.
Annotationes in Plinium. Appendix annotamentorum post Suetonii enarra-
tiones.*—Angelus Politianus, *Miscellaneorum centuria prima. Panepistemon.
Lamia.*—Domitius Calderinus, *Observationes.*—Johannes Baptista Pius,
Annotamenta. The correctors were Pius and Angelus Ugerius. Printed
by De Misintis for Angelus Britannicus.

Initial spaces, most with guide-letters, not filled in; without rubrication. Half modern vellum and decorated boards. MS marginalia.
Bookplate of William Norton Bullard.

HC 2946; Pr 7039; BMC 7:991 (IB.31254); Pell 2209; GW 4114; IGI 1583; Goff B-465; Sack 591; BSB-Ink B-361.

Countway Library (William Norton Bullard Collection)

3437 **Cleomedes:** De contemplatione orbium excelsorum. 3 April 1497.

4°. [72] leaves (64 blank); 207 x 150 mm.

Includes: Aelius Aristides, *Oratio ad Rhodienses de concordia.*–Dio Chrysostomus, *Oratio ad Nicomedios de concordia cum Nicenis componenda.*–Plutarchus, *De virtute morum. Praecepta connubalia.* Latin translations by Carolus Valgulius. Includes a poem by Johannes Franciscus Duccus. Printed by De Misintis for Angelus Britannicus.

Initial spaces, with guide-letters, not filled in; without rubrication. 19th-century marbled boards rebacked in modern leather. Booklabel of Georg Kloss (no. 1106 in the Sotheby sale catalogue, May 1835). Quire f misbound after g.

HC 5450*; Pr 7040; BMC 7:991 (IA.31256); Pell 3847; GW 7122; IGI 3039; Goff C-741; BSB-Ink C-460; Veneziani 248.

22 August 1856–Gift of Winslow Lewis. Inc 7040

3438 **Lanfranchinus, Christophorus:** Quaestio utrum praeferendus sit doctor an miles. 8 July 1497.

[For transcriptions see Reichling; but correct his "Bartholamaeus" in line 4 on a1r to "Bartholameus"; and the colophon should read "Inprimi Iussit Angelus Britanicus ..."] 4°. a–c⁴, d²; [14] leaves; 214 x 150 mm. a2r: 29 lines, 158 x 107 mm. Type: 4:110R. Woodcut initials.

Printed by De Misintis for Angelus Britannicus.

Without rubrication. 19th-century dark blue calf.

R 1244; IGI 5666; Veneziani 122 (under Britannicus).

5 July 1950–Received. Law Library

3439 **Politianus, Angelus:** Opera. 10 August 1499.

f°. [212] leaves (212 blank); 291 x 198 mm.

Of this edition Harvard has only quires s–u⁶, x⁴, y⁸, z⁶, and leaf A1, bound in at end of the Aldine edition of July 1498, of which it is an unauthorized reprint. See BMC and no. 2267 in vol. 2 of this catalogue. From the library of Richard Ashhurst Bowie.

HC 13219; Pr 6421=7046; BMC 7:992 (IB.31268); Polain 3234; IGI 7953; Goff P-887; CIBN P-540; Veneziani 259.

9 November 1908–Gift of Mrs. E. D. Brandegee. Inc 5567 (B)

Pavia

ANTONIUS DE CARCANO

3440 Albertus de Saxonia: Quaestiones in Aristotelis libros De caelo et mundo. 11 May 1481.

f°. [90] leaves; 262 x 185 mm.

GW gives a wrong collation, calling for quire A to consist of eight leaves, whereas it has only six.

Initial spaces, most with guide-letters, not filled in; without rubrication. 19th-century red morocco, gilt, edges gilt. Syston Park bookplate, with the monogram booklabel of Sir John H. Thorold (no. 50 in the Sotheby sale catalogue, December 1884); bookplate of James Frothingham Hunnewell. The first column on leaf E1v failed to print properly and has been partly traced over in MS.

H 575; Pell 329; Polain 4121; GW 795; IGI 250; Goff A-346; BSB-Ink A-138; Gasparrini Leporace 16.

January 1919–Deposited by James M. Hunnewell. Inc 7053.5

3441 Jacobus de Forlivio: Expositio in aphorismos Hippocratis. 1484/5.

a2r: Illustris medici Iacobi forliuiensis ī afforismos ‖ ypo. egregia expositio cū qōnibus feliciter incipiunt. ‖ (u⁶)Ita breuis ars uero lōga. ‖ x7v, COLOPHON: Iacobi forliuiensis Artium ⁊ medicine p̄stantissimi ⁊ ‖ celebērimi doctoris Cōmentationes ī ypo. afforismos ‖ Correcte per Egregium Artium ⁊ medicine doctorez ‖ dominum magistrum Franciscuȝ de Bobio Feliciter ‖ expliciunt. Impresse p̄p̄ per p̄stantem uirum ⁊ imp̄sso‖rie artis exptissimum. M. Antonium de carchão. An‖no dñi. 1484 ‖ Laus Deo ‖ Registrū huius libri incipit. ‖ ... sio in ‖

f°. a⁸, b⁶, c–m⁸, n⁶, o–p⁸, q⁴, r¹⁰, s⁸, t–u⁶, x⁸ (a1 and x8 blank); [158]

leaves (1 and 158 blank); 400 x 282 mm. 2 columns. a2r: 67 lines, 276 x 171 mm. Types: 2:105G, text of Hippocrates; 4:83G, commentary. Initial spaces.

Includes Marsilius de Sancta Sophia, *Expositio in particulam tertiam et septimam aphorismorum Hippocratis*. Edited by Franciscus de Bobbio. On dating see Gasparrini Leporace 29 and p.337.

Initials added in red and/or blue, paragraph marks in red or blue, capital strokes in red. Half 16th-century blind-stamped pigskin and wooden boards, with the abbatial arms of Placidius Hieber, abbot of Lambach, stamped in silver on front cover, with initials "PAZL"; brass clasp plates on front cover, latches on back, clasps with pigskin thongs. MS ownership notation on o5r and inside back cover, "Iste Liber est doctoris Andree Ram."

H 7249; Goff J–45; Gasparrini Leporace 29 (dated "1485 [gennaio-marzo]").

Countway Library (William Norton Bullard Collection)

3442 Concoregio, Johannes de: De aegritudinibus particularibus. Summula de curis febrium. 1485.

f° and 4°. 2 pts. in 1 vol. (pt. 1: [122] leaves, 1 blank; pt. 2: [66] leaves, 1 blank); 265 x 195 mm.

Initial spaces, some with guide-letters, not filled in; without rubrication. Half 19th-century vellum and paste-paper boards. MS marginalia. Bookplate of William Norton Bullard. Bookseller's ticket of C. E. Rappaport, Rome. In this copy the parts are bound in reverse order.

HC 5615*; Pr 7056; BMC 7:997 (IB.31334); Pell 3915; GW 7291; IGI 3120; Goff C–803; BSB-Ink C–505; Gasparrini Leporace 28.

Countway Library (William Norton Bullard Collection)

3443 Arnoldus de Villa Nova: Breviarium practicae medicinae. ca. 1485.

f°. [103] leaves (1 and 103 blank); 290 x 206 mm.

BSB catalogues this work under Pseudo-Arnoldus. The GW collation can be made more precise: g^{10} (–g6).

Large initial on a2r added in red and blue; initials elsewhere, paragraph marks, and underlinings added in red. Modern japanese vellum. Bookplate of W. G. Lennox. Blank leaves not present.

C 647; GW 2527; IGI 866; Goff A-1072; Sack 297; Gasparrini Leporace 25.

Countway Library

3444 Gentilis de Fulgineo: Super quinto libro Canonis Avicennae. ca. 1486.

f°. [54] leaves (1 and 54 blank); 254 x 182 mm.

Edited by Franciscus de Bobbio. Printed by De Carcano for Hieronymus de Durantibus.

Initial spaces, some with guide-letters, not filled in; without rubrication. Modern vellum.

HC(Add) 7568*; Pell 5027; GW 10616; IGI 4204; Goff G-143; BSB-Ink G-77; Gasparrini Leporace 31.

Countway Library (William Norton Bullard Collection)

3445 Gentilis de Fulgineo: Super secundo libro Canonis Avicennae. ca. 1486.

f°. [36] leaves (1 and 36 blank); 254 x 182 mm.

Printed by De Carcano for Hieronymus de Durantibus.

Initial spaces not filled in; without rubrication. Modern vellum.

H 7561*; Pr 7059; BMC 7:998 (IB.31337); Pell 5023; GW 10610; IGI 4198; Goff G-144; BSB-Ink G-78; Gasparrini Leporace 30.

Countway Library (William Norton Bullard Collection)

3446 Guainerius, Antonius: Opera medica. 10 January 1488.

f°. [256] leaves (1 blank); 296 x 205 mm.

Edited by Franciscus de Bobbio.

Initial spaces, some with guide-letters, not filled in; occasional paragraph marks, capital strokes, and underlinings added in red. Half 16th-century blind-stamped pigskin and wooden boards; brass clasp plates on back cover, latches on front, clasps and thongs gone; vellum index tabs; vellum label on front cover. MS marginalia.

HC 8098*; Pr 7057; BMC 7:998 (IB.31340); IGI 4507; Goff G-520; Gasparrini Leporace 35.

Countway Library (William Norton Bullard Collection)

3447 Gentilis de Fulgineo: Consilia medica. ca. 1488.

f°. [48] leaves (1 blank); 253 x 184 mm.

GW transcribes "Comedat" on g6r; this copy has error "Ccomedat."

Initial spaces, most with guide-letters, not filled in; without rubrication. Modern vellum. Occasional MS marginalia.

HC(Add) 7574*; Pell 5028; GW 10618 ("um 1486"); IGI 4205; Goff G–134; BSB-Ink G–71; not in Gasparrini Leporace.

Countway Library (William Norton Bullard Collection)

3448 Sancto Georgio, Johannes Antonius de: Lectura super usibus feudorum. 1 November 1490.

f°. [141] leaves (1 blank); 410 x 287 mm.

In this copy there is the stub of a blank leaf before k1, k2 is signed "k ii," k3–5 are signed k2–4 and have been corrected in MS to "k3–5"; stitching is visible between "k4" (i.e., k5) and [k]6. Initial spaces, most with guide-letters, not filled in; without rubrication. Paste-paper boards covered with vellum leaves of a Latin MS, so badly abraded that the writing can scarcely be seen. Blank leaf not present.

HC 7590*; Pr 7062; BMC 7:998 (IC.31352); IGI 8606; Goff S–131; Sack 3155; Gasparrini Leporace 40.

12 June 1944—Received. Law Library

3449 Avicenna: De anima [Latin]. ca. 1490.

f°. [52] leaves (1 blank); 290 x 200 mm.

A few initials added in brown and/or green, but most spaces, some with guide-letters, not filled in. Old limp vellum.

HR 2219; Pr 7058; BMC 12:71 (IB.31341); GW 3111; IGI 1111; Goff A–1415; Gasparrini Leporace 26 (dated ca. 1485).

10 April 1929—Gift of James Byrne. Inc 7058

3450 ——Another copy. 270 x 192 mm.

Initial spaces not filled in; without rubrication. Half modern pigskin and marbled boards. Imperfect: quire d^6 wanting.

Countway Library (William Norton Bullard Collection)

3451 Barzizius, Christophorus (Physician): Introductorium ad opus practicum medicinae. 20 August 1494.

f°. [1], 252 (i.e., 255), [1] leaves ([256] blank; 255 misnumbered 252; other misnumberings too numerous to record); 281 x 197 mm.

Includes Muhammad Rhazes, *Liber nonus ad Almansorem*, with commentary by Barzizius. Edited by Johannes Antonius Bassinus and corrected by Petrus Buzius. The GW collation can be made more precise: e^8 (–e3). Printed by De Carcano for Octavianus Scotus.

Initial spaces, some with guide-letters, not filled in; without rubrication. For binding description see no. 2282 in vol. 2, Muhammad Rhazes, *Liber nonus ad Almansorem* (Venice, Bonetus Locatellus for Octavianus Scotus, 10 April 1490), with which this is bound, along with Antonius Guainerius, *Opera medica* (Venice, Jacobus Pentius, 9 May 1508).

H 2666*=2665; Pr 7066; Pell 1975; GW 3672; IGI 1406; Goff B–260; Sack 527; BSB-Ink B–216; Gasparrini Leporace 51.

Countway Library (William Norton Bullard Collection)

3452 Barbatia, Andreas: Super titulo: De rebus ecclesiae alienandis vel non. 27 October 1497.

f°. [1], 2–80 (i.e., 90) leaves (38, 30–39, 58–59 repeated, 41, 43, 64 omitted in numbering; 40, 53, and 72 misnumbered 4, 26, and 7); 395 x 290 mm.

Initial spaces, most with guide-letters, not filled in; without rubrication. Half modern brown morocco and brown cloth.

HR 2437; GW 3372; IGI 1241; Goff B–114; Gasparrini Leporace 58.

Law Library

FRANCISCUS
DE SANCTO PETRO

3453 Mesue, Johannes: Opera medicinalia. 23 December 1478–9 February 1479.

A2r: [¹]Ncipit liber de cõsolatione medicina‖rū simpliciū solutiuaʁ Iohannis heben ‖ Mesue. ‖ [⁸]N nomīe Dei miβcor‖dis ... ‖ Q7r, line 35: Iohannis Mesue. Medici Singularis đ ‖ Medicinis particularium egritudinum. ‖ Liber feliciter finit. ‖ [For the rest of the transcriptions see IGI and Accurti (1930).]

f°. A–B¹⁰, C⁸, D¹⁰, E–G⁸, H⁴, I–K¹⁰, L–M⁸, N–O¹⁰, P–Q⁸, R¹⁰, S¹², T⁶ (A1, Q8, S12, and T6 blank); [166] leaves (1, 138, 160, and 166 blank); 307 x 215 mm. 2 columns. A2r: 50 lines, 268 x 167 mm. Type: 1:107R. Initial spaces.   Plate XI

Includes Petrus de Abano, *Additio in librum Mesue*, and Gentilis de Fulgineo, *De proportionibus medicinarum*.

Initials added in red and/or blue, many with marginal extensions; paragraph marks added in red or blue. Modern black morocco by Sangorski & Sutcliffe, London. Imperfect: quire T⁶ (Gentilis de Fulgineo) wanting; leaves A2-10, B1-9 partly remargined in upper corners; blank leaves A1 and S12 not present.

IGI 6386 (quires R–T only); Accurti (1930) 68 (quire T only); Goff M–512.

Countway Library

3454 **Abulkasim:** Liber Servitoris de praeparatione medicinarum simplicium. 1478 or 1479.

E1r: INCIPIT LIBER SERVITO‖RIS LIBER. xxviii. ‖ Bulchasim Benaberazerin trãslatus a ‖ Simone ianuēsi interpetre [*sic*] Abraã iudeo ‖ tortuosiensi. ‖ (d⁶)IXIT aggretator [sic] hui9 ‖ operis ... ‖ G6r, line 17: Finit liber Seruitoris de preparatiõe ‖ medicinarum simplicium. ‖ G6v: TRACTATVS DE VRINIS. ‖ (s⁵)Equntur [sic] nobilissima docu‖menta urinarū ... ‖ G7r, line 49: ... Et etiã beñ ‖ euacuare corpus ē optimum. ‖ .FINIS. ‖ G7v blank.

f°. E–G⁸ (G8 blank?); [24] leaves (24 blank?); 378 x 275 mm. 2 columns. E1r: 50 lines, 268 x 168 mm. Type: 1:107R. Initial spaces, some with guide-letters.   Plate XII

Rather than trying to construct a full description of this book from inadequate sources, I prefer to describe the fragment that is present at Harvard. It was clearly intended to accompany the same printer's edition of Mesue (see preceding entry), probably as a supplement to it. A complete copy would contain Nicolaus Salernitanus, *Antidotarium*. For an attempt at a complete description see E. P. Goldschmidt's catalogue 17 (1929), no. 73.

Initial spaces not filled in; without rubrication. Half modern calf and marbled boards. Blank (?) leaf not present.

Klebs 703.4; Goff N–161.

Countway Library (William Norton Bullard Collection)

FRANCISCUS GIRARDENGUS

3455 **Alexander de Ales:** Summa universae theologiae. 11 July–23 December 1489.

4°. 4 vols. (vol. 1: [224] leaves, 11 blank; vol. 2: [472] leaves, 14–15 blank; vol. 3: [360] leaves, 9 and 360 blank; vol. 4: [512] leaves, 11 blank); 210 x 150 mm.

Printed by Girardengus with Johannes Antonius Birreta.

Harvard has vol. 2 only. Initial spaces, with guide-letters, not filled in; without rubrication. 19th-century vellum. MS ownership notation on ᵖaa2r, "Ex libris Fr̄is Matthęi de Bonifatio."

H 644*; HC 644(1); Pr 7075A(1); BMC 7:1004 (IA.31412); Pell 432; Polain 113; GW 872; IGI 288; Goff A–384; Sack 106(4); BSB-Ink A–241.

1957—Bequest of Lee M. Friedman. Inc 7075A v.2

3456 **Johannes de Gaddesden:** Rosa anglica practica medicinae. 24 January 1492.

f°. [4], 173, [1] leaves ([174] blank); 282 x 204 mm.

Edited by Nicolaus Scyllatius. Printed by Girardengus with Johannes Antonius Birreta.

Initials and paragraph marks added in red in the first two quires, but the red has mostly washed away; initial spaces elsewhere, with guide-letters, not filled in. 19th-century blind-stamped brown calf, edges gilt, by W. Pratt. Stamp "Dupl Bibl Gott [i.e., Göttingen] vend" on title page; booklabels of C. Inglis (no. 409 in the Sotheby sale catalogue, June 1900) and of George Dunn, with his MS date of acquisition "June 1900" (no. 3347 in pt. 3 of the Sotheby sale catalogue, November 1917). An engraved title border has been pasted around the title on π1r, and other engravings are pasted inside the front and back covers, probably by J. B. Inglis. Sheets v3–4 misbound before v1.

HC 1108*; Pr 7106; BMC 7:1005 (IB.31417); Pell 764; Polain 1525; IGI 5249; Goff J-326; Sack 2069.

Countway Library (William Norton Bullard Collection)

3457 **Cepolla, Bartholomaeus:** De servitutibus urbanorum et rusticorum praediorum. Cautelae. 1 April 1492.

4°. 2 pts. in 1 vol. (pt. 1: [4], 37, [5], 38 leaves, [1] blank, 30 in the first count misnumbered 03; pt. 2: [2], 31, [1] leaves, [32] blank, 2 misnumbered 22); 395 x 275 mm.

The two parts are often recorded separately, but there seems no reason to do so, since only pt. 2 has a full colophon. Birreta alone is named in the colophon, but BMC considers this work the joint product of Birreta and Girardengus.

Initial spaces, with guide-letters, not filled in; without rubrication. Half modern vellum and blue boards.

H 4850* and 4866*; Pr 7064; BMC 7:1005 (IC.31418); GW 6501 and 6479; IGI 2698-A and 2688-A; Goff C-395 and C-383; BSB-Ink C-236 and C-225.

10 October 1947—Received. Law Library

3458 **Ferrariis de Gradibus, Johannes Matthaeus de:** Opera medica. 27 May 1497.

f°. [1], 2-247, [1] leaves ([120] and [248] blank); 400 x 284 mm.

There are variant titles; see BMC and GW. Includes Muhammad Rhazes, *Liber nonum ad Almansorem*. Edited by Johannes Antonius Bassinus. Printed by Girardengus for Aloysius de Castello and Bartholomaeus de Trottis.

This copy has the title of the main GW transcription. Initial spaces, with guide-letters, not filled in; without rubrication. Original half blind-stamped leather (of which only fragments remain) and wooden boards; leather thongs with brass clasps nailed to front cover, marks of latches on back, no longer present; spine gone; in a cloth case. Bookplate of William Norton Bullard. Imperfect: leaf a1 slightly mutilated, affecting text; blank leaf Q8 mostly torn away.

H 7838*; Pr 7110; BMC 7:1018 (IC.31613); GW 9832; IGI 3846; Goff F-120; BSB-Ink F-73.

Countway Library (William Norton Bullard Collection)

NICOLAUS GIRARDENGUS

3459 Paulus Venetus: Sophismata. 4 March 1483.

f°. [102] leaves (1 blank); 288 x 202 mm.

Polain (probably in error) calls for 104 leaves, with quire b in eights; this copy has b^6, as does that described by Sack. Edited by Manfredus de Medicis.

Paragraph marks added in red on a2-4, not thereafter; initial space on a2r, with guide-letter, not filled in. 19th-century gray boards. Bookplate of William Norton Bullard. Bookseller's ticket of C. E. Rappaport, Rome.

HR 12507; Polain 3018; IGI 7344; Goff P–236; Sack 2689.

Countway Library (William Norton Bullard Collection)

3460 Andreae, Johannes: Mercuriales quaestiones super regulis iuris. 17 May 1483.

f°. [146] leaves (1, 145–46 blank); 415 x 285 mm.

Printed by Girardengus for Johannes Franciscus de Pezanis.

Large initial on a2r added in red and blue, those elsewhere and paragraph marks in red or blue, capital strokes in red. Old vellum. MS ownership notation obliterated on a2r.

H 1059*; Pr 7082; BMC 7:1007 (IC.31435); Pell 654; GW 1738; IGI 495; Goff A–638.

5 May 1945—Received. Law Library

CHRISTOPHORUS
DE CANIBUS

3461 Burlaeus, Gualtherus: Expositio in Aristotelis Physica. 24 January 1488.

f°. [175] leaves (1 and 175 blank); 354 x 245 mm.

Includes the text of Aristotle in the Latin translation of Guillelmus de Moerbeka. Edited by Nicolettus Vernias. Printed by De Canibus for Hieronymus de Durantibus. The GW collation can be made more precise: i^8 (–i6).

Initial spaces, some with guide-letters, not filled in; without rubrication. Half modern vellum and marbled boards. Blank leaves not present.

HR 4138; GW 5776; IGI 2269; Goff B–1304.

13 December 1924—Bought with the Charles Minot fund. Inc 7084.5

3462 Ubaldis, Nicolaus de: De successionibus ab intestato. 22 October 1488.

[For transcriptions see Hain, supplemented by Copinger.] f°. a⁸, b–d⁶ (d6 blank); [26] leaves (26 blank); 375 x 275 mm. 2 columns. a4r: 63 lines, 278 x 180 mm. Types: 2:130G, headings; 6:85G, text. Initial spaces, with guide-letters.

Initials, paragraph marks, capital strokes, and underlinings added in red; leaves numbered in MS 52–77. Modern vellum.

HC 15895*; Pr 7085A; IGI 10005; Goff U–46; Sack 3597.

15 July 1938—Received. Law Library

LEONARDUS GERLA

3463 Ubaldis, Baldus de: Repetitio legis De longi temporis praescriptione. 2 January 1495.

[For transcriptions see Hain; but correct his ".M.cccclxxxv" to ".M.ccccxxxxv."] f°. a⁶; [6] leaves; 392 x 275 mm. 2 columns. a1r: 69 lines, 313 x 193 mm. Types: Haebler 1:90/1G and 2G. Initial spaces, with guide-letters, on a1r and a5r. Printer's device (Husung 80).   Plate XIII

Initial spaces not filled in; without rubrication. Bound in vellum leaves of a 15th-century Latin liturgical MS with musical notation.

H 2327*.

4 September 1940—Received. Law Library

3464 Cepolla, Bartholomaeus: De simulatione contractuum. 15 February 1498.

f°. [22] leaves; 395 x 280 mm.

Some copies are without printer's device on the title page and without colophon.

This copy is without printer's device and colophon. Initial spaces, some with guide-letters, not filled in; without rubrication. Half modern brown morocco and brown cloth.

HC 4874; BMC 12:72 (IC.31599); Pell 3486=3491; GW 6512; IGI 2706; Goff C-400; BSB-Ink C-240.

Law Library

3465 Bartolinis, Baldus de: Commentaria in paragraphum Cato libri IV Digestorum: De verborum obligatione. ca. 1498.

f°. [4] leaves; 433 x 287 mm.

Some copies have "DEO GRATIAS" inserted between the last line of text and the colophon.

This copy is without "DEO GRATIAS." Initial space on a1, with guide-letter, not filled in; without rubrication. Modern vellum.

H 2469*; Pell 1849; Polain 528; GW 3466; IGI 1272; Goff B-177; BSB-Ink B-117.

20 May 1946—Received. Law Library

M A R T I N U S   D E   L A V A L L E

3466 Costa, Stephanus: De consanguinitate et affinitate. 3 August 1489.

f°. [12] leaves (1 and 12 blank); ill.; 400 x 270 mm.

Initial spaces, with guide-letters, not filled in; without rubrication. Modern brown morocco by Lortic, with the arms of Victor Masséna, prince d'Essling, stamped in gilt on covers (no. 87 in the Galerie Fischer sale catalogue, May 1939); booklabel of Frances Hofer.

HC 5788; Pr 7094; BMC 7:1012 (IC.31524); GW 7807; IGI 3246; Goff C-945; Sack 1186; BSB-Ink C-684; Sander 2230.

31 December 1948—Gift of Frances Hofer. Typ Inc 7094

G A B R I E L   D E   G R A S S I S

3467 Petrus de Abano: Conciliator differentiarum philosophorum et medicorum. 6 November 1490.

4° and f°. [294] leaves (1 and 294 blank); 284 x 198 mm.

Includes his *De venenis* and Petrus de Carariis, *De terminatione veneno-rum*. Edited by Franciscus Argilagnes.

Initial spaces not filled in; without rubrication. Half 18th-century calf and decorated boards; in a cloth case. MS ownership notation on blank a1r, "Antonij Caietani Arimineñ ex dono. Anno Dñi 1702"; bookplate of William Norton Bullard.

HC 3*; Pr 7096; BMC 7:1013 (IB.31533); Pell 3; IGI 7599; Goff P–434.

Countway Library (William Norton Bullard Collection)

3468 Augustonus, Johannes Basilius: Prognosticon, 1491 [Latin]. After 12 November 1490.

4°. [6] leaves; 225 x 162 mm.

Initial spaces not filled in; without rubrication. For binding description see no. 2233 in vol. 2, the same author's *Prognosticon, 1493* (Venice, Johannes Hamann, 1492), with which this is bound. Imperfect: leaves [a]2–5 wanting.

GW 3068 (assigned to A. and J. Britannicus in Brescia); Accurti (1930) 3068; IGI 1076; Goff A–1378.

Countway Library (William Norton Bullard Collection)

J O H A N N E S   A N T O N I U S
D E   H O N A T E

3469 Mayno, Jason de: Commentaria in secundam partem Codicis. 31 January [i.e., after 13 February] 1493.

f°. [238] leaves (1 blank); 418 x 288 mm.

For transcriptions and type identification see IGI; but correct the leaf count and collation: a–f^8, g^6, h^4, l–n^8, o^6, p–y^8, z^6, ?^{6}, ?^{6}, A–C^8, D^{10}, E–G^8, H^{10}. IGI does not indicate that the heading on a2r is printed in red. The author's dedicatory letter is dated "Ex academia Ticinẽsi idibus februarij: anno salutis dominice. M.cccclxxxxiij."

Initial spaces, with guide-letters, not filled in; without rubrication. Old blind-stamped leather over wooden boards, rebacked; fragments of leather thongs nailed to front cover, brass latches on back, clasps and thongs gone. Bookstamps eradicated on a2r and H10v.

H 10956; IGI 5992.

18 July 1950—Received. Law Library

BERNARDINUS AND
AMBROSIUS DE ROVELLIS

3470 Zaccarias: De inductione formarum speculationes. 1493/95.

4°. [34] leaves; 213 x 154 mm.

Edited by Petrus Felix Hodeschus.

Initial spaces not filled in; without rubrication. Half old vellum and paste-paper boards. MS ownership notation on a1r, "Dom. Prof. Rom. S. J. Bibl. com."

CR 6610; Pr 7099; BMC 7:1014 (IB.31565); IGI 10427; Goff Z–10.

21 October 1919—Bought with the John Harvey Treat fund. Inc 7099

3471 Accoltis, Franciscus de: Super secundo libro Decretalium. 9 September 1496.

f°. [121] leaves (1 and 121 blank); 408 x 282 mm.

The GW collation can be made more precise: n^6 (–n6).

Initial spaces not filled in; without rubrication. Half 16th-century blind-stamped pigskin and wooden boards; brass clasp plates with fragments of pigskin thongs nailed to front cover, latches on back, clasps and thongs gone. Illegible autograph in a German hand dated 1835 on blank a1r. With this is bound Johannes Antonius de Sancto Georgio, *Commentum super quarto libro Decretalium* (Venice, Philippus Pincius, 13 January 1503). Blank leaf u6 not present. Wormed.

H 41*; GW 148; IGI 19; Goff A–21; BSB-Ink A–14.

23 May 1936—Received. Law Library

3472 Ubaldis, Angelus de: Consilia deficientia nonaginta. 10 May 1499.

f°. [56] leaves (1, 52, and 56 blank); 400 x 275 mm.

Initial spaces, the first with guide-letter, not filled in; without rubrication. Old vellum; vellum thongs slip into vellum clasps on front cover.

HC 15866; Pr 7105; BMC 7:1016 (IC.31577); IGI 9908; Goff U-5; Sack 3561.

17 May 1944—Received. Law Library

JOHANNES ANDREAS
DE BOSCHO,
MICHAEL AND BERNARDINUS
DE GARALDIS

3473 **Franchis, Philippus de:** Lectura super titulo De appellationibus. 15 December 1496.

f°. [15], II–LXXXXIIII (i.e., LXXXXIII), [1] leaves ([15] and [LXXXXIIII] blank; LXXXIIII omitted; XL–XLIIII misnumbered L–LIIII); 404 x 281 mm.

Initial spaces, some with guide-letters, not filled in; without rubrication. Old limp vellum. Blank leaf q4 not present.

H 7320; GW 10247; IGI 4079; Goff F–283; Sack 1477; BSB-Ink F–232.

Law Library

3474 **Hugo Senensis:** Expositio in primam fen quarti Canonis Avicennae. 29 October 1498.

[For transcriptions see Reichling.] f°. a⁸, b–d⁶, e⁴, f–i⁶, k⁴, l²; [60] leaves; 420 x 285 mm. 2 columns. a2r: 72 lines, 310 x 195 mm. Types: 2:136G (leaded to ca. 180), title and headings; Haebler 1*:86/7G, text. Initial spaces; device of the publisher, Franciscus Nebius de Burgo Franco, on title page.

Includes the Latin text of Avicenna. Edited by Johannes Tollentinus.

Initial spaces, with guide-letters, not filled in; without rubrication. 19th-century tan boards.

R 1766; IGI 4948; Goff H–547.

Countway Library

3475 Jacobus de Forlivio: Expositio in primum librum Canonis Avicennae. 17 November 1500.

[For transcriptions see IGI; but their type assignment is wrong.] f°. A–R⁸, S⁶; AA–CC⁸, DD¹⁰; [1], 2–142 leaves (141 misnumbered 140); 34 leaves (9 misnumbered 6); 420 x 290 mm. 2 columns. A2r: 82 lines, 310 x 191 mm. Types: Haebler 5:150G, title and headings; Haebler 4:100G, text; BMC 3:73G, commentary. Woodcut initials on A2r and AA1r; initial spaces, with guide-letters.

Includes additions by Jacobus de Partibus. Edited by Petrus Antonius Rusticus. Printed by the brothers De Garaldis for Aloysius Comensis, Bartholomaeus Trottus, and Balthasar Astensis.

Initial spaces not filled in; without rubrication. Original wooden boards with modern leather rebacking; fragments of leather thongs nailed to front cover, brass latches on back, clasps and thongs gone. Bookplate of William Norton Bullard.

Klebs 548.5; IGI 4987 (with facsim.); Goff J–53.

Countway Library (William Norton Bullard Collection)

F R A N C I S C U S   D E   G U A S C H I S

3476 Lanfrancus de Oriano: Aureus tractatus de arbitris. 10 May 1499.

[For transcriptions see Hain; but this copy reads "Lafrnchi [sic]" for his "Lāfrāchi" in the title and "praticabilis" for his "practicabilis" in the heading on a2r.] f°. a–e⁴ (e4 blank); [20] leaves (20 blank); 395 x 282 mm. 2 columns. a2r: 69 lines, 297 x 190 mm. Types: 1:87G, text; 2:180G, title and headings. Initial space on a2r, with guide-letter; printer's device (Husung 50) on title page.

Printed by De Guaschis for Johannes de Legnano and Girardus de Zeiis, whose names alone occur in the colophon.

Initial space not filled in; without rubrication. Half modern brown morocco and brown cloth.

H 9891*; Pr 7112; IGI 5672; Goff L–53.

Law Library

3477 Socinus, Bartholomaeus: Repetitio legis primae De vulgare et pupillari substitutione. ca. 1500.

f°. [26] leaves; 394 x 283 mm.

For transcriptions and collation see IGI.

Initial spaces, with guide-letters, not filled in; without rubrication. Half modern brown morocco and brown cloth.

IGI 9052.

Law Library

J A C O B U S   D E   P A U C I S   D R A P I S

3478 Jacobus de Voragine: Sermones de tempore, de sanctis, et quadragesimales. 2 September 1499–8 January 1500.

8°. 3 vols. (vol. 1: [16], 379 [i.e., 179], [1] leaves, [180] blank, 179 misnumbered 379; vol. 2: [8], 211, [1] leaves; vol. 3: [10], 117, [1] leaves, [118] blank); ill.; 167 x 114 mm.

Edited by Nicolaus Campanus and Hieronymus de Cherio.

Harvard has volume 3 only. A few initial spaces, with guide-letters, not filled in; without rubrication. Old leather, badly worn; vellum leaves of Latin MS bound in at front and back. MS ownership notation at end, "Hic: liber: est: f͞ris: valerii: De: Spoleto."

C 6526; R 789(2); Pr 7118(2); BMC 7:1019 (IA.31641)(3); Polain 2233(1-2); IGI 5070, 5062, 5056; Goff J-201; CIBN J-137; Sander 7734.

4 March 1921—Bought with the John Harvey Treat fund. Inc 7118.5

3479 ——Another copy. 150 x 106 mm.

Volume 3 only. Initial spaces not filled in; without rubrication. Modern vellum, with wallet edges. Blank leaf not present.

Countway Library

Sant'Orso

L E O N A R D U S   A C H A T E S

3480 Petrarca, Francesco: Canzoniere e Trionfi. 1474.

f°. [176] leaves (1 and 176 blank); 270 x 190 mm.

According to BMC, "The signatures are placed well below the last line of the page and have in consequence all been cut off by the binder." The Harvard copy is larger than that described by BMC and shows no sign of signatures. Includes Leonardus Brunus Aretinus, *Vita di Petrarca*.

Initial spaces, most with guide-letters, not filled in; without rubrication. 19th-century brown straight-grain morocco, gilt, edges gilt. Booklabel of Adriana R. Salem. Blank [r]8 not present.

HC 12759; Pr 7120 (assigned to Achates at Vicenza); BMC 7:1026 (IB.30944); IGI 7522; Goff P-377; CIBN P-181.

December 1964—Gift of Ward M. Canaday. Inc 7120

JOHANNES DE RENO

3481 Pseudo-Phalaris: Epistolae [Latin]. 1475.

4°. [52] leaves (52 blank); 205 x 142 mm.

The BMC records the last word in line 3 on [a]1r as divided "EPI ‖ STVLAS"; this copy has "EPIS ‖ TVLAS." Translated by Franciscus Griffolinus.

Initial spaces not filled in; without rubrication. Old sheep, rebacked. Bookplate of James Frothingham Hunnewell. Blank leaf not present.

HC(Add) 12894; Pr 6937; BMC 7:1027 (IA.30911); IGI 7692; Goff P-555; CIBN P-290.

January 1919—Deposited by James M. Hunnewell. Inc 7144.15

3482 Pius II, Pope: De duobus amantibus. ca. 1475.

4°. [34] leaves; 167 x 127 mm.

On the erroneous printing of a7v see BMC.

Initial spaces, most with guide-letters, not filled in; without rubrication. Modern brown morocco by Chambolle-Duru, edges gilt.

HC 218*; Pr 7146 (assigned to De Reno in Vicenza); BMC 7:1027 (IA.30914); Pell 150; IGI 7800; Goff P-676.

25 December 1957—Gift of I. Austin Kelly III. Inc 7146

3483 **Samuel Maroccanus, Rabbi:** Epistola contra Iudaeorum errores. ca. 1475.

4°. [28] leaves (1 blank); 202 x 143 mm.

Translated by Alphonsus Boni Hominis. Includes the Pseudo-Pontius Pilate epistle to Tiberius.

Initials added in red. 19th-century vellum. Bookplate of Lee M. Friedman.

H 14263*; Pr 7149 (assigned to De Reno in Vicenza); BMC 7:1028 (IA.30920); Polain 3435; IGI 8575; Goff S–104; CIBN S–54.

1957–Bequest of Lee M. Friedman. Inc 7149

Vicenza

L E O N A R D U S   A C H A T E S

3484 **Uberti, Fazio degli:** Dittamondo. November 1474.

f°. [106] leaves; 293 x 200 mm.

There is a variant on f5r; see BMC.

In this copy the last word on f5r is printed "strigido." The signatures are printed very low down on the first four leaves of each quire. Initials and paragraph marks added in red or blue. 18th-century red straight-grain morocco, gilt. Booklabel of Adriana R. Salem.

HC 15906; Pr 7119; BMC 7:1030 (IB.31702); IGI 10017; Goff U–53; CIBN U–18.

December 1959–Gift of Ward M. Canaday. Inc 7119

3485 **Cibaldone:** Cibaldone ovvero Libro terzo di Almansore. ca. 1480.

4°. [20] leaves; 184 x 135 mm.   Plate XIV

A verse paraphrase of book 3 of Muhammad Rhazes' *Liber ad Almansorem.* BMC has note, "The tract may be either Achates' first experiment with the type [114R] in or about 1480 or the work of some small printer using his material."

Without rubrication. 18th-century calf, rebacked in 19th-century sheep. With this were originally bound Lilius Giraldus, *Poematia* (Lug-

duni, 1536) and two other 16th-century works, which were removed
and bound separately. MS notes by Richard Heber, "This vol. sold at
Croft's for 10ˢ" (no. 1474 in the Paterson sale catalogue of Thomas
Crofts' library, April 1783), and "Fazakerley's sale 11.6" (no. 188 in
the King sale catalogue, February 1801; no. 4332 in pt. 3 of the
Sotheby sale catalogue of Heber's library, November 1834); no. 314
in the Sotheby sale catalogue of books from the Christie Miller library, July 1917; bookplate of Giuseppe Martini (no. 315 in his 1934
catalogue; no. 170 in pt. 2 of the Zürich sale catalogue, May 1935).

H 13904; Pr 7404 (Italian adespota); BMC 7:1034 (IA.31745); IGI
2789; Goff R–172.

Countway Library

3486 Crescentiis, Petrus de: Ruralia commoda [Italian]. 17 February 1490.

fº. [146] leaves (1 blank); ill.; 294 x 203 mm.

Initial spaces, with guide-letters, not filled in; without rubrication;
woodcut uncolored. Half 19th-century vellum and marbled boards.
Bookstamp of the Biblioteca municipale di Bologna, with its duplicate
stamp dated 1890; bookplate of Daniel B. Fearing. Imperfect: leaves
a3–4 inserted from another copy; last two leaves wormed, slightly
affecting text.

HC(+Add) 5838; Pr 7128; BMC 7:1033 (IB.31725); GW 7827; IGI
3267; Goff C–974; BSB-Ink C–700; Sander 2234.

30 June 1915—Gift of Daniel B. Fearing. Inc 7128

3487 Herbarius. 27 October 1491.

4°. [4], CL, [18] leaves (1 and 156 blank; CXIII and CXIX misnumbered CXIX and CXIII); ill.; 205 x 150 mm.

Because of the woodcut intended to depict Arnoldus de Villa Nova
and Avicenna at head of π2r, this edition has been wrongly ascribed
to Arnoldus. Printed by Achates with Guillelmus de Papia.

Initials and paragraph marks in the final two quires added in red or
blue; woodcuts colored; the border and woodcut on π2r have been illuminated in gold and colors heavily enough to obscure the original
lines; coat of arms in the lower border. Contemporary blind-stamped
leather over wooden boards; brass thong nails on front cover, brass
latches on back, clasps and thongs gone. 16th-century owner's MS

note in Italian on front flyleaf dated 10 April 1587.

HC(+Add) 8451; C 649a; Pr 7131; BMC 7:1033 (IA.31731); Pell 1314; IGI 4676; Goff H-68; Sander 610.

January 1919–Deposited by James M. Hunnewell. Inc 7131

3488 ——Another copy. 194 x 140 mm.

In this copy the initial spaces in the final two quires have not been filled in; only the first eight woodcuts of plants have been colored; woodcut and border on π2r uncolored. Modern brown blind-stamped morocco; edges gilt. Imperfect: leaf π4 wanting; x5–8 slightly mutilated in the margins; π2 remargined; blank π1 not present.

January 1918–Gift of Sarah C. Sears. Arnold Arboretum Library

3489 ——Another copy. 205 x 150 mm.

Initial spaces not filled in; woodcuts uncolored. Old vellum. Boston Medical Library bookplate, "ex dono Dr. William N. Bullard." Imperfect: [18] leaves at end wanting; leaf π2 mutilated; blank π1 not present.

Countway Library (William Norton Bullard Collection)

H E R M A N N U S   L I E C H T E N S T E I N

3490 Ptolemaeus, Claudius: Cosmographia. 13 September 1475.

f°. [143] leaves (1 blank); ill.; 294 x 203 mm.

Latin translation by Johannes Angelus. Edited by Angelus Vadius and Barnabas Picardus. Both Harvard copies are too tightly bound for me to determine the makeup of quire bb (described by BMC as "bb$^{8-1}$").

This copy originally had erroneous reading "Ptolomae, iuiri" in line 3 on aa2r, but it has been corrected in ink. Large initial on aa2r added in red and blue; those elsewhere, paragraph marks, capital strokes, and underlinings added in red. 19th-century calf. MS notation in lower margin of aa2r, "Anno dñi Millesimoquingentesimo iste liber datus fuit ad hoc monasteriũ pruffenĩg ord S Bñdictj ... per ... me ... Georgiũ Drechsel Can^{cũ} eccɫie Ratispoñ relictus ob sui memoriã et anĩe sue Remedium"; another in upper margin of the same leaf, "titulo commutationis Ex libris Monasterij S. Jacobi Scotorum

Ratisbonae. 1596"; Syston Park bookplate and monogram booklabel of Sir J. H. Thorold (no. 1654 in the Sotheby sale catalogue, December 1884). MS marginalia; blank leaf aa1r covered with Latin MS.

HC 13536*; Pr 7139; BMC 7:1035 (IB.31752); Polain 3281; IGI 8180; Goff P-1081; Sack 2985; CIBN P-681; Sander 5973.

21 February 1885–Bought with the J. B. Bright fund. Inc 7139

3491 ——Another copy. 301 x 200 mm.

Same MS correction on aa2r as in the above copy. Initial spaces, with guide-letters, not filled in; without rubrication. 18th-century red morocco; leather label on spine. MS note in Richard Heber's hand, "1816. Sale by Sotheby Dec. 1816" (no. 3725 in pt. 5 of the Wheatley sale catalogue of Heber's library, January 1835); from the library of Richard Ashhurst Bowie, with his MS note "Bot in Charleston S.C. Apl. 29 1868." Imperfect: leaves aa2–5 mutilated and backed in linen; blank leaf not present.

Countway Library (William Norton Bullard Collection)

3492 Statuta Veronae. 20 December 1475.

f°. [190] leaves (1 and 190 blank); 305 x 212 mm.

Occasional initials added in brown, but most spaces not filled in. 19th-century paste-paper boards, rebacked. Booklabel "Libreria Gonzati." Imperfect: leaf A2 slightly mutilated; many leaves remargined; blank leaves not present.

HC 10000; Pr 7141; BMC 7:1036 (IB.31754); IGI 10247; Goff S-726; CIBN S-412.

2 August 1920–Bought with the Bayard Cutting fund. Inc 7141

3493 Orosius, Paulus: Historiae adversus paganos. 1475?

f°. [100] leaves; 300 x 198 mm.

Edited by Aeneas Vulpes. Includes a poem by Bartholomaeus Paiellus.

Large initial on [a]2r added in black and red; initials elsewhere, capital strokes, and underlinings added in red; traces of MS quiring. Half modern brown morocco and green cloth. From the library of Richard Ashhurst Bowie, with a slip of his MS notes inserted at front.

H 12099*; Pr 7144; BMC 7:1035 (IB.31758a); IGI 7034; Goff O–97; CIBN O–59.

9 November 1908–Gift of Mrs. E. D. Brandegee. Inc 7144

3494 Duranti, Guillelmus: Rationale divinorum officiorum. 1478.

f°. [228] leaves (3 blank); 295 x 204 mm.

Edited by Johannes Aloisius Tuscanus.

Initials, paragraph marks, and underlinings added in red. Half old vellum and paste-paper boards. MS ownership notation and book-stamp obliterated in lower margin of π1r. Occasional MS marginalia. Blank leaf not present.

H 6480*; Pr 7155; BMC 7:1037 (IB.31812); Pell 4499; Polain 1375; GW 9115; IGI 3625; Goff D-417; Sack 1318; BSB–Ink D-334.

30 November 1945–Received. Law Library

3495 Ovidius Naso, Publius: Opera. 10 May–12 August 1480.

f°. 2 vols. (vol. 1: [250] leaves, 1 and 250 blank; vol. 2: [168] leaves, 1 and 168 blank); 288 x 197 and 294 x 204 mm.

Vol. 1: *Epistolae heroides. Amores. De arte amandi. De remedio amoris. Ibis. Fasti. De tristibus. De Ponto. De pulice. Consolatio ad Liviam.*–vol. 2: *Metamorphoses.* Edited by Barnabas Celsanus. Vol. 2 includes an introduction by Bonus Accursius, reprinted from earlier editions.

Initial spaces not filled in; without rubrication. The two volumes were originally of different provenance and are bound differently: vol. 1, 18th-century calf, spine gilt and repaired; edges stained red. Blank leaves at front and back covered with MS Latin verses. Vol. 2, old half leather and paste-paper boards. MS ownership notation obliterated at top of leaf π2r; from the library of Richard Ashhurst Bowie. Blank leaves not present.

HC(+Add) 12141*; Pr 7157; BMC 7:1037 (IB.31816); Polain 2953(2); IGI 7047; Goff O–131; Sack 2634; CIBN O–83.

9 November 1908–Gift of Mrs. E. D. Brandegee. Inc 7157

3496 Duranti, Guillelmus: Rationale divinorum officiorum. 1480.

f°. [224] leaves (3 and 224 blank); 310 x 205 mm.

Edited by Johannes Aloisius Tuscanus.

Large initial on A2r illuminated in colors, with marginal extension; initials at beginning of books also illuminated in colors; initials elsewhere added in red and purple or blue and red, paragraph marks in red or blue. Half old vellum and decorated boards; edges stained red. MS ownership notation on blank A1v, "Ex Libris Laurentii Giannetti Canonici Cortonensis."

HC 6482*; Pr 7159; Pell 4501; Polain 4342; GW 9120; IGI 3629; Goff D-423; BSB-Ink D-340.

2 March 1925—Gift of Denman W. Ross. Fogg Art Museum (Print Room)

3497 Silvaticus, Matthaeus: Liber pandectarum medicinae. ca. 1480.

f°. [322] leaves (7 and 322 blank); 300 x 210 mm.

Edited by Matthaeus Moretus.

Initial spaces, most with guide-letters, not filled in; without rubrication. Original (?) wooden boards, rebacked in leather; marks of clasp plates on front cover, latches on back, no longer present. Bookplate of William Norton Bullard.

HC 15193*; BMC 7:1038 (IB.31820); IGI 8981; Goff S-513.

Countway Library (William Norton Bullard Collection)

G I O V A N N I   L E O N A R D O   L O N G O

3498 Campora, Jacopo: Dell'immortalità dell'anima. 31 March 1477.

f°. [26] leaves (26 blank); 295 x 205 mm.

Includes a laudatory letter from Matteo Pigafetta urging Longo to print the work.

Initial spaces, with guide-letters, not filled in; without rubrication. Half modern calf and tan boards. Bookstamp "Ex libr. Fr. Franc. Raim. Adami"; MS note by the American Antiquarian Society on front flyleaf, "Exchange Acct. with D. G. Francis, June 1. 1891." Blank leaf not present.

HCR 4299; Pr 7152; BMC 7:1040 (IB.31785); Pell 3186; GW 5950; IGI 2394; Goff C-79.

July 1971—Bought with the Duplicate fund. Inc 7152

J O H A N N E S   D E   R E N O

3499 Leonicenus, Omnibonus: Commentum in Ciceronis Oratorem. 22 December 1476.

f°. [176] leaves; 286 x 202 mm.

BMC has note: "[De Reno's] connexions with Leonardus [Achates de Basilea] were evidently close, and it is not possible to be certain that the three books of 1476 and 1477 printed with type common to both men, which are here appended to his signed output, were not rather the work of Leonardus."—BMC 7:lxiv. Includes Omnibonus's *De laudibus eloquentiae.*

Initial spaces, with guide-letters, not filled in; without rubrication. Half modern brown morocco and green cloth. From the library of Richard Ashhurst Bowie, with his MS note "Quaritch. List n° 157 June 1882."

H 10030*=HR 10030; Pr 7145; BMC 7:1041 (IB.31765); IGI 7000; Goff L–171.

9 November 1908—Gift of Mrs. E. D. Brandegee. Inc 7145

3500 Catullus, Gaius Valerius: Carmina. 1481.

f°. [149] leaves (145 and 149 blank); 280 x 184 mm.

Edited by Johannes Calphurnius. Includes: Tibullus, *Elegiae.*—Propertius, *Elegiae.*—Statius, *Silvae.*—Calphurnius, *Mors et apotheosis Simonis infantis novi martyris.* Printed by De Reno with Dionysius Bertochus. The BMC and GW collations can be made more precise: q^8 (–q6).

Initial spaces, with guide-letters, not filled in; without rubrication. Pages numbered in MS 189–478. 18th-century calf, rehinged; edges speckled red and blue. Unidentified armorial bookplate inside front cover; from the library of Richard Ashhurst Bowie. Imperfect: quire y^4 at end (Calphurnius's poem) wanting; blank leaf x8 not present.

HC 4760*; Pr 7151; BMC 7:1041 (IB.31777); Pell 3443; Polain 1049; GW 6389; IGI 2615; Goff C–323; BSB-Ink C–198.

9 November 1908—Gift of Mrs. E. D. Brandegee. Inc 7151 (A)

3501 ——Another copy. 301 x 192 mm.

Initial spaces not filled in; without rubrication. Half 18th-century red morocco and green boards. MS ownership notation on blank a1r, "Ivlian. Ferruccij Piscientis"; another inside front cover, "di Giacomo Lucchesini"; from the library of Richard Ashhurst Bowie. Imperfect: all after quire o[6] (Statius and Calphurnius's poem) wanting.

9 November 1908—Gift of Mrs. E. D. Brandegee. Inc 7151 (B)

3502 **Lucanus, Marcus Annaeus:** Pharsalia. 11 May 1482.

4°. [136] leaves; 194 x 140 mm.

Initial spaces, some with guide-letters, not filled in; without rubrication. Old vellum; edges speckled red.

HR 10235; BMC 7:1041 (IA.31779); IGI 5816; Goff L–299; CIBN L–234.

22 March 1919—Bought with the Constantius fund. Inc 7151.8

S T E P H A N   K O B L I N G E R

3503 **Tortellius, Johannes:** Orthographia. 13 January 1479.

f°. [346] leaves (1–2 and 346 blank); 300 x 202 mm.

Edited by Hieronymus Bononius. The BMC collation should be corrected: A[12] (A1–2 blank).

Initial spaces not filled in; without rubrication. 16th-century blind-stamped pigskin stained red over wooden boards; leather thongs nailed to back cover, brass latches on front, brass clasps; marks of center and corner bosses, no longer present, on both covers; vellum fragments of Latin MS pasted down inside both covers. MS signature on blank A1r, "Christophorus Tschertonnides"; in other hands, "15 MK 75" and "1587"; bookplate of William Norton Bullard.

HC 15566*; Pr 7158; BMC 7:1043 (IB.31823); Polain 3792; IGI 9684; Goff T–397; CIBN T–293.

Countway Library (William Norton Bullard Collection)

HENRICUS DE SANCTO URSIO

3504 Petrus de Unzola: Aurora novissima. After 21 April 1485.

[For transcriptions see Hain; but this copy varies in having "in urbe" in line 10 of the colophon and in having line 11 end "ducis ‖."] f°. a–d⁸, e⁶, f–z⁸, &⁸, ꝑ⁸) a1 and ꝑ⁸ blank); [198] leaves (1 and 198 blank); 290 x 203 mm. 2 columns. a2r: 48 lines, 211 x 137 mm. Type: 3:88R. Initial spaces.

Edited by Franciscus de Anzolellis.

Initial spaces not filled in; without rubrication. Bound in part of a vellum leaf of Latin liturgical text with musical notation. Occasional MS marginalia. Imperfect: leaf ꝑ7 slightly mutilated; blank ꝑ8 not present.

H 16093*; IGI 10025; Goff U–63; CIBN P–274.

2 July 1950–Received. Law Library

3505 Thienis, Gaietanus de: Expositio in Aristotelem De anima. 21 September–16 October 1486.

f°. [125] leaves (124–25 blank); 302 x 207 mm.

Includes his *Quaestiones de sensu agente, de sensibilibus communibus, et de intellectu,* and Johannes de Janduno, *Expositio et quaestiones in Averrois librum De substantia orbis.* There is a variant *incipit* on a2r; see BMC (reprint edition). The BMC and BSB-Ink collations can be made more precise: a⁸ (–a6).

This copy has the *incipit* of the main BMC transcription. Initial spaces not filled in; without rubrication. Old limp vellum. Imperfect: leaf a1 and all after quire n⁸ wanting.

C 617=5824+5825; R 617(var.); Pr 7168; BMC 7:1046 (IB.31846); IGI 2340; Goff G–26; BSB-Ink C–35.

October 1951–Bequest of Frederick H. Lewis. Inc 7168

3506 ——Another copy. 271 x 195 mm.

This copy has the *incipit* of the main BMC transcription. Some initials and paragraph marks added in red, but the color has been mostly washed away. Old vellum. Bookplate of William Norton Bullard. Imperfect: leaf a1 inserted from another copy; several leaves slightly mutilated; blank leaves not present.

Countway Library (William Norton Bullard Collection)

3507 **Cicero:** Orationes Philippicae. 9 June 1488.

f°. [102] leaves; 312 x 215 mm.

Edited with a commentary by Franciscus Mataratius. Corrected by Johannes Maria Aureolus.

Initial spaces, with guide-letters, not filled in; without rubrication. Half modern brown morocco and green cloth. From the library of Richard Ashhurst Bowie.

HC 5138*; Pr 7171; BMC 7:1047 (IB.31850); Pell 3702; Polain 4098; GW 6796; IGI 2937; Goff C–556; Sack 1020; BSB-Ink C–389.

9 November 1908–Gift of Mrs. E. D. Brandegee. Inc 7171

3508 **Apuleius Madaurensis, Lucius:** Opera. 9 August 1488.

f°. [178] leaves (1 and 178 blank); 280 x 187 mm.

Mostly a reprint of the Sweynheym and Pannartz edition of 1469, edited by Giovanni Andrea Bussi. Includes Hermes Trismegistus, *Asclepius* (translated by Apuleius), and Albinus Platonicus, *Disciplinarum Platonis epitome* (translated by Petrus Balbus).

Initial spaces, with guide-letters, not filled in; without rubrication. Half 19th-century brown morocco and marbled boards. From the library of Richard Ashhurst Bowie, with his MS note at front, "Cohn Berlin Cat: CLI—1883." Blank leaves not present.

HC 1316* (incl. C 531); Pr 7172; BMC 7:1047 (IB.31851); Pell 924; Polain 285; GW 2302; IGI 770; Goff A–935; BSB-Ink A–659.

9 November 1908–Gift of Mrs. E. D. Brandegee. Inc 7172

3509 ——Another copy. 316 x 207 mm.

Initial spaces not filled in; without rubrication. Half 19th-century calf and marbled boards. Booklabel of Louis Thompson Rowe. Imperfect: leaf g8 wanting; blank leaves not present.

Countway Library

3510 **Natalibus, Petrus de:** Catalogus sanctorum et gestorum eorum. 12 December 1493.

f°. [332] leaves (332 blank); 305 x 204 mm.

Edited by Antonius Verlus.

Without rubrication. 18th-century vellum, spine gilt; edges speckled green and black. Booklabel of Count Paul Riant. Blank leaf not present.

HC 11676*; Pr 7173; BMC 7:1047 (IB.31854); Polain 2796; IGI 6769; Goff N-6; CIBN N-4.

28 December 1899—Gift of J. Randolph Coolidge and Archibald Cary Coolidge. Inc 7173

3511 **Martianus Capella:** De nuptiis Philologiae et Mercurii. 16 December 1499.

f°. [124] leaves; 297 x 205 mm.

Edited by Franciscus Vitalis Bodianus.

Initial spaces, with guide-letters, not filled in; without rubrication. Half 18th-century white pigskin and blue boards.

H 4370*; Pr 7174; BMC 7:1048 (IB.31860) and 12:74 (IB.31860b); Pell 3224; IGI 2426; Goff C-117.

February 1974—Gift of Morton Pepper in memory of C. Doris Hellman. Inc 7174

J A C O B U S   D E   D U S A

3512 **Claudianus, Claudius:** Opera. 27 May 1482.

f°. [102] leaves (1 blank); 300 x 187 mm.

Edited by Barnabas Celsanus.

Initials added in blue. 18th-century red morocco, gilt, rehinged. With Quaritch's Sunderland Library bookplate inside front cover (no. 3182 in pt. 2 of the Puttick & Simpson sale catalogue, April 1882); from the library of Richard Ashhurst Bowie, with a sheet of his MS notes inserted at front. Blank leaf not present.

HC 5370*; Pr 7175; BMC 7:1048 (IB.31862); Pell 3801; GW 7059; IGI 3010; Goff C-701; Sack 1035; BSB-Ink C-424.

9 November 1908—Gift of Mrs. E. D. Brandegee. Inc 7175

D I O N Y S I U S   B E R T O C H U S

3513 Crastonus, Johannes: Lexicon Graeco-Latinum. 10 November 1483.

f°. [264] leaves (1 blank); 310 x 208 mm.

This copy has error "um" (i.e., cum, corrected in MS) in line 2 on a3r. BMC points out that there are two settings of sheet f2 but gives no distinguishing readings; in this copy the type-page on f2r measures 197 mm. in length. As in BMC copy IB.31873, the text proper to c3v has changed places with that proper to c6r. Initial on a3r added in red; spaces elsewhere, some with guide-letters, not filled in. Half 19th-century calf and marbled boards, rehinged. MS ownership notation washed away on a3r but visible under ultraviolet light, "Du monastere des Celestins de Sens est ce present liure"; name "Johannes Lesourt" in Greek letters in lower margin of n6r; MS ownership notation partly torn away on blank a1r, "Celestino-r[um] ... liber iste ... sollicitudine f Jo ... transmissus p[er?] Vene ... Ioannem oger [=Auger?} tunc priorem ... lugdunensium Caelesti-nor[um]"; bookplate of Robert Proctor, with his note "Given me by S.C.C[ockerell]. 2 Apr. 1901"; from the library of Richard Ashhurst Bowie. Imperfect: leaf a2 (letter of Bonus Accursius, reprinted from his edition of 1478) wanting.

HCR 5813; Pr 7177; BMC 7:1049 (IC.31872); Pell 4040 and 4040A; Polain 1201; GW 7813; IGI 3253; Goff C–959; Sack 1187.

9 November 1908—Gift of Mrs. E. D. Brandegee. Inc 7177

S I M O N   B E V I L A Q U A

3514 Spirito, Lorenzo: Altro Marte. 9 April 1489.

f°. [88] leaves (1 blank); 302 x 205 mm.

Initial spaces, with guide-letters, not filled in; without rubrication. Old vellum; leather label on spine. Many leaves stained.

HC 14960*; Pr 7184 (Vicentine adespota); BMC 7:1051 (IB.31884); IGI 9136; Goff S–685.

11 December 1955—Bought with the Susan A. E. Morse fund. Inc 7179.5

3515 Brutus, Petrus: Victoria contra Iudaeos. 3 October 1489.

f°. [130] leaves; 308 x 212 mm.

Includes poems by Johannes Bonavitus and others.

Initial spaces, with guide-letters, not filled in; without rubrication. Old vellum; leather labels on spine; edges stained red. Bookplate of Francesco Orazio Beggi.

HC 4027*; Pr 7180; BMC 7:1051 (IB.31886); Pell 3047; Polain 922; GW 5659; IGI 2214; Goff B-1264; Sack 856; BSB-Ink B-951.

1957—Bequest of Lee M. Friedman. Inc 7180

Turin

J O H A N N E S   F A B R I

3516 Statuta Sabaudiae. 17 November 1477.

f°. [180] leaves (1, 166, and 180 blank); 267 x 195 mm.

Edited by Petrus Cara.

A few initials added in brown, but most spaces not filled in. 18th-century calf. Autograph on d5r and s7v, "Benedictus de Balma 1584"; MS ownership notation on front flyleaf, "Emptus die 20ª Martii 1766 [Stephanus] Parra." Blank leaves not present.

HC 14050; Pr 7217; BMC 7:1054 (IB.32415); IGI 8484; Goff S-1; CIBN S-405; Manzoni V.

17 November 1939—Received. Law Library

3517 Cicero: De officiis. 6 May 1481[?].

f°. [96] leaves (1 and 96 blank); 243 x 162 mm.

The settings of this and the following entry are identical except for the last two lines of the colophon, which in this issue read "Venetiis per cōsocios Magistri Nicholai Ianson De Anno ⁞ domini. M.cccc lxxxi die vi Maii." GW has note, "Demnach ist ein Teil der Auflage durch die Jensongesellschaft bezahlt und dementsprechend signiert worden; das Kolophon jedoch weist unzweifelhaft die Eigenheiten von Fabris Stilisierung auf ... so dass die Möglichkeit einer verloren-en, durch Fabri etwa mitsamt dem Kolophon nachgedruckten Ausgabe der Jensongesellschaft auszuschliessen ist." See also BMC 7:lxvi. Since the issue with Fabri's Turin colophon is dated 16 July 1481, it is perhaps doubtful that the date 6 May 1481 can be accepted without question.

Initial spaces not filled in; without rubrication. 18th-century calf, gilt; rehinged; edges speckled red. Autograph in upper margin of a2r, "J. Hume Bp. of Sarum 1777"; another on flyleaf at front, "Chas. F. Dunbar—Nov. 14, 1854." Quires b and h exchanged in binding; leaf m1 and the stub of blank m8 misbound after m4; blank leaves not present.

Pell 3740; GW 6943; not in IGI or Goff; not noted by Manzoni.

5 December 1941—From the estate of Charles F. Dunbar. Inc 7218.12

3518 Cicero: De officiis. 16 July 1481.

f°. [96] leaves (1 and 96 blank); 250 x 180 mm.

See previous entry for a variant. Includes the *De senectute*, *De amicitia*, and the *Paradoxa*.

Initial on a2r added in red; spaces elsewhere not filled in. Half 19th-century sheep and paste-paper boards. In MS inside front cover, "P. Balbus emit a. mdcccxix [an erasure] mdcccliii"; bookplate of James Frothingham Hunnewell. Top margin of a2 cut away, probably to remove an ownership notation; blank leaves not present; sheet b1 wrongly folded.

BMC 7:1054 (IB.32423); GW 6943; IGI 2903; Goff C–592; Manzoni VIII.

January 1919—Deposited by James M. Hunnewell. Inc 7218.10

NICOLAUS DE BENEDICTIS
AND JACOBINUS SUIGUS

3519 Juvenalis, Decimus Junius: Satirae. 8 October 1494.

f°. [136] leaves; 290 x 212 mm.

With the commentaries of Domitius Calderinus and Georgius Valla. Includes a poem and letter by Bonifacius Bugellanus and Calderinus's *Defensio adversus Brotheum*.

Initial spaces in the commentary not filled in; without rubrication. Modern blind-stamped brown morocco by Douglas Cockerell, dated 1900. Autographed, "H. C. Hoskier Jan. 1903" (no. 281 in the Sotheby sale catalogue, June 1908). Imperfect: leaf r8 slightly mutilated, affecting text.

HC 9707; Pr 7223; BMC 7:1058 (IB.32443); IGI 5599; Goff J–660; CIBN J–366; Manzoni XXII.

13 October 1916—Bought with the Constantius fund. Inc 7223

Modena

J O H A N N E S   V U R S T E R

3520 Mesue, Johannes: Opera medicinalia [Italian]. 25 June 1475.

f°. [224] leaves (1 and 224 blank); 301 x 200 mm.

BMC describes sheet f4 as quarto; it is folio in this copy. Large initial on [a]2r illuminated in gold and colors, with marginal extension; initials elsewhere added in red. The signatures are printed far down in the lower right-hand corners and have been trimmed away in many quires, with some replaced in MS. Modern brown morocco by Rivière; edges gilt. Blank leaves not present.

H 11114*; Pr 7191; BMC 7:1059 (IB.32207); IGI 6394; Goff M–518; CIBN M–328; Fava p.103.

Countway Library (William Norton Bullard Collection)

B A L T H A S A R   D E   S T R U C I I S

3521 Pseudo-Augustinus: Sermones ad heremitas. 25 April 1477.

4°. [178] leaves (3 blank); 209 x 145 mm.

BMC describes sheet g2 as octavo; this copy is quarto throughout. Initial spaces, most with guide-letters, not filled in; without rubrication. 18th-century mottled calf, spine gilt. No. 742 in pt. 1 of the Puttick & Simpson sale catalogue of the Sunderland library, December 1881; bookplate of James Frothingham Hunnewell. Imperfect: *tabula* (π^2) wanting; leaf i8 mutilated; the sizing has been removed from the leaves by washing, with resulting fragility.

HC 1994; Pr 7193; BMC 7:1060 (IA.32212); Pell 1510; GW 2999; IGI 1031; Goff A–1311; Fava p.104.

January 1919–Deposited by James M. Hunnewell. Inc 7193

D O M I N I C U S   R O C O C I O L U S

3522 Paganellus, Bartholomaeus: Elegiae. 7 October 1489.

4°. [44] leaves (44 blank); 194 x 142 mm.

Edited by Johannes Boiardus.

Initial spaces, with guide-letters, not filled in. For binding description see no. 3524, the same printer's edition of Paganellus's *De imperio Cupidinis* (23 May 1492), with which this is bound. No. 4354 (?) in pt. 2 of the Sotheby sale catalogue of Richard Heber's library, June 1834 (no mention being made of the first piece in the volume). Imperfect: sheet f1, including blank f4, wanting.

HC 12262; C 4577; Pr 7195; BMC 7:1062 (IA.32250); IGI 7136; Goff P–5; CIBN P–2; Fava p.107.

25 February 1920–Bought with the George Lyman Kittredge fund. Inc 7202

3523 Johannes de Hildesheim: Historia beatissimorum trium regum. 17 August 1490.

4°. [52] leaves; ill.; 186 x 135 mm.

Without rubrication; woodcut uncolored. Half modern black morocco and marbled boards. Booklabels of Count Giacomo Manzoni (no. 3603 in pt. 2 of the Sangiorgi sale catalogue, May–June 1893) and of Philip Hofer.

H 9399*; Pr 7196A; BMC 7:1062 (IA.32255); IGI 5276; Goff J–340; CIBN J–237; Fava p.107; Sander 3650.

9 November 1984–Bequest of Philip Hofer. Typ Inc 7196A

3524 Paganellus, Bartholomaeus: De imperio Cupidinis. 23 May 1492.

4°. [52] leaves; 194 x 142 mm.

Initial spaces at beginning of books, with guide-letters, not filled in; without rubrication. Old vellum. MS ownership notation in lower margin of a2r, "Congregationis S. Caroli"; "Bibliotheca Heberiana" bookstamp (not located in the 1834–37 sale catalogues). With this is bound the same printer's edition of Paganellus's *Elegiae* (7 October 1489).

H 12267*; C 4579; Pr 7202 (misreading the date as 1498); BMC 7:1063 (IA.32262); IGI 7138; Goff P-6; CIBN P-3; Fava p.109.

25 February 1920—Bought with the George Lyman Kittredge fund. Inc 7202

3525 Bigus, Ludovicus: Tumultuaria carmina. 7 June 1492.

4°. [116] leaves (116 blank); 208 x 150 mm.

Initial spaces, with guide-letters, not filled in; without rubrication. Old calf; front cover detached. Royal Society "ex dono Henr. Howard Norfolciensis" bookstamp on a1r, with its "Sold" stamp at end. Imperfect: 2 unsigned leaves at front wanting; blank leaf not present.

HCR 3200; Pr 7199; BMC 7:1063 (IA.32264); Pell 2402; GW 4355; IGI 1735; Goff B-673; Fava p.110.

Countway Library (William Norton Bullard Collection)

DIONYSIUS   BERTOCHUS

3526 Crastonus, Johannes: Lexicon Graeco-Latinum. 20 October 1499–not before 5 July 1500.

f°. 2 pts. in 1 vol. (pt. 1: [1], CXXVIII, [130] leaves, [1] blank, V, XXXII–III, XXXVI–VIII, XLI–XLIII, LXVII, and CVIII misnumbered III, XXXVI–VII, XXXIIII–VI, XXXIX–XXXXI, LXVI, and CVII; pt. 2: [36] leaves); 306 x 203 mm.

Pt. 2 consists of the Latin index of Ambrosius Regiensis and may have been printed by Bertochus at Reggio; see BMC. There are two settings of quires A–V; see BMC and GW. Includes a dedicatory letter by Bonus Accursius and a poem by Lucius Manius.

This copy has the setting, with foliation, of the main BMC and GW transcriptions of quires A–V. Initial spaces, most with guide-letters, not filled in; without rubrication. Half modern black morocco and green boards. MS ownership notation in lower margin of A2r, "Est Con:ˢ Sⁱⁱ [benedicti?] de Cingulo"; another on blank A1r, "Collegij

Societatis Jesu Perusini"; "Bibliotheca Heberiana" bookstamp on front flyleaf (no. 1519 in pt. 2 of the Sotheby sale catalogue, June 1834). Quire & misbound before Z.

H 5814*; Pr 7214; BMC 7:1067 (IB.32333); Pell 4043; Polain 1203; GW 7815; IGI 3256; Goff C-961; Sack 1189; BSB-Ink C-692; Fava p.115.

19 September 1846—Bought with the Donation fund of 1842. Inc 7214

3527 ——Another copy. 317 x 205 mm.

This copy has the secondary setting, without foliation, of quires A–V. Initial spaces not filled in; without rubrication. Old vellum with wallet edges. Booklabel of Leo S. Olschki, Florence. Imperfect: leaf e6 in pt. 2 mutilated, affecting text; blank leaf not present.

Countway Library (William Norton Bullard Collection)

3528 Martianus Capella: De nuptiis Philologiae et Mercurii. 15 May 1500.

f°. [100] leaves; 300 x 193 mm.

Apparently some copies have a four-sided strapwork border on the title page, but according to BMC this was separately printed and pasted on.

This copy is without a border on the title page. Initial spaces, most with guide-letters, not filled in; without rubrication. 18th-century sheep stained green, spine and edges gilt. Bookplate of Vincenzo Marini.

H 4371*; Pr 7215; BMC 7:1068 (IB.32338); Pell 3225; IGI 2427; Goff C-118; Fava p.115.

26 May 1959—Gift of Mrs. Augustus Paine. Inc 7215

3529 ——Another copy. 300 x 197 mm.

This copy is without a border on the title page. Initial spaces not filled in; without rubrication. 19th-century marbled paste-paper boards.

Countway Library

Cagli

ROBERTUS DE FANO AND BERNARDINUS DE BERGAMO

3530 Campanus, Johannes Antonius: Oratio funebris pro Baptista Sfortia. 1 March 1476.

8°. [25] leaves; 198 x 140 mm.

There are two issues of this edition, in the later of which the first sheet has been reprinted and a leaf containing verses by Laurentius Abstemius added at end; see BMC and GW.

This is the later issue, title agreeing with the main GW transcription; collation: [a–c⁸] ([c8+1). Initials added in red. Bookplate of James Frothingham Hunnewell, with his note "Bound by Mrs. Weir in red mor. with the Wodhull arms (No. 2346 in that library), but brass clasps added. Bought at the sale of the Klemm library, No. 376, Dresden, March, 1889." According to the Wodhull sale catalogue, this was originally bound with Servius Maurus's *Libellus de ultimis syllabis* (same printers, 15 October 1476), which has been removed and blank leaves inserted to fill up the space it occupied.

HCR 4292; R 1482; Pr 7229; BMC 7:1069 (IA.32505); Pell 3183; GW 5942 (described as 4°); IGI 2387; Goff C–77.

January 1919–Deposited by James M. Hunnewell. Inc 7229

Piacenza

JACOBUS DE TYELA

3531 Thomas de Hibernia: Manipulus florum, seu Sententiae Patrum. 5 September 1483.

f°. [182] leaves (1 and 182 blank); 272 x 183 mm.

For a detailed study of the two issues of this work see Curt F. Bühler, "The Two Issues of the First Edition of the *Manipulus Florum*" in his *Early Books and Manuscripts* (New York, 1973): [198]–204. Bühler has wrongly described the Harvard copy as his A rather than his B. Both Bühler and BMC say that this is the only book printed by De Tyela; but see the following entry.

Bühler's issue B. Initial on a1r illuminated in gold and colors, with marginal extension; initials elsewhere and paragraph marks added in red or blue. Old mottled sheep, mutilated, stamped on front cover "Bibliotheca Regia Parmensis"; booklabel of Frank Borton, with his MS date of acquisition "7/16 '94." Blank leaf at front not present.

HC 8542*; Pr 7237; BMC 7:1072 (IB.32891); IGI 9634; Goff H–149; CIBN T–220.

7 September 1928—Bought with the Charles Eliot Norton fund. Inc 7237

3532 **Gentilis de Fulgineo:** Quaestio de prolongatione febris. 1483?

f°. [18] leaves (1 and 18 blank); 402 x 278 mm.

Correct "secundam" to "secundum" in the GW transcription of the colophon. Both GW and IGI question the assignment to De Tyela; but the type is identical with that of the preceding entry.

Initial added in brown on a2r; spaces elsewhere not filled in. Half modern vellum and decorated boards. Bookplate of William Norton Bullard.

R 190 (assigned to Maufer in Padua); GW 10624; IGI 4208; Goff G–137 (Maufer).

Countway Library (William Norton Bullard Collection)

Pojano

FELIX ANTIQUARIUS
AND INNOCENS ZILETUS

3533 **Petrarca, Francesco:** De viris illustribus [Italian]. 1 October 1476.

f°. [240] leaves; 295 x 212 mm.

Italian translation by Donato degli Albanzani. Woodcut borders of two varieties occur throughout the text, one of strapwork disposed on a double frame, the other of branchwork disposed on a triple frame; they are intended to enclose portraits of the persons described in the biographies. There are variant settings of leaf [a]1r; see BMC.

This copy has the setting of BMC IB.32902; there are no portraits inserted in the borders. Initial spaces, with guide-letters, not filled in; without rubrication. Old vellum. Smudged bookstamp on [a]1r; book-label of Adriana R. Salem. Imperfect: quire π^4 wanting.

HC(+Add)R 12808; Pr 7238; BMC 7:1073 (IB.32902); Polain 3062; IGI 7584; Goff P-415; CIBN P-171.

December 1964—Gift of Ward M. Canaday. Inc 7238

Messina

G U I L L E L M U S   S C H O N B E R G E R

3534 **Dictys Cretensis:** Historia Troiana. 7-20 May 1498.

4°. [80] leaves (80 blank); 210 x 148 mm.

Latin translation by Lucius Septimius. Includes Dares Phrygius, *De excidio Troiae historia*, also in Latin translation. Edited by Franciscus Faragonius.

Without rubrication. 18th-century red morocco, spine and edges gilt. Autograph and marginal notes of Franciscus Silvius; autograph of Michael Wodhull on front flyleaf, with his MS date of acquisition "June 7th 1783" (no. 905 in the Sotheby sale catalogue, January 1886); from the library of Richard Ashhurst Bowie.

HC 6157*; Pr 6939; BMC 7:1077 (IA.33447); Pell 4241; GW 8327; IGI 3423; Goff D-186; BSB-Ink D-129.

9 November 1908—Gift of Mrs. E. D. Brandegee. Inc 6939

Colle di Valdelsa

B O N U S   G A L L U S

3535 **Gentilis de Fulgineo:** Consilium contra pestilentiam. ca. 1478/79.

4°. [20] leaves; 203 x 145 mm.

Initial spaces, with guide-letters, not filled in; without rubrication. Modern decorated boards.

R 530; Pr 7243A; BMC 7:1079 (IA.33518); Pell 5021; GW 10620; IGI 4207; Goff G–135.

Countway Library (William Norton Bullard Collection)

Pinerolo

JACOBUS RUBEUS

3536 **Ubaldis, Petrus de:** De duobus fratribus et aliis quibusdam sociis. ca. 1483.

f°. [82] leaves (1 blank); 422 x 287 mm.   Plate XV

I follow Vera Sack in assigning this to Jacobus Rubeus in Pinerolo. BMC catalogues it among the Venetian adespota, with note on the type, "88G., text type, as Jac. Rubeus 88G [P.5], Nic. Rubeus 88G [P.2]." Their description is prefaced by the note, "This book may conceivably have been produced by either Jacobus or Nicolaus Rubeus, but is more likely to be the work of some occasional printer using material discarded by Nicolaus." In the BMC Italian supplementary volume a work by Nicolaus de Tudeschis is catalogued as by Jacobus Rubeus at Pinerolo with the note, "... its appearance, however, is entirely Venetian, and it is possible that Rubeus commissioned it from some unidentified press at Venice." Sack, however, points out that the paper, with watermarks similar to Briquet 11149 and Heitz 176, is found in archives in southern Switzerland and northwest Italy and that no copy of this work is recorded by IGI, whereas copies are recorded in France. Pinerolo itself is in north Italy near the French border. Since Jacobus Rubeus is believed to have been printing in Pinerolo from 1479 to 1485, and since the types agree with those known to have been used by him, there is at least a strong probability that he was the printer of this book.

Initials added in red and/or blue, paragraph marks in red. Contemporary half blind-stamped leather and wooden boards; fragments of pigskin thongs nailed to front cover, brass latches on back, clasps and thongs gone; paper leaf of contemporary Latin legal MS inserted at end. Occasional MS marginalia.

H 15898*; BMC 5:585 (IC.25088); Goff U–50; Sack 3598.

17 April 1951–Received. Law Library

Reggio Emilia

BARTHOLOMAEUS
DE BRUSCHIS

3537 Scriptores rei rusticae. 5 June 1482.

f°. [304] leaves (15, 86–87, 242, and 304 blank); 329 x 230 mm.

This copy has a final quire χ^2, with the last leaf blank. There are two settings of sheets c1–4; see BMC. Edited by "M. B." after Georgius Merula and Franciscus Colucia. Includes the *De re rustica* of Marcus Porcius Cato, Marcus Terentius Varro, Lucius Junius Moderatus Columella, and Rutilius Taurus Palladius.

This copy has the setting of sheets c1–4 described for BMC IB.34008b. Initial spaces, most with guide-letters, not filled in; without rubrication. Old vellum; leather label on spine. Bookplate of the Duke of Sussex (not located in the Evans sale catalogues, 1844–45) and booklabel of George Dunn (no. 1585 in pt. 2 of the Sotheby sale catalogue, February 1914).

HC 14565*; Pr 7251; BMC 7:1086 (IB.34008b); IGI 8854; Goff S–347; Sack 3195; CIBN S–175; Fava p.150.

July 1914—Gift of Sarah C. Sears. Arnold Arboretum Library

ALBERTUS DE MAZALIBUS

3538 Tibullus, Albius: Elegiae. "19 Kl'.octo." 1481.

f°. [106] leaves (106 blank); 288 x 176 mm.

Includes the works of Catullus and Propertius. Printed by De Mazalibus with Prosper Odoardus.

Initial spaces, with guide-letters, not filled in; without rubrication. Old vellum. Unidentified episcopal bookstamp on a1v; autograph of Michael Wodhull on front flyleaf, with his MS date of acquisition "May 2d 1801" (no. 616 in the Sotheby sale catalogue, January 1886); bookplate of Boies Penrose II. Blank leaf not present.

HC(Add) 4757; Pr 7252; BMC 7:1087 (IB.34021); IGI 9661; Goff T–367; CIBN T–275; Fava p.149.

9 October 1945—Gift of Boies Penrose II. Inc 7252

A N D R E A S   P O R T I L I A

3539 **Albericus de Rosate:** Super prima parte Digesti veteris. 12 January 1484.

f°. [500] leaves (1 and 500 blank); 426 x 280 mm.

GW records error "utilie" in line 23 on HH4v; this copy has correct "utilis." Initial spaces, most with guide-letters, not filled in; without rubrication. 16th-century blind-stamped pigskin over wooden boards; one pigskin thong with brass clasp remains nailed to back cover, the other gone, latches on front; paper label on spine. MS ownership notation on a2r, "pro Conuentu frū [rest erased]." Imperfect: leaf a10 wanting, supplied in contemporary MS; only the stubs of the two blank leaves remain.

HR 14009; GW 526; IGI 138; Sack 45; Fava p.150.

20 August 1951—Received. Law Library

F R A N C I S C U S   D E   M A Z A L I B U S

3540 **Appianus:** Historia Romana [Pt. 2]. 22 October 1494.

f°. [136] leaves (136 blank); 289 x 199 mm.

Latin translation by Petrus Candidus Decembrius.

Initial spaces, most with guide-letters, not filled in; without rubrication. 19th-century dark blue morocco, edges gilt. From the library of Richard Ashhurst Bowie. Imperfect: leaf n3 wanting; blank leaf not present.

HC 1309*; Pr 7254; BMC 7:1088 (IB.34033a-b); Pell 916; Polain 4156; GW 2294; IGI 767; Goff A-932; Sack 253; BSB-Ink A-655; Fava p.151.

9 November 1908—Gift of Mrs. E. D. Brandegee. Inc 7254

3541 **Dionysius Halicarnassensis:** Antiquitates Romanae. 12 November 1498.

f°. [1], ii–ccxxvi leaves ([1] blank; xix, lviii, lxxiii–lxxv, clxx, clxxxv–

lxxxviii, and clxxxx–lxxxxii misnumbered xviii, vliii, lxxviii–lxxx, clxviii, clxxxiiii–lxxxvii, and clxxxix–lxxxxi); 284 x 185 mm.

Latin translation by Lampugninus Biragus. There are variant settings of sheet b1; cf. BMC and GW.

This copy has the setting of sheet b1 described in the GW *Anmerkung*. Initial spaces, a few with guide-letters, not filled in; without rubrication. Old vellum; edges marbled. Bookplate of Count Dmitri Boutourlin (no. 596 in the "Éditions du XV siècle" section of his 1831 catalogue); autograph in upper margin of a2r, "A. J. Odell"; from the library of Richard Ashhurst Bowie. Blank leaf not present.

HC(Add) 6240*; Pr 7256; BMC 7:1089 (IB.34040); Pell 4301; Polain 1313; GW 8424; IGI 3485; Goff D–251; BSB-Ink D–175; Fava p.152.

9 November 1908–Gift of Mrs. E. D. Brandegee. Inc 7256

3542 ——Another copy. 290 x 195 mm.

Two leaves (m5 and z7) only, removed from a binding and silked; bound in half 19th-century gray cloth and marbled boards, with MS note inside front cover, "Taken from the covers of Guevara–'Epistolas Familiares, 1673.'"

7 May 1866–Gift of J. O. Halliwell. Inc 7256.5

3543 **Scriptores rei rusticae.** 20 November 1499.

f°. [244] leaves (10 blank); 295 x 198 mm.

Edited after Georgius Merula and Franciscus Colucia by Philippus Beroaldus. Includes: Marcus Porcius Cato, *De re rustica.*—Marcus Terentius Varro, *De re rustica.*—Lucius Junius Moderatus Columella, *De re rustica* (with commentary of Pomponius Laetus).—Rutilius Taurus Palladius, *De re rustica* (with commentary of Antonius Urceus Codrus).—Poem by Bartholomaeus Ugerius. There is a variant on the title page; see below.

In this copy the last two lines of the title read "pi Bero aldi." Woodcut initials; one space, with guide-letter, on D1r not filled in; without rubrication. Half 19th-century vellum and marbled boards. Bookplate of Daniel B. Fearing. A few leaves at the end remargined; blank leaf not present.

HC(+Add) 14570*; Pr 7257; BMC 7:1089 (IB.34043); Polain 3480; IGI 8857; Goff S–350; CIBN S–178; Fava p.153.

30 June 1915—Gift of Daniel B. Fearing. Inc 7257

3544 ——Another copy. 293 x 200 mm.

In this copy the last two lines of the title red "pi Beroal‖di." Initial space not filled in; without rubrication. Old calf, spine gilt, edges speckled red. MS ownership notation on title page, "Res Pauli & Francisci Volaterranj et Amico[rum]"; another illegible one beneath it; armorial bookplate with motto "Anchor fast anchor" (Scottish family of Gray?).

15 August 1924—Gift of Sarah C. Sears. Arnold Arboretum Library

3545 ——Another copy. 300 x 205 mm.

In this copy the last two lines of the title read "pi Beroal‖di." Initial space not filled in; without rubrication. Old tree calf, rebacked; spine gilt. Blank leaf not present.

Countway Library (William Norton Bullard Collection)

D I O N Y S I U S   B E R T O C H U S

3546 Scriptores rei rusticae. 18 September 1496.

f°. [272] leaves; 305 x 202 mm.

Edited after Georgius Merula and Franciscus Colucia by Philippus Beroaldus. Includes the *De re rustica* of Marcus Porcius Cato, Marcus Terentius Varro, Lucius Junius Moderatus Columella (with commentary of Pomponius Laetus), and Rutilius Taurus Palladius (with commentary of Antonius Urceus Codrus). Also includes a poem by Bartholomaeus Ugerius.

Woodcut initials, also spaces, some with guide-letters, not filled in; without rubrication. Half 16th-century blind-stamped leather and wooden boards; marks of clasp plates and latches, clasps and thongs gone. MS ownership inscription inside front cover, "Sum Georgij Ludouici Gschwindij"; from the library of Richard Ashhurst Bowie, with a slip of his MS notes inserted at front.

HC 14569; Pr 7259; BMC 7:1090 (IB.34061a) and 12:77 (IB.34061); Polain 3479; IGI 8856; Goff S–349; Sack 3₁96; CIBN S–177; Fava p.152.

9 November 1908–Gift of Mrs. E. D. Brandegee. Inc 7259 (A)

3547 ——Another copy. 295 x 198 mm.

Initial spaces not filled in; without rubrication. Half modern brown morocco and marbled boards.

7 May 1913–Gift of Alain Campbell White. Inc 7259 (B)

3548 ——Another copy. 302 x 200 mm.

Initial spaces not filled in; without rubrication. 19th-century marbled boards; edges stained blue; leather label on spine.

January 1914–Gift of Sarah C. Sears. Arnold Arboretum Library

3549 **Aesopus:** Fabulae selectae [Greek and Latin]. 1497.

4°. [38] leaves; 215 x 150 mm.

Contains only the additional fables, as in the Milan edition of ca. 1480. Greek text with the Latin translation of Rinucius Aretinus in parallel columns. Edited by Bonus Accursius.

Initial spaces, with guide-letters, not filled in; without rubrication. Half modern brown morocco and marbled boards. From the library of Richard Ashhurst Bowie, with a slip of his MS notes inserted at front.

HR 266; Pr 7260; BMC 7:1091 (IA.34063); Pell 186; GW 314; IGI 62; Goff A–104; Fava p.152.

9 November 1908–Gift of Mrs. E. D. Brandegee. Inc 7260

3550 **Crastonus, Johannes:** Lexicon Latino-Graecum. 1497.

4°. [116] leaves (1 and 116 blank); 200 x 150 mm.

There are two settings of quire A; see BMC and GW. Printed by Bertochus with Marcus Antonius de Bazaleriis. With a dedicatory letter by Bonus Accursius.

In this copy the setting of quire A agrees with BMC IA.34069. Initial spaces, most with guide-letters, not filled in; without rubrication. Half old sheep and paste-paper boards, hinges broken; in a marbled cardboard box. Bookstamp of Robert F. Farington. MS marginalia in the first quire.

HC 5817; Pr 7261; BMC 7:1091 (IA.34069); Pell 38=4041A; GW 7818; IGI 3254; Goff C–964; BSB-Ink C–694; Fava p.152.

Countway Library (William Norton Bullard Collection)

B A Z A L E R I U S   D E   B A Z A L E R I I S

3551 Cicero: Scripta philosophica. 1498–10 April 1499.

f°. 4 pts. in 1 vol. (pt. 1: [32] leaves; pt. 2: [22] leaves; pt. 3: [18] leaves; pt. 4: [16] leaves); 298 x 195 mm.

Part 5 of this collection, containing the *De finibus bonorum et malorum* and other smaller works and continuing the signatures of the first four parts, was printed at Bologna by Caligula de Bazaleriis; see no. 3225. Includes: pt. 1, *De natura deorum.*–pt. 2, *De divinatione.*–pt. 3, *De fato. De legibus.*–pt. 4, *Academica priora.* Pomponius Laetus, *De re militari.*

Initial spaces, with guide-letters, and spaces for Greek not filled in; without rubrication. Half 19th-century calf and red boards, gilt. From the library of Richard Ashhurst Bowie. With this is bound pt. 5 (Bologna, Caligula de Bazaleriis, 20 June 1499).

H 5331(5); HR 5333*(1); H 5336(1–4); H 5338*(2); H 5339(2–3); H 5344*(3–5); Pr 7258A(1–5) and 6619A(5); BMC 7:1092 (IB.34058[1–4]) and 6:837 (IB.28998[5]); GW 6903; IGI 2883; Goff C–573; BSB-Ink C–378; Fava p.153.

9 November 1908—Gift of Mrs. E. D. Brandegee. Inc 7258A

U G O   R U G E R I U S

3552 Crottus, Bartholomaeus: Epigrammata et elegiae. 1 October 1500.

4°. [44] leaves (44 blank); 204 x 137 mm.

Includes Matteo Maria Boiardo, *Carmina bucolica.*

Initial spaces, one with guide-letter, not filled in; without rubrication. 19th–century brown morocco, gilt, edges gilt, by Clarke & Bedford. Leather booklabel of Robert Samuel Turner (no. 1204 in the Sotheby sale catalogue, June 1888).

HCR 5842=H 5841; Pr 7264; BMC 7:1093 (IA.34075); Pell 4044; GW 7842; IGI 3274; Goff C-979; BSB-Ink C-703; Fava p.154.

10 January 1952–Gift of Carleton R. Richmond. Inc 7264

Cividale

GERARDUS DE LISA

3553 Platina, Bartholomaeus: De honesta voluptate et valetudine. 24 October 1480.

4°. [94] leaves (94 blank); 197 x 128 mm.

Initials and paragraph marks added in red or green; traces of MS quiring. 18th-century calf, with the arms of Michael Wodhull stamped in gilt on front cover, with his MS date of acquisition "Apr. 16th 1789," and note "Pinelli Auction" (no. 6773 in the Pinelli sale catalogue, March–April 1789; no. 2007 in the Sotheby sale catalogue of books from Wodhull's library, January 1886); bookplate of James Frothingham Hunnewell.

HC(Add) 13052*; Pr 7266; BMC 7:1094 (IA.34201); Polain 3183; IGI 7850; Goff P-763; CIBN P-439.

January 1919–Deposited by James M. Hunnewell. Inc 7266

Pisa

LAURENTIUS [DE CENNIS?]
AND ANGELO DI FIRENZE

3554 Ficinus, Marsilius: De Christiana religione [Italian]. 2 June 1484.

f°. [114] leaves; 270 x 197 mm.

BMC transcribes "fidatissimo" in line 1 on p6v; this copy has "fidatisimo." Initial spaces, with guide-letters, not filled in; without rubrication. Half 19th-century black morocco and black cloth, edges gilt, by Zaehnsdorf. MS ownership notation in lower margin of a1r, "Collegij Solebani"; booklabel of E. P. Jacobsen. In this copy the table (π^2) is bound at end; lower margin of π1 repaired.

HR 7074; C 2500; Pr 7276; BMC 7:1095 (IA.34413); Pell 4788; GW 9879; IGI 3860; Goff F–151; Sack 1445.

23 December 1957—Gift of I. Austin Kelly III. Inc 7276

GREGORIUS DE GENTE

3555 Savonarola, Michael: De aqua ardenti. 22 September 1484.

4°. [28] leaves; 206 x 145 mm.

Initial spaces, with guide-letters, not filled in; without rubrication. 19th-century decorated boards. Bookstamp of Giuseppe Martini (not in his 1934 incunabula catalogue or in the Hoepli auction catalogues, 1934–35).

CR 5310; BMC 7:1096 (IA.34421); IGI 8804; Goff S–289.

Countway Library (William Norton Bullard Collection)

Siena

HENRICUS DE COLONIA

3556 Jacobus de Forlivio: Super capitulum Avicennae de generatione embryonis. 7 March 1485/6.

f°. [16] leaves; 404 x 274 mm.

Edited by Bernardinus Bitontus.

This copy varies from Accurti's transcription in having "tertiũ" rather than "tertiu3" in line 48 on c6v and in having colophon date "M.CCCCLXXXV." rather than "MCCCCLXXXV." Initial spaces, with guide-letters, not filled in; without rubrication. Half modern vellum and decorated boards. Bookplate of William Norton Bullard.

H 7235; Klebs 550.2; Accurti (1930) 83; IGI 4989; Goff J–43; Rhodes (S) 7.

Countway Library (William Norton Bullard Collection)

3557 Caccialupis, Johannes Baptista de: De debitoribus suspectis et fugitivis. 9 May 1486.

f°. [36] leaves (1 blank); 398 x 278 mm.

Includes his *De pactis* and *De transactionibus*. There are variants on [a]2r; see GW.

This copy has the readings of the main GW transcription on [a]2r. Initial spaces not filled in; without rubrication. Modern vellum.

H 4188*; BMC 12:78 (IC.34623); Pell 3129; Polain 4262; GW 5836; IGI 2295; Goff C-2; BSB-Ink C-14; Rhodes (S) 8.

16 May 1946—Received. Law Library

3558 Giocchis, Fabianus de: De emptione et venditione et de omnibus contractibus in genere. 1 April 1489.

f°. [40] leaves (1 and 40 blank); 400 x 280 mm.

Initial space on a2r not filled in; without rubrication. Modern vellum by K. Ebert, Munich.

H 11601; GW 10927; IGI 4301; Goff M-853; Rhodes (S) 26.

17 May 1946—Received. Law Library

3559 Socinus, Marianus: Repetitio paragraphi Quod si super positi de nominatione in iudicio. 1491.

f°. [10] leaves; 400 x 280 mm.

For collation and transcriptions see IGI. Edited by Benedetto Ciccolini. Printed by Henricus de Colonia with Henricus de Harlem.

Initial space on a1r not filled in; without rubrication. Modern vellum by K. Ebert, Munich.

H 14864; BMC 7:lxxxii (note); IGI 9077; Goff S-608; Rhodes (S) 33.

16 May 1946—Received. Law Library

HENRICUS DE HARLEM

3560 Socinus, Marianus: Repetitio super titulo De litis contestatione. 20 August 1492.

[For transcriptions see Hain.] f°. A-B⁶, C⁴, D-E⁶, F-G⁴, H², χ²; [40] leaves; 400 x 282 mm. 2 columns. A1r: 60 lines, 273 x 184 mm. Type: 1:91G.

Hain locates the *tabula* (χ^2) at front; it is found at the end in this copy and is not called for in the register.

Without rubrication. No. 9 in the volume described under no. 3576.

HC(Add) 14865*; IGI 9078; Goff S-609; Rhodes (S) 40.

22 May 1936—Received. Law Library

3561 Bulgarinis, Bulgarinus de: Disputatio de testamentis una cum Consilio. 4 April 1493.

f°. [12] leaves; 400 x 282 mm.

Initial spaces, one with guide-letter, not filled in; without rubrication. No. 6 in the volume described under no. 3576.

HC 4072*; Pr 7286; BMC 7:1101 (IC.34646); GW 5720; IGI 2222; Goff B-1277; Sack 862; BSB-Ink B-973; Rhodes (S) 44.

22 May 1936—Received. Law Library

3562 Caccialupis, Johannes Baptista de: Repetitio legum Imperium, Iubere cavere, More maiorum, Et quia. 11 May 1493.

f°. [16] leaves (16 blank); 400 x 282 mm.

Without rubrication. No. 13 in the volume described under no. 3576. Quires d of this and of no. 12 in the volume have changed places.

H 4194*; BMC 12:78 (IC.34647); GW 5845; IGI 2316; Goff C-9; Sack 888; BSB-Ink C-12; Rhodes (S) 45.

22 May 1936—Received. Law Library

3563 Cepolla, Bartholomaeus: De simulatione contractuum. 18 May 1493.

f°. [18] leaves; 400 x 282 mm.

Initial spaces not filled in; without rubrication. No. 2 in the volume described under no. 3576.

HC 4873*; Pr 7287; BMC 7:1101 (IC.34648); Pell 3490; Polain 1058; GW 6511; IGI 2705; Goff C-399; BSB-Ink C-239; Rhodes (S) 46.

22 May 1936—Received. Law Library

3564 Tyndarus de Perusio: Tractatus in materia compensationum. 26 June 1493.

[For transcriptions see Hain.] f°. a–b⁴, c²; [10] leaves; 400 x 282 mm. 2 columns. a1r: 62 lines and headline, 281 x 176 mm. Type: 1:91G. Initial space on a1r.

Initial space not filled in; without rubrication. No. 4 in the volume described under no. 3576.

H 15757*; IGI 9902; Goff T–568; Sack 3485; Rhodes (S) 47.

22 May 1936—Received. Law Library

3565 Periglis, Angelus de: Tractatus in materia societatum. 4 July 1493.

[For transcriptions see Hain; but change his "taȝ in iu‖re" to "taȝ de iu‖re" and "M CCCC.lxx‖xxiij." to "M.cccc.lxx‖xxiij."] f°. A⁴ (A4 blank); [4] leaves (4 blank); 400 x 282 mm. 2 columns. A1r: 62 lines, 281 x 176 mm. Initial space on A1r.

Initial space not filled in; without rubrication. No. 5 in the volume described under no. 3576.

H 12632*; IGI 7416; Goff P–286; Sack 2718; Rhodes (S) 48.

22 May 1936—Received. Law Library

3566 Castello, Amadeus Justinus de: De syndicatu officialium. 10 August 1493.

f°. [28] leaves; 400 x 282 mm.

Without rubrication. No. 3 in the volume described under no. 3576.

H 4587; R 866; BMC 12:79 (IC.34650); GW 6172; IGI 2557; Goff C–250; BSB-Ink C–177; Rhodes (S) 49.

22 May 1936—Received. Law Library

3567 Mattaselanus, Petrus: Repetitio legis Filium quem habentem. 1 October 1493.

f°. [16] leaves; 400 x 282 mm.

For transcriptions and collation see IGI. Edited by Sigismundus de Castellione.

Initial space on A1r not filled in; without rubrication. No. 7 in the volume described under no. 3576.

H 10917; IGI 6292; Goff M–365; Rhodes (S) 50.

22 May 1936—Received. Law Library

3568 **Bartolinis, Baldus de:** Repetitio rubricae De verborum obligationibus et paragraphi Si quis ita. 25 October 1493.

f°. [12] leaves; 392 x 273 mm.

Initial spaces not filled in; without rubrication. Modern vellum by K. Ebert, Munich. MS marginalia.

HC 2470*; Pr 7288; BMC 7:1102 (IC.34652); GW 3471; IGI 1276; Goff B-180; Rhodes (S) 51.

13 October 1931—Received. Law Library

3569 ——Another copy. 400 x 282 mm.

Without rubrication. No. 17 in the volume described under no. 3576.

22 May 1936—Received. Law Library

3570 **Caccialupis, Johannes Baptista de:** Repetitio legis Diem functo. 1493.

f°. [10] leaves; 400 x 282 mm.

Initial space on A1r, with guide-letter, not filled in; without rubrication. No. 11 in the volume described under no. 3576.

HR 4200; GW 5844; IGI 2306; Goff C-8; Rhodes (S) 43.

22 May 1936—Received. Law Library

3571 **Ubaldis, Petrus de:** Repetitio capituli Si diligenti. 8 January 1493/4.

f°. [8] leaves; 400 x 282 mm.

Includes a prefatory note by Leander Fabrinus. For transcriptions and collation see IGI.

Without rubrication. No. 8 in the volume described under no. 3576.

H 15903 (misdated 1483); IGI 10014; Goff U-52; Rhodes (S) 52.

22 May 1936—Received. Law Library

3572 **Periglis, Angelus de:** Repetitio legis In suis ff. De liberis et posthumis. 28 May 1494.

[For transcriptions see Hain; but correct his location of the colophon to "col. 1," not "col. 2."] f°. A-E⁴; [20] leaves; 400 x 282 mm. 2 columns. A1r: 62 lines and headline, 280 x 175 mm. Type: 1:91G. Initial spaces on A1r.

Initial spaces not filled in; without rubrication. No. 16 in the volume described under no. 3576.

H 12633*; IGI 7415; Goff P-285; Rhodes (S) 54.

22 May 1936—Received. Law Library

3573 Caccialupis, Johannes Baptista de: Tractatus de ludo. 10 October 1494.

f°. [8] leaves; 400 x 282 mm.

On the two issues of this work, one with 16 and the other with 8 leaves, see GW.

Without rubrication. No. 14 in the volume described under no. 3576.

H 4204; GW 5840; Goff C-5; BSB-Ink C-18.

22 May 1936—Received. Law Library

3574 Pepis, Franciscus de: Repetitio capituli Unde vir et uxor. 8 January 1494/5.

[For transcriptions see Hain.] f°. A-E⁴; [20] leaves; 400 x 282 mm. 2 columns. A1r: 62 lines and headline, 280 x 175 mm. Initial space on A1r.

Includes verses by Tullius Petrica. Hain counts only 19 leaves.

Initial space not filled in; without rubrication. No. 10 in the volume described under no. 3576.

H 12577*; IGI 7401; Goff P-261; Rhodes (S) 58.

22 May 1936—Received. Law Library

3575 Pontanus, Ludovicus: Super legem Si vero, paragraphi De viro. 18 March 1494/5.

f°. [16] leaves; 400 x 282 mm.

Without rubrication. No. 12 in the volume described under no. 3576. Quires d of this and of no. 13 in the volume have changed places.

HR 13284; BMC 7:1102 (IC.34654); IGI 8003; Goff P-923; Rhodes (S) 59.

22 May 1936–Received. Law Library

3576 **Brunus, Franciscus:** De indiciis et tortura. June 1495.

f°. [18] leaves; 400 x 282 mm.

Initial spaces, with guide-letters, not filled in; without rubrication. Half 16th-century blind-stamped pigskin and wooden boards (back board replaced); brass latches on front cover, clasps and thongs gone. No. 1 in a volume of 18 legal works printed by Henricus de Harlem from the Fürstlich Dietrichstein'sche Bibliothek, described in Rudolf Pindter's 1905-06 catalogue as no. 307 on p. 15, 24, 25, 28, 61, 70, 71, 75, 81, 84, and 89.

HR 4022; GW 5598; IGI 2183; Goff B-1229; BSB-Ink B-934; Rhodes (S) 63.

22 May 1936–Received. Law Library

3577 **Socinus, Marianus:** Repetitio fraternitatis de testibus. 6 August 1495.

[For transcriptions see Hain; but correct his error "inris" in line 2 of the caption on a1r to "iuris."] f°. a–c⁴, d²; [14] leaves; 400 x 282 mm. 2 columns. a1r: 62 lines, 282 x 180 mm. Type: 1:91G. Initial space on a1r, with guide-letter.

Initial space not filled in; without rubrication. No. 18 in the volume described under no. 3576. Imperfect: the last 3 lines of the colophon on d2r have failed to print.

H 14862*; Goff S-606; Rhodes (S) 64.

22 May 1936–Received. Law Library

3578 **Saliceto, Bartholomaeus de:** Repetitio legis Semel mora. 22 January 1495/6.

f°. [6] leaves; 400 x 282 mm.

For transcriptions and collation see IGI. Initial space on A1r not filled in; without rubrication. No. 15 in the volume described under no. 3576.

H 14141; IGI 8509; Goff S-24; Sack 3126; Rhodes (S) 65.

22 May 1936–Received. Law Library

SIGISMUNDUS RODT

3579 Florus, Lucius Annaeus: Epitome de Tito Livio. 1486/87.

4°. [56] leaves; 198 x 140 mm.

Edited by Philippus Beroaldus. Printed by Rodt for Henricus de Colonia.

Initial spaces, with guide-letters, not filled in; paragraph marks and capital strokes added in red, but the color has been largely washed away. Modern brown morocco by Sangorski & Sutcliffe. Bookplate of Boies Penrose II.

H 7201*; Pr 7290; BMC 7:1102 (IA.34666); Pell 4855; GW 10098; IGI 4011; Goff F–236; BSB-Ink F–169; Rhodes (S) 11.

9 October 1945–Gift of Boies Penrose II. Inc 7290

**3580 **——Another copy. 198 x 135 mm.

Initial spaces not filled in; without rubrication. For binding description see no. 3347, Caius Julius Solinus, *Polyhistor, siue De mirabilibus mundi* (Parma, Andreas Portilia, 20 December 1480), with which this is bound, along with Cornelius Nepos, *Vitae imperatorum* (Milan, Pachel and Scinzenzeler, 1480?).

January 1919–Deposited by James M. Hunnewell. Inc 6850 (B)

Pescia

PRINTER OF CANARO, *DE MATERIA EXCUSATORIS* (H 4 3 0 6)

3581 Decius, Philippus: Repetitio super rubrica De probationibus. 7 August 1490.

f°. [22] leaves (1 blank); 400 x 280 mm.

Includes a table by Bonifacius de Panicis. Printed for Bastianus and Raphael de Orlandis.

Initial spaces, with guide-letters, not filled in; without rubrication.

Modern vellum by K. Ebert, Munich. Blank leaf represented by a stub only.

H 6065*; GW 8221; IGI 3399; Goff D-121; BSB-Ink D-93.

16 May 1946—Received. Law Library

UNASSIGNED

3582 Savonarola, Hieronymus: De omnium scientiarum divisione. ca. 1492.

4°. [16] leaves; 208 x 138 mm.

Initial spaces not filled in; without rubrication. Modern red cloth.

HR 14475; Pr 7322; BMC 7:1110 (IA.35044); IGI 8676; Goff S-228.

21 May 1921—Bought with the Duplicate fund. Inc 7322

3583 ——Another copy. 203 x 130 mm.

Initial spaces not filled in; without rubrication. For binding description see no. 3004, his *Compendio di rivelazioni* (Florence, Lorenzo Morgiani and Johannes Petri, 1 September 1495), with which this is bound.

17 May 1921—From the Savonarola collection formed by Henry R. Newman. Gift of J. P. Morgan. Typ Inc 6358

Chivasso

JACOBINUS SUIGUS

3584 Angelus de Clavasio: Summa angelica de casibus conscientiae. 13 May 1486.

4°. [388] leaves (1, 377-78 blank); 202 x 144 mm.

With additions by Hieronymus Tornieli and a poem by Jacobinus Suigus.

Initials and paragraph marks added in red or blue. 16th-century blind-stamped leather over wooden boards, rebacked; fragments of leather thongs nailed to front cover, marks of latches on back, clasps

and thongs gone. Bound in at front are 16 leaves (a-b⁸) of corrections and additions keyed to this edition but adaptable to others as
well and obviously printed after several others had appeared. The
type is the 2:63G used by Uldericus Scinzenzeler at Milan, though no
edition of the *Summa angelica* is recorded by that printer; see no.
3124A for a full description. "Bibliothecae Portivncvlae" bookstamp;
MS ownership notation "Iste liber est ad vsũ frīs Bona[ventu]rae de
Palatio [?]"; bookplate of James Frothingham Hunnewell, with his
note "Bought in Berlin." Blank leaves z7-8 not present.

HC 5382; Pr 7323; BMC 7:1111 (IA.35202); Pell 3812; Polain 205;
GW 1923; IGI 559; Goff A-713.

January 1919–Deposited by James M. Hunnewell. Inc 7323

Scandiano

P E R E G R I N U S
D E   P A S Q U A L I B U S

3585 Appianus: Historia Romana [Pt. 1]. 10 January 1495.

f°. [80] leaves (80 blank); 288 x 198 mm.

Latin translation by Petrus Candidus Decembrius. There are variants
in the headlines of sheets C1 and D1; and there are two settings of
sheets D3 and E1; see BMC.

In this copy the headlines on C1r, C6v, D1r, and D6v read respectively LIBYCVS, LIBER, LIBYCVS, and LIEBR [sic]; sheets D3 and E1
are printed with the same 110R type as the rest of the book; the last
marginal note on E1r reads as in BMC IB.36201a. Initial spaces, some
with guide-letters, not filled in; without rubrication. 19th-century red
morocco, edges gilt. From the library of Richard Ashhurst Bowie.
Blank leaf bound at front.

HC(+Add) 1310; Pr 7325; BMC 7:1118 (IB.36201a); Pell 917; Polain
4155; GW 2292; IGI 765; Goff A-930; Fava p.169.

9 November 1908–Gift of Mrs. E. D. Brandegee. Inc 7325 (A)

3586 ——Another copy. 300 x 204 mm.

In this copy the headlines on C1r, C6v, D1r, and D6v read respectively LIBER, LIBYCVS, LIEBR [sic], and LIBYCVS; sheets D3 and E1 as described above. Initial spaces not filled in; without rubrication. Half modern red morocco and marbled boards. Imperfect: leaf N7 slightly mutilated; many leaves badly stained; blank leaf not present.

2 April 1900—Gift of James Read Chadwick. Inc 7325 (B)

Forlì

PAULUS GUARINUS AND JOHANNES JACOBUS DE BENEDICTIS

3587 Manilio, Antonio: Prognosticum dialogale usque ad annum 1500 et ultra. 26 July 1495.

a1r: SVMMI PON. IMPERATORIE MAESTATIS: CHRISTIANIS-SI ‖ mi Franchorum Regis: Ferdinandi Hispaniarum: Et Alfonsi Sicilię Se-‖renissimoꝫ Regum … ‖ … Vrbiũ locoꝫ & Principũ: Status. Casus: Ruinę ꝑ ‖ sperorũ aduersorũqꝫ successuũ: Ex astroꝫ spi ‖ rituũque p̄scientia: Vsque ad ãnum. M. ‖ cccc. & ultra. Excellentissimi & fa ‖ mosissimi Astrologi Antonii ‖ Manilii Dialogale ‖ pronosticon. ‖ d4r, COLOPHON: Impressum Forliuii hoc Excellentissimum & Verissimum Prognosticon ꝑ ‖ Paulum Guarinum Forliuiensem & Ioãnem Iacobum de Bene-‖dictis Bononiensem Anno Salutifere Incarnationis ‖ M.CCCC.LXXXXV. Die .XXVI ‖ Iulii. Ascendeñ. XII. ‖ Grad. Virginis ‖ Laus ‖ De ‖ o ‖ : ‖ SIC MEA VITALI PATRIA EST MIHI CARIOR AVRA. ‖ REGISTRVM … LAVS DEO. ‖ d4v, device.

4°. a–d⁴; [16] leaves; 218 x 138 mm. a2r: 44 lines, 172 x 117 mm. Type: 2:79R. Initial spaces. Plate XVI

Initial spaces not filled in; without rubrication. Modern blind-stamped brown morocco by Rivière; in a half morocco solander case.

BMC 7:1120 (note only); IGI 6121; Klebs 660.2; Goff M–199.

31 January 1955—Gift of Harrison D. Horblit. Inc 7327.5

Italy

NOT ASSIGNABLE
TO ANY TOWN

3588 Platea, Franciscus de: Opus restitutionum, usurarum, excommunicationum. Not after 1472.

f°. [136] leaves (135–36 blank); 313 x 215 mm.

Initials, paragraph marks, and capital strokes added in red or blue; rubricated heading at beginning of text on [a]1r; MS quiring. Half 18th-century sheep and tan boards. MS ownership notation at end, "Iste liber est canonicoʒ Regulariuʒ lateranẽsiuʒ sctī Augustinj cõmorantiuʒ in monast° sctoʒ quadraginta extra taruisium"; bookstamps of T. B. Reed and of the St. Bride Foundation, Passmore Edwards Library. Blank leaves represented by stubs only.

H 13034*; Pr 7394; BMC 7:1124 (IA.36851); IGI 7839; Goff P–751; Sack 2899; CIBN P–430 ("Padova?, imprimeur de Platea, *Opus restitutionum*").

16 March 1953–Received. Law Library

Indices

Author/Title Index

Index of Editors and Translators
and of Secondary Works,
Identified and Anonymous

Printers and Places

Provenance Index

A. G., 3093

A. S., 2878

ABBEY, JOHN ROLAND, 3095

ADAMUS, FRANCISCUS RAIMUNDUS, 2976, 3498

ALBANI LIBRARY, 3352

ALDRINGEN, PAULUS AB, 3133

ALESSIO, FILIPPO, 2873

ALIPRANDUS, JOHANNES ANGELUS, 3385

ALTEMPS, GIOVANNI ANGELO AND GAU-DENZIO, 3342

AMBROSINI, RAIMONDO, 3216, 3242

AMERICAN ANTIQUARIAN SOCIETY, 3498

ANCONA. BIBLIOTECA MUNICIPALE, 3324

ANDOVER-HARVARD THEOLOGICAL LI-BRARY, 3233

ANGUISSOLA (?), CAROLUS, 2874

ANTALDI, ANTALDO, 3176

ARNOLD ARBORETUM LIBRARY, 2811, 3384, 3488, 3537, 3544, 3548

ARNSBURG. CISTERCIANS, 3046

ARUNDEL, THOMAS HOWARD, 2D EARL OF, 3361

ASCOLO, ——, DUCA D' (?), 3267

ASHBURNER, WALTER, 2790, 2911, 3426

ASSISI. FRANCISCANS (BIBLIOTHECA POR-

TIUNCULAE), 3124A, 3584

ASTENSIS (?), JOHANNES MARIA, 3084

AUERSPERG, FRANZ KARL, PRINCE, 3085

AUGSBURG. FRANCISCANS (?), 3062

AUGUSTINIAN HERMITS (UNIDENTIFIED MONASTERY), 2980

AVARICUM see BOURGES

B., F. O. see BEGGI, FRANCESCO ORAZIO

B., I., 3171

B., N., 3328

BADEN (?) ORATORY (?), 3065

BAGLIONE, GALIOTTO, 2762

BALBUS, P., 3518

BALMA, BENEDICTUS DE, 3516

BALTUS, BERNARDUS, 3414

BALUZE, ÉTIENNE, 2774, 3209

BANDINI, ANGELO MARIA, 2850

BARBARINUS (?), JOHANNES ANTONIUS, 3200

BARBARO, FRANCESCO, 3346

BAROTTI, GIOVANNI ANDREA, 2923

BAUMBURG. AUGUSTINIAN CANONS, 3319

BAUMGARTENBERG. CISTERCIANS, 3271

BECKFORD, WILLIAM, 3072

Index of Incunabula Containing Manuscripts

Index of Incunabula
with Identified Bindings

Concordances

1. Hain/HUL

H	HUL	H	HUL	H	HUL
3	3467	418	(3035d)	1229	3170
7	3333–34	419	2855–58	1276	2845
10	3076	426	3204	1277	2993
12	2828	464	3115–16	1287	3142
16	3336–37	505	3428	1292	2964–65
18	2807	546	3339	1309	3540
41	3471	572	3280	1310	3585–86
55	3155	575	3440	1316	3508–09
57	3104	588	2777	1319	3249
70	3228	644	3455	1440	2806
72	3238	656	3431–32	1458	3335A
100	2821	822	2770–72	1540	3095
103	2822	893	3083	1543	3081
104	3000	899	3070	1558	2762
114	2831	908	3113	1563(1)	2905–06
157	3135–36	911	3113	1563(2)	2907–08
168	3049	938	3188	1574	2820
170	3066	989	2779	1623	3331
176–77	3296	990	2791	1653	3195
218	3482	1059	3460	1683	2790
266	3549	1108	3456	1709	2789
277	3048	1145	2962	1719	2830
345	3372	1211	3010	1729	3335
353	3283	1214	2998	1742	3178

H	HUL	H	HUL	H	HUL
1744?	3178	2758	3027-28	3675	3213
1805	3333-34	2778	2868	3677	3213
1806	3076	2784	2985	3678	3214
1863	3298	2785	3019	3763	3100
1878	2829	2788	3031	3987	3393
1930	3181	2806	3401	3999	3131-32
1952	3364	2813	2781-84	4009	3295
1994	3521	2850	3149	4022	3576
2001	3408	2860	3423	4027	3515
2018	2995	2873	3150-51	4072	3561
2031	3082	2898	3009	4096	3177
2053	3272	2919	3134	4138	3461
2132	3101	2934	3218	4188	3557
2133	3041	2945	2877-78	4194	3562
2152	3330	2946	3436	4196	3255
2181	3368	2949	3205-06	4200	3570
2189	2778	2953	3418	4204	3573
2219	3449-50	2955	3250	4216	3046
2245	2827	2957	3418	4217	3306
2284	3169	2963	3236	4232	3276
2289	3169	2966	3245-46	4234	2996
2327	3463	2967	3251	4266	2967
2330	3404	2968	3221	4292	3530
2364	3196	2969	3211-12	4299	3498
2371	3197	2971	3242	4321	2802
2386	3198	2974	3240-41	4370	3511
2394	3201	3200	3525	4371	3528-29
2401	3343	3243	3375	4397-98	3371
2429-30	3184	3245	3394	4505	3133
2437	3452	3247	3375	4536	3277A
2438	3175	3291	2792	4587	3566
2461	3390	3297	3086	4693	3435
2467	3290	3308	2776	4757	3538
2469	3465	3312	3203	4759	3040
2470	3568-69	3439	3180	4760	3500-01
2481	3075	3467	3433	4771	2844
2484	3087	3481	3433	4774	2992
2530	3144	3537	3427	4779	2999
2532	3281	3539	3309	4820-21	2968
2537	3256-57	3574	3058	4822-23	2862
2569(2)	3286	3602	3092	4835	2846-48
2623	3091	3667	3071-72	4847	3234-35
2665-66	3451	3669	3208-09	4850	3457
2712	3202	3671	3344	4866	3457
2752	2970	3672	2975-76	4872	3096

H	HUL	H	HUL	H	HUL
4873	3563	6095	2826	7406	3157
4874	3464	6139	3158-59	7407	3161
4882	3017	6157	3534	7408	3417
4888-89	2817	6184	3386	7434	3156
4899-4900	2894	6188	3171	7521	3398
4956	2859	6194	2989	7561	3445
5129	3243	6201	3406	7568	3444
5138	3507	6209	2987	7569	2824
5179	3043	6239	3316-18	7571	2805
5331	3225, 3551	6240	3541-42	7574	3447
5333	3551	6321	3429	7583	3130
5335	3231-32	6480	3494	7590	3448
5336	3551	6481	3304	7803(1)	2768
5338	3551	6482	3496	7804	2768
5339	3551	6585	3266	7838	3458
5344	3225, 3551	6599	2863	8098	3446
5361	3018	6702	3305	8128	2763
5370	3512	6711	3341-42	8129-30	2766
5382	3584	6716	3037	8132	2773
5450	3437	6962	3034	8343	3300
5483	2774-75	6963	2900	8451	3487-89
5492	2805	7003	3114	8456	3291-93
5498	2811	7065	2874-76	8467	3210
5543	3173-74	7069	2843	8542	3531
5615	3442	7074	3554	8545	2800-01
5731	3099	7075	2866-67	8557	3360-61
5736	3422	7076	2963	8566	2785-86
5741	3289	7077	2960	8649	2861
5788	3466	7078-79	2890	8672	2898
5813	3513	7082	2840	8772	2990-91
5814	3526-27	7115	3426	8774	3392
5817	3550	7132	3264	8799	2769
5838	3486	7159	3097	8881	2865
5841-42	3552	7166	3098	8925	2823
5881?	3061	7200	3354-55	9011	2780
5882	3061	7201	3579-80	9021	3110
5883?	3385	7226	2837	9087	3405
5884	3385	7231	2869	9096	3145
5888-89	2838	7235	3556	9110	2835-36
5943	3090	7249	3441	9128	2880
5946	2851-54	7268	2901	9130	2892
5948	3403	7274	3244	9131	2896-97
5954	2972-73	7320	3473	9312	3125-26
6065	3581	7392	3139-41	9355	2974
6093	3127	7393	3152	9399	3523

H	HUL	H	HUL	H	HUL
9452	3373–74	10765	3340	12282	3301
9460	2910	10771	3051	12302	2886
9469	3160	10776	3105	12507	3459
9561	2809	10807	3359	12577	3574
9582	2808	10820	3118	12632	3565
9583	3093	10836	3192	12633	3572
9650	3077	10880	3023	12719?	3329
9680	3053	10917	3567	12720	3329
9682	3042	10924	2796–97	12726	3121
9683	3057	10934	2873	12727	3329
9684	3047	10956	3469	12729	3393
9686	3062	10981	2899	12730	3409–10
9707	3519	10988	2978	12732	3424–25
9720	3307	11014	3036	12755	2795
9832	3236A	11045	3154	12759	3480
9891	3476	11091	3312	12775	3128–29
10000	3492	11113	2909	12780	2971
10024	2799	11114	3520	12793	3387
10030	3499	11542	3054	12797	3143
10092	3186	11544	3089	12808	3533
10101	2891	11553	2825	12809	2839
10102	3285	11589	2813	12882	3268
10103	2981	11601	3558	12890	3391
10133	3059	11608	3074	12892	3294
10136	3326–27	11617	2970	12894	3481
10235	3502	11676	3510	12897	2989
10243	3153	11774	2819	12903	2788
10258	2966	11903(2)	3363	12917	3078
10282	3383–84	11903(3)	3362	12954	3416
10334	2994	11909	3167	12956	3112
10386	3338	11920	3185	12965	2815
10427	3396	11968	3395	12992	3233
10428	3400	12042	3216	13000?	3284
10447	3356–58	12049	3216	13001	2903
10502	3297	12050	3216	13012	2949
10503	3434	12096	2816	13034	3588
10524	3199–3200	12099	3493	13036	2803–04
10525	2841	12106	3022	13048	3325
10539	3270	12141	3495	13052	3553
10540	3310	12160	3345	13056	3262–63
10690	3280	12239	3065	13062	2960–61
10691	3183	12241	3117	13068?	2960–61
10696	3187	12243	3117	13077	3119–20
10705	3069	12262	3522	13085	3137–38
10707	3176	12267	3524	13091	3350–53

H	HUL	H	HUL	H	HUL
13092	3302-03	14341	3032	14444	(3035e)
13094	3348-49	14342	2936	14445	2915
13112	3045	14345	2937-38	14446	3007
13113	3320-21	14347	2955	14449	2924
13115	3239	14348	(3035e)	14450	2944
13119	3064	14354?	2888-89	14451	2930-31
13121	2884-85	14355	2959	14453	2834
13144	3399	14357	3012	14458?	2926
13148	3407	14358	3014	14461	3003
13173	2907-08	14362	2888-89	14465	2921
13189	3079	14364	2954	14468	2933
13208	3123	14368	2919	14471	3024-25
13219	3439	14369	2977	14475	3582-83
13221	2871-72	14370	3015	14476	2949
13225	2882	14371	2928	14477	2950
13232	2883	14373	2916	14487	3220
13236	2879	14374	2917	14490	3217
13256	3274	14375	(3035e)	14493	2767
13257	3274A	14378	2940-42	14505	3237
13284	3575	14381	2952	14555	3258
13346	3389	14382	2986	14561	3038-39
13536	3490-91	14384	3030	14565	3537
13574	2870	14386	(3035e)	14568	3229-30
13577	2849	14387	2912	14569	3546-48
13581	2860	14389	3029	14570	3543-45
13608	3299	14390	2927	14590	3271
13615	3265	14392	2945	14591	3311
13625	2818	14393	3033	14662	2765
13648	3055-56	14394	2946	14691	3050
13898	2810	14395	2947	14707	2832
13901	3411	14396	2948	14708	3085
13904	3485	14397	(3035e)	14748	2806A
14008	3124	14399	2833	14753-54	3063
14009	3539	14402-03	(3035e)	14842	(3167a)
14050	3516	14404	2881	14862	3577
14131	3219	14405	2887	14864	3559
14141	3578	14410	(3035e)	14865	3560
14230	3430	14415	2951	14870	3189
14263	3483	14428-29?	3035	14873	3084
14264	3279	14431	2956-57	14875	3084
14269	3182	14433	2984	14878	3346-47
14275-76	2850	14435	2922	14886	3252
14334	2979	14436	3011	14960	3514
14335	3004	14439	3011	14996	3413-14
14339	2935	14442	3008	14998	3172

H	HUL	H	HUL	H	HUL
15007	3222–24	15195	3174A	15866	3472
15009(1)	3106–09	15219	3067–68	15880	3421
15009(2)–10	3094	15393	3328	15890	3288
15011	3162	15408	3308	15894	3102
15016	3365–67	15491	3314–15	15895	3462
15089	3319	15511	3322–24	15898	3536
15120	3060	15566	3503	15903	3571
15123	3122	15671	2793	15906	3484
15126	3226–27	15718	3420	15907	(3035c)
15132	2798	15757	3564	16093	3504
15134	3101	15780	3044	16220	3388
15135	3163–65	15832	2953	16227	3088
15136	2814	15847	3369–70	16285	3190–91
15193	3497	15848	3376–77	16288	2794
15194	3267	15849	3378		

2. Proctor/HUL

PR	HUL	PR	HUL	PR	HUL
3461	3088	5788	3052	5879	3077
3471	3262	5789	3054	5881	3078
3949	3279	5794	3055–56	5882	3079
4303	3040	5798	3058	5883	3082
5231	3388	5804	3063	5884	3083
5721	2762	5805	3059	5885	3084
5730	2763	5806	3060	5886	3085
5731	2765	5808	3061	5890	3086
5732	2766	5823	3066	5894	3087
5735	2776	5827	3069	5896	3090
5740	2777	5829	3070	5899A	3104
5748	2767	5831	3071–72	5902	3091
5753	2770–72	5832	3074	5904	3092
5754	2773	5837	3064	5906	3094
5755	2774–75	5838	3067–68	5908	3095
5759	2779	5845	3038–39	5924	3097
5762	2781–84	5851	3037	5926	3098
5764	2787	5852	3042	5934	3100
5765	2785-86	5855	3043	5953	3099
5768	3036	5859	3044	5955	3101
5773	3049	5860	3045	5957A	3103
5775	3050	5861	3046	5968–70	3127
5784	3051	5873	3048	5971	3106–09
5785	3053	5875	3075	5973	3110

PR	HUL	PR	HUL	PR	HUL
5975	3080	6125	2843	6220	2933
5977B	3081	6131	2855-58	6222	2934
5978	3145	6135	2859	6224	2937-38
5986	3146-47	6138	2863	6225	2936
5997	3149	6140	2864	6226	2935
5998	3150-51	6142	2865	6227	2943
5999	3152	6143	2866-67	6228	2944
6003	3154	6149	2871-72	6229	2945
6006	3113	6150	2873	6230	2947
6007	3114	6151	2874-76	6231	2954
6008	3115-16	6151A	2877-78	6233	2956-57
6012	3117	6152	2879	6234	2951
6015	3118	6153	2880	6236	3022
6016	3119-20	6156	2884-85	6245	2914
6018	3121	6157	2886	6270	2955
6021	3122	6160	2887	6272	2916
6022	3123	6162	2894	6274	2940-42
6026	3130	6163	2891	6279	2900
6028	3131-32	6165	2892	6283	2909
6030	3133	6166	2890	6284	2903
6031	3137-38	6167	2895	6286	2924
6032	3135-36	6169	2896-97	6288	2911
6037	3139-41	6171	2898	6290	2918
6038	3142	6175	2869	6292	2915
6039	3143	6178	2971	6293	2919
6042	3144	6180	2881	6294	2917
6051	3156	6183	2893	6295	2923
6055	3157	6184	2888-89	6296	2920
6056	3158-59	6192	2899	6298	2988
6065	3125-26	6194	2990-91	6301	2921
6067	3161	6194B	2901	6302	2922
6077	3163-65	6197	2905-06	6304	2959
6080	3168	6198	2907-08	6305	3035
6081	3089	6199	2910	6306	2970
6098	2837	6201	2912	6309	2972-73
6100	2838	6202	2913	6310	2974
6102	2839	6206	2927	6312	2975-76
6108	2840	6209	2986	6313	2979
6109	2841	6210	2952	6314	2980
6111	2842	6212	2948	6316	2981
6114	2845	6213	2926	6317	2985
6116	2846-48	6214	2939	6320	2986
6117	2850	6217	2928	6323	2868
6120	2851-54	6218	2930-31	6329A	2989
6124	2844	6219	2932	6339A	2861

PR	HUL	PR	HUL	PR	HUL
6342	2862	6454	3033	6573	3195
6349	2992	6456	3294	6574	3220
6350	2993	6458	3291-93	6585	3196
6351	2995	6459	3295	6586	3197
6352	2996	6464	3296	6587	3198
6355	2998	6466	3297	6588	3199-3200
6356	2999	6471	3304	6589	3202
6358	3004	6472	3302-03	6591	3204
6359	3009	6474	3305	6594	3205-06
6361	3011	6476	3306	6597	3208-09
6363	3012	6477	3307	6598	3210
6364	3014	6481	3308	6606	3211-12
6369	2986	6482	3309	6607	3215
6369A	3030	6483	3310	6609	3213
6370	3010	6484	3311	6610	3214
6372	2833	6486	3312	6611	3203
6374	2834	6489	3314-15	6615	3221
6375	2835-36	6490	3316-18	6619	3222-24
6378	3001	6493	3319	6619A	3225, 3551
6384	3019	6497	3320-21	6623	3226-27
6385	3018	6498	3325	6626	3229-30
6388	2997	6499	3326-27	6628	3231-32
6395	3005	6500	3322-24	6630-31	3233
6396	3006	6501	3328	6633	3234-35
6396A	3008	6502	3329	6635	3236
6397	3007	6506	3299	6636	3237
6398	3016	6507	3300	6638	3238
6399	3013	6509	3301	6639	3239
6405	2960-61	6515	3170	6640	3240-41
6406	2962	6516	3171	6641	3242
6407	2964-65	6524	3173-74	6642	3243
6408	2966	6525	3175	6643	3244
6409	2963	6526	3176	6645	3245-46
6412	2967	6532	3178	6646	3252
6414	2968	6536	3185	6647	3249
6415	3023	6548	3189	6648	3250
6417	3024-25	6556A	3190-91	6649	3251
6420	3027-28	6558A	3216	6651	3256-57
6421	3439	6558C	3216	6655	3182
6424	3031	6559	3217	6657	3183
6427	(3035e)	6560	3218	6661	3258
6429	3029	6561	3219	6662	3259
6430	3032	6563	3192	6663	3260
6444-48	(3035e)	6564	3180	6665	3261
6451-53	(3035e)	6567A	3181	6666	3262-63

PR	HUL	PR	HUL	PR	HUL
6669	3184	6845	3354–55	6965	3401
6676	3281	6850	3346–47	6973	3403
6680	3265	6851	3348–49	6978	3405
6682A	3280	6855	3360–61	6979	3406
6688	3269	6857	3363	6980	3407
6690	3266	6858	3362	6981	3408
6694	3271	6860	3356–58	6982	3409–10
6695	3270	6864	3364	6984	3411
6697	3272	6872	3365–67	6985A	3412
6706	3284	6873	3368	6987	3413–14
6708	3274	6880	3331	6989	3415
6709	3274A	6884	3333–34	6994	3416
6711	3276	6886	3335	6995	3417
6724	3283	6888A	3335A	6996	3419
6744	3285	6892	3336–37	6997	3420
6755	2792	6893	3338	7002	3423
6757	2793	6895	3339	7005	3422
6758	2794	6898	3340	7011	3424–25
6759	2795	6908	3341–42	7019	3429
6761	2796–97	6910	3343	7028	3430
6762	2799	6911	3344	7030	3431–32
6763	2800–01	6912	3369–70	7033	3433
6766	2802	6913	3371	7034	3435
6767	2798	6915	3372	7039	3436
6769	2791	6918	3373–74	7040	3437
6776	2803–04	6920	3375	7046	3439
6781	2806	6921	3376–77	7048	3395
6789	3380–81	6922	3378	7056	3442
6791	2807	6923	3383–84	7057	3446
6796	3290	6925	3385	7058	3449–50
6797	2808	6926	3386	7059	3445
6798	2809	6927	3387	7062	3448
6802	2813	6932	3389	7064	3457
6805	2814	6933	3390	7066	3451
6807	2817	6937	3481	7075A	3455
6808	2816	6939	3534	7082	3460
6813	2821	6944	3391	7085A	3462
6815	2822	6945	3392	7094	3466
6820	2823	6951	3393	7096	3467
6821	2825	6952	3394	7099	3470
6825	2826	6953	3396	7105	3472
6826	2828	6956	3397	7106	3456
6828	2824	6958	3398	7110	3458
6831	2831	6959	3399	7112	3476
6842	3350–53	6962	3400	7118	3478–79

PR	HUL	PR	HUL	PR	HUL
7119	3484	7184	3514	7260	3549
7120	3480	7185	3330	7261	3550
7128	3486	7189	3174A	7264	3552
7131	3487–89	7191	3520	7266	3553
7139	3490–91	7193	3521	7268	3112
7141	3492	7195	3522	7269	3111
7144	3493	7196A	3523	7276	3554
7145	3499	7199	3525	7286	3561
7146	3482	7202	3524	7287	3563
7149	3483	7214	3526–27	7288	3568–69
7151	3500–01	7215	3528–29	7290	3579–80
7152	3498	7217	3516	7322	3582–83
7155	3494	7223	3519	7323	3584
7157	3495	7229	3530	7325	3585–86
7158	3503	7237	3531	7331	2811
7159	3496	7238	3533	7347	2788
7168	3505–06	7243A	3535	7367	3287
7171	3507	7251	3537	7394	3588
7172	3508–09	7252	3538	7404	3485
7173	3510	7254	3540	7405	3359
7174	3511	7256	3541–42	7416	3179
7175	3512	7257	3543–45	7420	3194
7177	3513	7258A	3225, 3551		
7180	3515	7259	3546–48		

3. Gesamtkatalog/HUL

GW	HUL	GW	HUL	GW	HUL
148	3471	1268	2770–72	2430	2830
152	3155	1594	3083	2443	2790
185	3104	1601	3070	2452	3335
191	3238	1612	3113	2522	3333–34
192	3228	1620	2868	2524	3076
264	3388	1667	2791	2527	3443
266	3000	1668	2779	2621	3371
268	2822	1738	3460	2674	3298
269	2821	1919	2929	2709	2829
314	3549	1923	3584	2834	3181
339	3048	2048	2962	2867	3364
428	3372	2075	3170	2881	3272
441	3283	2079	2998	2894	3082
522	3124	2142	3010	2999	3521
526	3539	2204	2845	3001	3408
570	3204	2205	2993	3017	2995
579	2855–58	2271	2964–65	3068	3468
580	(3035d)	2292	3585–86	3094	3368
588	3339	2294	3540	3107	2778
682	3115–16	2302	3508–09	3111	3449–50
712	3428	2305	3249	3167	2827
795	3440	2329	3195	3244	3343
859	3431–32	2349	2789	3246	3198
872	3455	2369	3178	3256	3201

GW	HUL	GW	HUL	GW	HUL
3276	3196	4425	3394	5973	2802
3290	3197	4456	2792	6128	3133
3357	3175	4464	3086	6139	3277A
3372	3452	4499	2776	6172	3566
3379	3184	4502	3203	6211	2939
3392	3390	4637	3180	6226	3435
3449	3144	4649	3433	6387	3040
3466	3465	4657	3427	6389	3500-01
3467	3290	4658	3309	6400	2999
3471	3568-69	4662	3058	6409	2844
3473	3256-57	4775	2893	6410	2992
3477	3091	4780	3021	6420	3103
3593	3286	4870	3092	6442	2968
3672	3451	4952	3071-72	6443	2862
3739	3202	4954	3213	6456	2846-48
3802	3027-28	4955	2975-76	6471	3234-35
3819	3185	4956	3344	6479	3457
3838-39	2868	4958	3208-09	6494	3287
3847	3019	4960	3214	6501	3457
3849	2985	5073	3100	6510	3096
3850	3031	5556	3393	6511	3563
3907	3415	5577	3131-32	6512	3464
3927	3150-51	5598	3576	6513	3017
3938	3423	5600	2762	6518	3080
3946	3149	5613(1)	2905-06	6519	2817
4035	3134	5613(2)	2907-08	6534	2894
4053	3009	5623	2820	6540	3075
4087	2768	5659	3515	6545	3087
4099	3218	5720	3561	6606	2988
4114	3436	5739	3177	6771	3243
4117	2877-78	5748	2914	6796	3507
4126	3236	5776	3461	6824	3043
4127	3253	5836	3557	6903	3225, 3551
4131	3247-48	5840	3573	6906	3231-32
4132	3211-12	5844	3570	6943	3517-18
4133	3221	5845	3562	7059	3512
4134	3242	5851	3255	7122	3437
4138	3240-41	5859	3254	7164	2774-75
4142	3245-46	5867	3046	7181	2811
4143	3251	5868	3306	7213	2831
4144	3205-06	5883	3259	7291	3442
4146	3418	5884	2996	7460	2997
4148	3250	5917	2967	7565	3289
4355	3525	5942	3530	7574	3173-74
4423	3375	5950	3498	7579	2787

GW	HUL	GW	HUL	GW	HUL
7680	2809	8390	2987	10044	2900
7704	2808	8396	2989	10050	2913
7706	3093	8423	3316–18	10097	3354–55
7807	3466	8424	3541–42	10098	3579–80
7813	3513	8636	2932	10170	2837
7815	3526–27	8638	3429	10173	2869
7818	3550	9115	3494	10191	2901
7827	3486	9119	3304	10196	3244
7842	3552	9120	3496	10247	3473
7873	3061	9331	2863	10410	3215
7874	3385	9432	3037	10423	3139–41
7877	2838	9437	3341–42	10424	3152
7907	2812	9443	3305	10434	3161
7965	3090	9472	2861	10435	3417
7966	2851–54	9832	3458	10437	3157
7968	3403	9834	3114	10517	3331
7973	2972–73	9871	2963	10522	3278
8028	2902	9872	2840	10597	3398
8221	3581	9876	2843	10610	3445
8250	3127	9879	3554	10616	3444
8252	2826	9880	2890	10617	2805
8327	3534	9881	2866–67	10618	3447
8329	3111	9882	2874–76	10620	3535
8370	3386	9951	3426	10622	2824
8374	3171	9995	3264	10624	3532
8380	3406	10042	3034	10927	3558

4. Goff/HUL

Goff	HUL	Goff	HUL	Goff	HUL
A-20	3155	A-460	2770–72	A-1030	3335
A-21	3471	A-548	3083	A-1067	3333–34
A-33	3104	A-553	3070	A-1069	3076
A-37	3238	A-561	3113	A-1072	3443
A-38	3228	A-588	2791	A-1104	3371
A-61	3388	A-589	2779	A-1141	3298
A-63	3000	A-638	3460	A-1150	2829
A-81	2831	A-713	3584	A-1200	3181
A-92	2822	A-765	2962	A-1220	3364
A-93	2821	A-782	3170	A-1237	3272
A-101	3048	A-785	2998	A-1251	3082
A-104	3549	A-836	3010	A-1311	3521
A-148	3372	A-886	2845	A-1313	3408
A-155	3283	A-887	2993	A-1329	2995
A-190	3124	A-924	2964–65	A-1378	3468
A-210	3204	A-930	3585–86	A-1385	3041
A-215	2855–58	A-932	3540	A-1388	3101
A-216	(3035d)	A-935	3508–09	A-1404	3368
A-224	3339	A-938	3249	A-1411	2778
A-275	3115–16	A-956	3195	A-1415	3449–50
A-297	3428	A-969	2789		
A-346	3440	A-986	3178	B-11	2827
A-384	3455	A-1019	2830	B-53	3343
A-386	3431–32	A-1021	2790	B-58	3196

Goff	HUL	Goff	HUL	Goff	HUL
B-66	3197	B-673	3525	C-77	3530
B-85	3201	B-702	3375	C-79	3498
B-89	3198	B-704	3394	C-97	2802
B-107	3184	B-733	2792	C-117	3511
B-111	3175	B-741	3086	C-118	3528-29
B-114	3452	B-761	2776	C-198	3133
B-123	3390	B-762	3203	C-219	3277A
B-153	3075	B-842	3180	C-250	3566
B-158	3087	B-871	3427	C-273	2939
B-168	3144	B-872	3309	C-285	3435
B-177	3465	B-890	3058	C-322	3040
B-178	3290	B-911	2893	C-323	3500-01
B-180	3568-69	B-915	3021	C-331	2999
B-182	3256-57	B-929	3433	C-338	2844
B-186	3091	B-994	3092	C-339	2992
B-260	3451	B-1040	3071-72	C-347	3103
B-283	3202	B-1041	2975-76	C-356	2968
B-300	3027-28	B-1042	3344	C-357	2862
B-314	3185	B-1043	3213	C-364	2846-48
B-321-22	2868	B-1045	3208-09	C-376	3234-35
B-325	3019	B-1047	3214	C-383	3457
B-327	2985	B-1101	3100	C-388	3287
B-328	3031	B-1213	3393	C-395	3457
B-364	3415	B-1218	3131-32	C-398	3096
B-387	3150-51	B-1229	3576	C-399	3563
B-407	3134	B-1234	2762	C-400	3464
B-418	3009	B-1248	2905-06	C-401	3277
B-431	3423	B-1259	2820	C-405	3080
B-441	3149	B-1264	3515	C-407	2817
B-454	2768	B-1277	3561	C-419	2894
B-459	3218	B-1287	3177	C-443	2988
B-465	3436	B-1292	2914	C-449	2859
B-467	2877-78	B-1304	3461	C-518	3043
B-472	3247-48			C-549	3243
B-473	3236	C-2	3557	C-556	3507
B-474	3253	C-5	3573	C-571	3231-32
B-482	3211-12	C-8	3570	C-573	3225, 3551
B-483	3221	C-9	3562	C-592	3518
B-484	3242	C-10	3255	C-701	3512
B-487	3240-41	C-11	3254	C-741	3437
B-489	3245-46	C-20	3046	C-754	2774-75
B-490	3251	C-21	3306	C-763	2811
B-491	3205-06	C-33	3259	C-786	3173-74
B-493	3418	C-34	2996	C-803	3442
B-495	3250	C-61	2967	C-873	(3035a)

Goff	HUL	Goff	HUL	Goff	HUL
C-874	2997	F-63	3034	G-529	2766
C-916	3099	F-66	2900		
C-917	3422	F-120	3458	H-2	3300
C-921	3289	F-127	3114	H-68	3487–89
C-928	2787	F-148	2843	H-77	3291–93
C-945	3466	F-151	3554	H-86	3210
C-959	3513	F-152	2963	H-149	3531
C-961	3526–27	F-153	2840	H-151	2800–01
C-964	3550	F-156	2890	H-169	3360–61
C-974	3486	F-157	2866–67	H-178	2785–86
C-979	3552	F-158	2874–76	H-261	2861
C-1000	3061	F-186	3426	H-273	2898
C-1001	3385	F-195	3264	H-300	2990–91
C-1006	2838	F-207	2913	H-311	3392
		F-235	3354–55	H-320	2769
		F-236	3579–80	H-324	3158–59
D-7	2812	F-241	2837	H-336	2911
D-28	3090	F-243	2869	H-447	2865
D-29	2851–54	F-250	2901	H-540	2780
D-31	3403	F-252	3244	H-547	3474
D-36	2972–73	F-283	3473	H-548	3110
D-52	2902	F-326	3139–41	H-565	3193
D-121	3581	F-329	3152		
D-139	3127			I-9	3405
D-141	2826			I-18	3145
D-186	3534	G-3	3161	I-33	2835–36
D-188	3111	G-4	3417	I-48	2880
D-206	3386	G-6	3157	I-52	2892
D-210	3171	G-26	3505–06	I-53	2896–97
D-217	2989	G-43	3156	I-210	3125–26
D-221	3406	G-58	3331		
D-232	2987	G-59a	3278		
D-250	3316	G-122	3398	J-43	3556
D-251	3541–42	G-133	2805	J-45	3441
D-304	2932	G-134	3447	J-53	3475
D-305	3429	G-135	3535	J-201	3478–79
D-417	3494	G-137	3532	J-204	2781–84
D-419	3304	G-142	2824	J-209	3401
D-423	3496	G-143	2824	J-214	2974
		G-143	3444	J-214	2974
		G-144	3445	J-326	3456
		G-302	(3035b)	J-340	3523
E-45	2863	G-340	2994	J-484	3373–74
E-96	2958	G-434	3419	J-490	2910
E-116	3037	G-520	3446	J-496	3160
E-121	3305	G-527	2773	J-556	2809
E-127	3341–42	G-528	2763	J-568	2808

Goff	HUL	Goff	HUL	Goff	HUL
J-617	3077	M-303	3359	O-171	3065
J-631	3042	M-309	3118	O-173	3117
J-636	3053	M-321	3192	O-182	3345
J-636a	3042	M-342	3023		
J-637	3057	M-365	3567	P-5	3522
J-638	3047	M-380	2796–97	P-6	3524
J-640	3062	M-399	2873	P-14	3301
J-641	3168	M-417	2899	P-25	2886
J-660	3519	M-427	2978	P-55	3166
J-667	3307	M-447	3036	P-75	3018
		M-473	3154	P-178	3097
L-53	3476	M-502	3312	P-182	3098
L-70	3295	M-512	3453	P-204	3340
L-76	2970	M-518	3520	P-236	3459
L-170	3379	M-520	2909	P-261	3574
L-171	3499	M-550	3258	P-285	3572
L-174	2799	M-590	3266	P-286	3565
L-215	3186	M-704	3275	P-298	3380–81
L-218	2891	M-705	3073	P-342	3329
L-219	3285	M-808	3054	P-349	3121
L-221	2981	M-810	3089	P-350	3409–10
L-241	3059	M-817	2825	P-351	3424–25
L-244	3326–27	M-844	2813	P-355	3148
L-299	3502	M-853	3558	P-373	2795
L-308	3153	M-857	3074	P-377	3480
L-320	2966			P-389	3128–29
L-333	3383–84	N-6	3510	P-396	2971
		N-51	2819	P-409	3387
M-9	3396	N-59	3330	P-415	3533
M-11	3400	N-130	3338	P-419	3143
M-25	3356–58	N-161	3454	P-420	2839
M-59	3297	N-267(2)	3363	P-434	3467
M-64	3434	N-267(3)	3362	P-436	3336–37
M-77	3199–3200	N-268	3397	P-438	2807
M-80	2841	N-274	3167	P-442	2828
M-95	3270	N-279	3332	P-532	3194
M-96	3310			P-548	3294
M-192	3280	O-28	3395	P-551	3391
M-193	3183	O-38	3273	P-553	3268
M-196	3187	O-73	3216	P-555	3481
M-199	3587	O-94	2823	P-566	2788
M-203	3176	O-97	3493	P-570	3269
M-205	3069	O-103	3022	P-604	2815
M-274	3051	O-131	3495	P-605	3112
M-276	3105	O-151	3282	P-606	3416

Goff	HUL	Goff	HUL	Goff	HUL
P-615	3078	P-1120	2904	S-201	3007
P-632	3233	P-1139	3299	S-202–03	(3035e)
P-635	3284	P-1140	3265	S-208	2951
P-641	2903	P-1146	2818	S-216	3035
P-676	3482			S-217	2956–57
P-700	3296	Q-27	3055–56	S-220	2984
P-721	3135–36			S-221	2922
P-724	3049	R-172	3485	S-222	3011
P-726	3066	R-178	3411	S-225	3008
P-751	3588	R-179	2810	S-226	2925
P-753	2803–04	R-199	2929	S-227	2955
P-763	3553	R-243	2816	S-228	3582–83
P-766	3262–63			S-229	2959
P-770	3325	S-1	3516	S-231	2881
P-771	2960–61	S-19	3219	S-232	2920
P-781	3119–20	S-24	3578	S-234	3013
P-783	3137–38	S-82	3430	S-235	3024–25
P-790	3350–53	S-104	3483	S-236	2943
P-791	3302–03	S-107	3279	S-237	2954
P-793	3348–49	S-112	3182	S-239	2888–89
P-807	3045	S-117	2850	S-242	(3035e)
P-808	3320–21	S-131	3448	S-243	2986
P-810	3239	S-160a	3179	S-244	2952
P-813	3064	S-168	3001	S-245	2912
P-815	2884–85	S-169	2915	S-247	3030
P-819	3399	S-172	(3035e)	S-248	3029
P-824	3407	S-174	2934	S-250	2927
P-829	2764	S-175	2940–42	S-251	3020
P-861	3079	S-179(a)	2979	S-253	2945
P-874	2907–08	S-179(b)	2980	S-254	3033
P-875	3123	S-180	3004	S-255	2946
P-887	3439	S-181	2982–83	S-256	2947
P-888	3207	S-182	2949	S-257	2948
P-890	2871–72	S-183	3005	S-258	(3035e)
P-894	2882	S-184	3006	S-259	2833
P-896	2883	S-187	3003	S-263–64	(3035e)
P-898	2879	S-188	2921	S-265	2887
P-918	3274	S-191	2834	S-266	2923
P-920	3274A	S-193	2928	S-267	3016
P-923	3575	S-194	2933	S-269	(3035e)
P-1078	3026	S-195	2926	S-271	3012
P-1081	3490–91	S-196	2930–31	S-272	3014
P-1108	2870	S-197	2924	S-274	2936
P-1109	2849	S-198	(3035e)	S-275	2937–38
P-1119	3002	S-199	2918	S-278	2917

Goff	HUL	Goff	HUL	Goff	HUL
S-279	2916	S-608	3559	T-397	3503
S-281	(3035e)	S-609	3560	T-478	2777
S-282	2935	S-613	3189	T-500	2793
S-283	3032	S-618	3084	T-548	3420
S-284	2944	S-619	3346–47	T-568	3564
S-285	2977	S-625	3252		
S-287	2919	S-685	3514	U-5	3472
S-288	3015	S-699	3040	U-11	3421
S-289	3555	S-706	3413–14	U-13	3169
S-290	2767	S-707	3172	U-22	3404
S-293	3220	S-710	3412	U-43	3288
S-299	3217	S-714	3222–24	U-45	3102
S-304	3237	S-716	3106–09	U-46	3462
S-340	3038–39	S-717	3094	U-50	3536
S-345	3215	S-718	3162	U-52	3571
S-347	3537	S-721	3365–67	U-53	3484
S-348	3229–30	S-722	3402	U-56	(3035c)
S-349	3546–48	S-726	3492	U-63	3504
S-350	3543–45	S-758	2969	U-69	3281
S-368	3271	S-789	3276		
S-369	3311	S-796	3319	V-21	2842
S-433	2765	S-812	2798	V-29	3044
S-467	3050	S-821	3060	V-74	2953
S-477	3382	S-823	3122	V-88	3369–70
S-481	2832	S-825	3226–27	V-89	3376–77
S-482	3085	S-829	3163–65	V-90	3378
S-494	3142	S-830	2814	V-181	3313
S-510	3267			V-216	2864
S-511	3174A	T-7	3067–68	V-217	2895
S-513	3497	T-75	3308	V-267	3260
S-519	3389	T-79	3328	V-272	3146–47
S-527	2806A	T-155	3314–15	V-273	3052
S-532	3063	T-197	2806		
S-590	(3167a)	T-213	3335A	X-5	3088
S-593	(3167a)	T-259	3095		
S-601	(3167a)	T-262	3081	Z-10	3470
S-603	(3167a)	T-359	3322–24	Z-27	3190–91
S-606	3577	T-367	3538	Z-28	2794

Not in Goff

HUL	HUL	HUL
2860	3130	3463
2950	3188	3469
3017	3236A	3477
(3035b)	3261	3517
3093	3286	3539
3124A	3438	

Plates

e GO SVM DANIEL PROHETA VNVS DE ISRAHELITIS Q VI

captiui ducti ſūt de ſancta ciuitate ieru
ſalem hec omnia a deo facta ſunt nihil tamen
p memet addidi ſed omnia a deo facta accepi.

Aerem ſerenū uidere lucrum ſignificat.
A beſtiis iſeſtari q ſe uiderit ab īimicis ſupabit.
Aerē lentū. uel nebuloſū uidere expedicióe₃.
Aerē turpē uidere laborem ſig.
Aerem limpidum uidere expectatione₃ ſig.
Aerem clarū uidere expurgationem ſig.
Acetum potare moleſtia₃ ſig.
Ad ſacrificia acceder leticiā magnam ſig.
Agnos uel edos edere uel habere deſolatione₃.
Agrimonia edere nuutiū bonum ſig.
Albā ueſtem habere uel induere leticiā ſig.
Albū uel dalmaticū ueſtir leticiam ſig.
Alas dare uel pdere detrimentū ſig.
Amaros fructus comedere infirmitate₃ ſig.
Anulos dare uel pdere dolorem ſig.
Alciorem q ſe uiderit grauē languorem ſig.
Anulos accipere ' ſecuritatem ſig.
Apes uolantes uidere pūgnam ſig.

Plate I

z

Ad huc non est zelotipus homo ille
Vir preposita tibi valebit
Judex est tibi propitius
In hac causa hes amicos bene fideles

Aries. f. z. Beraxon.

Quod uis in coniugio cito capies
Matrionium habes b° mese ul' ano ad pl's
Amore serui melius gaudebis
Tempus meliorabitur anno futuro
Hic bene potando proficis
Hic promouebitur cum labore
Nuntius fatuus et nihil agit
Hic erit sapiens sed tarde
Appellatus uincet τ morietur
Vix potes soluere quod debes
Hic est zelotipus manifestus
Vade secure quia lucraberis hac via

Aries. f. Mensor

Matrimonium contrahes anno futuro
Amore deductus es τ gaudebis
Tempus erit contrarium electo anno
Hic in scola proficiet in ribaldriis
Nuncius nihil faciet quia stultus est
Hic promouebitur per symoniam
Hic erit sapiens et malitiosus
Illi pugiles non pugnabunt
Tua solues debita fugiendo
Hic est zelotipus sed non palam
Hec uia non proficiet maiori
Causam tuam perdes in iudicio

Plate II

CYRIFFO CALVANEO COMPO
STO PER LVCA DEPVLCI AD
PETITIONE DEL MAGNIFICO
LORENZO DEMEDICI.

i   O CANTERO CY
          riffo caluaneo
          Cyriffo ilquale per
          paesi diuersi
Errando ando per farsi almondo iddeo
Nuoui amori:nuoui casi:& nuoui uersi
Porteran forse al gran Gioue tropheo
Non pur gli assiri egiptii parthi o persi
Et prestandomi ilcelo qui del suo aiuto
Comincieremo al Poueroadueduto
E t non inuoco uoi sacre che al monte
  Scandete iuersi oue ilcaual pegaso
  Fece nel saxo quel famoso fonte
  Ma Vener che damore colma ogni uaso
  Aspiri:& uolga labenigna fronte
  Dipaliprenda al doloroso caso
  Che sola in selua misera & infelice
  Se stessa piange & poi mormora & dice

                              a

Plate IV

Vt tuus iste nepos:Ad se ipsum in secunda persona cum indignatiõe maiore loquitur . Nepos autem propterea luxuriosus & prodigus dicitur.quod sub auo educati solutiorem delicatiorem que uitam degunt.Hora.Discinctus aut perdam nepos. Satur anseris extis sapientiores:ut Pli. x.libro refert:iecur anseris probauerunt fartilibusque in magnam amplitudinem crescit.Exẽptũ quoque lacte mulso augetur.De eo Horatius:Pinguibus & ficis pastum iecur anseris albi. Ingui

Vt tuus iste nepos olim satur anseris extis
Cum morbosa uago singultiet inguine uenã
Patriciæ immeiat uuluæ mihi trama figuræ
Sit reliqua:ast illi tremat omento popa uenter
Vẽde animã lucro mercare:atcp excute solers
Omne latus mundi:ne sit præstantior alter
Capadocas rigida pingues clausisse catasta.
Rẽ duplica:feci iam triplex:iam mihi quarto
Iam decies:redit in rugam:depinge:ubi sistam
Inuẽtus chrysippe tui finitor acerui:

A.Persii Flacci Satyrarum finis.

Magister Vlderic°scizẽzeleꞇ Mediolãi ipressiꞇ
M.CCCC.L.XXXx.

ne uago:ab inguinis uicinitate inguen pro mẽbro uirili ponitur Vagum au tem dicendo rem turpem honesto uo cabulo contegens maronianum illud expressit.Iã primũ satis hic libidiosus alternis & eundo & exeundo porta te faciet patentiorẽ. Morosa uena: cum proprie uẽa sit per quã sanguinis riuus meat:quia tamen per penẽ quoque ge nitura trãscurrit:genitalis seminis iter in inguine uenam denomiat :quod pla ne per singultũ expressit . Nã ut singul tiunt fauces ita quoque genitura fluen te singultire uidetur penis . Morosã au tem dicens:id mutoni : quod est homi nis in amore uetita & negata petentis dedit. Patriciæ imeiat uuluæ cũ gene rosa & nobili fœmina coeat . Mihi trama figuræ sit reliqua : ast illi tremat omento popa uenter:sensus est : ut ego parcius uiuens emacream:eo per luxũ pinguescente: sibi enim tramã hoc est uiliora obsonia relinqui dicit.Trama

enim silũ est:quod intra stamen discurrit.Staminis autem fila preciosiora quã tramæ sũt. Omẽ tum uero membrana tenuis est:quæ intestina contegit.Popa autẽ pingue significat:unde & popi na deducitur:Nam quod a quodã scribitur panem esse.quo sacerdotes:uel corũ ministri uescebã tur:unde & popeanum ungnentũ dicitur:fide caret.Popeanum enim a popea Neronis uxore ap pellari.Pli.testimonio:uolumine undecimo planuest.Ait eni . Crassissimũ asinæ lac ut coaguli uice utantur.conferre aliquid & candori in mulierũ cure existimatur.Popea certe Domitii Nero nis coniunx quingentas per omnia secũ fœtas trahens balneatũ etiam solio totum corpus illo la cte macerabat:extendi quocp cutẽ credens.Itẽ.viii.&.xx.cutem in facie erugari & tenerescere & candorẽ custodiri lacte asinino putant notique est quasdam quotidie septingentarũ custodito numero souere Popeaque hoc uxor Neronis principis instituit:his quoque Iuue.accedit. aut pin guia popeana spirat:& hinc miseti uscantur labra mariti. Vẽde animã lucro:hæc ab eodem non sine stomacho dicuntur qui demens ut patrimonium grande relinqueret:multos labores pe riculaque pertulerit . Ne sit præstantior alter: Capadocas rigida pingues clausisse catasta.Ne uenaliũ seruorum alter maiorem gregẽ possideat.Catasta autẽ locus erat:ubi serui uenales expo nebantur.a uerbo græco catasto.quod expono significat:appellata:Papini.in siluis.Nõ te barba ricæ uersabat turba catastæ. Tibullus.Nota loquor regnũ ipse tenet quẽ sæpe coegit barbara gypsatos ferre catasta pedes.Pli.v.&.xxx.Talem in catasta uidere chrysogonũ syllæ:Cappado cia uero Solino auctore põtica regio est:que læuo latere utrascp armenias cõmagenecp tangens: dextro multis asiæ populis circunfusa ad tauri iuga & solis ortus attollitur. Appianus uero mi noris armeniæ partẽ:ptolomæus ipsam minorẽ armeniã esse scribunt.Iam decies redit in rugam iam rem decies geminaui:necp tamen cupiditati modum adhibui Depinge ubi sistam inuentus chrysippe tui finitor acerui:nescius auariciæ suæ finem impõete Chrysippum rogat: quo tandẽ in numero diuitiarum consistat.Chrysippus uero apollonii solensis siue tarsensis filius Cleantis zenonisque auditor:ut refert laertius:undecim & trecenta uolumina in logicis scripsit :in quibus omnia ad eam artẽ spectantia & coaceruauit & diligenter absoluit.Ob quod ait sui acerui: hoc ẽ dialecticotum librorum cumuli finitorem Chrysippum repertum esse.

Plate V

Ui vult habere summaz an
gelicam correctissimã que
... primo impressã clausu
... postea attẽdat ad cor
rec... infrascriptuz in
... iueniet multa que ui
tio transcriptorz et ipresso
ru corrupta sũt uel ommissa. Quod qdez
e facti cũ exemplari pprio ipsius fratris
Angeli. In quo noto prio capitulũ i quo
est corruptio. secũdo paragraphũ . tertio
lineãm ponẽdo aliquod uerbũ precedens
z subsequens i cuius medio uel additur
quod e ommissum uel corrigitur quod e
falsum i dicta summa primo impressa. nisi
quãdo ommissio ut corruptio e in fine. s.
qz tunc quãdo nõ ponitur hic nisi uerbũ
precedens: tũc oia sequẽtia sunt corrup
ta uel ommittẽda z ideo corrigẽda ut sup
plenda aut ommittẽda sunt secũdũ qp in
infrascripto correctezio iuenies . Et sic
si eã secũdũ infrascriptũ correctoriuz
emendabis iustissimũ codicẽ habebis. Ut
si non habes predictã summã impressam
clausu: sed aliam ipressaz uenetiis uel ali
bi: tũc aduerte qp pdicta summa impressa
clausũ habet quinquagita quincz lineas
pro qualibet colũna: z qualibet linea hẽt
32 uel circa litteras alphabeti. Ex quo po
teris facillime iuenire i qua linea est cor
rupta z iuenire verbũ precedẽs z subse
quens in cuius medio ponitur correctio
secudum qp supra dictũ e: quia cũ omnes
ipresse ab illa prio ipressa clausũ sũpse
rit exemplũ cõiter omnes ubi prio impres
sa est corrupta uel diminuta sic z alie po
stea impresse licet in aliquibus posterius
ipresse fuerint correcte sz non plene.

Abbas. s.4.linea.6. ẽ laudunũ in cle.
s.6.li.fi.z panor.in c.
s.17.li.pẽt.cõcedere et cũ z iste.s. est ma
le signatus vscz ad. s.23.
s.12.li.secũda Pa.i dicto.c.cũ ad mona
steriũ per c.fi.de regula.quod.
s.ultio li.fi.a platis nisi ex approbata cõ
suetudine uel priuilegio aliud habeatur
ut ibi.

Abbatissa i pricipio li.tertia in quo prefi
cienda est.
s.5.li.4. tamen ab officio z a beneficio
monachas.

Absolutio primo. s.i.li.5.nuper. s. in se
cũda de sen.exco.ubi et archiepiscopo.
s.2.li.10.di.18.q.ultia. z li.zi.uel quãdo
excõicatus adire non
s.3.li.13.itelligit etiam de proprijs.
Absolutio. z.i pri.li.fi.hosti. z ber.in.c.
s.i.li.13 spirituale extra curiã... ut
excõicet est.
s.2.li.4.z c.venerabilibus de sen.exco.
s.4.li.i.an talis valeat.
s.5.li.19.nouit z c.excõicat̃ õ offi.dele.
s.ultimo li.5.offi.02.idem dic de
Absolutioz. s.i.li.4. hug. i criminibus
horrendis.
s.2.li.17.de iudit facit ... z.
s.10.li.12.de offi.02.nisi petisset generali
ter absolutione ab oibus excõicationibs
z generaliter fuisset cõcessa: ga licet fieri
nõ debeat nisi exprimãtur specialiter tñ
facta tenet. si vero fuit excõicatus soluz
vna excõicatione: sz ppter plures causas
tũc dicendũ qp aut vna causa . Et li.13.c.
super litteris de rescrip.
s.2.li.penultia no. voc.in dicto c. officij
nisi si sit.
s.i3.li.i.heres. s.4.
Acceptio psonaz. s.i.li.t.ar.32.q.4.
s.4.li.19.ad dãdũ cõsanguineo dũmodo
s.6.li.pria vir meliori bono z li.3.aliud
est i maiori Et li.8.sit honus ga secũdũ
Actiones. s.5.li.2.pscriptio. s.34.
Actus i prin k.fi.comoda.l.si pñ i fi.l.3
s.3.deficit z e sic Actus legitimus e ille
q obuenit uel firmatur a lege.ff. de ucr
si.l.lege obuenire.ut e emãcipatio accep
tilatio aditio hereditatis. cõtractio matri
monij Zuzoris datio z huiusmõi: qui nõ
sunt actus contractuũ. s̃m vero ordinez
minorũ est regere. predicare. cõfessiones
audire. leger. visitare. diffinire.eliger.c i
gi.accusare .testificari. z ad ordices prio
uert qui omnes intelliguntur noie actuũ
legitimorũ solum z non alii.
Accusatio s.2.li.13.furti. s.pact̃.ff. de
s.3.li.12. z 3.cã.q.4.z.5. z de accu. z li
antepenult.clarus i c.plane de hõi.li. 6
z lis.quod sequitur ad li. 6 e cassãdũ .
s.8.li.4.crimen iponit.
s.10.li.4.ultio 35.q.9. ve iam
Administratio Deficit. s.3.Qui z vicatur
hẽre administrationẽ ecctiasticã v.ide infra

Aut humor faciuntq3 deum per quatuor artus
Et mundi struxere globum: prohibentq3 requiri
Vltra se quidq̃ tum per se cuncta creantur.
Frigida nec calidis desint: aut humida siccis:
Spiritus aut solidis: sitq3 hæc discordia concors.
Quem nexus habilis & opus generabile fingit:
Atq3 omnis partus elementa rapacia reddunt:
Semper erit genus in pugna. dubiumq3 manebit:
Quod latet & tantum superest hominumq3 deumq3.
Sed facies qua cunq3 tamen sub origine rerum
Conuenit & certo digestum est ordine corpus.
Ignis in ætbereas uolucer se sustulit auras.
Summaq3 complexus stellantis culmina cæli
Flamarum uallo naturæ mœnia fecit.
Proximus in tenuis descendit spiritus auras.
Aeraq3 extendit medium per inania mundi.
Ignem flatus alit uicinis subditus astris.
Tertia sors undas strauit flatusq3 natantis
Aequora perfudit toto nascentia ponto.
Vt liquor exhalet tenuis: atq3 euomat auras.
Aeraq3 ex ipso ducentem semina pascat.
Vltima subsedit glomerato pondere tellus.
Conuenitq3 uagis limus permixtus harenis
Paulatim ad summum tenui fugiente liquore.
Quoq3 magis puras humor secessit in undas:
Et siccata magis strinxerunt æquora terras:
Adiacuitq3 cauis fluuidum couallibus æquor
Emersere fretis montes orbisq3 per undas
Exiliit: uasto clausus tamen undiq3 ponto.
Imaq3 de cunctis mediam tenet undiq3 sedem.
Id circoq3 manet stabilis: quia totus ab illo
Tantundem refugit mundus. fecitq3 cadendo
Vndiq3 ne caderet: medium totius & imum est.
Ictaq3 contractis consistunt corpora plagis.
Et concurrendo prohibent in longius ire.

Plate VIII

Incipit ordo missalis scdm
psuetudinez Romane curie.
Dominica prima de aduentu.
Statio ad sanctam Mariam
maiore Ad missaz. Introit⁹.

D te le
uaui ani
maz me
az deus
meus in
te confi
do non
erubes/
cã. neq3
irrideant me inimici mei. etenim
uniuersi q te expectãt non ofun
dent. ps. Vias tuas dñe demon
stra mihi. 7 semitas tuas edoce
me. Sequit imediate. V. Gla
pri. 7 Sicut erat. Quo finito re
petit Introit⁹. Ad te leuaui.
Et iste modus repetédi itro
itũ seruat p totũ annũ cũ di
citur. Gloria pri. post itroitũ
Etiã in festis duplicib⁹. Oio
Xcita qs dñe potétiã tu
am 7 ueni: ut ab imine
tib⁹peccatoꝛ nfoꝛ piculis:
te mereamur protegente eri
pi. te liberãte saluari. Qui ui
uis. Ab hac die usq3 ad uigi
liaz natiuitatis dñi post oꝛa
tionem diei dr oio de sancta
maria. s. Deus qui de beate
marie. Tertia oro. Ecclesie
tue. Vel. Deus omniũ fideli
u3 pastoꝛ. Infra ebdomadã
si tuerit festuz. prima oro de

festo: scda de dñica: tertia de
sancta Maria. Lectio episto
le beati pauli apli ad Roma
nos. xiij. capitulo.
Ratres. Sciétes: qꝛ ho
ra est iam nos de somno sur
gere. Auc aut proprioꝛ é nfa
sal⁹: q3 cũ credidim⁹. Aoꝝ p
cessit: dies aut appropinquit.
Abijciamus ergo opa tene
bꝛaruz: 7 induamur arma lu
cis. Sic ut in die honeste am
bulemus. Nõ in comessatio
nib⁹7 ebꝛietatibus. nõ in cu
bilib⁹ 7 ipudicitijs: nõ in cõ
tétione 7 emulatõe. Sed idu
imini dñm iesum xpm. Gra.
Vniuersi q te expectãt nõ ofun
dent dñe. V. Vias tuas dñe no
tas fac mihi. 7 semitas tuas edo
ce me. Alla. V. Ostéde nobis do
mine misericoꝛdiã tuã. 7 salutare
tuũ da nobis. Sequétia sancti
euãgelij ꝑm lucam. xxi. capi.
A illo tpe. Dixit iesus
discipulis suis. Erunt si
gna in sole 7 luna 7 stellis. et
in tris pssura gentiũ pꝛe ofu
sione sonit⁹ maris 7 fluctuũ.
arescétib⁹ boib⁹ pꝛe timoꝛe
7 expectatõe. q supueniét uni
uerso oꝛbi. Nã uirtutes celo
rũ. mouebunt. Et túc uide
bunt filiũ hois ueniente i nu
be: cũ potestate magna 7 ma
iestate. Dijs aut fieri incipié
tib⁹. respicite 7 leuate capita
uestra. qm appropinquat re

a

restium quia non ualet/potest etiam opponi
q̃ restes non reddunt caᷤ sui vidi et ma.suf
ficiente mut.l.solam.et ibi bar.et bal.C.ᵹ te
stibus et actui corporeo congruentem ut.l. q
testamento.§.fi.ff.de testibus ꝛc.

℄Quib⁹ omnibus pactis censetur conclusũ
in causa non autem puto q̃ in criminali ꝯclu
datur et causa q̃ ꝓcediᵗ officio iudiciᷤ
ut.l.ii.§.qui publico.ff.de adul.cum si. ſz q̃
ꝓceditur officio iudicis non concluditur in
cã nec etiam quando ordinarie ꝓcedit iudi
ci nunᴄq̃ intelligitur esse conclusum sed par
ti sic ut.l.vbicuᴄꝗ.ff.de interroga. actio. ita
no.glo.ĩ cle. sepe in.ᵹ.item rogatur extra
de ᵛbo.sig. Pret⁹.video q̃ ad defensam et
ad offensam et testes post aperturam testiu̅ꝗ
possunt non tantum instrumenta produci ut
no.bar.in.l.i. in fi.ff. de questionibus et no.
bar.in.l.fi.C.si publico.ff.de adul.in.ᵹ.ulteri
us quero utrum et in.l.diui fratres.ff.de pe.
ergo non concluditur in cã quinnimo usᴄꝗ ſ
calculo ferendum sentẽcie potest tam ad ᵭfẽ
sam ᴄꝗ ad offensam actitari nisi statuta aliter
pᷓueant/alias si iudex non recipet ᷤensiõeᷤ
usᴄꝗ ad calculum ferende sentencie tenet ĩ sin
vicatu de denegata iusticia et q̃ fecerit litem
suam ut.l.fi.C.de uariis et extra.ordin.cri.ᴄꝗ
bene no.et tene menti ne erres ſz q̃ dixi aᵭ
offensam intelligas ut no.iac.de ate.et cy.et
sali.in.l.fi.C.de quest.et aduertas an testis sit
torquendus dic q̃ non etiam in criminalibus
regulariter quando est liber bᵓ ffalsᷤ in cer
tis casibus ut.l.er libero ĩ prin.ꝛ.l.diuus.in
prin.§.fi.et utrobiᴄꝗ bar.ff.de questionibus
de quo late per sali.in.l.fi.in.ii.q.C.de questi
onibus. Sis tamen cautus q̃ non excipit có
tra testem q̃ sit criminosus q̃ debent in exep
tione poni omnes circunstacie crimnis sicuᵗ
in libello accusatorio ut locus et tempus ut
extra de testibus.c.iii.in.ᵛi. ita dicit bar. in.l.
iii.§.l.iuᷤ.ff.de testibus in glo.et videas que
dixi sup in glo.ꝓxime predenti Ang.

℄Qui iudex commisit blasio publico preco
ni q̃ banniat aᵭ consilium generale ꝓ sen
tencijs in criminalibus ferendis ꝛc.

℄Nõ.q̃ non est necesse q̃ reꝰ specialiter ꝛ
noiatim citetur ad audiendum sentẽciã nã
in ciuilibus non valeret sentencia nisi speci
aliter ꝛ noiatim ꝑsonaliter uel ad domũ uel
etiam pemptorie fuerit citatus ut no.bar. in
extrauag.ad reprimendam sup ᵛbo p nunci
um tñ in criminalibus hoc non requiritur et
hoc ꝓpter licentiam quam inquisiᵗ dedit iu
dici de qua p bar.in.l.is qui reus.ff.de pub.
iudi.et.l.inter accusatorem e.ti.et dix. sup in
glo.sup ᵛbo et iudici licentiam dedit ꝛc. ac
etiã ꝓpter monitionẽ iudicis subsecurã quã
postea fecit iudex q monuit dictum reũ ꝛ ſin
gulis diebus et horis usᴄꝗ ad sentenciam in
clusiue ꝛc.que monitio habᷓ viᷤ peremptorii
ut.l.ii.et ibi glo.et doc. C. quomoᷤᴄꝗñ iudex
ergo talis cõmonitio iudicis sufficit nec alia

specialis citacio requiritur ar.no.p bar.in .l.
si finita.§.iuᷤ.ff.de dam.infec.in.ii.colum.ꝛ in
l.edictum.ff.de iudi.et ꝓdicta ꝓcedunt quan
do ingstus conparuit ꝛ fuit monitus et ᷤdie
licentiam iudici alias aũt si fuerit absens ꝛ ñ
compuit vt q̃ nᵗlomõ põt condẽnari nisi spe
cialiter et noiatim fuerit citatus sicut in ciui
li mᵗtomagis in criminali.vbi ᵛtitur magis
piculum facit cle.pastorali.de re iudicata sed
de consuetudine non citatur et hoc ꝓcediᵗ
totum ex forma statutoᷤ et aduertas q̃ có
suetudo est q̃ p ꝓconem bannitur ad consiliũ
generale et q̃ dictum consiliũ generale mo
neatur uel campana uel cornu uel tuba scᷤᷤ
morem locoᷤ ut no.glo.in.l.ii.C.de decur.li.x
facit no.in.l.i.C.que sit longa consue.que
oĩa facias appere in actis et ideo etiã ferun̅t
sentencie criminales citato publico et genera
li consilio ut siquis esset qui vellet appellare
uel dicere de nullitate uel aliquid allegare ad
defensam rei ꝛ sponte mori decernẽtis q̃ pos
sit ut.l.non tantum cum sua materia.ff. ᵭ ap
pella.et etiam siᴄꝗ uellet dicere et allegare tu
ra fisci et reipublice quia hic agitur de uin
dicta publica q̃ possunt ne fiscus uel respup
lica fraudentur et ne delicta remaneant impu
nita si forte absoluerit iudex non absoluen
dum igitur sit talis citacio consiᵗu generalis
facit aũt. si omnis.C.ut si se absti.q̃ no.ibi
p doc.Et tene menti q̃ in criminalibus utpu
ta Et in accusatione potest fieri sentencia Et
nulla parte instante ut est casus in.l.Cꝗuis in
dubii.ut.C.de adul. ꝛc.

Anzel'.de Aretio.

IN NOMINE DO MINI AMEN.

Ꝭc est quedam sentencia
condemnatoria prim̅ cor
poralis et prim̅ pecunia
ria lata data p drm.L. ᵭ
sano honorabilem potes
tatem bononie ꝛc.

℄Quod sña dicatur lata per dñm Thomã
potestatem et sic per ꝑsidem puincie ꝓut
est necessariũ quonĩ q̃ mors ᵗ membri mutila
cio nam p eius uicarium seu eiꝰ uice gerentẽ
sentencia corporalis executiua fieri non pot
non tantum presente preside ſz etiã eo absen
te. Nam uicarius potestaris ꝛ eius uice gerẽs
omnia potest absente preside que potest ipse
preses preterᴄq̃ inferre mortem uel membri
abscisionem realiter.nam in contumacia bene
posset quem condẽnare ad mortẽ presᴅe ex
istente absente ꝛ ꝛ rex.et glo.ordinaria ꝛ ibi
doc.in.l.iii.ff.ᵭe officio eiꝰ qui uic.alter.ge.
Et hoc nõ.q̃ ᵭ facto ciuitat͛habui pusi̅ me
assistente pluries ꝫsente meo presiᵭe. et hoc
tenet bar.in.l.obseruare in prin.ff.de offici. p
consul.et lega.facit q̃ no.in.l.i.§.i.ff.de leg.
iii.quod tamen intellige uerum si sit uicarius

Ern Stot

2

¶Ncipit liber de cōsolatione medicinā
rū simpliciū solutiuaꝛ Iohannis heben
Mesue.

In nomie Dei misicor
dis cuꝭ nutu ſmo reci
pit gratia. & doctrina
pfectione·principiū ꝥ
boꝛ Iohānis filii Me
ſue filii Hamech filii
Helii filii Abdela regis
Damaſci uerbū cecidit
iꝗretes ſcirē quid est quoniā reme
morati ſunt ꝗ de retificatione medicina
rū ſimpliciū ſolutiaꝛ multi ſapiētes ſcri
pſerūt i diſpſione tamen nec qſquā eoꝛ
plenā traditione ex hac itētione edidit,
ſed per diuerſa capſa de diuerſis reme
morati ſunt diſpſa doctrinā hanc dimit
tētes quidā uero ex dillectiſſimis nͬis q
bus ex caritate tenemur ,nos deprecati
ſunt ut opus unū ex hac diſpertiōe col
lectū in unā pceptorū aggregatione trāſ
feramꝰ quoꝛ iuſtas exaudientes preces
hoc opus agredimur cuꝛ auxilio & boni
tate dei q ſit benedictus. ¶Fac ergo pie
deus pceptoꝛ hoꝛ agregatione felicem
de theſauris largitatis tue oīa felicitans.
¶Ponamus aūt opus noſtrū ſectiōes du
as.In prima ſciētia uniuerſalē de retifica
tiōe mediciaꝛ cū ꝏdictōnibus & modis
ſuis.In ſecūda pticulares ſmones in una
quaq; mediciaꝛ de eſſe & poſſe & retiſi
catiōe ſcribamus & i hoc terminabimus.
¶Diſtinctio capituloꝛ primi libri.

Quatuor itentiōū aggregabimus
ſermone i hoc primo noſtro libro.
¶Prima itētio poit ꝏdictiōes i ellectōe
& poſſe mediciaꝛ ſolutiōeꝛ facietiū. ¶Se
cūda poit ꝏdictiones i emēdatōne mali
tiaꝛ in ipſis ,
¶Tertia ponit ꝏdictōes i emēdatōe ma
litiaꝛ redūdātiū ab ipſis i corpore i hora
ſolutionis,
¶Quarta ponit ꝏdictiōes i emēdatiōe
nocuītoꝛ derelictoꝛ poſt purgatione,

Prima itētio duo capſa ꝏtinet.
¶Capſm primū ē de ellectiōe me
diciaꝛ ꝗ ſit p ꝑprehēſione iudicioꝛ eaꝛ
ſecūdū eſſe ꝑpriū.

¶Capitulꝑm ſecūdum eſt de ellectiōe
mediciaꝛ que ſit p ꝑprehēſione iudici
oꝛ eaꝛ ſm poſſe ipſaꝛ.
¶Secūda intētio continet duas ſum
mas.
¶Prima ſumma ē de retificatione medi
cinaꝛ cum ſocietate alteriꝰ medicine &
cōtinet quatuor capitula.
¶Capſm primū ē de retificatiōe medi
cinaꝛ. cū eo ꝙ oppoiſ eis ꝑprietate ſua
¶Capſm ſecūdū ē de retificatione eaꝛ
cū eo quod opponitur eis ꝏplexione ſua.
¶Capſm tertiū ē de retificatione eaꝛ
cū eo quod opponiſ eis effectu ſuo.
¶Capſm quartū ē de ꝑportione rerum
ſibi iuīce aſſociandaꝛ.
¶Secūda ſumma ē de retificatione me
dicinaꝛ cū boitate que acquiriſ p parte
& ꝏtinet quatuor capitula.
¶Capſm primū eſt de modis coctionis
medicinaꝛ.
¶Capſm ſecūdū ē de modis lauationis
medicinarum.
¶Capſm tertiū ē de modis infuſionis
medicinarum.
¶Capſm quartū ē de modis tirturatio
nis medicinarum.
¶Tertia itētio ē de emēdatione nocu
mētoꝛ i hora purgationis & conti
net tria capitula.
¶Capſm primū ſi medicia mouet & nō
euacuet.
¶Capſm ſecūdū ſi medicina idebite &
laborioſe ſoluit.
¶Capſm tertiū ſi medicina ſoluit ultra
ꝗ oportet.
¶Quarta itētio ē dē emēdatione nocu
mētoꝛ poſt purgatione & ꝏtinet
xꝛ. capitula ,
¶Capſm primū de febre poſt purgati
onem.
¶Capſm ſecūdū de dolore capitis poſt
purgatione,
¶Capitulum tertium de uertigine poſt
purgatione.
¶Capſm quartum de debilitate uiſus
poſt purgationem.
¶Capſm quintū de debilitate ſtomaci
poſt purgationem,
¶Capſm ſextū de ſiti poſt purgatione

·A·i·

Plate XI

Bulchaſim Benaberazerin trãſlatus a
Simone ianueſi interpetre Abraã iudeo
tortuoſienſi.

d IXIT aggregator hui⁹
operis Poſtq̃ ego colle-
gi libꝛ hũc magnũ i me
dicis ꝺpoſitis.q̃ ẽ liber
magni iuuamenti. quẽ
nominaui libruȝ ſerui
torem. & cõpleui libros ſuos oẽs ſecũdũ
uoluntatẽ meã.inueni in multis medicis
compoſitis libri huius medicinas multas
ſimplices que indigẽt preparatione ãte
horã neceſſitatis magne earũ quẽadmo-
dum ſuccos exprimere.et medicias cõbu
rere abluere & conficere aliquas ex eis.
Et diſcernere que ex eis bõa ſunt.& que
nõ bona.& alia ſecundũ hanc formã.Pre
uidi igĩt aggregare omne q̃ eſt neceſſa
rium in hoc ſecundũ rememorationem
meã.Et ordinaui hũc librũ i tres tract⁹.
Primus eorũ ẽ de prepatiõe lapidũ & mi
neralium ſolũ.& de ablutione eoꝛ.& de
aduſtione & cõfectione eoꝛ ſicut ẽ mar-
chaſita & atramentum & calcantũ & col
cotar & ſpẽs aluminum & ſpẽs ſalis.&
plumbũ & ferrũ & es & cohol & ſcoria
argẽti & ſcoria auri.& ẽ de ablutiõe thu
cie & calcis.& ẽ de ſublimatione argenti
uiui & arſenici.et de medicinis petratis.i.
pſilotris. & de operatione medicinarum
acutarum & de oꝑatiõe ȝenȝiſur.& .de
prepatiõe iſtorum oĩum.et declaratiõe
ſcie iuuamentorum iſtorũ omnium.
Tractatus ſecundus ẽ de prepatiõe radi
cum plantarũ & operatione expreſſiõis
ſuccorũ earum. & qualiter extrahuntur
mucillagines & cortices ſeminum & me
dulle ſeminuȝ.& de ablutione olei & de
preparatione ſecis eius & de ablutione aceti & de collectione ſecis eius.
& de oꝑatione aceti ſq̍liitici.& de diſtil
latione aque ipſi⁹ ſquille & de aſſatione
ipſius.& de diſtillatiõe aque cãphore.&
de operatione amilli ex frumento.& de
ordeo & ſiligine.& de ablutione corali
& karabe.& de operatione medicinarũ
acutaꝛ & laxatiuarum ſicut ẽ ſcamonea

& coloqntida turbit & mȝȝerẽon & ana
cardi & ſcebram .i.eſula & ſpecies ei⁹.Et
ad ſciendũ tẽpus quo debent colligi her
be neceſſarie reſeruationi.& qualiter de
bent ſeruari que colligunt ex radicibus
& floribꝰ & oleis eorum & ſimilibus.
Tertius tractatus ẽ de ꝑparatione medicinarum ſumptarũ ex animalibus ſicut
de aduſtiõe cõchiliũ & oſtracorũ & cor-
nuum & ſolearum & unguiũ.& oſſium
& de aduſtiõe corticũ ouoꝛ.& ꝺ aduſtio
ne lete & de aduſtiõe ſartam.i. cancrorũ
& ſcorpionum & tyriorũ & lepoꝛ.& ue
ſpertilionum & yrundinum & de modo
colligẽdi ſanguinem ex animalibus uiuẽ
tibꝰ.& de candidatione cere & de ꝺſec
tione.urine infantium & qualiter ſit glu
tem ex coriis & qualiter colligunt fella
& exſiccãt ad neceſſitatem alcohol & de
cognitiõe iſtorum oiuȝ q̃ ſunt bona & q̃
ñbona ex eis Tractatus primus capⁱⁱ
primi de ablutiõe litargiri & de aduſtiõe
eius & electiõe boni ex eo.

T de primo tractatu eſt mod⁹ ab
lutionis litargiri & de aduſtiõe
ipſius & electionis boni & non
boni ex eo.Spẽs igitur litargiri multe ſũt
quia quedam ſpecies eius eſt q̃ fit ex plũ
bo & q̃dã fit ex argẽto & quedã fit ex au
ro & q̃dã ex eis ẽ nigri coloris & ꞌq̃dã au
tei que quidẽ melior eſt.ceteris.Nam un
guẽta que fiunt ex tali litargiro declinãt
ad albedinem & ſunt nobiliſſime bonita
tis ſed ſi litargirum fuerit nigrũ aut hñs
in ſe aliquid plumbi erit unguẽtum qd̓
fiet ex eo nigrum & turpe.Si ergo uolu
eris ipſuȝ abluere & de-albare neceſſe
ẽ q̃ eligas id q̃ habet colorem auri & qd̓
ſit graue & mundũ a plũbo & frãgas idẽ
in fruſta quantitaſis ſabe & accipias quã
titatem ex eo quã uolueris & pone in ola
rudi & proiicias ſuper idẽ aquam & ponas ſup id de frumẽto bono & purgato q̃
titatẽ quandam & accipias de ordeo pu-
gillũ unum & liga eũ in pãno lineo nouo ſubtili & ſuſpẽdas eũ ligatũ in orificio
olle intra ipſam & facias feruere donec
crepet ordeũ.deinde auferas ollã ab igne
& ponas idquod ẽ in olla in parua paraſ
ſide munda & proiicias frumentum &

E. i

Repetitio solénis & egregia.l.ñ.C.ve long.temp.p̃-
scriptio.in qua ad plenum tractat materia prescriptio
nun̄ .Edita per subtilissimū vtriusq̃ iuris illumina-
torem.d. Baldum de vbaldis de perusio.

Um in longi. In soléni ac vti-
lissima repetione huī aurate.l.
ñ.C. v longi tempo.pscrip. Húc
ordíné obseruabo. Et pᵒ eam
dinidá 7 actualiter subdiuidaꝫ.
Secūdo ponā sūmariū intelle
ctū. Tertio pro faciliori intro-
ductione aliqua ad euidétiā.pre
mittam.casum figurando. Quarto colligā notabilia et
formabo plura ꝫria que hanc.l.planā efficient. Quinto
7 vltimo subnectam.qōnes plures quotidianas 7 in
materia pscriptionū necessarias. Pᵒrimo lex ista princ-
cipaliter diuidit in qnq; ptes.q̃ in primo ponit quali-
veteribus dubitatoibus res emergebāt circa pscriptio
né longi téporis. Scᵇo impator illas dubitatoes soluit. Tertio impator in mā ꝯcludit. Quarto imperator
remouet aliā dubitátoem. Quinto impator oñdit qua
liter ista pscriptio longi téporis in rebus mobilib̄ 7 ꝯr-
poralibus ét .pcedit in rebus imobilib̄ 7 incorpalibus
puta in seruituti. Secūda ibi sancimus. Tertia ibi igit
Quarta ibi nulla scia. Quira ibi eodé. Secūda ps sub
diuidit in tres ptes. In pria ponit thema 7 qō. Scᵇo
soluit qōne. Tertio ponit rōne solutōis. Secūda ibi de
rebus ait. Tertia ibi nihil eniꝫ. Sic sūmariū possidés
bona fide 7 titulo vero vel putatiuo er iustȯ errore. Cō
tinue tñ pscribit.r.ānis inter pñtes.rr.inter abñtes.7
pñtes dicūt qñ sunt in eadé prouincia. Absentes dicūt
qñ sunt in diuersis prouincijs possidés suna. Ille vero
ꝫ quē pscribit in alia 7 pscriptio longi temporis .pcedit
tā ꝫtra sciente q̃ ꝫtra ignorāte tam in rcb̄ ꝯporalib̄.
corporalib̄ nulla habita distinctōe reꝫ in quo loco sunt
b.d. Ad euidétiā é sciendū q̃ nos habemus res. imobi
les. 7 in istis tñ béat locū vsucapio triéniũ nō aut h̄ꝫ. lo
eū pscriptio longi téporis vt.l.ij.ꝭ.in quib̄ can.cet.lon.
temp.pscrip. 7 i.l.vnica.ꝭ.de vsuc.trāsf. Habem̄ etiaꝫ
res imobiles ꝯporales 7 in istis nō hab̄ꝫ locū vsucapio
triénij vt.l.vnica.ꝭ.allegata. Habemus res ꝯporales
vt in mā 7 iste sunt duplicis generis. Quedā sunt iura
que quasi possidétur puta per vsum meū 7 per patien-
tiam aduersarij vt.l.quotiés.ff.de serui.titulo genera
li. Et vtruꝫ in istis .pcedat pscriptio inferius dicemus.
Quedam sunt iura que nō possidétur nec quasi vt sunt
obligatoés 7 actoes. Et vtꝫ i istis .pcedat pscriptio lō-
gi téporis statiꝫ subiciā. Ité vberis scire ad euidétiā q̃
nos habem̄ aetoem psonalé 7 in ista nō .pcedit prescriptio longi temporis sed solum longissimi vt.l.sicut
supra de consti.pecu.7 que sit ratio statiꝫ dicā 7 habemus etiā actionem realem 7 ista est duplex quedam ē
actio realis que assumat rei ven. 7 vtrūi ista procedat
pscriptio longi temporis statim subiciā . Item habe
mus aliam actiōem realem que vocat vpothecaria 7
ista comperit creditori nec potest ꝯpetere domino
regulariter cuꝫ quis nō possit habere dominiū 7 cade
re 7 vpothecaria vt.l.neꝫ pignus.ff.de reg.iur. 7 vtrū
in istis habeat locum pscriptio longi temporis statim
subiciam. Tertio est sciēdū ad euidétiaꝫ q̃ in fruitutib̄
bém̄ q̃i possessionem 7 qualiter in istis querat quali
possessio seruitutis infra subiciam. Item habemus ipꝫ
ius seruitutis. Casus in terminis sic figuratur dñe imperator ego vidi in.l.i.ꝭ.de vsuc.7.ꝭ.l.piece. quod
possidens bona fide 7 ti.prescribit longo tempore.r.an
norum inter psentes.rr.annoꝫ inter absentes mō domine imperator circa prescriptionem de tribus veteri

bus emergebant tres dubitatōes. Pᵒria circa res vtrū
ad h̄ .vt procedat longi temporis pscriptio sit necesse q̃
sint res presentes cōstitute vbi dominus é vel creditor
cōtra quos prescribitur. Et scᵇa dubitario é inter per
sonas. Vtruꝫ hoc q̃ prescriptio dicat .pcessisse iter
presentes requiratur presentia vtriuᶊ q̃ partis. an alte-
rius tñ. Tertia dubitatio vtrum ad hoc vt prescriptio
dicatur pcessisse iter presentes requiratur q̃ prescribens 7 ille cōtra quem prescribitur sint in eadeꝫ ciuitate
an sufficiat q̃ sint in eadem prouincia 7 imperator rñ.7
dicit q̃ oēs dubitatiōes intendit per distinctiōes pñtis
l.tollere.7 primo respondet ad fam 7 tertiam dubita-
tiōe i q̃ dicit q̃ ad hoc vt prescriptio longi tempo. di
catur pcessisse iter ābentes 7 ꝯcluditur spatio 7 quem
quem prescribitur q̃ prescribes sint presentes 7 dicāt
pñtes.7 per hoc respondet ad fam questionem no ñ tñ
si habeat domiciliū in eadeꝫ ciuitate sed si habeat in ea
dem prouincia . Vnde si ille cōtra quem prescribere 7
pscribens dicant habere domicilium in eadeꝫ prouincia
pcessisse dicitur prescriptio cōtra presentes 7 ꝯcluditur spatio.r.annoruꝫ. Si vero ille cōtra quem prescribitur sit in vna prouincia 7 prescribens sit in alia dicit
pcessisse prescriptio iter absentes 7 ꝯcluditur spatio
rr.annorum sed domine imperator vos respōdetis ad
secūdam 7 tertiaꝫ qōes. respōdeatis ad primā in qua
querit an prescriptio longi temporis dicat pcessisse inter presentes 7 anteꝫ .pcedat sit necesse q̃ ambo sint i-
stitute in eadeꝫ prouincia vbi dñs degit vel creditor ꝫ quē
prescribitur respondet impator q̃ siue res sint cōstitute
in eadem prouincia in qua degit sine in alia q̃ procedit
prescriptio longi temporis 7 ratio est nihil enim prohi-
bet siue res sit in eadem prouincia in qua degit dominus
vel creditor: domino 7 creditori moueri cōtrouersiā 7
pscriptionem interrumpere dñs rōne dñi creditor. rōne
vtilis pignori ad se aduocatus. ratio q̃ ius vendicā-
tis 7 incorporale et vbicunꝫ sunt res posite dñs potest
védicare ré per rei vendicatiōem 7 ad se trahere rē do
minij 7 creditor rōne pignoꝝ 7 ideo nostri veteres sub
tilissime 7 diuino quodā motu actiōes 7 actionuꝫ mate
riam cōstituere.quẹ quidem cū sint incorporales possūt
vbicūꝫ ius suū 7 effectum extendere quo bene sequitur
q̃ ille cōtra quē prescribitur: vbicunꝫ sit res siue ad se
possit trahere rem suā per rei vendicatōem vel p actio
nem ypothecariaꝫ 7 si non secerit d̄ꝫ sibi imputari 7 cōtra ipsum procedit prescriptio siue inter presentes siue
inter ābentes nulla habita distinctiōe reruꝫ vbi posite
sint. Sed domine imperator nūquid procedit ita cōtra
sciēntem q̃ cōtra ignorantem. Respondet q̃ sic 7 q̃ dictum est de prescriptione longi temporis verum é nō ta
tuꝫ in rebus corporalibus sed etiaꝫ incorporalibus vt
puta vsusfru. 7 in alijs seruitutibus hoc vult h.l.Mo.p
mo q̃ presentes dicant q̃i sunt in eadem prouincia q̃
tuꝫ ad prescriptiōem. Ratio est in puptu. Nam ad h̄
vt ille contra quem pscribitur 7 prescribens dicant pre
sentes lex cōsiderauit subtilitatem.conueniendi 7 inter-
rumpendi prescriptionem ymo olim regna nō distin-
guebantur per ciuitates.sed per prouincias ita q̃ queli
bet prouincia habebat vnuꝫ regē tñ sub quo homines
illius prouincie potera̅t cōuenri 7 iste appellabat pa-
tes prouincie illius vt.l.ꝫgandez.ff.de accesso.modo si
prescribens 7 ille cōtra quem prescribitur moverēt in di
uersis ciuitatibus nō tamē in eadem prouincia. Ita est
facilitas cōueniendi possessorem illius prouincie q̃ad-
modum si essent in eadem ciuitate 7 pro tanto dicit gl.
attenta ista ratione hodie quelibet ciuitas h̄ꝫ suū regi-
mē. Nō esset ita facilitas cōueniendi possessorem 7 interui
pēdi prescriptiōem.si domiciliū habeat in diuersis ciui
tatibus quẹadmodum est in eadē ciuitate. Certe ad h̄
vt dicat pcessisse prescriptio lon.tempo. iter presentes

𝕒

Pefcie cotto cõ altre cofe infieme
E bono a chi ha calida natura
Pur e uifcofo e fa ria nutritura
Pefci che uãno infieme e uãno a fchiera
Quei fõ meliori di quelli fe uol prĕder
Non fon nociui e meno fol offendere
Quelli che la foa carne han men uifcofa
E che men groffa e tofto fe corrũpe
Meno offendeno il corpo e men il rũpe
Quelli che ftãno in quetta aq̃ o mal herba
O in lochi paludofi che non foni
E quei che troppo grandi:nõ fon boni
Se le falato fene manzi poco
Se ne quando fe prende medicina
Ne freddo fe de ufar fera o matina
Il piper caccia la uentofitade
Digefte e bon al petto & al polmone
Al ftomaco:ala flegma ogni ftagiõe
Croco molto rifolue ma e ftitico
Fa bon color:cõforta il core el ftomaco
Luxuria induce e orina fuga il ftomaco
Cenamo e caldo e fecco e defopila
Il figato e lo ftomaco conforta
Ogna corota cofa de fuor porta
Zenzero e bono alo ftomaco freddo
Alarga il uentre e fecca li humorofi
Digefte ben e fecca ochi mendofi

Plate XIV

cmg3.

¶ Tuero pro clariori
intelligentia in xv. ptes pncipales diuide
dū aſſumptū ❡ Primo namq3 cōſideradū
arbitror ſocietatū genera quot ſint ❡ Se
cūdo ſocietas quatr̄ cōtrahatur ❡ Tertio
qō genus ſocietatis cōtractu eſſe itelliga
tur ❡ Quarto quatr̄ inter ſocios porti
oēs ſocietatis ſint faciēde ❡ Quito que lu
cra iter ſocios ueniāt cōicanda ❡ Sexto
que expēſe inter ſocios debeāt fieri de cōi
❡ Septimo quale diligētia ſocius ſocio in
re cōi adhibere teneatur ❡ Octauo an
dāpna cōtigētia cōi corpori ſocietatis ul
uni ex ſocis cō.ter iter oēs debeāt iparti
ri at3 iputari ❡ Nono an facto unius ex
ſociis uel corū inſtitoris ceteri obligēt et
ſimilr̄ ecōtra an ceteris acquiratr̄ ❡ Decio
ſi unus ex ſociis i ſocietate aliū ſociū ſine
cōſeſu aliorū aſſūpſit an ex facto aſſūpti
ipe ul aſſumēs ceteris teneat et ecōtra an
ceteri eorum facto aſſūpto ul aſſūmtiob3
ligēt ❡ Undecimo quatr̄ et quando ſocie
tas finiat ❡ Duodecimo quis rōne3 geſti
onis reddere teneat ❡ Decimotertio an et
qn iuri reddendi rōne3 adminiſtratois pre
ſcribatur ❡ Decimo quarto que actio
cōpetat inter ſocios z an unus ab altero
conueniatur ❡ Decimoquinto qliter ſo
cius ſocio teneatur

❡ Irca primā3

partem principalem ſex
genera diuerſarum ſo
cietatum principalr̄ ēē cōſi
dero ❡ Prima ē quedā3
ſocietas que ſocietas ui
te nucupat ut cū duo fra
tres uel plu. es ſimul ad
unū pane z unū uinū in
eā domo cōiter uiuūt. Tūc eni quedam
ſocietas uite cōtracta uidet ſecūdū bar.
i.l. ſi. L.ō colla. z i.c. ſi duo fres i cōi ca
ſa poſt morte patris remāſerit. de duob3
fratribus de nouo biſficio i ueſtitis i uſib3
pheudor ❡ Secūda ſocietas eſt rei unius
: l. ſocietatē. ff. pro ſocio. ut cū animo
ſocietatis cōtrahede aliqua rem emimus
ut · l. cū. p. L. p ſo. facit · l. ij. ff. cōi diuidū
do. uel pduximus: ut. ff. pro ſocio. l. ut
ſit pro ſocio actio z l. cū duobg i prin.
z i. §. Ite mela: z i l. actione. §. Ite ſi
ſocietate incamus ad aliquā rem enien
dam. ff. pro ſocio. Alias ſi non animo ſo
cietatis cōtrahede i re coe3 incidimus nō
eſt ſocietas cū cōiter etiā citra ſocietate3
res agi poteſt utputa cū nō affectioe ſoci

---

etatis icidimus i cōione3 ut euēit i re duo
bus legata uel ſi a duobus res ſit empta
ſit uel cōdūcta ut i pductioibus publicor
uel hāditas. Aut donatio nobis cōiter ob
ueniat. Aut ſi a duobus ſeparati enimp
nō ſocij futuri ❡ Quibus caibus nō ſoci
etatis iudicio locus eſt ut. d. l. ut ſit pro
ſocio actio. cū duab3 ſ. quétibg. z l. cum
duob3 i pri. z. l. ſi d qō unus ex ſocijs. i
pn. ff. p ſo. z. l. ij. ff. cōi diuidūdo. ff. In
dubio aūt bar. z bal. i. l. cū pponas. L.
. p ſocio. Uidēt uelle p iducatur ſocietas
ō quo ibi per eos ❡ Tertia ſocietas ē ne
gociationis alicuius ut. d. l. ſocietates cō
trahūt. qō eſt cum ad aliquam arte exer
cēdā puta argentariā mercatiā uel ſ les
ſocietates cōtrahūt ut. ō. l. cū duobus. §.
cū duo erant argentarij: z. l. ij. §. de illo
z. l. duo ſocietate cōtraxerūt. ff. p ſocio.
❡ Quarta ſocietas ē uectigalis: ut d. l. ſo
cietates ptrahūt ut cū aliq ſocietatis Zhcō
a re publica uectigal emptū eſt ut: l. a ō
ff. p ſo. ❡ Quinta eſt ſocietas uniuerſor
q̄ ex queſtu z opea deſcēdit ut cū ſocie
tas ſimpliciter coita ē nec diſtictū fuit qō
genus ſocietatis ſit. ❡ Tūc enim intelligit
coita ſocietas uniuerſorum que ex queſtu
z opea deſcēdit ideſt uniuerſorū. q̄ ex o
pera z iduſtria ac diligētia acquiruntur
ff. pro ſo. l. coir. cū3 ſequétibus ❡ Sexta
ſocietas eſt uniuerſor ſeu omiū3 bonor
ut. d. l. ſocietates cōtrahūt ut cū ē cōtra
cta ſocietas ut hereditates legata donata
aut alia quacūq3 ratione acquiſita cōicē
tur: ut. l. i. l. §. cum ſpecialiter z. l. cū duo
bus. §. idē pap. ſi inter fratres. z. §. ſociū
uniuerſa z l. ſi ſocietate3 uniuerſatū for
tunarum. ff. pro ſocio.

❡ Irca ſecundam p

tem principalem aduertendum
ſocietatem expreſſe contrahi
poſſe. l. ſocietatem coire. ff. pro
ſo: ut cū uerbis interuenete ſti
pulatione uel pacto ſocij ſocietatem ieūt
ut dicit ibi glo. z et tex. i. l. ut ſit. p ſocio
actio. z i l. nam cū tractatu habito. z in
d. l. duo ſocietate. ff. p ſo. z tacite actus
exercendo ſociales ut per Ja. de hare.
Oldra. Ricar. Malib. z Bar in. l. titiū
z mciui. §. altero de admi. tu z per eūdē
bar. in. l. i. §. ſi quis hoc interdicto. de iti
ne. actuq3 priua. z p Cy. z bal. in. l. ſi
patruus. L. cōia utriuſq̄ iudi ❡ Nam ſo
cietas cōtrahitur ſolo cōſenſu ut. qui ad
mittitur. z l. plāe. ff. pro ſocio. z iſtituto
ob. que ex cōſenſu naſcirca pn. z cōſen
ſus declaratur nō ſolum uerbis ſed etiā
ſcis. ff. de legibus. l. de qbus. de his q̄ ſiūt
a ma. parte cap. i. c. ex ore. de appel. c.
dilecti. ff. de edili. edicto. l. ſi cum. §. ei q̄.

SVMMI PON.IMPERATORIE MAESTATIS: CHRISTIANISSI
mi Franchorum Regis:Ferdinandi Hispaniarum:Et Alfonsi Sicilię Se/
renissimoȝ Regum. ILlustrissimoȝ Venetorū. Excellentissimi Me
diolani Archiducis. Ferrarie Ducis.Florentinoȝ. Mantue Mar
chionis. Senensium. Pisanoȝ. Ianuensium. Lucensiū.
BONONIENSIVM. PerfidoȝMaumetanoȝ.Antichri
sti ortusEt totius, Italię : & ultramontanaȝ partiū.
Vrbiū locoȝ & Principū:Status.Casus:Ruinę: ȝ
speroru aduersoruᵭ successuū:Ex astroȝ spi
rituūque pscientia:Vsque ad ānum.M.
ccccc.& ultra.Excellentissimi & sa
mosissimi Astrologi Antonii
Manilii Dialogale
pronosticon.

De reuolutione mundi.
Antonius Manilius Reuereñ.D.Nicolao Flisco Genueñ.epo Forii iulieñ. de
reuolutione mundi Dialogum mittit.

  Olim Reuereñ.pręsul ulla te affici admiratione:si pro amore meo
 n in te singulari tibi ac mihi hodie'cōgratulari me aspicias .Fateor me
   nusᵭ cōtinere potuisse:& maxime cū nouerim : Alexandrum sum
mū pōtificē tuę prudentię tuęque sactimonie spem adhibuisse'plurimā dū
Cesenā urbem:ac prouinciā suā Romandiolā factionibus depopulationibo:
homicidiis:& assiduis incendiis tumultuātē uideret:quā armis & bello cū
domare nequiret imitatus est Nnmām pompilium Rege romanoȝ:religiōe
ac tua sanctimon a moliri ac refrenari posse sperans te ceteris ȝponēs ad hāc
ȝuinciam & Cesenā regendā:& gubemādā idoneū elegit atque misit :Et
ut ipse pater sanctissimus excogitauerat:ita euenisse manifestū est:nō solum
tuo aduentu sed etiā solo tuo nomine pacata & sedata est subito.Qua de cā
te assiduum cū deo habere comerciū atque ex eius gremio in terrā demissū
fatemur oēs.Et ut corā te magis lectari possem.die quo sol in Arietis prirci
piā introiret Cesenā profectus sum.Erat enim hora cōuiuii dum te ac Ioā/
nē ambrosium fratrē tuū una cū aliis uirıs ȝclaris reperissem in cōuiuio:in/
terrogatus sui de rebus futuris:& de enigmatibus Promethei spiritus Fer/
rariēñ.quę'frater tuus paulo post mihi ȝposuit.Cū ut Ionas ȝpheta diu ob
stitissem:rogatu tuo & ui quadā fratris tui ac alioȝ cōuiuaȝ respōdere coa/
ctus sum.De genituris siue dicā quadriuiratū Regū quattuor & quoruᶜdā
principū & ciuitatū horoscopis:& de responsione Promethei dignū fore exi
stimaui celebrare hoc nostrū cōuiuiū ex quorū sermone de reuolutiōe mūdi
Dialogū scribere ac tuo sacro nomini dedicare cōstituo :& si aliquid erroris
uideretur :tuo arbitrio castigādū relinquo,eo maxime:cum te ac Ioannem
ambrosiū & Antonium Maniliū loquentes uideas.Accipe igitur leto aīo:
& sub tua tutela hūc dia.ogū :& in eo uidere te interdū loquctem delectabe

           (1)   a

Plate XVI

A Catalogue of the Fifteenth-Century Printed Books in the Harvard University Library, Vol. 3: Books Printed in Italy with the Exception of Rome and Venice is the third of a series of four volumes which catalogue the extensive holdings of incunabula in the various libraries affiliated with Harvard University.

Representing one of the largest collections of incunabula in the western hemisphere, this catalogue will become a basic reference tool for all students of European civilization in the fifteenth century. The descriptions provide information about format, size, binding, illuminations, marginalia, bookplates and labels, and imperfections, as well as contents, names of editors and translators, and variants, together with cross-references to other standard catalogues.

Like its predecessors, this volume includes representative plates and indices to authors and anonymous titles, editors and translators, printers and places, provenances, concordances, and identifiable bindings. These indices will be cumulated in the fifth and final volume, which will also include a history of the collection.

James E. Walsh is Keeper of Printed Books at the Houghton Library, Harvard University. In addition to having compiled several other library catalogues, Mr. Walsh is the author of numerous exhibition catalogues and journal articles.

ORTS

medieval & renaissance texts & studies
is the publishing program of the
Center for Medieval and Early Renaissance Studies
at the State University of New York at Binghamton.

ORTS emphasizes books that are needed —
texts, translations, and major research tools.

ORTS aims to publish the highest quality scholarship
in attractive and durable format at modest cost.